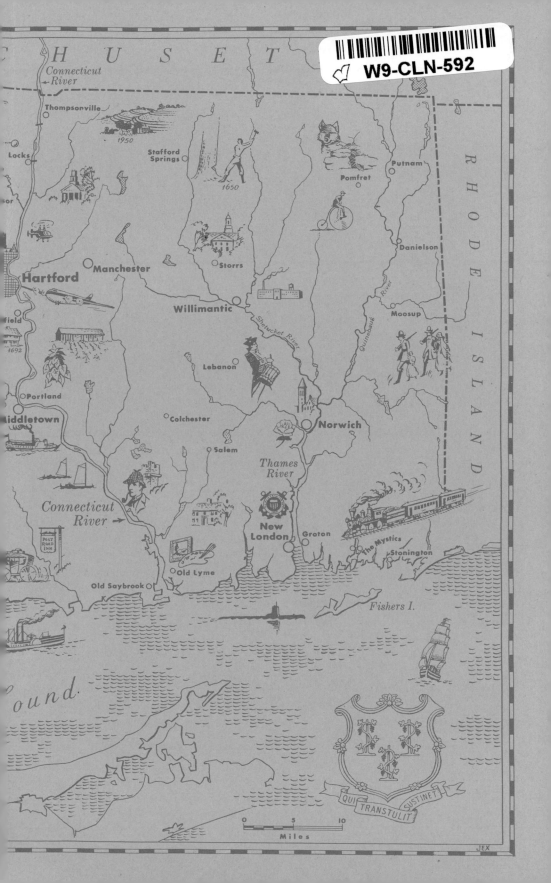

The Yankees of Connecticut

Other Books by the Same Author:

FATHER WENT TO COLLEGE

STAGECOACH NORTH

FOOTPATH IN THE WILDERNESS (*Editor*)

BREAD LOAF ANTHOLOGY (*Editor*)

TOWN FATHER

THE GREEN MOUNTAINS OF VERMONT

THE
YANKEES OF
CONNECTICUT

W. STORRS LEE

Illustrations by Ralph Lee

HENRY HOLT AND COMPANY

New York

F
94
L4
copy 2

4/22 Burgess

85378

To Ralph S. Minor

ACKNOWLEDGMENTS

To the following friends I wish to express formal thanks for kindly criticism and patient assistance in the preparation of this book: Mr. Howard Cady, the Reverend James F. English, Mr. Arthur K. D. Healy, Miss Virginia A. Knox, Dr. Ralph S. Minor, Dr. Howard Munford, Mr. Don Parry, Miss Elizabeth Thompson, Dr. Viola White, and particularly my wife, Mary Louise. Gratitude is also due a long list of authors and publishers, noted under Quotation Sources, for permission to quote from their works.

MARK TWAIN FIXED THE BIRTHPLACE FOR HIS FAVORITE YANKEE AT Hartford, but he was quick to caution the uninformed that such a location shouldn't be taken too literally; actually his man came from "just over the river, in the country"—as though Greater Hartford, the state of Connecticut, and Yankeedom were all one and the same. Typed as the son of a blacksmith, nephew of a horse doctor, Twain's Yankee was incorrigibly practical, loquacious, destitute of sentiment (and therefore of poetry). Like his father and his uncle before him, he too worked for a spell at blacksmithing and horse doctoring, then, following the path of thousands of other country lads, went over to the "arms factory" to become a master hand at producing guns and revolvers and cannon and boilers and all manner of labor-saving machinery—"anything a body wanted, anything in the world, it didn't make any difference what; and if there wasn't any quick new-fangled way to make a thing, he could invent one, and do it as easily as rolling off a log"— the Yankee prototype.

To Mark Twain a Connecticut native was the "Yankee of the Yankees." He transferred him to King Arthur's Court. Josh Billings went one step further and put his character in the Garden of Eden, "where he could alter it to advantage." None of the spinners of Yankee yarns and cataloguers of Yankee character left any doubt that the sons of Connecticut were the most resourceful, the most long-headed, the most voluble, the most far-flung of all the American strains. They out-Puritaned the men of Massachusetts, out-bargained the Yorkers, occasionally outmaneuvered the Pennsylvania Dutch, outtalked the talkative of North Carolina, Georgia, and Alabama; in fact, they spread themselves so indiscriminately across the continent that after a time their character and their trademarks were mistaken for American character and American trademarks.

The Yankee tradition wasn't exclusively a product of Connecticut. All of New England contributed, but Connecticut undoubtedly begat the original Yankees. They were dispersed because they couldn't stay put and they couldn't get on with each other. They were such a migrant lot that they turned up in the Green Mountain country as Vermont Yankees, in the Berkshires as Massachusetts Yankees, in western New York as Genesee Yankees, on Lake Erie as Ohio Yankees, and, perish the thought, in the deep South as Mississippi and Texas Yankees. They were a phenomenon of the eighteenth century, despised and beloved, welcomed and rejected, thoroughly inconsistent and always unpredictable.

Mark Twain and Josh Billings didn't need to spirit them off to King Arthur's Court or the Garden of Eden. The fact of their migration was no less fantastic than the fiction. In 1797 the sophisticated British analyst of men and manners, John Bernard, characterized the typical Yankee as a "cunning, calculating, persevering personage with an infusion of Scotch hardiness and love of wandering," preferably remaining just within the law ("Going to jail he considers not so much a disgrace as a waste of time"), but Bernard also observed that the children of Connecticut had already ranged so far that "Yankee" had become a term denoting character rather than locality. The diffusion of Yankeeism was well under way before 1776; after the Revolution there was no confining it.

The cunning, calculating migrants from Connecticut took their rough manners, their Congregationalism, and their clever gadgetry with them to northern New England, then West and South. They shipped out from Long Island Sound and set their compasses for Africa and the West Indies to help supply the South with slaves they would later help set free. As whalers they explored the far corners of the Arctic and the Antarctic. They turned up arrogantly in British ports, where the relatives they had disowned cast aspersions on them for their Yankeefied English, their talent for shrewd bartering, and their inelegance. "I'll be damned if ever I saw a Yankee that didn't bolt his food whole like a Boa Constrictor," exclaimed Judge Thomas C. Haliburton.

Actually there was a wonderful strength of character about them, a sharp wit, and a fairly sound philosophy, but because of their garrulity, their contempt for amenities, and their cheeseparing, they were their own worst enemies in presenting the right impression of what they stood for. No contemporary spokesman ever gave them adequate credit for the erudition they carried with them. In their westward movement they left a trail of white-steepled New England churches and stalwart college halls all the way across the nation. Ohio, a thousand miles from Connecticut, everywhere was identified—and not always politely—as "the Yankee State," not because of the schools, colleges, churches, and factories planted there, but because of the standing joke among Ohio boatmen about the endless cargoes of "wooden nutmegs, straw baskets, and Yankee notions" they had to carry.

Far beyond Ohio went the peddlers of nutmegs, the gospel bearers, and the college presidents—all the way to the Pacific. Often they left Connecticut, or the states in which they had paused for a generation, as indigents, and struck it rich at the next point of call. In the Gold Rush days of the Far West they left the same disenchanted impression dropped earlier in the ports of Great Britain or the wilds of Ohio—"California with its gold and its cornfields, its conifers and its grizzlies, its diggers and hidalgos, its heathen Chinese and its Yankee millionaires."

Nor did the Yankee influence halt in California. During the last decades of the nineteenth century, the reputation spread even across the Pacific until a complaint was made that "Japan is getting Yankeefied," and a traveler in Mongolia reported that Connecticut goods had "suddenly made their appearance in the village shops"— lanterns, kerosene lamps, tinware and the inevitable Yankee notions. Their tradition in a little over a century circumscribed the globe.

For better or for worse, the qualities once attributed to the Yankee forefathers in particular have been passed on to the nation as a whole. To outsiders we are still a materialistic people with a gift for ingenuity, mobile, impatient for action, uninspired in our diplomacy. In Connecticut, those traits, somehow combined, led to the first conception of mass production, the assembly line, the interchangable precision part, the insistency of salesmanship—as well as the republican ideas that were translated into the Constitution of the United States. It was an extraordinary bequest, and inadvertently it brought an extraordinary weight of responsibility to the American heirs. Sam Slick, once looked down upon with derision or indifference, is now looked up to with deference. He has assumed a very important place in global affairs; he is a success; the world is betting on him and thinks he ought to know the answers. In view of the prominence he has acquired, a reappraisal of him is in order; and these seventeen essays on as many aspects of the Yankees of Connecticut are a fresh inquiry for his critics to assess.

W. Storrs Lee

Middlebury, Vermont
May 23, 1957

CONTENTS

The Yankees of Connecticut

· 1 ·

FOREFATHERS

"JOHNNIES" THE DUTCH CALLED THEM—"JOHNNIES" OR "JANKINS."
All the lads and gentry of the Connecticut settlement carried the
Johnnie label. They might be fishermen testing their lines on the
Shrewsbury banks in Yorker waters, or trappers stalking the game
runs east of Hartford; they might be coastal peddlers tying up at
the jetties of New Amsterdam with deck cargoes of pelts and potashes, tobacco and turnips. Everywhere British paths crossed those
of the Dutch, the same derisive sobriquet followed. Whether the
Connecticut colonial was one of the seven pillars of the Congregational church or a young ruffian spoiling for an international
brawl, to the Hollanders he was always "Jankin." But the English
"J" was difficult for Germanic tongues, and after a while the
"Jankin" degenerated into "Yankee," and the neighbors in Manhattan had fixed for all time a title on the sons of Connecticut.

These were the haughty, God-fearing, obdurate frontiersmen
who shortly bluffed the Dutch out of a stake in Connecticut soil
and went about the business of purging their chosen land of other
evils—rabble-rousing Quakers, wolves, witches, Baptists, rattlesnakes, Massachusetts pretenders, the Devil, and finally their own
red-coated cousins dressed as defenders of George III.

It was as incongruous as any moment in American history, for
they had been neither bred nor schooled for the effort. They were

Englishmen of distinction turned dirt farmers, scholars turned swordsmen, eminent divines turned backwoods diplomats and barterers, genteel aristocrats learning how to swing an ax or drive an ox. Attached to them, of course, was a motley throng of servants, middle-class yeomen, and craftsmen, with a sprinkling of crackpots and adventure-seekers—dissenters all. But the great majority of early Connecticut settlers were from families of repute, entitled to respectable coats of arms, and proud enough of their distinguished lineage to make early arrangements for chipping reasonable facsimiles of the heraldry on their gravestones.

They were graduates of Cambridge and Oxford, families with court connections, London merchants of wealth, men whose names had been mentioned in Parliament—though not always with favor. They were by-products of Elizabethan England and the religious contentions brought on by the good Queen's royal successors; by-products of the times of Shakespeare, Bunyan, and Oliver Cromwell; of Scrooby church; of that nursery of Puritanism and Congregationalism—Emmanuel College; and they were also by-products of the opinionated squabbles of Boston and Cape Cod. They represented the revolt among revolutionaries, men with a mission who wanted only to establish exclusive freedom villages along the Connecticut River and Long Island Sound, where without too much interference they could propagate the Gospel according to Thomas Hooker.

"We play mock-holy-day with God," the fiery Hooker had warned his little congregation in Chelmsford before he was forced to flee from England. "The Gospell we make it our packhorse; God is going, his glory is departing, England hath seen her best dayes, and now evill dayes are befalling us; God is packing up his Gospell, because no body will buy his wares, nor come to his price. . . . He is going, stop him, and let not Thy God depart, lay seige against him with humble and hearty closing with him." And so they came to Connecticut where God, personified as Hooker's impatient peddler, would find more steady customers.

From the beginning the church was the center. At first it was a windowless barn with slabs for pews and a barrelhead for a pulpit, but it soon became a white, steepled edifice with boxed pews, a high pulpit, and a gallery for borderline Christians. It was the "meeting house" in the most elemental sense, where the village gathered for political powwows and military mobilization as well as spiritual edification. It was town hall, civic center, arena, and church under one roof—the pride of young and old. Everything radiated from the meetinghouse. It faced the town commons where the local militia drilled and where fairs were held in summer. The one-room schoolhouse or academy was next door; the general store, the blacksmith shop, and the parsonage were on the other side of the green; and the lawyer's office, the cooper, tinsmith, the doctor, and a few deacons were not far down the road.

Where one would least expect to find a caste system, it was most conspicuous: seating in church was strictly by rank, the most desirable pews going to the highest bidder—families arranged in proximity to the pulpit according to their prominence and affluence. And the placing of homesteads followed the same principle: the worthier and the more useful citizens were expected to take up residence as close to the church as their social and economic position warranted, or, as an acceptable substitute for proximity, one of the loftier elevations of the countryside would do, provided the site offered a commanding view of the church, and provided the homestead were on a large enough scale to offset the distance. From hill and vale all roads led directly to the meetinghouse.

The homes of the less exalted were spread over an area of a mile or two. They were solid, blunt-faced structures, ungracious and ungainly, utilitarian in every way, built to accommodate a great number of children and to house a family industry that included everything from butter churning and apple storage to shoemaking and shirting. Yet somewhere on a staircase or on the parlor paneling there was always a bit of daring decoration inserted by the builder with uncanny subtlety, as though he wanted to leave for posterity a reminder that he did have a sense of whimsy or a feeling for elegance, and could have constructed a more gracious building if the taboos of Puritanism had only allowed it.

This was the Yankee village that grew from the tenets of Thomas Hooker and his contemporaries. Into the community melting pot Hooker had thrown his outspoken zeal for evangelism. Roger Ludlow, Oxford graduate, member of London's Inner Temple and as good an attorney as there was in North America, had contributed a canny sense for making a tough colonial law sound reasonable. Preacher John Davenport, another Oxford alumnus, son of the mayor of Canterbury, and one of the Seven Pillars of New Haven's separate civil government, offered his intolerance of compromise and indifference to the opinions of others. Theophilus Eaton, one of London's richest and most prominent merchants, ex-agent of Charles I to the court of Denmark, contributed a business man's spirit of enterprise.

The wealthy John Haynes, "a gentleman of great estate" who had given up Copland Manor in Essex to pioneer in New England, subscribed his enthusiasm for self-adequacy. Edward Hopkins, an immoderately wealthy merchant who knew all the trade lingo of London and Constantinople, added his shrewdness for barter and a better bargain. Captain John Mason, who had served Great Britain with distinction in the Low Countries and had headed Dorchester's militia, threw in his resourcefulness for eliminating the objectionable. Then John Winthrop, sophisticate, scientist, and diplomat, had come along with the energy and assets to establish factories and forges, ironworks, saltworks, leadworks, and, taking unto himself most of the idealistic qualities the others possessed, had modeled himself into the symbolic Yankee.

Together this sampling of men, with their compatriots, set the first stamp of Connecticut character. From them descended the generations of shrewd bargainers, conscientious pietists, and resourceful craftsmen; the outspoken individualists and inquisitive inventors, the enterprising traders, the stable scholars, the intellectuals, and the droll humorists. And through them all was a strain of respect for expediency: whether their affairs were of the pulpit or of the purse, the conviction persisted that attainment of a glorious end could justify the employment of an opportune means. Such were the enduring qualities of the Yankees of Connecticut.

During the century after the first generation had departed, hecklers and antagonists poured into the colony by the thousands, but there were always enough of the old school to keep the newcomers within bounds, to keep the Connecticut tradition well fed and protected, and a long line of competent successors adding rich ore to the melting pot. Jared Eliott, a D.D. with an enthusiasm for field husbandry and physic, was a good example. He was one of the early graduates of Yale, class of 1706, and from the graduation ceremonies he went directly to Clinton where he occupied the pulpit for the rest of his life, delivering some four thousand sermons from the same lectern and establishing a record of never failing to preach at least once every Sunday for a period of over forty years. But like his neighbors, who were never content unless they had their fingers in half a dozen pies, he went into many more endeavors than just preparing sermons. He was a pioneer in applied science, and studied and practiced medicine until he became the leading physician in the New England colonies. He helped the president of Yale introduce silk culture to Connecticut. His essays on field husbandry were the most widely read agricultural treatises in America. Then, on a hunch that there was commercial value in the black sand along the coast, he put a successful smelter into operation and wrote an essay called *The Invention or Art of Making Very Good, If Not the Best Iron, from Black Sea Sand*. Among British scientists, the treatise was received with such acclaim that the author was issued a gold medal and made a life member of the Royal Society of London.

Dr. Eliott had a good education, but mastery of Latin and Greek were not essential to success even in this classically minded society. Until he was twenty-five, Matthew Griswold of Lyme could read and write; that was about all. The responsibilities of his father's farm had occupied all his time. But at the age of twenty-five, he decided to become a lawyer. He couldn't desert the farm for school, and he couldn't afford to spend the necessary time in a law office, so he borrowed books and purchased books, absorbing everything he read. Without the aid of a single instructor, he was admitted to the bar, and soon put out his shingle. So successful was his practice that he was appointed king's attorney, and then successively he became representative in the general assembly, state councilman, superior court judge, lieutenant governor, chief justice of the state, and governor. And through all the distinguished career, his contemporaries noted that "the social sweetly blended with the Christian virtues. . . . The children of want he never sent empty from his door, but guided by a real sympathy, he fed the hungry, clothed the naked, and relieved the distressed."

Roger Sherman was equally successful in demonstrating that Yale didn't offer the only route to fame. Sitting at a cobbler's bench in New Milford with a book propped against his box of awls, he read theology, history, mathematics, law, and philosophy, and started his civic life by serving as juryman, town gauger, town clerk pro tem, church clerk, school committeeman. For a decade he published a series of almanacs incorporating astronomical data based on his own calculations, and interlarded with quotations from Milton, Pope, and Dryden. When finally admitted to the bar, he quickly rose from justice of peace to become justice of the county court, legislator, judge of the Superior Court of Connecticut, member of the first Continental Congress, and one of the authors of the Constitution of the United States. And Yale, respecting at last the validity of his education in the cobbler's shop, conferred upon him an honorary master's degree.

Participation in politics was the recognized route to importance. Village democracy was everyone's job. Farmer Samuel Hill ran for so many offices in Guilford that in the year of his death, 1752, he was not only town clerk and clerk of proprietors, but also a probate judge and representative in the legislature. In fact, Judge Hill had done so much political running that his fellow townsmen coined for him and for the English language the "run like Sam Hill" epithet. Everybody in Connecticut was running like Sam Hill in the interests of democracy, as though they had to make up for lost time.

These men, and hundreds like them, were all products of the village, men who had taken their indoctrination from grainfields and workbenches, and hard-to-digest morsels from the pulpit of the meetinghouse. The life of the pioneer was rough and demanding. Spadework was done in the early decades, but the conquering of Connecticut elements went on for two long centuries, and considering what the frontiersmen had to contend with in natural environment alone, it was little short of a miracle that they had energy left to devote to refinements—political or spiritual.

None of the Connecticut communities lost its rural setting before the big industries of the 1820's and 1830's began to move in. Until then every town, even those with metropolitan ambitions, had a pastoral outlook with a forest on the hill and cows in the back yards. Out of the hills for two centuries came an assortment of enemies. Wolves and rattlesnakes continued to be the terror of farm hands and housewives. The rattler was so common over much of the state that it often crept through cracks of loosely framed houses and was encountered in kitchens, bedrooms, and cellars. Bounties were placed on the rattles, but still the snakes multiplied—particularly in imagination, and particularly around Norwich, where a Pied Piper with a violin allegedly decoyed them to Waweekus Hill, and where land was of such little value, because of the infestation, that the legislature granted the Reverend Gurdon Saltonstall of New London an enormous tract as compensation for preaching a single election sermon.

As for wolves, heavy stone slabs known as "wolf stones" had to be placed over graves in the Stonington cemetery as protection against the marauders. In 1786, a Thanksgiving service was broken up at civilized Litchfield when an excited report was delivered to the pulpit that the "voracious animals intended an attack on the harmless tenants of the fold" as they left the meetinghouse. Wolf hunts were such a popular sport and Thanksgiving sermons so notoriously long that historical analysts have found it hard to believe that the delivery of this message might not have been delayed for another hour. But whether or not it was a put-up job, the men of the congregation reverently filed out. Eighty of them rushed home for their muskets, and "the whole of this formidable body, well armed, moved in a circular form, to an adjacent mountain, the supposed retreat of these carnivorous unwelcome guests." Four magnificent wolves were captured in a fine display of fearlessness and frivolity. Unfortunately the church service was over by the time the hunters got back to town, so instead of returning to their pews to express prayerful thanksgiving for their merciful delivery, "the whole party retired to an inn and spent the day in joy and festivity."

At Pomfret a few years earlier a farmer named Israel Putnam counted a total of seventy dead sheep and goats and many more maimed lambs and kids after a single night's assault by a wolf and her whelps. Israel lost his temper; he was already "sufficiently occupied in building a house and barn, making fences, sowing grain, planting orchards and taking care of his stock" without having to encounter in turn "the calamities occasioned by drought in summer, blast in harvest, loss of cattle in winter and the desolation of his sheep-fold by wolves." He called in five neighbors to survey the havoc, and the five shook hands on a vow of vengeance to pursue the wolf day and night until she was done for. It was no ordinary sportsman's wolf hunt. The beast didn't have a chance, and from the exploit that followed Israel Putnam garnered more fame than from all his conquests as a general in the American Revolution.

Halfway across Connecticut they tracked her until she doubled back and was at last cornered several days later in a narrow cave that ran some fifteen or twenty feet back into a Pomfret ledge. Toward midnight most of the town assembled outside the entrance to witness the *coup de grace*. Dogs were sent in to make the attack, but one by one they came out mangled and humbled. Bonfires of blazing straw and sulphur were poked into the long passageway, but the wolf refused to be smoked out. Putnam tried to persuade his Negro to crawl into the cave with a gun, but, despite accusations of cowardice, the slave declined the privilege. Having made the dare to another, Putnam had no choice but to go himself. With a rope tied to his ankles so that his audience could haul him out at the appropriate moment, he snaked his way down the passage, carrying a blazing brand of birch bark.

His contemporaries, their children, and grandchildren never tired of retelling the story and elaborating upon it: "The most terrifying darkness appeared in front of the dim circle of light

afforded by his torch. It was silent as the house of death. None
but the monsters of the desert had ever before explored this solitary mansion of horror. He, cautiously proceeding onward, came to
the ascent, which he slowly mounted on his hands and knees until he discovered the glaring eyeballs of the wolf, who was sitting at the extremity of the cavern. Startled at the sight of fire,
she gnashed her teeth, and gave a sudden growl. As soon as he
had made the necessary discovery, he kicked the rope as a signal
for pulling him out.

"The people at the mouth of the den, who had listened with
painful anxiety, hearing the growl of the wolf, and supposing
their friend to be in the most imminent danger, drew him forth
with such celerity that his shirt was stripped over his head and his
skin severely lacerated. After he had adjusted his clothes, and
loaded his gun with nine buck-shot, holding a torch in one hand
and the musket in the other, he descended the second time. When
he drew nearer than before, the wolf, assuming a still more fierce
and terrible appearance, howling, rolling her eyes, snapping her
teeth, and dropping her head between her legs, was evidently in
the attitude and on the point of springing at him. At this critical
instant he leveled and fired at her head.

"Stunned by the shock and suffocated with the smoke, he immediately found himself drawn out of the cave. But having re-
freshed himself, and permitted the smoke to dissipate, he went
down the third time. Once more he came within sight of the
wolf, who appearing very passive, he applied the torch to her nose,
and perceiving her dead, he took hold of her ears, and then kick-
ing the rope (still tied round his legs,) the people above, with
no small exultation, dragged them both out together."

While wolves ravaged the livestock of the pioneers, crows and
blackbirds ravaged the crops. They came in clouds that would
shadow the sun with their passing, and the great flocks would
light in a corn field or a stand of rye to ruin a crop within an
hour. From July to September the farmer or one of his children
had to stand daily watches over the grain. In 1711 the affliction
was so great at Hartford that the freemen voted a vindictive
mandate that "every rateable person in this town shall be obliged
in the months of March, April, May and June, to kill one dozen
of blackbirds, or else pay one shilling for the town's use." Bounty
of a penny a head was also approved for those who exceeded their
quota; the selectmen were ordered to execute the order and to
keep it in "full force and virtue until the town shall see cause
to alter it." At Wethersfield a similar law was on the books, ex-

cept that it distinguished between venerable and youthful fowl; only the *old* birds drew the penny bounty, and the selectmen were saddled with the task of determining the age when the citizens trooped in with their killings.

Even pigeons were a pest. "I have often seen a hundred, or two hundred of these splendid birds, come upon us, with a noise absolutely deafening, and sweeping the air with a sudden gust, like the breath of a thunder cloud," recalled Samuel Goodrich, who liked to net them from a blind. "Sometimes our brush hut, where we lay concealed, was covered all over with pigeons, and we dared not move a finger, as their red piercing eyes were upon us. When at last with a sudden pull of the rope, the net was sprung, and we went to secure our booty—often fifty, and sometimes even a hundred birds—I felt a fullness of triumph, which words are wholly inadequate to express!"

The settlers seemed to have picked out sites that invariably intercepted flyways or game runs, for wolves and bears as well as deer migrated toward the rivers or the seacoast in seasons of drought, and always in the winter. Panthers roamed through the colony, taking their toll and keeping the public on edge, and even in a populated center like Windsor, a bounty of five pounds was paid William Phelps in 1767 for bringing down a big cat half a mile from his house after it had slaughtered nine sheep.

Bears were more common, particularly along the seacoast. Nathan Bradley, the ranking huntsman of Madison, shot deer by the hundred and bears by the score, but was remembered most for the one bear he didn't catch. In his old age he went out unarmed to pay a visit to a neighbor and was halted by an enormous bruin and her cubs. The bear commanded the right of way and refused to let him pass. Nathan backed away and tried another route, but every time he approached, the animal reared up on her haunches and glared defiance. The old man wasn't used to taking dictation from bears, but in the end he had to make his retreat to his home, with tears streaming down his face and sobbing like a child over his one defeat.

Near New Haven, as late as 1766, bears still were exerting their claim of winter passage to fishing areas on the coast, and one clever marauder paused en route at Bethany long enough to wrench six tenpenny nails out of the hinges on a door guarding a young calf. The bear got the calf, and over a period of several nights killed sheep, mangled a dog, destroyed a hive of bees, and then returned to the dairy, "unnailed the wooden bars which defended the window of a milk room, got in and feasted on a tray of milk, turned another over and spilt it, then took up a punch bowl containing about three quarts of cream, carefully carried it through the window, near fifteen feet from the house without spilling; and after he had drunk or lapped it, genteelly turned the bowl bottom side upwards (as if he had drunk a dish of tea for breakfast) and left it whole." The farmer and his wife, who witnessed the scene from a window, had the courage at last to express objections, and were attacked by the bear, which "rose up like a lion rampant, and struck at them with his paws." But the visitor also had to face a loaded gun, and the next day Bethany was treated to the sight of a massive carcass.

The aborigines, of course, were sometimes an even greater menace than the wild life, but after the destruction of the Pequots in 1637 and the termination of King Philip's war in 1676, the Indians were more of a nuisance than a terror. Intertribal wars, as well as the conflicts with colonists, had decimated them; they were reduced to remnants of tribes living in small villages and encampments scattered throughout the state. In petty trade they had sold off their lands until they lived in squalor and pitiful poverty, resentful of the Yankee encroachments but lacking the strength or resolution to do anything about it. For example, Norwalk, a substantial area between the Saugatuck and the Norwalk Rivers, extending "from sea, Indian one day walk into the country," had originally gone for "8 fathom wampum, 6 coats, 10 hatchets, 10 hoes, 10 knives, 10 scizers, 10 juseharps, 10 fathom tobacco, 3 kettles, 3 hands-about, and 10 looking glasses." Later this tract was extended west to the Five Mile River, still "from sea, Indian one day in country," for an additional assessment of "10 fathom wampum, 3 hatchets, 3 hoes when ships come, 6 glasses, 12 tobacco pipes, 3 knives, 10 drillers, 10 needles." The whole of Milford had been auctioned off for six coats, ten blankets, a kettle, and an assortment of hoes, knives, hatchets, and glasses, and Norwich went for a canoeload of beef, corn, and peas given to the Mohegans while they were in a benevolent mood, under siege of the Narragansetts.

The Indians soon regretted the easy bargains they had made, but for the most part they were sporting about them, respected the marks that ancient sachems had affixed to documents filed in the offices of town clerks, and expressed their resentment in petty pilfering, obnoxious drunkenness, and begging. At Killingly the harmless Nipmucks made a perennial nuisance of themselves simply by squatting on the doorsteps of their white neighbors hour after hour, day after day. They begged for food and usually got it, but a friendly handout to the few constituted an invitation to the rest of the clan to drop in for a meal. After a time they would come in family groups of fifty or sixty and settle silently in a dooryard until they were fed. They would arrive for supper, spend the night, and stay for breakfast. To complaints from a farmer that he couldn't afford such hospitality, the Indians had the stock reply that they hadn't received a fair price for their lost hunting lands and were merely collecting the balance in provisions. It went on for years. In a poor season the visits sometimes came daily. A half-dozen would gain access to a kitchen, and shortly twice that number would appear from nowhere to join them; or, as biscuit were being passed in the yard, additional children would appear from underneath papoose blankets or from behind shrubs.

Their greatest enjoyment came from little games and contests; they wanted to try their strength against the strength of white men. Joseph Cady was mowing brush one day in 1720 at the foot of Mashentuck Hill in northeastern Connecticut when a young warrior strolled out of the woods challenging the farmer to a wrestling match. Without hesitation Cady dropped his scythe, knowing full well that he would have to worst his challenger or face him as an insolent braggart for life. For a long time they grappled in an even match. Then, with a desperate effort, Cady flung his antagonist to the ground. Quite by accident the Indian landed full weight on the stubs of brush, fresh cut. His head was pierced by a sharp point and he was instantly killed. It was an embarrassing accident, but when the circumstances were explained to the friends of the deceased, there was no ill will. The white man had won in an honest tussle.

At Derby another Indian was accidentally shot by a prominent hunter, Noah Durand. Noah was waiting in the dusk at a deer run and mistook the Indian for his game. For a time there were scandalous reverberations, but in a powwow the tribesmen were convinced that the shooting was not intentional. Noah was exonerated, but he paid tribute the rest of his life. His home became the rendezvous of the family of the victim, their Indian friends, and friends of friends.

The Indians, however, made at least token repayments for some of the charity. They were generous with their venison, tobacco, corn, dried clams, and whortleberries when the white neighbors were short of staples. And not infrequently the neighbors had opportunities to return favors that were never forgotten. Onto a hayfield in East Windsor one afternoon dashed a frantic young chieftain pleading for sanctuary from his pursuers. The field was dotted with haycocks, and, without an interruption in his stacking, the farmer flung an ample forkload over the prone supplicator and went on about his labors. Pursuers appeared a minute later with an inquiry as to the direction in which the fugitive was running. The oracle leaned on his fork and pensively allowed as how he had seen a running Indian cross the field to the north. Gratefully accepting the intelligence, the avengers hurried off. Farmer Bissell had made friends in both camps.

Occasionally a tear-fetching idyl grew from the close relationship of Indians and white men, and romance between brown maidens and Yankee swains was not unknown. The Indian love call sounded most poignantly up on the Housatonic south of New Milford, where "Lover's Leap," a high wooded crag overlooking the rapids, still marks the spot where one romance turned to tragedy. Lillinoah, daughter of Chief Waramaug, lived there, and one winter's day, while wandering in the forest, she came upon a stricken youth, weak from exhaustion. Lillinoah took him into camp, nursed him back to health over a period of many months, and at the end of summer father Waramaug finally gave consent to their marriage. The prospective groom begged off until he could go back to his village to make peace with his family; then he would return to claim his bride.

"Through the long winter Lillinoah hoped and waited," the story went. "In spring she decked her hair with woodland blossoms and wandered down the trail in the vain hope of meeting her returning lover. When autumn came, she grew pale and listless. The worried chief suggested to Eagle Feather, his most stalwart aid, 'The girl sickens in loneliness. You shall wed her.'"

"Lillinoah overheard the conversation. That evening she stole down to the river and pushed a canoe out into the stream. Tossing away the paddle, she drifted swiftly toward the rapids. Suddenly, above the roaring waters, she heard the voice she had waited so many months to hear, joyously singing a song that she knew. The branches on the crag above her parted and for one agonized instant her lover looked down on the doomed canoe. Lillinoah raised her arms beseeching his help. Unhesitatingly the white man leaped into the river, just as the canoe, careening in the current, capsized. On the brink of the falls, he reached her and together they were dashed on the rocks below."

But love for the Indians was seldom so impassioned. Unquestionably the settlers were opportunists in most of their relations with the savages, and the opportunism extended to religious conversion as well as favor-currying. Many an Indian soul was tem-

porarily won to Christianity by the Reverend James Fitch of
Norwich in one afternoon at Montville. Chief Uncas came to the
pastor pleading for divine intercession against a drought that had
parched the cornfields and driven the game out of the country;
none of the violent Mohegan prayers had brought so much as a
morning fog to relieve the scourge.

"If God shall send you rain," said Mr. Fitch, "will you not
attribute it to your powwows?"

Uncas vowed that he would not, for everything they had done
was in vain.

"If you will declare it before these Indians," replied the minister, "you shall see what God will do for us."

Mr. Fitch went to his knees and Uncas went back to his tribe,
and in a dramatic speech informed his people that if rain came,
the Englishman's God would have to be given the credit, rather
than their own powwowing. "On that very day the clouds became
more extended; and the day following, there was such a copious
rain that their river rose more than two feet in height." The long
record of the Mohegan Congregational Church can be ascribed
in part to the successful intervention of rain-maker Fitch far back
in the colonial days.

Many an Indian was converted to Christianity by the ardent
Congregational pioneers and was assigned a back seat in church
or a place in the gallery along with the Negro servants and slaves.
A few even turned evangelist and became apostles among their
degenerate tribesmen. But the general attitude of the Yankees was
one of tolerance rather than charity toward their Indian brethren. Pretty widely they agreed with the distinguished spokesman
John Buckley, lawyer, minister, and physician, who contended
that "the Indians had no just claims to any lands, but such as
they subdued and improved by their own labor, and that the
English had a perfect right to occupy all other lands without compensation to the natives."

Nevertheless, pioneer grandsons were still settling up for the
easy land bargains many decades after their sires had passed on.
The tribute was just another form of hidden tax the villagers were
assessed. Yet despite the toll of beasts and savage, the Yankees
managed to tend their culture as tirelessly as they tended their
crops. It was a hand-me-down process; mothers taught daughters
and fathers taught sons; the schoolmaster filled in a few months
of the year, and the pastor took over when brave thoughts of
preparing for higher education began to emerge. The lawyer,
the cooper, the blacksmith, the cobbler all took on apprentices.

There were academies and there was Yale, but the real educating was a home process, for that was where frugality developed into a code of economy, where hard work became industry, where necessity became the mother of invention and enterprise, where discipline took shape as a philosophy, and paternal principles bred filial character.

From these homes the sons went forth in ever increasing numbers to test their strength on new pioneer ventures—Jonathan Trumbull from his father's country store in Lebanon to become an outstanding figure in Connecticut commerce with Great Britain, provider for the Continental army and Revolutionary War governor; Jeremiah Wadsworth from a broken home in Middletown as a deck hand to become founder and president of banks, head of an insurance company and a wool factory; William Eaton from Woodstock as a runaway army private to become consul in Tunis and a soldier of fortune in Egypt; Jonathan Edwards from East Windsor as a thirteen-year-old Yale freshman to become New England's most controversial theologist; Lemuel Hopkins from his father's cornfields in Waterbury to become a fair poet and a far better physician.

There were giants among them, but only one Timothy Dwight. He learned the alphabet from his mother in one lesson, was reading the Bible with ease and comprehension at four, picked up Latin during school recesses while the boys were at play; he could have been ready for Yale at the age of eight if his grammar school hadn't suddenly been discontinued. So he was held back for five years while his mother spread a secondary school curriculum before him, and he wasn't able to enter college until he was thirteen. It was at Yale that he acquired the ambition to make a conquest of all knowledge, and he was making good progress toward it when his eyesight began to give out from fourteen hours of concentrated reading each day.

To avoid having to take time out for exercise, he had reduced his diet to exactly twelve mouthfuls a meal, and he had a complete physical breakdown. The regaining of his health became a fetish as fixed as his educational discipline; he walked two thousand miles and rode horseback three thousand more, then returned full of vigor and vitality to serve as president of his alma mater for over twenty years, instructing the senior class on the side in rhetoric, logic, metaphysics, and ethics, acting as professor of theology, and filling the college pulpit. "Pope Dwight" they called him, brilliant teacher and educator, clergyman, poet, legislator, historian, geographer, a man of excesses if Connecticut ever reared one.

But the product of the Yankee village was not all genius, nor all stable citizenry. The genes of conscientious objectors and discontented extremists also produced a full quota of fanatics, crackpots, and unpleasant people. And they multiplied in the latter decades of the eighteenth century when Congregationalism began to yield its hard and fast grip.

At Enfield were the Shakers, "singing and dancing, shaking and shouting . . . working miracles, prophesying and speaking with new tongues" while waiting for the second coming of Christ. At Danbury and New Haven were the Sandemanians, sitting around a huge circular table, instead of in pews, on Thursday afternoons and on Sunday, exhorting each other, convinced that theirs was the only true church and that faith was a mere intellectual belief. At Hampton were the Christ-ians in their Goshen meetinghouse "so noisey as to be heard at the distance of two miles," striving to be as humble as little children, crawling and creeping about the floor, rolling over one another in their humility, and generally enjoying their "love-feasts" in childish hoots of ecstasy. Prospect had its Perfectionists who disregarded all orthodox ordinances, including keeping of the Sabbath, in their contention that all days were holy and only they could be eternally secure. New London had its Rogerene Quakers, Groton its Spiritualists, New Milford its Jemimaites, and many another town had similar little sects of religious deviates, colorful, pitiful, and alarming.

When a nonconformist failed to gather a following to share his unorthodoxy, he courageously stood alone. Sarah Bishop turned female anchorite and lived with her Bible and an assortment of wild animals in a cave near Ridgefield most of her life, cultivating a half-dozen peach trees, a grapevine, and a few hills of beans, cucumbers and potatoes, and gathering berries, nuts, and roots for a subsistence. "Like nature in its first state, she was without form," observed one visitor. "Her dress appeared little else than one confused and shapeless mass of rags, patched together without any order, which obscured all human shape, excepting her head, which was clothed with a luxuriancy of lank grey hair, depending on every side, as time had formed it." Barricaded in her tiny rock fortress, she spent her days in fasting, prayer and Bible reading, eschewing the devil, and being as hospitable to birds and beasts as St. Francis.

At North Stratford lived Hannah Herman "of good understanding, strict religion, solid piety," firm in her belief that she had "a guardian angel." In a visitation when Hannah was seventy-nine, the angel had told her, "You will not live to a hundred years, but almost; you will live to be ninety-nine, and then die." She died on her ninety-ninth birthday.

There were even a few agnostics like Ethan Allen of Litchfield, who believed that "man after death would transmigrate into beasts, birds, fishes, reptiles, etc., and often informed his friends that he himself expected to live again in the form of a large white horse."

Though the state was spared intrusions such as Greater Boston experienced, Connecticut was infested with an ample number of witches, particularly around New Haven—hags that preceded horses through lonely stretches of road on moonlit nights, leaving only their riding hoods in the road as token of their actuality when help from the Almighty was summoned; specters that lodged themselves in the upper branches of fruit trees and aimed showers of apples at gatherers underneath; tormentors that possessed children and stuck needles into their legs; and one New Haven demon that took a fancy to hogs, made them run about on hind legs and squeal "as though possessed by legions of unclean spirits," until one day the keeper of the hogs sliced off the right ear of a demented animal; thereafter a suspected old woman about town always wore a muffler over the right side of her head.

Nor was the pioneer state immune to culprits and criminals. Horse thieves made periodic tours, forgers and counterfeiters were not uncommon, impersonators and confidence men preyed on tavern keepers and housewives alike, and even murderers invaded the Yankee utopia.

A ride on the wooden horse was a common punishment for horse thieves, and in 1785 Moses Parker rode it in Hartford to the delight of the assembled townspeople: "The terrible machine was prepared—consisting of one simple stick of wood, supported by four legs. . . . Hither the prisoner was conducted, and being previously well booted and spurred by the officer, was mounted on the oaken stud. Here he continued for half an hour, laughing at his own fate, and making diversion for a numerous body of spectators who honored him with their company. He took several starts for a race with the best horses in the city; and it was difficult to determine who were most pleased with the exhibition, the criminal or the spectators." However, his arrogance was tempered

later by the faithful application of fifteen stripes at the whipping
post, an assessment of a ten-pound fine, and confinement of three
months in the workhouse.

Bearing witness to the punishment of malefactors was one of the
esteemed privileges of the populace. An estimated ten thousand
gathered at Hartford on June 10, 1797, for the hanging of Richard
Done, convicted murderer. They listened to a powerful pre-execu-
tion sermon on the text, "I desired mercy and not sacrifice"; they
listened to Richard's proclamations of innocence to the last, but
"at half past four, the scaffold was dropped from under him,"
and a reporter from the Hartford *Courant* affirmed that "every
part of the exercise was performed with the greatest decency and
propriety; and we are happy to add, that amid such a number of
people, no unfortunate incident took place."

Through the larger towns wandered a few outcasts of society
wearing halters about their necks and carrying conspicuous
brands on their foreheads—"A" for adultery, "B" for burglary,
"C" for counterfeiting, and on down the alphabet of crime. For
lesser offences the culprit might suffer banishment without the
branding, as did Goodman Love from New Haven, "being not
only a disorderly person himself, but an encourager of others to
disorderly drinking parties." Others sat in the stocks for hours or
days, wore irons "during the magistrate's pleasure," or endured
unmerciful lashings at the public whipping post.

Sometimes the villagers entered into the spirit of the chastise-
ment in an enthusiastic way and, after the law was through with
a criminal, added their own retribution. In December, 1782, the
deranged William Beadle murdered his whole family and then
killed himself in one of the bloodiest crimes of Wethersfield history, but no allowance was made for the maniac's mental condition. Since the law was silent on what might be done with the
body of a murderer, the enraged townspeople demanded it, and
made arrangements to display it at a crossroads "perforated by a
stake," but "no one would consent it should be near his house or
land," so they finally came to a compromise, and on the shore of
a river "tumbled it into a hole . . . like the carcase of a beast,
. . . the bloody knife tied on his breast."

For murders conducted with more subtlety, where no law could
be found to cover the case, the press and a caustic spokesman
were usually effective in riding the criminal out of town, as happened to a cancer quack at Hartford after Lemuel Hopkins' facile
pen had exposed the imposter:

Here lies a fool flat on his back,
The victim of a cancer quack;
Who lost his money and his life
By plaster, caustic, and by knife.
The case was this—a pimple rose,
Southeast a little of his nose;
Which daily reddened and grew bigger
As too much drinking gave it vigor. . . .

According to Hopkins, "threescore different modes of cure" were tried before the famed cancer magician appeared with his faked endorsements, plasters, vials, jalaps, caustics. But none of them served the advertised purpose, and the quack finally had to resort to surgery:

"Courage, 'tis done," the doctor cried
And quick the incision knife applied:
That with three cuts made such a hole,
Out flew the patient's tortured soul.
Go, readers, gentle, eke, and simple,
If you have wart, or corn, or pimple;
To quack infallible apply;
Here's room enough for you to lie. . . .

No, the disciples of Hooker and Davenport, Trumbull and Dwight, did not always embody the qualities of their leaders. Connecticut was the refuge for dissidents, and the dissidents inevitably bred paradox. The state was crowded with men of nobility, genius, compassion, and integrity, but the democratic society they created left room for any number of eccentrics and libertines waiting to take advantage of liberty. The pioneers kindled a busy fire under the Connecticut melting pot. Over the two centuries between the 1630's and the 1830's, they kept the furnace aglow and the pot well filled. It bubbled and boiled, and occasionally erupted as new ores were added. But the assay was kept high.

In the spring of 1636 Thomas Hooker led his congregation and their herd of a hundred and sixty cattle over the hills from Boston and down the valley of the long River through "the hideous and trackless wilderness," carrying his invalid wife on a litter. The spirited preacher was always in the lead. He knew the libraries of Cambridge and the streets of London, and he knew his Hebrew and Greek, but the knowledge helped little in deciphering the blazes along the Indian trails or in composing sign language to convey abstract ideas of friendship at the Indian encampments. He assisted with the herding of the cattle, carried his own pack and arms like the others. Mornings, he offered up community prayers and then did his share of the milking. Evenings, he prayed again and milked again. And with such utensils and furniture as they had been able to bring along, they set up housekeeping and churchgoing in the fertile fields of Hartford. It was a lean existence.

Less than two hundred years later Hartford was a thriving city with six churches and a dozen district schools, a score of taverns and nearly as many taprooms, fourteen shipping companies, and over sixty provision stores. There were grain mills, oil mills, and eight distilleries; cotton factories, woolen factories, hat factories, and fifteen shoe factories. There were blacksmiths, coppersmiths, gold- and silversmiths; carriage makers, coopers, confectioners; every kind of craftsman from umbrella makers and engravers to master house-joiners and wheelwrights. The town was producing bells, wallpaper, pewter, morocco leather goods, buttons, whip lashes. There were two resident portrait painters, six bookbinders, and seven bookstores. There were commodities and there was culture. And what was going on at Hartford was going on all over Connecticut.

It looked as though the "Jankins" were making a success of their venture.

· 2 ·

LAWGIVERS

YALE SOMETIMES GRADUATED ALMOST AS MANY LAWYERS AS MINIS-
ters, and from Tapping Reeve's one-room law school at Litchfield went forth some of the greatest barristers of the nation, but
the pastors were Connecticut's politicians par excellence. During
the colonial days, during the Revolution, and down to the bitter
years of the War of 1812, the clergy were the effective lawgivers.
The ministerial politicking was not always in the open, not always
demonstrative, but it was prevalent; at conferences and consociation meetings, the party line was drawn; in sermons and in parish
calls the word got to the freemen; and when voting time came,
the proper, conservative law went into the books, the right man
somehow took the governor's chair or the constable's mace.

A twentieth-century electorate has often been critical of less
righteous behind-scenes scheming and maneuvering, has often
been astonished over the tally at the polls or over the yield in
legislation wrought by their representatives at Hartford. The precedents, however, were all set long ago by politicos of the pulpit
who went into matters of law as conscientiously as they went into
matters of salvation.

"On election day they had a festival," admitted the Reverend
Lyman Beecher, who had attended many such gatherings. "All
the clergy used to go, walk in the procession, smoke pipes, and

drink. And, fact is, when they got together, they would talk over who should be governor, and who lieutenant governor, and who in the Upper House, and their counsels would prevail. . . . The ministers had always managed things themselves, for in those days the ministers were all politicians, they had always been used to it from the beginning."

Parson Thomas Hooker outlined in a notable sermon the kind of government Connecticut should have, and seven months later lawyer Roger Ludlow put the ideas into proper constitutional phraseology: "For as much as it hath pleased the Almighty God . . . to Order and dispose of things that we the Inhabitants and Residents of Windsor, Hartford, and Weathersfield are now Cohabiting and dwelling in and upon the River of Conectecotte, . . . And well knowing where a people are gathered togather, the word of God requires that to mayntayne the peace and Union of such a people, there should be an Orderly and decent government established . . . We doe therefore assotiate and conioyne our selves to be as one Publicke State and Commonwelth, and doe . . . enter into Combination and Confederation togather to mayntayne and presearve the liberty and purity of the gospell of our lord Jesus."

In the colony at New Haven it was the same. Puritan clergyman John Davenport and man-of-affairs Theophilus Eaton edited the Plantation Covenant: "Whereas we all come into these parts of America, with one and the same end and ayme, namely, to advance the kingdom of our Lord Jesus Christ, and to enjoy the liberties of the gospel, in purity and peace . . . we therefore doe conceive it our bounden duty, without delay, to enter into present consolation amongst ourselves. . . . That as in nation, and Religion, so in other respects, we be, and continue, one. . . ."

Out of these documents, inspired by church fathers—the "Fundamental Orders" of the River colony and the Plantation Covenant of New Haven—emerged the "Blue Laws" with which Connecticut was to be twitted as long as oaks grow on her hills and acorns on the oaks.

Actually the statutes weren't a shade bluer than those of Great Britain at the time, or of Massachusetts, from whose laws they were freely plagiarized. But because Connecticut occasionally tried to be very thorough about enforcing them, and because her own people often made comedy of them, the color held fast. Besides, the laws *were* blue, and continued so, long after they could be blamed on the Puritans. Colonial Connecticut never went so far as Massachusetts to decree that women's dresses should be long enough to hide their shoe buckles, that sleeves must cover the wrists, or that men couldn't wear "immoderate breeches" with knots of "ribin," double ruffs, and silk roses; but in modern Connecticut as recently as the 1930's, any male who appeared on a state-owned beach with a bare chest or without an apron over his shorts was running the risk of being summarily ejected for indecent exposure.

Just how blue New Haven's laws were it is unlikely that anyone will ever know, for apparently the first code was never published. The colony lawgivers relied strictly on the word of God, backed up every important statute with a Biblical reference to book, chapter, and verse, and then freely implemented the divine ordinance with their own interpretation and application to the local scene. "The Laws for holiness, and Righteousnesse, are already made," noted the preamble, "and given us in the scriptures, which in matters morrall, or of morall equity, may not be altered by humane power, . . . yet civill Rulers and Courts . . . are the ministers of Good People and have the power to declare, publish, and establish orders for smaller matters, not particularly determined in scripture, according to the more Generall Rules of Righteousness."

The Fourth Commandment ordained that the Sabbath be kept holy and that no work be done thereon. In an agricultural community, the magistrates readily recognized the necessity of performing certain farm chores before going to meeting—chores like watering the horses and pasturing the cattle—but a careful line was drawn between these works of necessity and works of convenience. There may have been a law forbidding manufacture of beer on Saturday "to prevent the commission of sin by its working on the Sabbath"; there may even have been a law against physical expression of affection on Sunday, for presumably a New Haven gentleman, returning home after a long absence, was caught in the act of kissing his spouse "with appetite" and was arraigned the next day before the court.

But whether or not such blue laws were ever on the books, the general law was broad enough to cover these violations under the head of "sport, recreation, or otherwise": "Whosoever shal profane the Lord's Day, or any part of it, either by sinful servile work, or by unlawful sport, recreation or otherwise, whether wilfully, or in careless neglect, shal be duly punished by fine, imprisonment, or corporally, according to the nature and measure of the sinn, and offence. But if the court upon examination, by clear and satisfying evidence, find that the sin was proudly, presumptuously, and with a high hand committed against the known command and authority of the blessed God, such a person . . . shal be put to death . . ." The impassioned New Haven husband was lucky to have gotten away with his life.

Swearing was an equally invidious offense—particularly when it was "rash, vain, from tempered passion or otherwise." It wasn't a capital crime, like kissing on Sunday, but it could draw a ten-shilling fine for the first instance, twenty shillings for the second. And when the blasphemer couldn't pay the fine, he was committed to the stocks "betwixt one and two hours" for the initial breach, "betwixt three and four hours" for the second. "But if the same person, notwithstanding such former proceedings, shal offend the third time, by such swearing, or cursing, he shal be whipped, for his incorigible profaneness. If swearing and cursing go both together, or he be accompanied by other sinful aggravations, such miscarriages shal be punished with a higher fine, or corporally with due severity, as the court shal judge meet."

Long after New Haven had reluctantly yielded its status as an independent colony and become identified with Connecticut and the U.S.A., its blue law against profanity persisted and was widely enforced in other parts of the state. P. T. Barnum, who kept a store in Bethel where swearing "was according to custom, but contrary to law," reported the infraction of Crofut, a frequent visitor from New York, "a man of property, and equally noted for his self-will and his really terrible profanity."

"One day he was in my little establishment engaged in conversation," Barnum recalled, "when Nathan Seelye, Esq., one of our village justices of the peace, and a man of strict religious principles, came in, and hearing Crofut's profane language, he told him he considered it his duty to fine him one dollar for swearing. Crofut responded immediately with an oath that he did not care a damn for the Connecticut blue-laws. 'That will make two dollars,' said Mr. Seelye. This brought forth another oath. 'Three dollars,' said the sturdy justice. Nothing but oaths were given in reply, until Esquire Seelye declared the damage to the Connecticut laws to amount to fifteen dollars. Crofut took out a twenty-dollar bill, and handed it to the justice of the peace, with an oath. 'Sixteen dollars,' said Mr. Seelye, counting out four dollars to hand to Mr. Crofut as his change. 'Oh, keep it, keep it,' said Crofut, 'I don't want any change, I'll damn soon swear out the balance.' He did so, after which he was more circumspect with his conversation, remarking that twenty dollars a day for swearing was about as much as he could stand." "Blue-laws were something more than a dead letter," in the 1820's, acknowledged Barnum.

Matters of sex had clearly gotten out of hand in colonial New Haven, or the authors of her statutes were unduly preoccupied with the perils of procreation. For the long, detailed *lex scripta* on sex offences, the pages of the Bible had been combed for Hebraic irregularities, and every last one of them incorporated by name. A spade was called a spade, and what Moses and the Lord had prescribed as penalties were conferred upon the offending citizenry. Adultery, sodomy, lesbianism, harlotry, rape, incest, bestiality were all capital crimes. "Birth control," of the only kind they knew, brought the death sentence, too—if the magistrates ever found out—yet, inconsistently enough, carrying on with a single woman might merit only the penalty of enforced marriage.

Practical provision was even made for the reputations of married people whose respective wives or husbands were left behind in the old country—banishment for any suspect: "Whereas some persons . . . whose wives or Husbands are in England or elsewhere, by means whereof they are exposed to great temptations, and some of them live under suspition of uncleanesse, if they do not fal into lewd and sinful courses, it is therefore ordered, that all such persons, living within this Jurisdiction, shall by the first opportunity repair to the said relations. . . ."

The original laws of the River settlement were a little less rigid and a little less specific, but in spirit the differences were not significant—except that New Haven leaned more heavily on the Bible for legal inspiration and on Congregationalism for the privilege of franchise.

Yet compared to the severity and brutality of British laws, Connecticut's code was a model of humanitarianism. In 1603 England had 31 offenses punishable by death, and the list steadily expanded until there were 223 by 1819. Hartford never had more than 12. While the Yankees were framing their laws, larceny above twelve pence was still a capital crime in Great Britain; killing a deer in the king's preserve, or theft of a horse, a hawk, or a piece of woolen cloth brought death by hanging. For idleness, an offender was branded and placed in slavery for two years; and if the slave ran away, he was branded on both cheeks and became a slave for life.

Settlers remembered all too vividly the cases of Englishmen who, for bringing minor displeasure to the king or one of his functionaries, had stood in the pillory with both ears lopped off, paid fines of several thousand pounds, and been condemned to life imprisonment. They had seen female lawbreakers drawn on a hurdle to the place of execution and burned alive; knew of men who had been boiled to death for expressing dissent, or, worse, had been slung up on a block and tackle to be dipped to death in the slow process of raising and lowering over a cauldron of boiling oil.

In the name of witchcraft, thousands of neurotics and cranks in the home country were ruthlessly tortured, burned, or imprisoned, and the fad was at its height during the colonial period; yet cautious Connecticut magistrates did away with only ten unfortunates during the whole period of the craze—despite the impression left to posterity that they had a morbid solicitude for those who put creases in kettles, unbewitched sick children, made oxen frisky, and entertained too great a familiarity with Satan.

It was to escape such a vicious penal code that emigrants had moved to America. They had social perspective that was a century or two ahead of their time, but they could not cast off abruptly all conception of the criminal law under which they had been brought up. The blue laws were mere vestiges of the harsh law of England, and in all likelihood the "blue" label would have faded and been forgotten before the end of the Revolution if one Samuel Peters hadn't, about that time, touched up the color in a fabricated *History of Connecticut* published abroad.

Peters was a Tory and a Church of England cleric who had been tarred and feathered and ridden out of the town of Hebron for his unpopular oratory. "For my telling the Church people not to take up arms, etc., it being high treason, etc.," he wrote to a sympathizer after his informal departure, "the Sons of Liberty have destroyed my windows, rent my clothes, even my gown, etc., crying out, down with the Church, the rags of Popery, etc.; their rebellion is obvious—treason is common—and robbery is their daily diversion: the Lord deliver us from anarchy."

Peters escaped to England and there vented his spleen against the American insurrectionists by concocting an amazing account of life under the frightful blue laws of a Connecticut where no one danced, played cards, made mince pies, or played musical instruments, excepting in defiance of law and order. He pictured a typical Sabbath day on which no one dared cook victuals, make beds, sweep house, kiss children, cut hair, shave, run, or travel "except reverently to and from meeting house," and labored the issue by adding that "a clergyman, who had been in orders about twenty years, once broke their sabbatical law by combing a discomposed lock of hair on the top of his wig; at another time by making a humming noise, which they called whistling; at a third time, by walking too fast from church; at a fourth by running into church when it rained; at a fifth by walking in his garden and picking a bunch of grapes: for which several crimes he was complained of by the grand jury, had warrants against him, was seized, brought to trial, and paid a considerable sum of money."

He outlined the quaint law under which all males were obliged to have their hair "cut round, according to a cap" or the dried shell of a pumpkin. He ranted about the "infamous villainy of Hooker, who spread death upon the leaves of his Bible, and struck Connecticote (a great sachem) mad with disease." And to any but the most gullible, he revealed his propensity to exaggeration by describing a waterfall where the water was harder than marble—"so consolidated by pressure, by swiftness, between the pinching, sturdy rocks, to such a degree of induration that no iron crow can be forced into it."

Historian Benjamin Trumbull had known Peters since his youth, and dismissed him with the quip, "Of all men with whom I have ever been acquainted, he is the least to be depended upon as to any matter of fact." But in England, readers of the *History of Connecticut* did not have first-hand knowledge of the author with which they could discount his effusions so abruptly. All through the volume there was enough proximity to truth to make the whole almost plausible—though a perspicacious British reviewer observed in it "so many marks of party spleen and idle credulity, that we do not hesitate to pronounce it altogether unworthy of public attention"; and in America it was discredited with such uncharitable epithets as "extravagant and incredible," "ludicrous and apocryphal."

Nevertheless the book was circulated widely and quoted more widely. Whenever an archbishop or a statesman, a humanist or a historian, wished to poke prejudiced fun at Connecticut lawmakers, he merely had to quote Peters without bothering to note that the work was a fraud. The blue laws, as compiled by the excommunicated Hebron cleric, became the popular conception of Purtianical New Haven and Hartford legislation even in his native state. Peters convinced the world that Connecticut courts daily subjected their clientele to penalties of banishment, confiscation of property, extortion of fines, cruel lashings, cutting off of ears, burnings of the tongue, and death for the most trivial offences. His attack heaped vengeance manifold upon the rough lads of Hebron who broke his windows and rent his gown. And the intervening years have done little to alter his mendacity. He is still quoted in good faith.

The colorful statutes, however, were not the only legislative enigma. From the beginning, Connecticut's most incendiary wrangles were over just what territory made up Connecticut—in what direction the boundaries ran; where the New York lines were, the Massachusetts line, the Rhode Island line; who had settlement rights along the Sound and along the Connecticut River; who had the right to give immigrants their plantation privileges. It was a hopeless tangle for all of the decades that Connecticut was a colony, and continued to be a tangle through most of the following century.

Seldom were the lawgivers quite sure how far the arm of their law extended. If Connecticut had lost all the claims against her territory, she would have been reduced to a modest area east of the Connecticut River and could have vied with Rhode Island for the distinction of being the smallest state in the Union. If she had won all of her claims, she would have been the largest state, with jurisdiction over Rhode Island and Long Island, substantial slices of New York, Pennsylvania, Ohio, Indiana, Illinois, Iowa, Nebraska, Wyoming, the Salt Lake region of Utah, Nevada, and a chunk of northern California including Mount Shasta and the Klamath River.

Quinnehtukqut—beside-the-long-tidal-river—was what the Indians called it. When the first English settlers moved into the territory and ousted the Dutch by the cold-war process of bluffing and ignoring them, they were squatters. Presumptuously, Massachusetts had given them permission to establish subcolonies on the River at Windsor, Wethersfield, and Hartford, and also allowed John Davenport to lead his band of dissidents from Boston to Quinnipiac—New Haven. If John Smith had sent up a group of Virginians to colonize Quinnehtukqut, the action would have been no less audacious, for Massachusetts had no claim to the land. The first temporary frame house was set up at Windsor in the fall of 1633; John Oldham took up residence with his disciples at Wethersfield the following year; sixty pioneers from Newton moved into Hartford in October, 1635, and Thomas Hooker came overland with his caravan the next spring; New Haven was settled in April, 1683, as an entirely independent colony. And all had their private lawgivers.

Meantime on October 5, 1635, John Winthrop, Jr., son of the Massachusetts governor, who had officially represented the Bay Colony in London during the previous year, arrived in New England carrying a commission that identified him as the over-all "governor of the River Connecticut, with the places adjoining there unto for and during the space of one whole year." His commission granted him "full power to do and execute any such lawful thing . . . as the dignity and office of a governor doth."

Possibly even Winthrop was unaware of how tenuous was the document he flourished, for it did not give him authority to impose an independent legislative system and was inconsiderately sketchy in defining territorial limitations. More than three years earlier, the Earl of Warwick had drafted a patent requesting a block of land extending "thirty miles along the coast southwesterly from Narragansett River" and reaching fifty miles inland. The request was filed with the British Council for New England, and the council had ignored it. But that did not deter the good-hearted earl from then making out a further deed to a distinguished group of "Lords and Gentlemen" for a parcel of land running for 120 miles along the coast and extending west to the Pacific Ocean, including the land that Massachusetts had already parceled out. Winthrop was such an eager advocate of New England colonization that he accepted his nebulous governorship as a convenient wedge for advancement of the cause, and in accordance with his instructions shortly set up headquarters at Saybrook, notifying the Connecticut squatters that, since their settlements were outside the jurisdiction of Massachusetts, they would submit to his counsel or leave.

There was a shallowness in Winthrop's threat, for he well knew that his commission was temporary. The "Lords and Gentlemen" needed settlers, and the settlers needed what the "Lords and Gentlemen" had to offer. The comedy of confusion threatened to become a tragic impasse until it was resolved after months of debate by an ingenious device of letting the Massachusetts General Court serve as a sort of governmental "broker." Assuming a pose of patronage, the court issued a document granting a committee of eight, for one year, full executive and judicial authority to order decrees, to inflict punishments, to regulate trade, planting, and building, and "to convene the said inhabitants of the towns to any convenient place that they shall think meet" to set up a government. For a people staking all they owned on a venture into the wilderness, it was a compromise of more than dubious value; nevertheless Hooker and his followers accepted it, and out of this fallible warranty evolved the stable laws, blue and otherwise, of a new dominion.

Winthrop's commission soon expired, but he decided to stay on anyway and give the colony the benefit of his counsel and support. In a few months the influx of Massachusetts malcontents into the Connecticut valley swelled to a migration. Hartford, Wethersfield, and Windsor burgeoned into sizable settlements, without benefit of charter or official sponsor. The bureaucrats of London were much too engrossed in other affairs to check into the geography of the New England coast or investigate the governmental processes of a bothersome plantation across the Atlantic. So the Connecticut settlers proceeded as though they themselves possessed the divine right of kings. From the Indians they purchased their land; they quietly divorced Massachusetts; and, making believe that the authority received from their "broker" had permanent validity, on January 14, 1639, in a mass meeting, freemen from the three Connecticut River towns met at Hartford to set up a legal code of their own—"the first example in history of a written constitution, a distinct organic law constituting a government and defining its powers."

"The Fundamental Orders," as the constitution soon came to be known, provided that the state would be made up of towns, each regulating certain local affairs; that all state powers would return to the people once a year in annual elections; that town representatives would act coordinately in all legislation; that judicial and executive authority would be distinguished from legislative. The governor, elected annually, could not hold office more often than every other year, and he had to be "a member of some approved congregation"; his executive and judicial powers were shared by six magistrates.

By implication, the Orders renounced the laws of England, both common and statute, and justice was administered "according to the laws here established, or for want thereof according to the word of God." It was a long step in the direction of democratic government, for it gave the community, if not the individual, a new place in a social order, but the interests of the town and church came first. In everything from distributing land and building roads to burning timber and killing blackbirds, the individual took a secondary place. Town liberty was of major importance, and although a freeman could have a vote in selecting a pastor, the law of the church—indistinguishable from the law of the town—prevailed. As an observer noted, the two were so closely identified that "practically the church had selectmen and the town had deacons."

But the Fundamental Orders complicated rather than settled questions of boundaries and allegiance. For more than two decades the complications multiplied. And the one man who finally brought the chaos to a head was Winthrop himself. By 1657 he had become the colony's first citizen, duly elected colonial governor. He was such a towering success as executive that the Assembly soon set aside the constitutional provision which decreed that a governor was not eligible for appointment more often than every other year, and after 1659 he was re-elected annually for the rest of his life, a total of eighteen years.

But he served *in absentia* during his fourth term. That year he spent in London. Charles II had just been restored to the throne, and Governor Winthrop had the right Stuart connections for approaching the sovereign in behalf of Connecticut. From his grandfather, John had inherited an extraordinary ring originally presented by Charles I. The Governor was ready to swap the ring for a clear-cut Connecticut charter.

Armed with the jewelry, a copy of the dubious Warwick deed to the "River Connecticut," and instructions from the Assembly, Winthrop arrived in England and, as an entry to His Majesty, sent in the precious heirloom as a gift. The ruse worked. "With uncommon grace and favor," he was received by Charles II and invited to request a return favor. John spread out the Warwick deed and asked for a verification. His Majesty was astonished to learn that Warwick had promoted such an enormous plantation in New England, but he was also very ignorant of American topography and political machinations. Reaffirming the deed was the least he could do for a man so loyal to the throne.

On April 20, 1662, Charles had his initials affixed to a new charter granting Connecticut all the territory bounded on the east by "the Narragansett River, commonly called Narragansett Bay, where the said river falleth into the sea; on the north the line of the Massachusetts plantation; on the south, the sea; and, in longitude as the line of the Massachusetts Colony runneth from east to the west, that is to say, from the said Narragansett Bay on the east, to the South Sea on the west part, with the islands thereto adjoining."

It included a great deal of territory that neither Winthrop nor his constituency wanted. The three-thousand-mile strip stretching across the continent was an inconsequential detail, but he knew there would be ferment on the other side of the Atlantic when New Englanders learned that Charles had inadvertently ceded to Connecticut virtually all of Rhode Island, a substantial cross section of New York, Long Island, a chunk of land between the Mystic and Pawcatuck Rivers claimed by Massachusetts as her reward for participation in the Pequot War, and the whole controversial colony of New Haven. To question the King's wisdom and generosity, to embarrass him and his advisers by pointing out their geographical confusion, would have been highly inappropriate, so Winthrop wrapped up his precious charter and hurried back to Hartford.

Governor Winthrop's triumphal homecoming was a sensation; no one had expected such overwhelming success. And as word of the new boundaries spread among the colonies, the lusty wrangle Winthrop envisaged was not long in coming. It lasted for over two centuries. New Haven fought bitterly against falling under the new jurisdiction, but when it became evident that she had to choose between New York and Connecticut, she accepted the lesser of two evils and gave in after three years of contention.

Bounds for heretic Rhode Island were aligned and realigned, accepted and repudiated, added to and subtracted from for eighty years, while the two colonies verged on a state of war. Massachusetts reluctantly withdrew her Pequot claim and concentrated on the east-west line; for years the border towns were in and out of Connecticut, complaining about Bay State encroachments and pleading for protection, while errors in surveying were compounded by errors in judgment, and the final compromise of a somewhat irregular line was not reached until 1826. The controversy with New York called for the intercession of a long line of British kings, and eventually of the United States Congress, before agreement was reached in 1881. Like the other states, Connecticut gave up her rights to Pacific shore line, and finally settled the western claims in a sale of nearly three and a half million Ohio acres in "the Western Reserve of Connecticut."

Besides establishing equivocal boundaries, the royal charter outlined the processes of government for the colony as "One Body Corporate and Politique in fact and name by the Name of Governour and Company of the English Collony of Conecticut in New England"; it gave a free hand in the exploitation of "Soyles, Grounds, Havens, Ports, Rivers, Waters, Fishings, Mynes, Myneralls, Precious Stones, Quarries and all and singuler other Comodities"; it authorized creation of a military "to encounter, expulse, repell and resist by force of Armes as well by Sea as by land and alsoe to kill, slay, and destroy by all fitting wayes, enterprizes, and means whatsoever all and every such Person or Persons as shall att any tyme hereafter Attempt or enterprize the destruccon, invasion, detriment or annoyance of the said Inhabitants"; it invited the colony to make "all manner of wholesome and reasonable Laws . . . not contrary to the lawes of this Realme of England"; to promote expansion, it urged that transportation be arranged for "such of our loveing Subjects and Strangers as shall or will willingly accompany them in and to their said Collony and Plantation."

If Roger Ludlow and Thomas Hooker, along with John Winthrop, had dictated the document, they could not have done much better. With few changes, it placed the stamp of approval on the government that was already in operation. It virtually made Connecticut an independent republic.

During the century that the colony existed under Great Britain, neither town nor assembly ever hesitated to take full advantage of the charter rights in augmenting legislation, wiping out old laws, and establishing new ones—with relatively little regard for the warning against adopting statutes "contrary to the lawes of this Realme of England." The basic principles of democratic government had been defined, and that definition was adhered to even after the colonial tie was broken.

In blunders almost as large as those made in creating the colony, slices of Connecticut were occasionally parceled out to new petitioners, and would-be usurpers had to be repulsed. On the insistence of New Haven, the established church became more firmly established; the General Court became a General Assembly and expanded into two houses of Deputies and Magistrates, later the House and Senate; a new constitution was edited in 1818; judicial authority was divorced from the executive branch, and a modern system of state, county, and municipal courts evolved; judges saw a new light and exchanged the common laws of Moses and Connecticut for the common law of England; but the only parliamentary law that has remained on the books to commemorate the decades when Connecticut was a British colony is an act of 1762 that established the Gregorian calendar. To the last, the state was thorough in maintaining a legislative independence of Whitehall.

For a long time the lawgivers even shied away from giving government any of the symbols of dignity associated with parliament. The Assembly met as informally as a committee of church deacons around private dining room tables, until they discovered Jeremy Adams' tavern at Hartford. This was so much to their liking, with its spacious chambers, convenient outbuildings, and hospitable bar, that they adopted it as their statehouse, absorbed Jeremy's mortgage on the tavern, and contracted to meet there as long as he would provide "wine and liquors and other provision for food and comfortable refreshing, both for man and beast . . . and a chamber for the meeting of the court, furnished with

chairs and tables, a large leather chair and carpet, with accomoda-
tion for forty or fifty people." That was as near as they came in
Hartford to the dignity of a statehouse for over fifty years, and
then the only reason they moved into another tavern was that
the original had become so run down and dilapidated.

In the carpeted room at Adams' they made appropriations for
Indian wars, established the early Connecticut towns, swore in
freemen, argued against kings and Quakers, arbitrated squabbles
between Congregationalists and Episcopalians, studied the sur-
veys for post roads, and issued ordinances on trade and commerce.
It was there, too, that the lights were inexplicably extinguished
during a session in October, 1687, when Sir Edmund Andros arrived as short-lived Governor of New England to demand the
surrender of the charter, and the parchment disappeared in the
darkness to find temporary security in a hollow oak.

Not until 1720 did the legislature have a sedate wooden statehouse, not until 1795 a brick one, and it had to wait almost another century for the present three-and-a-third-million-dollar edifice. New Haven, which shared the honor of entertaining the
legislature, erected a statehouse three years before Hartford, built
another in 1764, and an imposing Parthenon on the Green as
as added attraction in 1831. On odd years the legislature met
there until 1875, when the circuit riders found a final destination.

The roving legislature provided an opportunity for a far greater
number of freemen and their families to get in on the act. The
people loved nothing better than hobnobbing with the dignitaries, bearing witness to their arguing, their churchgoing, and their
tippling, while elders with axes to grind could confront the representatives with ideas of their own. In fact, so much lobbying went
on that the practice was heatedly and perennially criticized.

"I was at Hartford a little while ago," complained a laywoman
to her newspaper, "and I see folks running about streets after the
gentlemen that belonged to the General Assembly; and I asked
what it was for, and an old woman told me that they came a
great way, mater of forty miles easily, to find fault with what the
Assembly was going to do. And what I want of you is, to com-
plain of it; for it does not seem clever to have them gentlemen
pestered so by cats-paws."

The only legislative ceremony in which the public was lavish
came with the opening of Assembly. Election Day was a holiday
throughout the state. It helped make up for the loss of festivals
like Christmas, Easter, and Whitsuntide. Families exchanged visits; all the preserved luxuries came out of the cupboards; and to

every guest went ample slices of election cake. But the big to-do was at Hartford, which happened to be the capital for 1808. In the morning, before a mass of spectators from Hartford and the countryside for miles around, the troops and Governor's guard paraded at the Statehouse in a ceremony as colorful as any Whitehall show—the troops in blue, foot guards in white waist-coats and pantaloons with jackets of scarlet, and mounted guards in regalia as elaborate. At eleven o'clock sharp the Governor descended the steps of the Statehouse to the deafening cheers of spectators, and the mile-long procession to the South Meeting-house formed—the Governor, fife and drum bands, the blue troops and the scarlet guards, the Lieutenant Governor, assistants, high sheriffs, members of the lower house, and all the clergymen of the state.

The election sermon, given by an honored pastor of the state, was the *pièce de résistance* of the service, and many a minister made or broke his reputation before the august and critical audience. It was an occasion calling for exactly the right message of stimulation in keeping with the political tempo of the moment; sometimes the stimulation went too far, and sometimes it fell short. But the speaker fortunately did not have to reckon with the reaction of women, for the only females admitted were the choristers deep in the recesses of the balcony. There were invocations, prayers, hymns, and a benediction—all calculated to connect the reasoning of the hour with the Rock of Ages. Then followed another parade, a luxurious repast with the clergy as guests, the swearing in of new officers at the Statehouse, fireworks and an illumination, and a gala ball in the evening. No other day of the Connecticut calendar could match it for excitement.

Regardless of these doings at the capitol, the heart of the government was at the town level, though that did not mean anything approaching universal suffrage. Apprentices, servants, women, and malefactors were automatically excluded from any kind of participation in town or colony government; then there was a broad difference between "admitted inhabitants" and "freemen." An admitted inhabitant was a resident of "honest conversation," a godly man and substantial landowner who had taken an oath of allegiance to the commonwealth testifying that he was neither Jew, Quaker, nor atheist. When voted in at the town meeting, he could take part in town affairs, cast a ballot for town officials or for deputies to the General Court; he was eligible for election to an inconspicuous local office, but had no eligibility for participation in state government.

Freemen were the more distinguished "admitted inhabitants," who through exemplary citizenship and churchgoing had been approved by the General Court itself or by a magistrate authorized through the Court to admit freemen. Only the freemen could vote for higher officials, run for the office of magistrate, attend the General Court, or participate in affairs of the larger commonwealth. The freemen were the tight little fraternity in control of the colony, constituting probably less than a third of the "admitted inhabitants."

Anyone of good character, however, with proper political and religious credentials could rise to the stature of freeman. And the town organization shortly enveloped such a variety of officers that widespread interest in local affairs was inevitable. A responsible post awaited almost any aspirant. As the selectmen and constables gradually relinquished some of their duties, the list of official titles grew larger and longer: there were fence-viewers, haywards or bound-viewers, rate-collectors, surveyors, chimney-viewers (laddies to enforce the requirement that every house have a ladder handy in case of fire), listers, bailiffs, various inspectors, packers of meat, branders of horses, sealers of leather, examiners of yarn, sealers of weights and measures, public whippers, cattle herders, sheepmasters, tithingmen, drum-beaters, ordinary keepers, ensigns for town bands, town criers, town warners, town clerks. Just because an "admitted inhabitant" couldn't hold a colonial or state office did not mean that there were not many other government positions open to him.

The townsmen or selectmen carried the major weight of responsibility on their shoulders. Their duties ranged all the way from overseeing the construction of roads and ferries to payment of bounties for wolves and blackbirds; and, since the affairs of town were the affairs of church, the townsmen also had to make sure that the meetinghouse and parsonage were kept in repair, that there was an ample number of pews and psalm books, that the drum-beater, bell-ringer, and tithingmen were on the job.

The right-hand man of the townsmen and the law was the constable—an office of great distinction, which permitted the wearing of impressive military regalia with such embellishments in braid, ribbon, and headgear as the incumbent cared to add, and the carrying of a badge of office in the form of a stout black staff. It was he who had charge of military discipline; he patrolled the town against intruders, summoned inhabitants to town meetings, "put forth hue and cry after murderers, thieves and robbers," arrested Sabbath-breakers, and dropped in at the tavern to caution anyone inclined toward overindulgence.

These were the important town officers that helped set the character of the conservative Connecticut village. Over the years, county, state, and federal officials gradually absorbed many of their prerogatives; part-time voluntary servants of the town became full-time salaried servants; the limited franchise lost its limitations; the small town became a larger town with big-town ways; but the original idea that a well-ordered community should look after its own never disappeared.

As political propagandists, the Congregational ministers lost their popularity early in the 1800's during the upheaval that swept the Federalist party out of power. A new generation of dissenters attacked the closely knit church-town combine and called for "toleration." "We have never had sufficient elbow-room in this holy state," cried a typical rebel against the old order. "From the beginning, no man could hold an office and occupy one half the broad road. We have been hemmed in by *laws* and *steady habits*, and been compelled to go to hell in a road not much wider than the narrow path to life."

The clergy suffered a stinging setback. "The Democrats have beaten us all to pieces. . . . They slung us out like a stone from a sling," moaned a defeatist. A state auditor one year refused to approve the free dinners for ministers at the Election Day banquet, and after that there were fewer parsons in the parades. Little by little, they relinquished their enthusiasm for politics and substututed enthusiasm for revivals and good works. "They say ministers have lost their influence," cheerfully remarked one man of the cloth. "The fact is, they have gained. By voluntary efforts, societies, missions and revivals, they exert deeper influence than ever they could by queues, and shoe-buckles, and cocked hats, and gold-beaded canes."

But the early lawgivers of Connecticut, including the pastors, did not limit their giving to the state. They established the political foundations for other states; promoted the first law school in America at Litchfield in 1782; published the first American lawbooks; and contributed in large measure to the creation of a democratic constitution for the United States. Although the state didn't bother to ratify the Bill of Rights until April 19, 1939, it was Connecticut that possessed "the first properly American constitution—a work in which the framers were permitted to give body and shape for the first time to the genuine republican idea" —despite the deep blue tint and the politicians from the parsonage.

· 3 ·

PULPITEERS AND PROPHETS

THROUGH FOUR GENERATIONS NOW, THE ANCESTRAL PURITAN PASTORS have been superciliously maligned for their longitudinal sermons and arid oratory, for their interminable prayers, for their monopolizing too large a portion of the dull Congregational Sabbath. To be sure, the parishioners received more generous returns in eloquence than they ever paid for, but this posthumous belittling of pastors is unwarranted. The Connecticut gospel minister was the community leader; he was respected, honored, and revered by a people starving for information and enlightenment. They chose him in town meeting and could dismiss him in town meeting, but the fact that pastorates often extended over half a century is evidence there were few complaints of excessive spiritual counsel.

Nowhere in New England was there a higher quality of religious philosophy—conflicting though it was. Connecticut gave birth to the theologian, reformer, and creator of creeds, Jonathan Edwards, who fathered "The Great Awakening." It also gave birth to the master of fine oratory Henry Ward Beecher, and to Horace Bushnell, "the preacher's preacher," who used the energetic language of the people and the poets to convey his message of practical Christianity, an educator whose talents were so widely recognized that he was offered (and declined) in 1840 the presidency of Vermont's Middlebury College on one side of the continent, and a few years later the presidency of the University of California on the far side. The most inconspicuous community frequently had a distinguished author, philosopher, and statesman occupying its parsonage. The people demanded a high standard in spiritual guidance; the pastor met it.

Six days a week villagers labored on remote farms without access to the news of the world, totally uninformed. On the seventh, they went to meeting to find out what was going on about them, and incidentally to satisfy the craving for a little intellectual stimulation of the only kind they knew—biblical. They were so inured to feats of endurance that four, five, and six hours of sedentary confinement in the box pew of a church was not overtaxing. It was a relaxation from the hardships of the six profane days of the week. The two long Sunday services, and the social hour between at the "Sabba Day," "Noon," or "cider" house, were anticipated with something more than indifference and antipathy. It was the caesura in the prosaic rural routine; it was a holy day or *holiday* in the elemental sense.

The enjoyment, of course, was not unalloyed. It took stamina to warm the frigid climate of the house of God for the body as well as the soul; there were the distasteful blue laws to be reckoned with; the eye of a spiteful beadle to be avoided. And there were always a few resentful communities, notably those in the eastern counties, that did not approve of the established ecclesiastical order at all. But in the great majority of Connecticut towns, the pastor and his ministrations were accepted with warm admiration and enthusiasm. The restrictive regimen of the Sabbath was more than offset by the illuminating message and the newsy bulletins issued from the rostrum.

The pulpit was not only the source of latest intelligence from the Kingdom; it was also the local newspaper, the editorial column, the head of a political round table, the theater. The minister on Sunday morning was prophet, news chronicler, politician, and actor wrapped into one. His sermons contained erudite treatises on the wisdom of Isaiah, the acts of Jeroboam, the teachings of Hosea; but he did not shy away from commentary on what Thomas Jefferson, Napoleon Bonaparte, or Governor Trumbull were up to. And the prayers got down to intimate details of village life in revealing, by innuendo or specific reference, which of the local lads needed divine guidance because of carousing too noisily on the waterfront, which of the lassies was suspected of excesses in careless bundling, who was down with the measles and mumps, who had just completed an unsavory deal with the

Tories. Every good prayer had to have a few eye-openers, and the petitioner furnished enough food for thought and gossip to last from one Sabbath to the next. The prayers certainly swayed opinion in local circles as well as in a higher realm.

The minister was the best-informed man in town, and it was his duty to disperse that information. When the governor and council stole the march on the Continental Congress by issuing a Connecticut Declaration of Independence sixteen days prior to the adoption of the Philadelphia document, the press, magistrates, town clerks, and criers were ignored as agents for disseminating information on the greatest event in the history of the colony. Written into the proclamation were the specific instructions: "And all the Ministers of the gospel in this Colony, are directed and desired to publish this Proclamation in their several churches and congregations, and to enforce the Exhortations thereof by their own pious Example and public instructions." Although the separation from Great Britain was clearly political action, the task of conditioning the public to acceptance of it was entrusted solely to the clergy.

Whether the news was of intramural or of international importance, the preacher did not spread it in any spirit of petty gabbling; his motives were the highest. According to the fundamental tenets of Congregationalism, every individual, regardless of his station in life, was "called to the work," and that call was a kind of investiture to join in the home-front struggle against sin, physical suffering, moral depravity, and the British. The minister was not fulfilling his office unless he kept his flock on the job. His injunctions to the congregation were as broad as they were long. He was concerned about national interests as well as village interests, and his prayers reflected the same. He pulled no punches in naming names or referring to familiar incidents when addressing the Almighty. In anticipation of the imminent arrival of Cornwallis on the American coast during the Revolution, Judah Champion of Litchfield interceded for his congregation with minimum charity for the invaders: "Oh Lord, we view with terror and dismay, the approach of the enemies of thy holy religion; wilt thou send storm and tempest and scatter them to the uttermost parts of the earth; but, peradventure, should any escape thy vengeance, collect them together again, Oh Lord, as in the hollow of thy hand, and let thy lightenings play upon them."

For two centuries the Congregational clergy exercised authoritarian control over the masses in Connecticut. They were never granted this power; and generally the congregation would have been the last to concede that they had it. It was a benevolent oligarchy. The pastors molded political opinion, set the pattern for proper family and community life, guided intellectual and cultural pursuits, and often stood as the authority on matters of agriculture, economy, education, and industry as well as theology. For a colony and state founded on democratic principles, it was a frightening concentration of power. And if they had not borne it with amazing skill and sublety, they alone could have provoked a revolution.

These pastors have been pictured as a stodgy group, wholesome, intelligent, and of high character, but lost in their stuffy libraries, remote and pompous in their pulpit approach, dull, somber, colorless. A few undoubtedly answered that description, but they would have been overthrown within a decade had the majority been of that ilk. During the two centuries they were in power, they were undoubtedly the most vital professional men in the state, men of purpose and principles, good scholars and good orators, the more promising sons of Yale and Harvard. Yale was their principal breeding ground, and at that time preparation of graduates for the ministry was the major objective of most colleges. The teachings of Yale were plowed back into Connecticut soil. Through the ministers, the liberal education of New Haven became the learning of the state.

Since Connecticut was made up primarily of agricultural communities, there was a social homogeneity in the respective congregations. The pastor usually became a farmer too, for the salary of a few hundred dollars a year could not begin to support the substantial family that filled the parsonage. Provision of farm and home for the minister was as essential as provision of a church, and usually the parsonage, like the church, was either built by men of the parish or paid for in subscriptions of nails, lumber, window glass, cartage, bricks, and hours of labor. And when a family couldn't afford to pay the church taxes, it could substitute the equivalent in construction of stone walls, plowing, planting, or haying on the parsonage grounds. Altogether the minister lived rather well. He set the social as well as moral tone for the town.

The clergyman had to be an energetic machine, for in addition to tilling the soil and preparing the long sermons, enormous demands were made on his time. At every occasion he was expected to be on hand ready with a prayer and a few profound remarks, whether it was the town meeting at the church or a dinner party at the deacon's. There was the routine of pastoral calls, funerals, and patriotic rallies. Before high schools came into existence, his mornings and evenings were taken up with tutoring boys for entrance to Yale, supplementing the learning that went beyond the scope of the schoolmaster. All travelers of distinction called at his door expecting an invitation for dinner or for the night. His bookshelves became a lending library until he organized one in the village. There were ministerial conferences and consociation meetings to attend, and annually he put in his appearance for the election sermon of the legislature when the ministers gathered at the capital with the government representatives for a day of prayer, eloquence, and a great deal of incidental lobbying. The local pastor had knowledge of every phase of life in the state. It was from that orientation that his power grew. He was a man of vitality, stamina, and consequence. He had views on every burning question of the hour, and he had to be listened to on Sunday, for Connecticut law made church attendance compulsory.

The ministers formed a tight organization, so tight that if, for instance, they had united in the choice of a path of compromise and pacification, they could well have persuaded their constituents to retain allegiance to Great Britain, and could have postponed the Revolution. The governor, many political leaders, and state judges demonstrated no intention of putting up resistance to the Stamp Act. Then a professor of divinity at Yale, Naphtali Daggett, stepped to the fore and attacked the newly appointed stampmaster in a pungent letter of defiance published in *The Connecticut Gazette* on August 9, 1765: "Where are the mercenary Publicans who delight in Nothing so much as the dearest Blood of their Country? Will the Cries of your despairing, dying Brethren be Music pleasing to your ears? If so, go on! bend the Knee to your Master Horseleach, and beg a Share in the Pillage of your Country. . . . That same repacious and base Spirit which prompted you to undertake the ignominious task, will urge you on to every cruel and oppressive Measure. You will serve to put us continually in Mind of our abject Condition. . . . For one of our Fellow Slaves, who equally shares in our Plans, to rise up and beg the Favor of inflicting them, is intolerable."

Newspapers in other parts of New England took up the cry of resistance, but ministers, schooled in the Yale tradition, cried louder. At Lyme, Stephen Johnson, Yale '43, sharpened his quill and wrote seethingly: "If the British Parliament have a right to impose a Stamp Tax, they have a right to lay on us a Poll Tax, a Lard Tax, a Malt Tax, a Cyder Tax, a Window Tax, a Smoke

Tax, and why not Tax us for the Light of the Sun, the Air we Breathe, and the Ground we are Buried in?"

In Windham, Lebanon, Griswold, Woodstock, Stonington, Wallingford, South Windham, Farmington, Hebron, Hanover, Branford, Sharon, Stamford, powerful sermons of resistance scorched the Sabbath air. During the next decade floods of pamphlets, sermons, and articles poured out from the studies of small-town pastors. And when the Revolution broke, the same spirit lived on.

At North Haven, in 1775, Benjamin Trumbull stepped down from his pulpit one Sunday morning after a fiery sermon, turned up the leaf of the communion table, and invited his congregation to enlist then and there. Forty-six responded. Two years later he again assumed the part of recruiting officer. Periodically he went off to war as chaplain, was appointed captain of a volunteer company, and stood behind the earthworks, musket loaded, ready to defend life, liberty, and Calvinism.

At Durham, Elizur Goodrich preached resistance long and eloquently, urging his congregation to give up their property and lives, if necessary, to the cause, and "advising the young women to give their hearts and hands to those young men only who had given theirs to the war for independence."

At Sharon, Cotton Mather Smith announced the news of Lexington from the pulpit, dismissed his congregation, and retired to the village green to help assemble and equip a company of a hundred men, ready for immediate march.

At Danbury, Ebenezer Baldwin preached a bellicose sermon in which he prophesied that the war could mark the beginning of a vast American empire, founded on principles of liberty and freedom, which in two hundred years would grow in population to 192,000,000. He left his pulpit as chaplain of a Danbury regiment he had helped to recruit, and died of illness contracted in the army.

Litchfield's Judah Champion took periodic leave to serve as chaplain, recruited soldiers, solicited money, devoted much of his sermons to war news, and even permitted the women to spin on the Sabbath.

At Lebanon, during the winter of 1780, the pastor preached such a provocative sermon on the terrible suffering of the army that the Governor's wife, seated in the congregation, modestly moved forward to the altar and laid on it the rich scarlet cloak she was wearing, and over the scarlet cloak shortly were heaped other contributions to the cause from other members of the church: rings, brooches, chains, purses, more cloaks, greatcoats, caps, mittens, boots, money, stockings.

There were a few tired, lukewarm pastors here and there, fence-sitters occasionally, torn between Tory and colonial interests, but most of them were just more Champions, Baldwins, Smiths, Goodriches, Trumbulls, and Johnsons. The challenge of the Revolution brought out the true stature of the Congregational pastors, who wielded such vast power in the state and used that power magnanimously to promote the interests of their congregations and the state.

The "established" church of Connecticut was Congregational, and until 1791 when free incorporation was granted to other sects, its pastors virtually had a monopoly on religious propagation. Church and State were one. The agenda of town meetings included propositions related to the "fixing" of churches and the election of pastors, as well as the surveying of roads and the appointment of wardens. Into the minutes often crept such paragraphs as the one in the records of Simsbury, where a controversy raged for thirteen years over whether or not to locate a meeting-house at Hop Meadow: "May ye 7th 1683. Whereas there has been a difference arising amongst us, concerning ye setling the place of ye meeting house; that a settled peace may be obtained amongst us, to ye Glory of God, and the comfort of ourselves and ours, we . . . do so agree and appoint as soon as may be comfortably obtained a day solemnly to meet together, in a solemn manner to cast lots for ye place where ye meeting-house shall stand."

Although the Fundamental Orders of the colony of Connecticut clearly called for separation of civil privilege from church membership, the principle was freely disregarded. The colony was also dedicated to "mayntayne and presearue the liberty and purity of the gospell of our Lord Jesus which we now professe, as also the disciplyne of the Churches which according to the truth of the said gospell is now practised amongst vs." To the Puritans that meant the suppression of heresy—as they defined heresy. Any beliefs that strayed even minutely from Congregationalism were heretical, and the offender became subject to civil law. Moreover, by the terms of the Royal Charter the magistrates had a free hand to control all religious matters. The state was the secular arm of the church, and, as such, it was compelled to uphold and defend the established religion. In a regularly constituted town meeting, for instance, there was nothing irregular—or arrogant —about the resolution of 1640 attributed to Milford:

Voted: That the earth is the Lord's, and the fullness thereof.
Voted: That the earth is given to the Saints.
Voted: That we are the Saints.

For almost two centuries the people were caught in this church-town dilemma, which they were reluctant to recognize as a dilemma. In the early years, the conflict was of little significance because of the absence of any appreciable number of dissenters. But, as Quakers moved in from Rhode Island, as Baptists, Separatists, and Anglicans demanded the right to worship as they chose, Congregational hierarchy was repeatedly confronted with legal squabbles that had to be solved amicably—or the very charter of the colony might be withdrawn. Restrictive laws were enacted, rescinded, and re-enacted; new platforms were adopted, abolished, and modified; but through it all, Congregationalism remained firmly "established." Baptists and Anglicans were reluctantly released from the requirement of paying taxes for the support of Congregationalists. Any widening of religious privilege came with remarkable resistance until after the adoption of a new constitution in 1818, and that was brought on by a protracted series of conflicts—the Great Awakening inspired by Jonathan Edwards, the division of Congregationalists into Old Lights and New Lights, the breakdown of the Federalist party which long supported the established church, and later reminders that the Connecticut Constitution was at variance with the federal constitution on the question of religious freedom.

The clergy demonstrated a broad-mindedness in other affairs, prudence and shrewdness in handling matters of greater moment; but any heresy, any conflict with their church was treated with utter intolerance. As a class, they were not men who would enter into learned arguments on the number of angels that could dance on the head of a pin, but they held the conviction that orthodox Connecticut Congregationalists had the best chance of entering into the Kingdom of Heaven, and their profession was the preparation of souls for that entrance. They guarded their convictions zealously.

The order of Sabbath service, where the convictions were enunciated, altered little during the seventeenth century, the eighteenth, and the first half of the nineteenth. The summons was sounded at nine in the morning by a bell, if the town had the wealth to procure one; otherwise by a drum, a horn, or a conch. The congregation arrived on foot preferably, for that was the least ostentatious manner of moving about on Sunday; the more distant members came on horseback, and later in carts or carriages, but it took many years for carriages to be accepted as a suitable means of travel to church; they entailed far too much display.

The families solemnly took their places in the deep, square boxes and closed the doors behind them. The minister climbed to the high pulpit, where he could look down into the pews and where the occupants could look up to him without being distracted by neighbors in other pews. In the coldest days of winter, the church was entirely without heat except for the footstoves in the forward boxes, where sat the wealthier and more distinguished families.

Against the creaking of paneling, the objections of babies, the coughing, sneezing, and nose-blowing of a chilled January congregation, the pastor called the service to order by reading several chapters from the Old Testament and sometimes a few additional chapters from the New. Then followed a half-hour interlude of intonation, for which a pitch was set on a tuning fork or pitch pipe by a ranking dignitary of the church, as judiciously elected as the committee on pews. The songs were no rollicking gospel hymns. At best, there were not more than half a dozen tunes in the repertoire during the more Puritanical era, and these never sung quite the same on two occasions or in two places. But the words for a great many psalms were somehow squeezed into the melody, regardless of meter and feet. The pastor recited a line, and the congregation then sang it back to him; he "lined" another verse, and that was referred back to him in the same fashion. The half-hour was just about long enough to exhaust the available tunes on the multiversed hymns. Occasionally the pastor was obliged to interrupt the proceedings to reprimand a full-throated group of youths for putting too much unction into their rendition, a tone-deaf deacon for getting ahead of the rest, or a well-meaning matron for introducing too many unnecessary "quavers."

Then came the sermon, which was good for an hour or longer, and the newsy prayer almost as long. By noon, even the more reserved of the elders were ready for a change of body position and location. The congregation quietly withdrew to the "Noon" house for a midday break, a basket lunch, and alcoholic fortification. A few out-of-town families maintained private structures, but generally the "Noon" house was a community institution, located close to the church and constructed around a cavernous fireplace; here the women could thaw out and surreptitiously turn over the latest news imparted in the parson's prayer, while the men over their flips pompously "felt over" the morning's discourse. Some parishes went so far as to set up barrels of hard cider, at which all could freely quench their thirst and renew their spirits. Presently the bell, the drum, or the horn sounded again, and the congregation filed back into the church for the second installment of the Sabbath program—quite on the order of the first.

The only marked change in the service up to the middle of the nineteenth century was in the psalm-singing and music-making, and this alteration aroused a fury of dispute fully as warm as the legal squabbles with the Anglicans and Baptists. From the Massachusetts Puritans, the Connecticut Congregationalists inherited the *Bay Psalm Book*, which had been edited by three ministers, none of whom knew anything about either music or poetry. "If the verses are not alwayes so smooth and elegant as some may desire or expect," read their apology in the preface, "let them consider that God's altar needs not any polishings. Exodus 20."

This question of polishing was what disturbed the sensitive souls who did have an ear for music, and the battle raged for more than a century. On the one hand, an archdeacon trying to keep his conducting within traditional bounds was punished for singing paslms with "a jesticulous tone and antitonant voyce, viz., squeaking like a pigg which doth not only interrupt the other voyces but is altogether dissonant and disagreeing unto any musicall harmonie." On the other hand, the Reverend Timothy Woodbridge brazenly preached a "Singing Lecture" in East Hartford one Sabbath in 1727, making a stirring appeal "for the encouragement of Regular Singing, a comely and commendable practice; which for want of Care in preserving and skilful Instructors to receive, has languished in the Country till it is in a manner lost and Dead; yea it has been so long Dead, as with some it stinketh. . . ."

Exponents of euphony intent on introducing musical instruments into churches fought bitterly with those who were convinced that it was a travesty against the Almighty. Those who would "sing by rote" struggled with those who would "sing by rule." "If we once begin to sing by rote," an opponent shouted, "the next thing will be to pray by rule, and then comes Popery." And the advocate of singing by rule pointed out that the principal reason the rote singers didn't want to give in was because they "use Quavers and Semi-Quavers, &c., and on this account it is it, and so loathe to part with

n meetings, the burning issue
nging by rule was at last made
argument. In Glastonbury, af-
ruary, 1733, the congregation
day by rote and the other half
election." But almost a century
ter introduced their "new fan-
nsion arose that Pastor Russel
to the quarrel among his hard-
headed church folk, finally stepped down from the pulpit and
went into the hardware business. As inventor of the "new fan-
gled" extension bit, carpenters the world over still sing his praises.

Little by little, the conservatives were shown that words sung to
a set tune and illustrated on an instrument did not deprive the
service of its solemnity. Gradually the "lining" was given up, and
the tuning forks and pipes were replaced by a fiddle, a bass viol,
a clarinet, flutes, cellos, pipes, or hautboys—and eventually the
first church organ in New England was installed in the Kensington
meetinghouse. Harmony at last came to the Congregational
church.

Against this stormy cloud of witnesses for Congregationalism,
other Protestant denominations had little opportunity to flourish,
and the Roman Catholics had scarcely a chance. At Meriden, while
ground was being broken for a new Baptist church, the Congregationalists resorted to an injunction to prevent the erection of the
building next door—not that they had any objection to the Baptists "as Christian people, as good neighbors and as worthy citizens," but they took exception to the rasping voice of the proposed
pastor, who, they feared, would drown out the quiet-spoken Congregational pastor on Sunday mornings.

The Puritans seemed to have forgotten that their original
antagonism in the mother country had been against persecution.
In Connecticut they could practice what they had preached
against. Civic privileges were virtually dependent on adherence to
Yankee Calvinism until at last the revolutionary 1818 state bill of
rights provided that: "No preference shall be given by law to any
Christian sect or mode of worship. . . . The exercise and enjoyment of religious profession and worship, without discrimination,
shall forever be free to all persons in this state; provided, that the
right . . . shall not be so construed as to excuse acts of licentious-

ness, or to justify practices inconsistent with the peace and safety
of the state." Although this did not take care of social censure,
which was to continue for many more decades, it did end official
castigation of the French and Irish who chose to cling to the
church of their fathers.

The Connecticut Catholics had had a rough time; when some
four hundred French neutrals were deported to Connecticut from
Nova Scotia by the British government in 1775, the exiles had no
benefit of Catholic clergy in the fifty towns where they were distributed. Indentured servants from the Emerald Isle assigned to
Connecticut following the Cromwellian settlement of Ireland had
no Father O'Donnell or O'Connell to hear their confessions, and
though a considerable number of voluntary Irish migrants were
admitted to Connecticut after 1762, on Sundays they were expected to attend the white Congregational church on the village
green.

Oddly enough, it was the army of France that inspired the
first open-mindedness toward papacy in Connecticut villages. In
1780, some five thousand French soldiers, coming to the relief of a
desperate little colony that wanted to be part of an independent
nation, marched into Connecticut with their polite generals, spirited cavalry, stirring music—and Roman Catholic priests. They
brought their own munitions, their own supplies, and their own
money. The townspeople watched these Catholic infidels doing
their close-order drill, saw them parading resplendently on the
village green, danced with them at exhilarating parties, did a little
Yankee trading with them. "A gay June for Lebanon was that," reflected a town historian, "when those six brilliant French regiments
with their gorgeous banners and martial bands were daily displayed on this spacious and lovely village green." For six months,
a thousand infantry and five hundred mounted hussars were quar-
tered in Lebanon and other key towns. It was evident that their
iniquities did not vary appreciably from Congregational iniquities.
In Hartford, a vast open-air Mass was witnessed by the Congregationalists for whom these idolators were fighting. Even Washington
took it upon himself to remind his constituents that they should
not forget "the important assistance which they received from a nation in which the Roman Catholic faith is professed."

They did not forget. The reluctance was still present after the
Revolution, but the attitude was more charitable, and instances
of kindliness toward brethren of other faiths more frequent. With
political independence came institutional independence when the
Anglican Church in America severed its connection with Great

Britain. In 1784, Dr. Samuel Seabury of Connecticut became the first Episcopalian bishop in the United States, and the acceptance of this official claiming spiritual jurisdiction over a denomination in the new republic established a precedent for Roman Catholic hierarchy. Five years later, Pope Pius VI appointed the first bishop in the United States, and the bishop shortly paid an exploratory visit to New London.

However, a few prominent conversions from Congregationalism to Catholicism accomplished more than all the spiritual dignitaries in invoking a new attitude toward the offensive religion. Daniel Barber was the first apostate. He was the great-grandson of the builder of the church at Simsbury, born and bred in the faith of four Congregational generations. By an Episcopalian zealot he was led to espouse the apostolic order, was soon ordained a deacon, and later became an Episcopal bishop and rector. Then finally he went all the way over to Catholicism, and became an eloquent spokesman for his new-found faith, as demonstrated in his popular tract, *Catholic Worship and Piety Explained and Recommended in Sundry Letters to a Very Dear Friend and Others.* Barber's conversion shook the foundations of the village churches of Connecticut. Fanny Allen, daughter of the Connecticut-born hero of Ticonderoga, Ethan Allen, caused almost as much of a sensation among her Puritan relatives and acquaintances in Litchfield County when they learned that she had taken to a nunnery in Vermont. Jerusha Booth, of Newton, wife of a minister, mother of five children, received special papal permission to enter a Visitation convent and became Sister Mary Augustine. Her husband was admitted to the Jesuit novitiate.

These shockng occurrences were followed by others, and, as decades passed, the Puritans of Connecticut gradually became inured to the encroachment of Rome. New legislation at last provided a climate in which Catholics no longer needed to fear persecution. Here and there, outgrown Protestant churches were graciously turned over to the new order. "Well, Bishop Fenwick, as we have a fine new church building, we will let you have the old one," a Protestant representative with a Hartford church to dispose of, jovially told the Catholic representative in 1829. And Bishop Fenwick replied, "Yes, and you have a fine new religion, and we will keep the old one."

Not until 1872 did Connecticut become a Catholic diocese conterminous with the state. The construction of the New York and New Haven Railroad brought thousands of Irish laborers during the 1840's, and in the cities and towns along its route

Catholic congregations grew with remarkable rapidity. The mill towns beckoned migrations of French Canadians to the eastern part of the state. German, Polish, and Lithuanian immigrants flowed into the tenements of Hartford, New Britain, and towns of the Naugatuck valley, where hardware and metal manufacturing was developing. Italians in great numbers moved into New Haven, and Slovak groups into Bridgeport. In 1835 there were only seven hundred twenty Catholics and two wooden church buildings in the state; within a century, the number had grown to more than a half million attending some three hundred Catholic churches. Two decades later it was estimated that well over half the population of the state was attending Sunday Mass rather than Sunday "meeting."

During the years of the great foreign influx, the outnumbered Congregationalists easily made up for the intolerance of their forbears. They did a complete about face, welcoming with open arms the people of many lands, introducing them to the ways of democracy through educational programs and evangelistic work, without stress on any narrow religious dogma. The Americaniza- tion programs conducted by church groups were one of the major social achievements of a generation. To new sects the warmest hospitality was shown, and efforts to establish churches of their own were freely abetted. Frequently the charity extended even to giving up the old established order, as congregations of differing tenets merged into one of broader outlook.

In northern New England many a Protestant church stands neg- lected and abandoned on a deserted hilltop, but few of the Connecticut meetinghouses have suffered this indignity. As rural communities expanded into suburban and rural-urban centers, the old churches have seen a corresponding growth. Most of the original Congregational church doors are still open on Sunday morning. The sermons are shorter, the doctrine less platitudinous, the music more melodious, but the basic faith of the Connecticut fathers lives on, refined and revitalized.

· 4 ·

HUSBANDMEN

MILLER GAY GROOMED THE GRUBBIEST FIELDS IN THE TOWN OF Lebanon. The soil was thin and strewn with boulders, soggy in spring and dry in summer, and the land all slanted up hill at an angle steep enough to wind a horse. It took the life out of a man to coax life into the acres. But Gay was a good farmer. There was no tiller of the soil in the whole of Lebanon more tireless or more diligent. Despite the handicaps under which he labored, his hay was rank and weedless; people paused along the highway to marvel at his potato patch; his cornfield was the envy of the countryside. He was a good citizen, too—not distinguished, but a good average citizen, attentive in fulfilling his religious duties, ready to take his turn at road building and raising bees, never entertaining any holier-than-thou attitude.

The only public office to which he had ever aspired and been elected was drum-beater. Winter and summer, for years, he had summoned Lebanon to church services and town meetings. His one indulgence and avocation was drumming. From the head of his bass, Gay could raise a resonance that could be heard clear over to Liberty Hill, and the rhythm of his sticks on a side drum would set the laziest feet into action. Sometimes he was carried away with his own sound; in fancy the beat sent the beater a long distance from his fields toward the horizon, and even over the horizon into a world much more exciting than the one he knew in the routine of plowing and planting and harvesting. He had learned to curb such flights, learned to repress any urgings to investigate more fertile and more profitable fields. Nevertheless, the lust of the wanderer was in him.

One morning late in the spring of 1775 he was moodily hoeing the seventh row of corn, his mind far away from the slim green shoots that he was trying to encourage. Mechanically he knocked his hoe on a rock to rap off the packed dirt. He raised it again, as a spirited "Hello" from the road startled him back into the realm of reality. Gay leaned on his hoe, looked toward the intruder, and recognized his pious neighbor Captain James Clark sitting erect on his horse and dressed in an outfit that was meant to resemble a uniform.

"I've left the Lord to look after my crops, Neighbor Gay," the captain called.

The young farmer knew that Clark wasn't talking about garden crops.

"I am getting up a company to join Prescott and Putnam; I want you as drummer," the captain added.

Gay tried to shape a response that was worth shouting back across the seven rows, but he wasn't the articulate sort. Without a word he left his hoe standing in the row and crossed the field to his little house.

"Mag," he said, interrupting his wife at her spinning wheel, "Captain Clark says I'm to beat the drum for his company."

Maggie knew there was no holding him back, no protest that would take effect. She courageously helped him bundle a few things into a kerchief, kissed him a tearful good-by; then he was off down the road following Captain Clark toward Boston and Bunker Hill, already sounding a tentative rhythm on his drum.

Gay was a patriot. He was also bored enough with farming to make patriotism come easy. Whether he left the cornfield more out of love for liberty than out of affection for adventure, there is no telling. Nor is there any honest way of sorting out the real reasons why thousands of other Connecticut farmers followed Gay in their abandonment of hillside fields. Over the centuries they have quit for causes less worthy, but the quitting has been no less enthusiastic. Once a farmer set his hand to the plow, he didn't like to turn back, yet out of sheer boredom, out of impatience with the stubborn soil, out of soul-galling fatigue, they did turn back. They have turned to more regimented and more remunerative routine of the factory; overwhelmed by frustration, they have sold the works and gone West; driven to distraction by rocks, weeds, and untimely rains, they have turned peddler. They have answered faint but unmistakably alluring calls into fields as diversified as shopkeeping, doctoring, shipping, even the ministry. Any occupation seemed preferable to the labors of general farming—crop-and-cattle farming.

Those who gave up their overextended acres for specialties like poultry or peaches, truck gardening or dairying, weren't farmers at all in the accepted Connecticut tradition. They were merely making an industry out of some one phase of farming. The true Yankee farmer was a professional Jack-of-all-trades; he had horses, cows, sheep, fruit trees, grain fields, and vegetable plots, fifty acres of pasture, and twice as much in woodland. Perhaps he set out on too ambitious a scale, perhaps the whole idea was wrong. It was a challenge to generations of families, a noble undertaking, successful and then unsuccessful; but the record of Connecticut crop-and-cattle farming is a story of alternate aggression and retreat, high hopes and second- or third-generation surrender.

Eighteenth-century farms were established on a dynastic basis. Barns, homestead, and outbuildings were constructed not alone for the generation of the builder. He built and acquired property on the assumption that his son, grandsons, and great-grandsons would carry on where he left off. "The most valuable crop a Connecticut farmer can raise is seven stalwart sons," was the saying. From north to south, east to west, the state was dotted with thousands of homesteads that would house a family of fifteen; barns that would shelter twenty cattle, two or three teams of horses, lumber wagons, threshing machines, rakes, tedders, and a vast tonnage of hay; and sprawling sheds for all the asides. But few of the heirs lived up to the expectations of the elders. The farms remained in the family for a few generations, but long before the middle of the twentieth century the majority of them had been won over by submarginal-farm immigrants, by the keepers of Rhode Island Reds and Plymouth Rocks, by slicks from the city— or the buildings had settled into the oblivion of cavernous cellar holes. So many farmers went over the hill to greener pastures, so many accepted the invitation to more lucrative ways of life, that they left behind them an amplitude of evidence to question whether Connecticut ever was cut out for crop-and-cattle tenure. Too often, the farm ran the farmer, and finally ran him out.

The first great exodus of farm people occurred in the decades immediately after the Revolution. "Within the last thirty years the current of emigration from this State has swelled to a torrent," reported Pease and Niles in their 1819 *Gazetteer*. "It may be safely estimated that at the present time the emigrants from Connecticut, and their descendants, amount to more than 700,000 souls"—and the escapists left the state a total population of less than half that number. Nevertheless, agriculture, in one form or another, was the principal pursuit until 1850, and during the two centuries of its dominance there was no relenting in the formidable obstacles tenants had to buck.

The Ice Age created the first unkind obstruction to the future farmers of Connecticut. Mountainous glaciers, thundering down from the north ten thousand years before Hooker came on from Boston, bulldozed much of the topsoil into Long Island Sound and the Atlantic beyond. Gushing floods of ice water from retracting glaciers scoured surfaces thin and dumped the residue unevenly over southern counties, and the slowly melting ice sheet, heavy as a raisin pudding with souvenir boulders and rock chips from New Hampshire and Vermont, left its load of debris liberally scattered over the state for the plows of settlers to encounter.

The valley of the Connecticut and other river basins were more fortunate, for here ancient floods and tidal estuaries made deposits of more workable soil, but in the upland regions, the land consisted mostly of veneer spread haphazard by the ice sheet. The natural processes of soil building had been at work for a long time before the white men took their turn at it, but the land was still in pretty bad shape in the middle 1600's. Thanks to the glacier, the upland farmers had little besides second-hand borrowed soil to begin with, and often they did not improve it. The rocks went into endless chains of stone walls and gigantic stone heaps, and the inclined fields lost their more cumbersome impedimenta, but the settlers had a profound ignorance of the simplest principles of plant nutrition. The first generation of poor settlers disregarded every law of agriculture. They burned forests and destroyed layers of leaf mold in the process of getting a cash crop of pot- and pearl-ashes for the British textile, soap, and glass industries. They helped along the process of soil erosion by plowing the land downhill. They had little appreciation for the value of good seed, and less for the value of common horse manure. They exhausted themselves in trying to coax crops out of sterile soil, and exhausted good soil by raising the same crop in the same field year after year.

"My father planted corn on a certain piece of land; it answered well. . . . I do the same, though it does not answer well," complained a discouraged apologist in 1791. "I do not like new things. . . . So it goes until soil is exhausted. . . . One knows not how to fertilize and take benefit of nature's manure. This does for the present. When the land is impoverished, one goes off to Kentucky, or . . . to the Genesee. . . . Farmers, when they have used land till it would bear no crops, let it lie without feeding it. . . . The man does not work it right, but he says, this will do for the present."

Fertilizing crops with manure was a European fad with which settlers rarely experimented. Except in the rawest weather, the animals were turned to pasture, and their droppings were never preserved for fortifying cultivated lands, though on the shore farms, progressive agronomists went to the trouble of fishing for fertilizer, seining tons of whitefish to strew on the fields. It was a trick they learned from the Indians; the schools of fish at the mouth of the Connecticut near Saybrook were the prized crop-booster. "The lightest soils, enriched by them, have produced forty bushels of rye to the acre," asserted historian John Barber, "and they have an equally advantageous effect upon the growth of corn, potatoes and other productions."

The early farmers chose to do things the hard way, and so they had a battle on their hands from the start. In addition to the lean terrain, there were pests aplenty. The year 1666 brought the first scourge of caterpillars and cankerworms; later came an invasion of palmer worms to attack the rye, wheat, and apple trees, and white grubs to ruin the corn. Blasts and blight could be explained away only as retribution from the Almighty in return for community misconduct. Deer fed on the corn, and wolves fed on the livestock. Farm folk had to fight off bears and wildcats, coons and crows, muskrats and rattlesnakes, blackbirds, foxes, and woodchucks. There appeared to be no end to the assailants.

But as if the cause were righteous, they went at farming as they would go into battle. They organized by families and by a community of families to wage war in a conquest of the soil and to force the spare earth to yield them subsistence. Everyone was a farmer, and that did not exclude the doctor, the lawyer, the schoolmaster, and the minister. Self-sufficiency was the rule of their economy. Farm and home together became a family factory where everything from fabrics to cider brandy was created. The household satisfied its essential demands with what it could make, and its remaining requirements by the labor of handymen living in the immediate vicinity, through the process of swapping.

In addition to raising crops and pasturing cattle, the farmer doubled as his own carpenter, cooper, woodsman, road-builder, mechanic, veterinarian, and frequently his own blacksmith. He raised the flax, sheared the wool, and tanned the leather that went onto the backs of his children and his own back. He patched and reshod the family footwear, often modeled the only awkward shoes the children had to wear. He turned craftsman in shaping household furniture or inventing little labor-saving devices like butter churns and winnowing machines. To be sure, there was a specialist in all these things living a few miles down the road, but they became luxuries when made outside, and farm economy decreed that every article that could be manufactured at home should be produced there to avoid drawing on the thin cash purse. The coins were saved up for the purchase of pins and needles, a bit of fancy ribbon, a few tin utensils, perhaps even a clock when the peddler next put in his appearance.

Rye and Indian corn were the principal grains, with wheat and oats almost as common; in the barnyard were cattle, sheep, swine, and variety of fowl. From the dairy came kitchen-made butter and cheese; from the orchards, apples, pears, and a few coveted peaches. In better homes potatoes, carrots, and turnips were still regarded as roots fit only for cattle, but potatoes were served three times a day on farm tables, supplemented with peas and parsnips, beets and beans, cabbage and cucumbers from the kitchen garden, kept as neat as a pantry by a tireless housewife. And for breakfast there were always the poorer cuts of pork and beef. The best cuts had to be pickled for shipment to New London and the West Indies for cash—along with the bundles of oak staves and a colt or two.

In the fall, after the pests had taken their toll, as one third-generation pioneer recalled, "they gathered their scanty crops of corn, rye, pumpkins, turnips, beans and peas; they swingled their flax and hatcheled their tow; they ate of wild turkey, bear's meat, and venison . . . rendering thanks 'for such things as ye Lorde gives his people.' The women spun and wove, and made and mended, keeping their hearts as well as they kept their houses." The women worried and worked; the men sweated and worked, and for a long time did not count it as undue hardship. Year in and year out there was the back-breaking drudgery: conquering more of the forest, belaboring stumps in the path of the plow, dragging off boulders that came to the surface as regularly as the potato crop, persuading rye to sprout in soil that was too wet in spring and too dry in summer, stalking evasive game, contending with everlasting frustrations that ate into the soul and wearied the muscles.

And the farm hands were always badgered by threats of a turn for the worse in the weather—winter weather so cold that "the cow's milk shrunk away from under the cream" in the cooling pans, summer weather so wet that "the bottles of heaven" were colloquially declared to be "uncorked." In one unprecedented storm of July 3, 1788, nineteen inches of hailstones were dumped on the fields of Canterbury.

Then the predictions in the almanac came true just often enough to serve as warning for the wary: "Now comes rain"; "It may gather up for a storm"; "Looks likely for rain but there will probably be none"; "The clouds denote wind and rain"; "It may thunder in some places"; "Unusual weather"; "A sudden combustion after a long calm"; "Cloudy if not wet"; "Some unexpected change"; "A cold New England storm"; "Warm showers if not thunder"; "Freezing cold weather, after which comes storm of snow, but how long after I don't say."

When the weather itself failed to keep people on edge, there were any number of augurs that would, like *Poor Roger's American Country Almanack*, *The Freebetter Almanack*, *The Astronomical Diary*, or *The Farmer's Almanack by J. Weatherwise*. With the weather rested the success or failure of crops, more than with any other uncontrollable factor; there was always too much of it.

No one attempted to minimize the adversities of farming. It was an exacting, exhausting round—a fourteen-hour day, seven days a week, except that on Sunday there was nothing to do but milk and pasture the cows, feed the pigs, water and bed the horses, tend the hens, cope with the innumerable little emergencies that arose without respect for Sabbath regulations, and go to church—twice. Three hundred sixty-five days a year the same chores had to be repeated. And winter was no siesta, for it was then that the wood chopping and lumbering had to be done, the shoe repairing, the threshing, the hatcheling, and the snow shoveling.

Rewards there were, of course—the life of independence, the satisfaction of accomplishing the impossible, the pleasure of watching a field of rye change color from verdant green to butter yellow, the warmth of a stable on a blustery winter night, the sadness and the pride of seeing a fine horse, raised from a foal, leaving the yard for the last time, reined by a good driver, and a supper table rimmed with ten sons and daughters who had taken their start through the sweat of respectable labor.

Over a period of two centuries the pattern of the crop-and-cattle farm remained essentially the same, from the middle 1600's to the middle 1800's. And the principal changes in the farm village were in size and number. The big industrial towns were rural and the little towns industrial. There was small difference between them. Every town had a sawmill, a gristmill, a cider mill, a blacksmith, and a wheelwright, and if the home community were deficient, the next town had a tannery, a cabinet-maker, harness-maker, tinsmith, and hatter—all of whom were farmers, too, in their spare time.

There was enough food, but there was never enough cash. After 1810 the demand for potash and pearlash dropped off; income from trade with the West Indies was as uncertain as the vagaries of politics in France and Great Britain. Very early, the farmer decided that he needed some dependable specialty, a cash-producing enterprise that would bring in enough additional revenue to piece out the lean subsistence. And in a successful search for the remunerative side line, he often found the beginning of an escape from farming, for after a trial run of a few years, the spare-time occupation developed into a full-time occupation. It was one way of earning emancipation from the rigors of agriculture.

The first escapes were into agricultural specialties. In Hartford and Middlesex counties, the best route was in orchard planting—not with the prospect of raising a fine edible fruit, but rather with producing quantities of pippins, spitzenburghs, redstreaks and guelderlengs for vinegar, cider, and cider brandy. On farms with modest-sized orchards, production of five or six hundred—even a thousand—barrels of applejack was not uncommon; but when the apple-grower got into the thousand-barrel category, with his own cider press and distillery, he was far along the road toward being more of an industrialist than a farmer. Scores of tired tillers found a new occupation in a cider mill.

"A great quantity of cider is annually made, which is used extensively, as a common drink," observed a back-country editor; "and a small portion of the surplus is exported; but the principal part of it is manufactured into spirituous liquor, called cider brandy. There is probably no part of the United States, in which the growth of the apple is so sure as upon the Connecticut River. Here it never entirely fails. Cider is an excellent and wholesome beverage; but its quality depends in a great measure upon the attention which is bestowed upon its manufacture and preservation; and it is much to be regretted that so important an article should in general be so much neglected." Considering the fact that there were five distilleries for converting cider into brandy in the apple town of Farmington, eight at Canton, and twelve in Berlin, the editor obviously set a high industrial standard or was opposed to immoderate consumption of brook water.

He was happier about conditions in the Windsor-Enfield area, where there was a total of twenty-one gin distilleries, in which farmers had found another kind of escape. "The business is pursued extensively and advantageously," he asserted pridefully, "and employs a great amount of capital. The gin manufactured in the aforesaid towns is of an excellent quality and is mostly sent abroad for a market. These towns having engaged so extensively in the manufacture, and taken the lead of all others, it is not improbable that some of them may become the Scheidam of America. This business furnishes a ready and advantageous market for grain and wood, and contributes in no small degree to the agricultural prosperity of the county. . . . Gin forms a large and valuable staple for exportation, greatly exceeding any other manufactured article in the State."

For its export of liquors in 1816, the town of East Windsor alone paid duties to the Collector of the District totaling $23,913, and could boast of six distilleries, "four of which are on an extensive scale and continue the business without interruption throughout the year. . . . There is probably no town in the United States where there is as great a quantity of spirit made from grain as in East Windsor." At the time, farmers were raising annually some 70,000 bushels of rye, most of which went directly to the gin distilleries of East Windsor and Warehouse Point. During those rich and productive years, many a farmer on both sides of the river in the upper part of the Connecticut valley found amelioration from the rugged farm life, both financial and spirituous.

At Wethersfield, there was sanctuary in another specialty—absurd at first, but soon expanding into a magnificent trade that reeked all the way from New York to the West Indies. Onions. There was no Hartford clay in the soil of Wethersfield, and none of the Windham County glacial debris. It was richly productive alluvial, a sandy loam with a mixture of "garden mold"; and some back-yard gardener discovered soon after settlement that onions thrived in it. The rows got longer and longer and the esculent roots bigger. When an absorption point had been reached in the local market, they were bunched and roped, Latin-style, and shipped experimentally in small quantities, along with horses, beef, and barrel staves, to the West Indies. They never came back.

The market expanded until Wethersfield was shipping them out by the ton in the early 1800's, over a million and a half bunches a year, more onions than were grown in any other town on the continent. The smell of Wethersfield was the butt of jokes everywhere along the Atlantic shipping lanes; boatloads of onions passing down the Connecticut provoked cheers and jeers from the shore towns, and travelers made long detours to sniff and sample the phenomenon of Onion Town. One elated visitor wrote ecstatically: "It is peculiarly novel and interesting, on passing through the town in the month of June, to behold in every direction the extensive fields of onions. Whilst in a luxuriant state of vegetation, the growing vegetable exhales its strong savour. The atmosphere becomes impregnated, and the luscious qualities of the onion are wafted far and wide upon every passing breeze."

Every conceivable kind of experiment was faithfully tried in an effort to squeeze profit out of the reluctant Connecticut soil. Hemp-raising and flax were explored on a large scale, and groves of mulberry trees were set out to feed silkworms; great acreages of watermelons were planted in East Hartford; Norfolk went into maple sugar and in one year produced 21,000 pounds; at Enfield, the Shakers devoted themselves to improvements in horticulture and made a specialty of raising garden seeds for the market. At New Haven, the firm of Jacobs & Israel decided that men of the soil should produce their own rum, as well as their own gin and applejack, and advertised for public scrutiny: "Any Gentlemen, Farmers or others, that have any juice extracted from Corn-stalks which they are desirous of having distilled into Rum are hereby notified that the subscribers, Distillers in the town of New Haven, will distill the same on shares, or otherwise, as they can agree. And those who please to favor them with their employ, may depend on having the strictest justice done them, and their liquor distilled to the fullest proof. Or any person that would rather dispose of said juice or Corn-stalks, on delivering it at the Distillery, will receive the Market Price; and every favor will be most gratefully acknowledged by the Public's very obedient servants, Jacobs and Israel."

Despite all its industry, New Haven was considered predominately bucolic well into the first decades of the 1800's, and so great was the urge to escape from agriculture that many a husbandman gave up cattle farming for oyster farming, "the leading business of the inhabitants and steadily increasing" in 1836, when 130,841 bushels passed through the markets.

But the great diversion from crop-and-cattle farming was tobacco. Unlike most of the other plants with which they were experimenting, tobacco was indigenous. When the first settlers arrived, the Indians were cultivating plots of poke or ottomauch. It

was a weed with a small round leaf, quite different from the familiar Virginia type, which had been imported from the West Indies under the label of "tobacko." The Indians mixed the dried
leaves with sumac and smoked it in pipes for ceremonial occasions,
or concocted a thin brown beverage which was remarkably effective in relieving the drinker of his problems of the hour. Squaws
planted, fertilized, and guarded the patches of corn and pumpkins, but so important was the crop of poke to Indian sociology
that men retained the sacred privilege of cultivating it.

In no time the Puritans adopted the bad habits of their aboriginal associates, took to puffing their own pipes, and developed
a taste for the foul tobacco punch. The rows of tobacco in the
home garden were as essential as the rows of cucumbers and potatoes. And the magistrates were not long in discovering the wisdom of placing some limitation on the consumption. Within four
years after the first residents had moved into the Connecticut valley, the Court ordered that no one should "drinke" any tobacco,
without sanction from the authorities, except what had been
"planted within these libertyes." It was the first food-and-drug act,
designed to protect habitual users from contaminated supplies
from outside, and, incidentally to encourage the home-grown
product.

But the first law was hardly adequate to cover the excesses of ad-
dicts or the juvenile delinquents. "Many abuses are crept in, and
committed, by frequent taking of tobacko," decried the General
Court, and thereupon ordered in 1647: "that no person under the
age of twenty one years, nor any other, that hath not already ac-
costumed himselfe to the use thereof, shall take any tobacko, untill
hee hath brought a certificate under the hands of some who are
approved for knowledge and skill in phisick, that it is useful for
him. . . ." The legislators were notably charitable toward those
who already had the tobacco habit—those who "by their former
taking it, have to their own apprehension made it necessary to
them." To such, the law permitted smoking in their own kitchens
and parlors, but forbade it under penalty of sixpence for each offence "in the streett, highwayes, or any barne yards, or uppon
training days, in any open places."

Nevertheless, tobacco culture and tobacco smoking had arrived in Connecticut to stay. During the next two centuries,
amendments in tobacco legislation came almost as frequently as
the meetings of the legislators, and culture of the weed had as
many ups and downs. The broad-leafed Virginia variety was substituted for the native type. Periodically, it was exported in quan-

tity to the land of its origin—the West Indies. Shipments went to England and the other colonies. Tobacco was grown in every town, and to prevent fraud and safeguard quality production, every town had two or more inspectors—tobacco surveyors and tobacco packers. Israel Putnam returned from his expedition against Havana in 1762 bursting with enthusiasm for the cigar, and to the good Colonel goes the credit for popularizing the redolent Connecticut cheroot—Supers, Windsor Particulars, and Long Nines, as the first of them were called.

By the second decade of the nineteenth century, the Viets cigar factories in Suffield and East Windsor were daily turning out hand-rolled cigars by the thousand, and most of the back-yard nicotine patches that had been scattered over the uplands were abandoned, out of deference to the more productive soil of the Connecticut River valley. The farmers in that area had found another escape from the rigors of crop-and-cattle farming and had gone into the tobacco specialty in a big way.

Back on the hill farms, there was never a letup in the labor as the years went by. What a father saw as a reward, a son saw only as prosaic drudgery. The second generation stayed on, and sometimes the third, but there was a thinning out in each. The idea of farm dynasty was dying. Cash was still hard to come by, and the cotton mills and woolen mills came to the inland rivers with their invitations of easier money. It took cash now to replenish the impoverished soil. Even the pastures were worn thin. The virgin forest was gone, and there were fewer acorns, beechnuts, and chestnuts for the hogs. Descriptions of rich, stoneless fields stretching for unfenced miles beyond the Mississippi came back to New England. The great farm machinery, the reapers and six-bank plows, were good for the plains, but they didn't fit into the two-acre plots buttressed by stone walls. And swarms of new pests, insects, and blights swept over the farms. There were new mechanical sprayers, better plows and horse rakes, and finally a tractor with all the attachments; but the sons of the old-timers had already gone to the factories, the brokerage houses, or just West. Connecticut agriculture moved into the era of the specialist and began to take dictation from Yale's Agricultural Experiment Station or Storrs Agricultural College. But by then few of the crop-and-cattle farms were left.

Yet farming in Yankeedom is far from done for. It has merely taken another course to supplant an old order that couldn't survive the intrusions of high-geared industry. The grandsons of the American Revolution relinquished their barnyards and chicken runs to the sons of Sweden, Italy, Poland, Germany, and Austria, and the new tenants became technicians and mechanics on agricultural plants as dependent on gasoline and power lines as a cotton factory. Farm land has advanced in average value until Connecticut soil has become more precious than any other tillage in the country—not because it is richer than the San Joaquin Valley or more productive than the flatlands of Kansas, but because of its demand for other purposes, the encroachment of industry, and the proximity to the most concentrated population center in the nation. Pressures from outside have dictated a policy of intensive rather than extensive cultivation, scientific crop alternation rather than soil-depleting crop repetition, mechanization of every kind of equipment, from planes for dusting to egg-graders.

Where it was necessary a generation back to take produce to market under tedious horse power plodding over rutted and rocky country roads, trucks now roll over surfaced highways that border the acres of every orchard and vegetable patch. Farm buildings, once cheaply constructed out of lumber from the back wood lot, and sheltering a few homemade implements and home-raised stock, are replaced by costly buildings and expensive equipment, representing capital investment of enormous sums. And the consumer is reminded of that investment every time he pays two bits for a bottle of milk instead of a nickel, seventy-five cents for a basket of berries instead of fifteen, a quarter for a bunch of carrots rather than five cents for two bunches.

On diminutive Connecticut fields, it is more profitable to raise hay and corn silage than wheat, oats, rye, barley, and buckwheat, so the farmer has given up these once profitable crops, concentrates on his timothy and hybrid maize, and buys his grain. His potato crops yield in income almost as much as his tobacco. Dead fish was the first fertilizer to be abandoned, and the sprinklings of barn-yard manure and wood ashes weren't enough; after the Civil War guano was replaced by commercial fertilizer, and in the current decade the annual bill for phosphates and bone meal alone represents considerably more than the total income of a two-hundred-acre farm in 1800.

With the cost of insecticides, hire, interest, taxes, seed, advertising, and general mechanization, farming has become an expensive enterprise, and the one factor that makes it pay at all in Connecticut is that the market has come to the farmer; he no longer has to travel very far to find it. Fluid milk is sold within a few miles of the homogenizing plant; no longer does it have to be converted into cheese and butter for preservation and easy transport. Small fruits and vegetables—including the persistent onion—are harvested from some twenty-five thousand acres and delivered directly to waiting city markets. Eggs and friers are picked up by dealers who back their trucks up to the coops. Apples that aren't sold at roadside stands go directly to retailers, commission men, or wholesalers.

In dollar value, poultry has taken the lead among farm products, relegating the dairy to second place, and tobacco, which long held supremacy, to third. In fact, palatial chicken barracks are the most conspicuous feature of the agricultural landscape, and Connecticut's gallinaceous birds are coveted wherever poultry is raised. Forty per cent of the meat poultry in the United States took its ancestry from a single farm in Glastonbury—the Arbor Acres White Rocks.

The Connecticut farmer can still have a good living, and a rewarding one, and he is spared many of the difficulties of his predecessor, but he will do well to fortify himself with a technician's training, a scientist's patience, and a degree from the University of Connecticut. He is as indispensable now as Miller Gay was to Lebanon in 1775.

· 5 ·

MARINERS

ON JANUARY 21, 1954, MRS. DWIGHT D. EISENHOWER SWUNG A BOTTLE against a sleek hull slanted down the ways of a shipyard in Groton, and the *Nautilus,* with screeches of resistance, slowly slid into the Thames River. For the ceremony there were the usual brief speeches, the usual platform of celebrities, the usual display of patriotic color, and the packed throng of many thousand spectators; but there was something most extraordinary in this great event: the crowd was bearing witness to the launching of the first atom-powered submarine.

Many of the witnesses that day could remember reciting from grammar school exercise books, when they were forty years younger, the undisputed axiom "Atoms aren't divisible." But the atom had been divided, and, as a result, this thirty-million-dollar monster was to be driven by turbines supplied with steam generated from the heat of an atomic reactor. The Navy was not revealing publicly what speed the submarine was capable of doing, but it was no secret that she could travel submerged around the world without touching port.

If this proved feasible for a submarine, imaginations could be permitted to run wild on what the split atom might do for giant transports and for industry. The crowd was witnessing not only the launching of a new warship, but the launching of a whole new era for mankind. It was one of the great moments in nautical and in global history.

No one has counted the thousands of ship launchings that have taken place on the Thames estuary. In the years before steel, steam, and electronics, a new ship skidding down the ways was much too common an occurrence to attract any mass observance. Another vessel, added to the vast fleet already in the harbor, brought little excitement. In recent decades, New Londoners have watched gray warships mysteriously sweeping in and out of the harbor, a tug occasionally puffing up toward Norwich with a barge in tow, the flotilla of yachts in summer, and the ferries shoving off on schedule for Fisher's Island and Montauk Point; but for most of the year it is a sluggish harbor.

The pageantry of the *Nautilus* launching and the routine movements about the estuary are most unspectacular, compared to the extravaganza of nautical activity that crowded the mouth of the Thames between New London and Groton during the golden days of West Indian traffic before the Revolution; or the era of whaling ships in the middle 1800's, when New London vied with Nantucket and New Bedford as capital of an industry extending to the far horizons of the Atlantic and the Pacific, the Arctic and the Antarctic. The harbor was then a forest of hundreds of masts, and sailings to distant corners of the globe were everyday occurrences.

The enormous warehouses and docks on either side of the river flowed with ponderous activity and reverberated with the thunder of a great port, while the endless procession of teams leading to the New London wharves backed up all the way to Norwich, and the shipping yards were mountains of barrels, gear, and supplies.

Unlike the men of Nantucket, the New Londoners were seamen from the beginning, not primarily fishermen. The epoch of West Indian trade began with Master John Coit, who in 1664 went into the business of building shallops and pinnaces for trading voyages along the coast, to other Connecticut ports, to Boston and New York. His pinnaces of a modest twenty or thirty tons gradually went farther afield on commercial explorations—as far north as Newfoundland, as far south as Virginia. The cargoes of pelts and wampum, the country-cured hams and salted beef, found such a ready market among the other colonies that the business gave him and his sons the courage and capital to invest in larger ventures.

The shallops were replaced by three fine barques toward the end of the seventeenth century, and off to the Caribbean Captain Samuel Chester sailed in the *Endeavor*, with a shipment of more cured pork and beef, staves for thousands of barrels, hogsheads, tuns, and casks from the shops of Connecticut coopers, and a few ponies that the enterprising Coits estimated might net a pretty profit from some West Indian plantation.

Twenty-eight days later Captain Chester made fast his hawsers at a Barbados quay and found that Coit had not been overly optimistic about the demand for New England farm products in the Caribbees. The *Endeavor* was back in New London less than two months after she had sailed, her hold filled with hogsheads of sugar and molasses, and one contraband cask of rum. During the brief voyage of the ship, the magistrates of the colony had gotten wind of the *Endeavor's* destination and slyly passed an ordinance forbidding the importation of any of this Barbados kill-devil that had brought so much trouble to Massachusetts. Captain Chester reluctantly surrendered his prize to the magistrates, but no group of Connecticut Yankees could long endure the torture of seeing adjacent colonies cleaning up on a profitable trade; the ban on Barbados rum did not remain long on the books.

Dreams of fortunes to be made in West Indies trade were forming before the hold of the *Endeavor* was emptied. The rush was on. New companies sprouted overnight. A master shipbuilder of Portsmouth, England, Captain John Jeffrey, was lured to Groton with the gift of land for a shipyard and promises of a wad of contracts for new construction. On both sides of the Thames, the shore line slowly disappeared behind acres of wharves, warehouses, ways, and depots. The fervor was not localized, for farmers and factory owners, trappers and traders all the way up the valleys of the Thames, the Shetucket, the Willimantic, and over toward the Connecticut, were as much interested in reaping the rewards of Caribbean trade as the linen-clad merchants and shrewd skippers who maintained offices close to the piers.

By 1715 and 1720, the plush days of the West Indies traffic had arrived. They lasted for fifty years—until the threat of war with Great Britain and the bloody European contest for Caribbean real estate brought an end to it. During that half-century, New London and Groton flourished. At the height of the summer season, on one day, four or five great merchantmen might be loading at once, bound for Martinique, Antigua, Barbados, Jamaica, or Paramaribo. And the traffic they drew from the inland hills and valleys strung out for miles back into the countryside.

A hundred great wagons, each drawn by a dozen horses, or huge oxcarts would lumber through the streets of New London during a single morning, in a confusion of dust, shouts, whipcrackings, and cussings of teamsters. And down the Thames from Norwich plied scores of small craft, low in the water from their heavy cargoes. Sacks of wheat and dried peas from the farms of Mansfield, barrels of kiln-dried corn from Pomfret, tierces of ham from Coventry, casks of pickled pork and beef from Norwich, tubs of butter from Plainfield and Moosup, rich round cheeses from Lebanon and Colchester, wagons piled high with spruce pipe staves and hickory hoops shaped, shaved, and steamed in remote workshops. There were few towns in the counties of Windham, Tolland, and New London that were not represented in the processions. Then, interspersing the wagons, came the drovers with herds of steers or strings of colts.

During some of those fabulous days, it appeared that eastern Connecticut was denuding itself for the benefit of the West Indies trade, but by dint of hard labor back in the hills there were always more products where these came from. Shipments out inspired larger farm industry and kept a few men of the soil from migrating, and on the returns many of the spacious homesteads all the way north to Putnam, Woodstock, and Stafford were built. As a by-product, the drovers, teamsters, and farm boys also picked up many of the ways of the world in the New London taverns and grog shops. And after a night of carousing, imbibing strong tobacco and stronger Barbados liquors, they carried their heavy heads and ponderous loads of sugar, molasses, and rum back north to the dull village, where they could spread the spicy gospel of New London among their awed companions.

As abruptly as they began, the tumultuous and profitable days of the West Indies trade terminated with the end of the American colonial period. The first naval expedition of the new Continental Congress was fitted out at New London in January, 1776, and returned three months later with eighty-eight captured cannons, seventy prisoners, and a wealth of pilfered British supplies. The ships that had carried beef and molasses up and down the coast mounted odd mortars and fieldpieces on their decks and went forth as privateers to worry the British fleet. But the most lively activity during the Revolution was the performance of the whaleboats.

All along the shore on both sides of the Sound, from Stamford to New London and from Throgg's Neck to Sag Harbor, little whaling "companies" had carried on a sportive existence for years. A dozen or twenty youths in a waterfront community would get together and build or buy a forty-foot craft on the order of a sloop, designed for easy maneuverability as well as competitive speed. In order to avoid dependence on wind or tide, they were outfitted with eight long oars as well as sails. The original purpose of the craft was capturing offshore whales, but they had been put to as many uses as the shallops of the early colonists—fishing, freighting and short-haul ventures. Although they were seldom used for catching whales by 1775, the informal "companies" existed in every port for sport as well as utilitarian interests.

At the outbreak of the Revolution, they were natural units to volunteer as task forces for swift, surreptitious missions across the Sound; for four years they did yeoman duty. On a dark night a squad would set out on a spying errand; in full daylight an outfit would brazenly take off on a trading expedition with goods declared contraband by the British. There were scavenging parties, abduction parties, reprisal parties, pillaging parties. Minor Long Island strongholds were captured in commando raids, enemy ships were burned or taken in bold boardings. The whaleboats disrupted traffic in and out of New York Harbor, and pounced upon so many unwary fishermen at the Shrewsbury banks that the fishing grounds on which Manhattan depended were virtually deserted.

It was on a whaleboat that Nathan Hale, disguised as a schoolmaster, was ferried to Long Island on his fateful spying expedition in 1776, and it was while he was waiting for his return whaleboat transportation that he was captured—a delay that was responsible for the line: "I regret only that I have but one life to give for my country."

Captain Caleb Brewster of Fairfield was perhaps the most prominent hero of the whaleboat service. He already had the capture of one enemy warship on his record when on December 7, 1782, he took command of a half-dozen of the little whalers, intercepted an armed enemy fleet, and forced his boats into their midst. In the hand-to-hand conflict that ensued, scores were killed and wounded on both sides, and the captain had a rifle ball in his shoulder, but the enemy was repulsed and two of the vessels captured. The wound had healed enough by the following March to permit another whaleboat attack on the *Fox*, a sizable British gunboat anchored in the Sound for the specific purpose of eliminating the traffic of the whaling privateersmen. Brewster stole up on the *Fox* one dark night; he leaped aboard with his men, bayonets fixed; in two minutes the British captain and several of his men were dead, and the vessel was in the possession of the rebels.

The surrender at Yorktown did not bring a restoration of the rich West Indies trade to New London. Faint-hearted attempts were made to re-establish commerce along the Atlantic seaboard, and occasionally a vessel cleared for the West Indies, London, Liverpool, Cadiz, or Ireland, but the former activity of the port was gone. Norwich, which had suffered far less during the war, succeeded in usurping its full share of the commerce and for a time half a hundred seaworthy ships proudly advertised the home port across their sterns. Between 1795 and 1805, some of the traffic was renewed at New London, but as long as France and Great Britain were at war, neutral commerce was in jeopardy on the high seas. The thriving seaport became a derelict waterfront town; the barques and merchantmen gathered barnacles and rotted at their anchorages. Wharves and warehouses fell into dilapidation. Self-appointed economists tried to indicate that whaling was the answer to all the depression of the town, but a few unsuccessful trips robbed both skippers and merchants of their ardor for going into the oil business. Stubbornly refusing to believe that the lush trade with Barbados and Martinique would not be restored, they were above the indignity of turning whalers.

During the early days of the New London settlement, whales had abounded in Long Island Sound and had been captured by boats from shore by both the Indians and settlers, but a century had made them a far less common sight, and whalers now had to go farther afield. In 1785, two brigs went out from Long Island and brought back munificent cargoes of oil—enough for the New London *Gazette* to make the waggish proposal: "Now, my horse jockeys, beat your horses and cattle into spears, lances, harpoons and whaling-gear, and let us all strike out. Many spouts ahead; whales are aplenty, and to be had for the catching." A company was formed, but the conservative merchants failed to heed the injunction; they still had their eyes on the Caribbean. Then the Embargo Act and the second war with Great Britain put a quietus on further plans.

The gradual passing of the stalwarts in the old school of West Indies trade, the general depression in a town that had to be actively seafaring or nothing, and the high price that whale oil commanded in 1819, finally brought New London back to life. The fever for whaling struck as suddenly and as contagiously as the fever for Caribbean commerce a century earlier. Every kind of craft that could be leased, purchased, or commandeered on the northeast seaboard was brought into the harbor to be converted into a whaling vessel—brigs, barques, merchantmen, schooners. A stout frame and a capacious hold were the two features that mattered, and the whaling fleet of miscellaneous vessels gathered in the Thames estuary was the sight of Connecticut.

The brig *Mary* set sail down the Atlantic coast to the Brazil Banks and returned less than a year later with 744 barrels of whale oil and 78 of sperm—twice the cargo of any ship that had gone out in previous decades on experimental runs. The *Carrier* put in with a haul of 928 barrels, and enthusiasm for the new industry mounted. When the *Mary* returned from a second voyage of a year with 2000 barrels, all thought of returning to the West Indies trade vanished. Within ten years New London had six thriving whale-oil companies, some eighty vessels, and three thousand men in the business.

Once more the farm wagons from the up-state villages rumbled into town, carrying provisions to supply two-year expeditions, for a single ship with its crew of thirty or forty required "two hundred and fifty barrels of pork, two hundred barrels of beef, and fifty of flour, with bread, corn, vinegar, codfish, pease and molasses in proportion." Blacksmith shops had a new occupation in supplying lances, harpoons, and spades, and the coopers all over the state were kept busy furnishing thousands upon thousands of stout barrels. Along the waterfront, on both sides of the Thames, the mountains of oil barrels were stacked tier on tier, with a layer of soaked seaweed on top to keep them moist and to preserve the oil.

To the Brazil Banks the ships went forth from New London to Patagonia and the islands of the Pacific, to Kamchatka and Baffin Bay, and far north to the Arctic. A favored two-year voyage took a whaler around the Cape of Good Hope, through the Indian and Pacific Oceans to the Sea of Kamchatka, then south to the Hawaiian and Society Islands, back along the Chilean coast, around Cape Horn, north across the Brazil Banks, and through the West Indies. As if returning from a great naval conquest, the "full" ship rounded Fisher's Island with banners flying, to be greeted with booming cannon and cheering throngs on the docks.

For much of the rest of the century, New London was teeming with the industry of whalers and whale oil. In 1865, the whaling barque *Nile*, which had already made close to a dozen trips around the globe, was scouring the frigid Bering Straights with a great fleet of other vessels from New London, Nantucket, and New Bedford, when the daring Confederate steamship *Shenandoah* slipped into their midst. The Civil War had extended even to the remote waters of the Arctic. Nine ships were pillaged and burned by the swift steamer, and the *Nile* captured and looted, but the

Shenandoah had other missions to carry out. The crews of the captured vessels were crowded aboard the bonded *Nile,* and she made her way down to San Francisco, only to learn that the war had ended weeks before the engagement. The *Nile* returned to New London; she was the pride of the New London fleet—"square at the bows, wide amidships, lined with six feet of solid oak forward as a protection against Arctic ice, three-decked, capacious and clumsy." If any one ship could symbolize the nineteenth-century whaling vessel from the Thames, the *Nile* was that symbol, and she survived to make many more voyages.

The industry received a mortal blow in September, 1871, when an entire fleet was wiped out in an Arctic ice floe on the opposite side of the Pole. The whaling had been good off Greenland that year, and was still good. The holds of thirty-four vessels were almost filled. Ice was closing in, warned the Eskimos, but the killing was too good to leave. So the captains chose to ignore the counsel of the natives. They waited too long. The wind suddenly veered, blocking off the escape of the fleet assembled in a narrow bay. The massive blanket of ice extended to the horizon. Not one of the thirty-four ships escaped the crushing assault, and the crews were rescued only after torturous exposure of two weeks—rescued by a whaler that had managed to remain free outside the bay.

Petroleum and Thomas Edison's new lamp finished off New London's profitable industry. The last whaler came to port in 1909, and remained there with scores of others to rot in picturesque squalor in the harbor. Steamship companies, yachtsmen, and the Navy took over in the following decades; the nautical glory and romance that were New London's during the epochs of West Indies trade and the whaling ships were never to return.

The fortunes of that one harbor were not very different from the fortunes of the other harbors lying between Greenwich and Stonington, except that the mouth of the Thames gave New London the superior port, and both her prosperity and her adversities were accordingly more spectacular. Every cove that could shelter a ship in a storm shared in the state's maritime history, and each community with a seaworthy outlook contrived to develop a specialty.

Derby, at the head of tidewater twelve miles up the Housatonic, started shipbuilding in 1657, and long before Bridgeport or New Haven had expanded into major ports, Derby was the shipping center for the inland towns of the southwestern section of the state. The Derby Fishing Company was as well known in the Mediterranean and the West Indies as in Manhattan. Mystic became the center for clipper ships during the Gold Rush period, and from her ways Captain John E. Williams took the *Andrew Jackson* in 1860 on a run around the horn to California to establish the record of eighty-nine days and four hours—outdoing the famous *Flying Cloud* by nine hours. Stonington, "the Nursery of Seamen" and an early port of entry, built whalers and gave birth to scores of whaler captains. Before steamships stole the march on her trade, she was destined to be an important enough port for the federal government to expend $35,000 on a breakwater.

New Haven was late in getting into the commercial race, but just before 1800 she had begun to concentrate on Oriental trade, with as many as a hundred ships clearing the port annually for a flourishing trade in the Pacific, China, the East Indies, and the South Seas. In 1797, the *Neptune* sailed from New Haven with the ardent trader Captain Townsend at the helm, a general cargo in the hold, and five hundred gold dollars in the skipper's locker. He headed for the West Indies, where he picked up rum and sugar; at Rio he took on sandalwood and indigo; off the Falkland Islands and Tierra del Fuego the crew spent a few weeks sealing. Then the *Neptune* set sail for the South Seas, where calico, cottons, brass wire, and hardware were swapped for more dyes, pearls, and pearl shell. In Shanghai, the captain bartered his sealskins and the last of his original cargo for teas, silks, lacquer ware, porcelain, and ivory. When he returned to New Haven, two and a half years after shipping out, he had a cargo worth a quarter of a million dollars and the original purse of five hundred dollars intact.

The Long Wharf was built at New Haven in 1802, and it became the center for a new sealing fleet and a booming commerce in sealskins as well as the Oriental trade. In fact, one of the scourges of the town was the insufferable odor of thousands of sealskins drying in the sun on New Haven Green. The War of 1812 threw some six hundred registered seamen out of jobs, and after the opening of the Farmington Canal in 1828 and the Hartford and New Haven Railroad five years later, manufacturing, rather than shipping, became the principal interest of the city. With Bridgeport, the story was much the same; its lusty trade and interest in seafaring declined with the coming of a railroad in 1840 and the start of an industrial boom.

On the Connecticut River, every other town and village conjured up spectacular dreams of developing into a major port for seagoing ships. In fact, Wethersfield, far up the River, in 1649 built the first vessel in the colony and took an early lead in export of hides, salt beef, bricks, fish, and onions. Middletown, the wealthiest town in Connecticut during the second half of the nineteenth century, vied with New Haven for Oriental trade and reaped enormous profits in African slave trade. Warehouses and wharves reached into the river at Windsor, Hartford, Gildersleeve, Portland, Middle Haddam, East Haddam, Essex, Old Lyme, and Old Saybrook. A schooner of ninety tons slid down the ways at Portland in 1741; some of the famed fighting ships of the Revolution came from the same yards, and when a line between New York and Charleston was established in 1836, the company placed its contracts for ships with the Portland firm. Old Lyme registered some sixty skippers who guided clipper ships and packets to Calcutta and Liverpool, Le Havre and Hong Kong. Shipyards appeared even on the tributaries of the Connecticut; Leesville on the Salmon River held a monopoly on inland construction of sloops.

At Windsor, locks were built around the rapids in the Connecticut in 1829, when it was assumed that the River would become the major New England traffic artery, and plans were afoot to make the stream navigable all the way north to Barnet, Vermont. Indeed, much of the lumber and produce of New Hampshire, Vermont, and Central Massachusetts was making its way down the Connecticut. Canals and dredging were all that was needed to convert a great outlet into a history-making avenue to the sea.

The promoters of New Haven didn't like the looks of it. They coveted the trade that was heading toward Hartford, Middletown, and Saybrook, and started working on schemes for turning the commerce in their direction. After the opening of the Erie Canal, whenever two business designers got together, the conversation inevitably turned to canals. The whole future of American transportation lay in the construction of canals—canals of the scope that New York had possessed the foresight to build. Engineers were demonstrating how readily a connection could be made between the St. Lawrence River and the Hudson, between Boston, Massachusetts, Dover, New Hampshire, Portland, Maine, and the Connecticut; Vermonters were projecting a ditch through the Green Mountains from the Connecticut River to Lake Champlain. New Haven had to tie into this system. The Farmington Canal was their answer, so the landlubber mariners of New Haven expended their enterprise and capital in a magnificent attempt to drain off their share of the inland commerce.

On July 4, 1825, with festivities appropriate to the day, the first earth was moved for a great waterway that could eventually connect the St. Lawrence with Long Island Sound—at New Haven. The route would give Hartford a wide berth. It followed up through Hamden, Cheshire, Southington, Plainville, Farmington, Avon, and Granby, then across the Massachusetts border to North- ampton. Within three years, the fifteen-mile stretch and the nine- teen locks between the Long Wharf at New Haven and Cheshire were completed; later in 1828, the canal reached to Farmington, and the following year to Westfield, Massachusetts; in 1835, it was carried to Northampton. The first leg of the waterway that was to bring riches to New Haven was in operation. As the first boats passed through, most of the citizens of central Connecticut were on the banks or the bridges to wave hilarious greetings. Horses and carriages were bedecked in ribbons; flags were flying, bands play- ing, guns saluting. At night the boats passed down the canal in the glow of hundreds of bonfires. "My God," cried the octoge- narian John North, standing on a Farmington bridge, "what would our fathers have said! Who'd a-thought of a boat going across the great plain!"

The canal was indeed a great achievement. On the Connecticut section alone there were twenty-eight locks; close to a dozen stone culverts were built under the canal where brooks and creeks had been intercepted; and south of Avon the waterway crossed the Farmington River on an amazing wooden aqueduct supported by stone piers. To little towns like Avon, the canal brought a spurt of business such as had never been dreamed of; to manufacturers, it brought reductions in fuel costs; to the farm boys en route, it brought a luster of excitement, good fishing in summer, and good skating in winter; to the merchants in New Haven, it brought new commerce, but not the deluge they had expected; to its owners, it brought nothing but headaches.

The troubles started almost before the first boats had passed through the sixty locks between Northampton and the Canal Basin at Long Wharf. There were landslides and washouts, leak- ages and lawsuits. Freshets gouged out the banks, and summer droughts left empty mud flats. In one flood, a boat broke away from its towline, swept through a breach in the dike, and reached Avon before it could be stopped. Two deacons in Cheshire who owned a gristmill were convinced that the canal men had ap- propriated their water. "On dark nights they took a long iron rod and tested the bank, which hence often washed away there, and the deacons had plenty of water to grind with." The gaily painted canal boats carried appealing names like *The Rising Sun* and *Wild- fire*, but despite the names, it took a full week for a New Haven businessman to make the round trip to Northampton and back.

The canal was a failure from the start. The management was

changed; New Haven banks poured more money into its operation; New York investors were persuaded to buy more stock. Still
the toll charges added up to a pittance compared with the cost of
construction and operation. The only dividends ever paid to stockholders were from the hay that was cut along the banks. Ten years
after the great enterprise was completed, the managers gave up trying to collect new subscriptions for stock; in 1847 operations were
suspended; the canal was abandoned and the right of way sold to
the Consolidated Railroad. To the last, a few die-hards maintained
that there was money in the canal. "So there proved to be," replied the cynic, "over one and a quarter million of dollars in it, and
no one able to get it out."

Other attempts at operating Connecticut canals followed the
same pattern as the Farmington: the Blackstone and Middlesex,
the Quinebaug in 1824, the Sharon in 1826, the Saugatuck and
New Milford in 1829. Connecticut was too rough and too hilly
for any canal project to become a paying venture. The inland
mariners lacked the know-how of the mariners on the high seas or
on Long Island Sound.

The fresh-water sailors on the Connecticut saw far greater prosperity than those of the Farmington valley. During the middle decades of the century, before the railroads stole a complete monopoly on swift transportation, the River was the liveliest and noisiest
thoroughfare crossing the state. Scores of flat-bottomed, cabinless
freight scows, and enormous log rafts from the forest slopes of New
Hampshire and Vermont, cluttered the channels from Thompsonville south to Saybrook. And between Hartford and Springfield
paddled the impressive passenger steamers: the *James Dwight*, the
Agawam, the *Greenfield*, the *Massachusetts*, and the *Vermont*. No
one in central Connecticut had lived until he had made the exciting voyage of twenty-five miles between the two metropolises—at
the extortionate rate of two dollars a round trip. There was the
thrilling churn of the heavy paddles as the river steamer forced a
way against the current; the tooting of the whistle as the ship
passed a dock, a village, or another craft; the grumble and hiss of
the mighty engines; the waving and shouting to neighbors on
shore; and the importance of walking down the gangway under
scrutiny of the less fortunate spectators gathered at the docks.

Then there was the *Goodsell*, strictly a freighter, carrying fifty
tons and used for towing the three or four scows of Abbe, Wood-
ward and Company between Saybrook and Holyoke. She
freighted corn up river and freighted corn down; the sacks of
Green Mountain and White Mountain corn went to the southern

Connecticut market, and the sacks of western corn that had been shipped through the Erie Canal and down the Hudson went to the northern Connecticut market. Distilleries at Scitico and Warehouse Point used three hundred bushels a day, and the *Goodsell* had to keep them supplied. Downstream, along with the more modest tonnage of New England grain, she carried lumber, paper, tobacco, and barrels of gin. On one of her fenced scows she often towed a seething mass of fat black hogs from Vermont farms, squealing and grunting disputatiously in the wake of her paddles.

But the river traffic with the real picturesque appeal was the fleet of flatboats—independent of steam—as many as forty at a time moving downriver under full sail, ahead of a brisk north wind and carrying everything from lumber and maple syrup to silk and stone. On the flatboats, too, came the powder from the mills at Hazardville, packed in kegs weighing from six to twenty-five pounds, destined for the magazines in the Jersey flats. As many as thirteen thousand kegs might be stacked on a single barge, and the crew for these trips was not easy to come by, in view of the vulnerable cargo. On one occasion, a skipper watching the approach of a lowering thunderstorm finally tossed over an anchor and set out for shore with the entire crew—except for one intrepid member who chose to remain on board, and called after the disappearing skiff: "God Almighty'll have to shoot pretty straight to hit this old hulk." The challenge was accepted from on high; the captain and crew returned to find the powder kegs miraculously intact and the defiant protector of their cargo sprawled unconscious in the companionway, where a bolt had felled him.

The upstream traffic moved at a dawdling pace except under the propulsion of a stiff south wind. Lacking the wind, the crew of the scows took to their fourteen-foot poles and had to walk the heavy craft up the river in a tedious tread from bow to mast-board, mast-board to bow, with the heavy pole under the arm and against the shoulder. The process could go on for hours or days, unless the wind veered. At night, the boatmen cast anchor and rowed ashore to the comfort of one of the taverns that catered to them, at twenty-five cents a meal and twenty-five cents a night. Windsor was the station to which boatmen headed far up the river looked forward with the greatest anticipation, for the locks there brought everyone to a halt and made it the natural headquarters for all the drovers, passengers, captains, and crews. They could choose between the Windsor Hill Tavern on the east shore or the Point Rocks on the west, the Hinsdale Inn at Windsor or the Old Yellow Tavern at the locks.

There was many a hazard on the river to be avoided: the treacherous sand bars, the competition for the channel with boats going in the opposite direction, the rapids at Enfield, low water after a drought, and high, rushing water after a freshet. Even the *Goodsell* on many occasions came close to falling victim of the moody river. During the flood of April, 1854, when an unprecedented accumulation of winter snows was washed off the upstate mountains in three days of torrential rain, the ship lay at Warehouse Point for almost a week with hawsers and anchor chains straining against the flood, unable to unload a cargo of sixteen hundred bushels of corn. When the storm subsided, the water was so high that she steamed up Main Street and made a landing just off the porch of the American Hotel. After dropping her cargo, the *Goodsell's* skipper rescued a shipload of stranded citizens and, at the risk of his ship on the rampaging river, sailed south to Hartford. Since he was unable to pass under the bridge, he steamed into the East Hartford meadows, recrossed the river, and landed his passengers at a drugstore on State Street.

The hazards confronting the river skippers, however, were far less awe-inspiring than those to which the mariners on the Sound were exposed. Fisher's Island, lying four miles off the mouth of the Thames, was the dread of navigators approaching or leaving the coast in inclement weather. Its sunken reefs and sharp ledges, the bars, swift currents, and shoals were the terror of every sailor. Race Point and Race Rock time and again took their toll: the *John and Lucy* in 1671, the *Providence* in 1679, staunch whaling vessels in 1735 and 1775, and the most notable victim of Race Point, the steamboat *Atlantic*, on November 25, 1846.

The *Atlantic* plied between Norwich and New York. On the night of November 25, she cleared the mouth of the Thames and, with some reluctance on the part of her captain, headed into a vicious storm with mountainous seas. The ship had hardly reached open water when the comforting thud of her engines came to a grinding halt. Frantically the engineers worked below in the dim lantern light trying to make repairs, as the *Atlantic* wallowed in the high seas. The currents all headed toward Fisher's Island, and the wind, too, carried in that direction. The engineers reported to the captain that the damage could be mended only in a shipyard. The vessel didn't have a chance. To the horror of passengers crowding the decks, she was swept across the Sound out of control, headed directly for Race Point. There she crashed and broke up, pounded to pieces in the surf and rocks, and through it all the ship's bell kept tolling pitilessly. Forty-two persons perished in the catastrophe. Lydia Sigourney, always holding her pen poised to record the latest dramatic incident in a singing stanza, commemorated the tragedy with "The Bell of the Wreck," adding a program note: "The bell of the steamer *Atlantic*, lost in Long Island Sound Nov. 25, 1846, being supported by portions of the wreck and the contiguous rock, continued to toll, swept by wind and surge, the requiem of the dead."

> *Toll, toll, toll*
> *Thou bell by billows swung,*
> *And night and day thy warning words*
> *Repeat with mournful tongue!*
> *Toll for the queenly boat*
> *Wreck'd on yon rocky shore;*
> *Sea-wind is in her palace-halls,*
> *She rides the surge no more.*

Captain Glass set sail from New London on August 20, 1872, in open defiance of terrors far more tragic than a great many Race Rocks and Race Points, and returned to tell the story. His was the first voyage of a steamer to Antarctica; he left with a commission to explore for new sealing grounds in the uncharted waters south of the Shetland Islands, and as a bonus, P. T. Barnum had offered a prize of $10,000 if the *Francis Allyn* would bring back alive a full-grown sea elephant.

For over a year the steamer rolled through the frigid waters of Scotia Sea, from the Falkland Islands and Cape Horn to the Shetlands. Captain and crew explored the northern coast of Antarctica, and went as far east as South Georgia. In a gale off Cape Horn, a man was swept overboard and miraculously washed back into the rigging by a returning billow; on Ragged Island, they rescued a beachcomber who had been shipwrecked two years before off Cape Horn and had survived on a diet of penguin legs; on the Shetland Islands, they battled clouds of stormy petrels that attacked them in flocks of hundreds of thousands; on Elephant Island, they discovered "pure copper" that had flowed out of a mountain crevasse in a stream several hundred feet wide; on snowless Maria Island, they anchored in the forbidding crater of a slumbering volcano and returned a short time later to find that their anchorage had vanished in an upheaval they had barely missed; at Frenchmen's Bay, they anchored to explore the South Georgia Islands, where the wreckage of hundreds of ships lost off Cape Horn was piled up.

There was never an hour free of peril for the *Francis Allyn*. They found sea lions, sea elephants, sea leopards, and sea dogs. And despite the constant buffeting of fierce blizzards, they caught thousands of seals, but they were unsuccessful in capturing Barnum's ten-thousand-dollar elephant. On May 10, 1874, they steamed into New London with 9275 sealskins and 42,000 gallons of sea-elephant oil. The voyage had netted a profit of $130,000. The success was so prodigious that five other ships were at once fitted out and sent to the same waters. Not one of them was ever heard from again.

Along the miles of Long Island Sound, up and down the navigable rivers, in remote inlets now cut off by bridges and highways, are innumerable sites of once flourishing ventures in maritime industry. The yachting center at Southport was a capital for nineteenth-century peddler ships carrying on a lively trade with Boston and New York. At Old Lyme, a sea captain traditionally lived in every house; and his sons and brothers were engaged in shipping, in fishing, in salt manufacture, or in building clippers on the Lieutenant River. Pleasure boats and trawlers have taken the place of the fleet of merchantmen anchored off Clinton. No one would suspect that two shipyards formerly made Gales Ferry one of the busiest spots on the Thames, or that Greenfield Hill was the favored village where retiring privateersmen and whaleboat warriors took up residence to raise chickens and tend flower gardens. Famous ships were launched at what are now ranked as quiet little agricultural towns like Essex, Middle Haddam, and Hamburg. In fact, shipbuilder Thomas Child alone sent almost 250 vessels down the ways at Middle Haddam—London packets and ships for the China trade, vessels with elaborate interiors of mahogany, rosewood, black walnut, and fine woods brought from the West Indies.

In the Marine Museum at Mystic have been gathered up the mementos of these forgotten epochs of the Connecticut struggle against the sea. There are clipper-ship models, old barque heads, the whittlings and decorations of sailors afloat, the paraphernalia of whaling and sailing days; there is a ropewalk of 1824, a rigging loft, spar shed, counting room, ship builder's home; there are sample ships, typical shops that served them, and the buildings that made up a sea-front village of past centuries. The symbols are all there, but even a fine museum cannot give a fair representation of the impregnable courage, the stamina, the human strength, and the lust for life of the sea that created the epochs.

· 6 ·

HIGHWAY STRATEGISTS

THE MOST UNEXPECTED LEGACY THE FIRST SETTLERS OF WINDHAM
County found in their wilderness was a well-beaten Indian trail
leading from Canterbury and Plainfield all the way east to Narragansett Bay—a better outlet than they could have surveyed
through trial and error in ten years of sporadic labor. To be sure,
it was a warpath—but a trade thoroughfare too, the link they
needed with civilization and commerce. Over long stretches, moc-
casined feet had trod it two feet deep into the forest sod, and for
an Indian trail it was remarkably straight; generations of Narragansetts and Mohawks shuttling east and west in hurried transit
had eliminated most of the windings, located the shallowest
river fords, and broken out enough underbrush to make it easy
to follow, even for a white man.

The Windham pioneers appropriated the trail. Widened, it became the main street for scattered villages; cleared of overhanging
branches, it became their bridle path to meetinghouse and market;
broadened still further, it became a road for oxcarts. Unfortunately, the traffic headed toward Providence and the colony of
Rhode Island, rather than to Norwich and New London, and
intercolonial trafficking was not favored by the British overseers,
but that was the last concern of independent Connecticut Yan-

kees. Gradually it took on the appearance of a highway. In the dry season, the way was just about passable; in spring or fall, no one thought of venturing over it; in winter, with a surface of packed snow and ice, it was as good as any of the king's highways back in the homeland. The cart path was soon extended west to Windham, where it connected with other Indian trails and through-ways down the Shetucket to Norwich, and with routes leading west to Hartford and north to Massachusetts. Most of the Connecticut colonists with business in Providence went by way of Canterbury.

The converted Indian warpath became known as the "Great Road," though there was nothing "great" about it, except that it presented fewer obstructions and more headroom than a compass route. The sloughs were still there, the stumps and the boulders, the risky stream crossings, and the long reaches of silent forest between villages. The sloughs became deeper with use; in a few seasons, the hoofs of cattle obliterated all the surface packing the Indians had given it; frosts pushed up more boulders into the tracks. The "Great Road" was a rutted, rocky quagmire, without a bridge or causeway over the stretch of fifty miles, yet it was one of the best highways in the colony of Connecticut.

In 1712, the legislature recognized the importance of the route, commended the towns for their achievement in commandeering it, and made a few apologetic recommendations for further improvement. The town of Plainfield got busy, pridefully hauled out some of the stumps, and laid a few rods of corduroy through the worst swamps. Other farmers en route, for their own convenience in reaching a meetinghouse or a distant hayfield, smoothed similar patches, but until 1799 the surface of the road differed little from what it was in 1699.

On September 28, 1795, a committee of surveyors made a report to the Assembly recommending two changes in the layout of the road through Windham, seven in Canterbury, six in Plainfield. "We would further observe," they summarized, "that upon a view of said road we find it proceeds in a very direct course from Windham to Providence; that it is a road of great travelling, but extremely rough and out of repair in many places; that it is capable of being made a pleasant road for carriages; but in some of the worst parts of it the inhabitants are thinly settled and the least able to repair it, and it is the opinion of your committee that after suitable repairs are made upon said road there ought to be a Turnpike Erected and Established on said road in the town of Canterbury . . . and that the avails thereof will probably be sufficient to support and maintain said road with a reasonable toll."

The recommendations were accepted and approved, but the approval also set off an endless series of wrangles over who was going to be accommodated by the road, whose pasture it was to skirt, whose potato field it was to divide. It took four years to settle the worst of the squabbles and to summon sufficient courage and capital to proceed with the project. In 1799, the Windham Turnpike Company was finally incorporated, with a franchise extending from North Coventry, along Wamgumbaug Lake, through Willimantic, Windham, Scotland, Westminster, and Canterbury to Plainfield. The road stopped at Plainfield, for in the years occupied with local polemics and fund-raising, another turnpike company with a more direct line between Norwich and Rhode Island had horned in and taken over the east section of the old Indian trail.

The "Great Road" was improved by the addition of a few bridges; it was widened, and more logs were laid for corduroy foundation; but the hills were just as steep and the March mud as soft. For the privilege of passing over it, tolls on the order of sixpence and threepence were extorted at four gates along the route for half a century. The Windham Turnpike Corporation did not pass out of existence until 1852. Section by section, the ownership then reverted to the towns through which it passed, and within the memory of residents along the way, it became a macadam-topped highway. Although there may be more direct routes to Providence, State Highway 14 stands as a forgotten memorial to the Indians who first cut it through the wilderness, and to the white settlers who stole the right of way from them three centuries ago.

There is nothing unique about the history of the "Great Road." It differs only in detail from the story of many hundreds of miles of Connecticut highway. For other roads a preliminary Indian trail did not always exist, or it was so circuitous that only its general direction could be followed; squabbles over private versus public ownership varied in intensity; arguments about location of thoroughfares, the most advantageous river crossings, and who was to foot the bills, were as variable as the terrain and the families occupying it, but the pattern was the same: the long period of indifference to road surfaces until after the Revolutionary War, the common surrender of an essential public utility to private ownership, the slow recognition of town responsibility, and finally the absorption of traffic interests by the state. Connecticut has a current reputation for maintaining one of the finest highway systems in the nation, but it also has a memorable history of some of the worst highways that ever existed in any nation.

Until about 1800 the condition of Connecticut roads was incredible. Down the center of the state, through the tobacco and onion country, was a fairly even thoroughfare, offering a magnificent scenic tour—in clement weather. "To describe the neighborhood of Hartford is to describe Connecticut," exclaimed one overenthusiastic French tourist, Brissot de Warville, in 1788. ". . . Nature and Art have here displayed all their treasures; it is really the Paradise of the United States."

But M. de Warville's travels in the state were very limited. He carefully avoided the more remote interior highways, and the very day after passing through "Paradise" encountered more typical road conditions that gave him reason to withhold some of his enthusiasm: "Heaven preserved us from accident, at which I was much astonished," he sighed with relief. "At Fairfield finished the agreeable part of our journey. From this town to Rye, thirty-three miles, we had to struggle against rocks and precipices. I knew not which to admire most in the driver, his intrepidity or dexterity. I cannot conceive how he avoided twenty times dashing the carriage in pieces and how his horses could retain themselves in descending the staircases of rocks. One of these is called Horseneck; a chain of rocks so steep, that if a horse should slip, the carriage must be thrown into the valley two or three hundred feet."

Nowhere in Connecticut—not even in the paradisiacal Hartford region—was there a single stretch of highway that could measure up to the more traveled roads of Massachusetts and New York. Connecticut topography wasn't designed to make things easy for road-builders. No road could be laid out in any direction without crossing a stream or swamp. Tidal estuaries called for circuitous zigzags along the coast. The long ridges of hills, stretching like gnarled fingers from Massachusetts to the Sound, discouraged any attempt to run a straight road east and west. Except in the broad river valleys, glacial boulders, rocks, and ledge outcroppings were everywhere. Then the natural timber growth offered impedimenta as challenging as the terrain. Virgin trees with four- and five-foot trunks and heights of 150 feet blocked progress in any direction, and clearing a prospective roadbed of a pair of them could occupy a team of road-builders for a full day. The Indians had burned the forest floor over vast tracts of greenwood; still the jungle of undergrowth came back every year, and the burning had only helped to preserve gigantic fallen trunks that blanketed the virgin land.

Contrary as was the inland country, the towns along the Sound actually had the roughest going, for the bogs and inlets made anything but the most circuitous highway an impossibility. Moreover, bridges across navigable streams were forbidden because they would be an obstruction to traffic afloat. Accordingly, coastal settlers gave up in despair and became as dependent on water transportation as Venice. At Middlesex Parish—Darien—families couldn't always afford a horse and wagon, but they all owned sloops, anchored at Pear Tree Cove or somewhere along the Five Mile River. And later, at the height of water-borne traffic, Clock's Landing was a principal port of call for some of the forty or fifty steamboats engaged in Sound trade. Repeatedly the commercial center of Darien was moved to intercept the traffic, and it wasn't until after 1848, when the New Haven Railroad erected passenger stations, that Darien began to settle down and count as much on highways as on waterways.

But all these natural obstructions were also common in Massachusetts, New York, and everywhere else along the Atlantic seaboard: Connecticut had to reckon with human obstruction as well as natural. A Yankee orneryness made things much harder for visionary road-builders than any of the natural obstacles. "So strongly individualistic were they," summarized one analyst, "that neither persons nor towns would cooperate in any enterprise which required the subordination of their own particular rights to the general good of the community unless they could see some immediate benefit to themselves. Self-contained and independent, they resented any supervision by a higher authority. . . . Just as Connecticut succeeded as a colony in evading more skillfully than any of the other thirteen, the orders of the British Crown, so the towns had a like success in relation to the General Court, and nowhere was it greater than in connection with the roads." It was a large and vicious cycle: "Bad roads discouraged intercourse, lack of intercourse increased isolation, isolation developed independence and a lack of cooperation, which in turn caused the roads to suffer."

For two centuries, there was little incentive for good roads. Population was scattered, manufacturing interests were minor, pioneering farmers didn't travel. It was an agricultural state. Regardless of law, selectmen, and the General Court, the obstinate Yankee farmer continued to regard a public road crossing his property as an invasion of his private domain. When cows were turned to pasture, a fence or gate, likely as not, went up across the road as a "pent." It was a lighter inconvenience, the farmer figured, for travelers to open gates or take down and replace fences when passing through than for him to have to circumscribe his property with a half-mile of barrier. He had no interest in building roads for a speculative future, and he was loath to inconvenience himself in any way for the convenience of transient intruders. His whole conception of rural society was one of self-sufficiency. Basically, the farm was an independent economic unit, where every essential from beef and blankets to shingles and shoes was home-produced. For items like salt, molasses, and foolscap, the household leaned on the general store; for their grist, they depended on the miller; for their edification, they turned to the minister. Both the storekeeper and the minister had to get out of town occasionally to replenish their respective wares, and four or five times a year the adult males of a village formed a great caravan and set out for Hartford, Providence, New London, or Norwich, where surpluses were traded off for cash. Many a farmer made a good thing out of these expeditions, but they were not pleasure trips; the vehicles were tough enough to plow through unbroken terrain if necessary. In such an economy, groomed highways were a luxury no one could afford. The rutted slough became an accepted institution.

There were two classes of roads. First came the town "ways," radiating from the village green or meetinghouse and meandering back over the hills to the most remote farmyard within the town limits, dead-end roads all, connecting with nothing beyond unless they accidentally crossed another highway. Then there were the "King's Highways" or "country roads," ordered and planned by some executive body higher than the town and intended to associate one town with the next. In both categories, however, construction and repair were the responsibility of the town, and over that point most of the contention welled up.

The arrangement of town ways made no sense topographically or socially—except that they were all oriented to the village church. In settling a town, the first arrivals took first choice of lands, usually with a house lot near the meetinghouse and the farm proper farther away. They took care of themselves in spacing their buildings along some main route they could agree upon. But when subsequent residents moved in and bought blocks of land that fronted on no highway, the real confusion started. A right of way to a new farm was the last consideration of either the town fathers or the purchasers. Frequently a plot of several hundred acres was entirely boxed in, leaving the owner at the mercy of his contentious neighbors. For a time, the trespassing across pastures and

potato fields, the sharing of lanes and wood paths, was tolerated
with charity. But sooner or later the trespasser grew tired of letting
down bars and being accused of not replacing them; disagreements
mounted; and then his only recourse was to petition the town for
a highway. In Thompson, a frustrated Squire Hookell petitioned
for a public road out of his hemmed-in acres because he had to
pass through twelve sets of bars before he reached a recognized
road. At Lebanon, a backwoods pariah complained that he was
weary of having threats thrown at him on the way to church as he
crossed four miles of private property and passed through "thirteen
or fourteen fences and many mirey places."

To the selectmen fell the chore of mediating the feuds, and until 1771 there was no appeal from their decision, but after that, the
petitioner could go to the county court or even to the Assembly.
The farmer who objected to having a public way cut through his
property was not unreasonable, for it meant that he would have
to go to the expense of building new fences on either side of the
new route and have his fields divided. The small compensation
he might expect from condemnation proceedings would nowhere
nearly meet the cost of rearranging his farm. It was through this
tedious process that the local roads of the state came into their
haphazard existence.

In the King's Highways there was a little more order; they were
straighter and better marked, but since the town ways did not
necessarily connect with them, the confusion persisted. Travelers
going east to Providence in 1712, for instance, would arrive at
Plainfield to find a dead end in the King's Highway; Plainfield
hadn't bothered to extend it through the village—and objected to
such intrusion on general principles anyway.

The King's Highways were an insult to the title. Like the town
ways, they were merely wide swaths cut through the woods. Rocks
and stumps remained where nature had placed them. There was
no foundation or surface. If a bog or a brook lay in the path,
crossing it was the traveler's problem. Culverts and runoffs had not
yet entered the road builders' lingo. Anyone traveling by cart without an ax, a saw, and a handy shovel was an untutored optimist;
and despite occasional markers and milestones, the route was not
distinguishable from the private cart paths that branched off from
it. At every village, an outsider paused to get his bearings and to
try to remember the directives: "You follow up the hill to Ebenezer Baxter's house, down through his pasture to his brother Nathaniel's. The dog will come after you but he's more noise than
bite. Pay no heed to the way that leaves off there to the north.

You cross the lower fordway of Becket's Creek. Water's high, but passable. Keep along the right bank till you come to the upper fordway where you'll have to use care 'count of its being fast. Down the hill to Grosset's barn and ploughed land to the old road at the northeast corner of Ezekiel Corwin's young apple orchard, foreside the meetinghouse." To an outlander, it was all as clear as a faded daguerreotype.

Under a law of 1643, all able-bodied males between the ages of sixteen and sixty were required to put in one day's labor a year on the town highways, with their teams, or pay a penalty of five shillings. There were no exceptions, but road-working was obviously an inglorious occupation for some of the dignitaries like magistrates and ministers, physicians and schoolmasters; they were soon exempt, and their places taken by slaves, servants, mulattoes, and Indians. But one day's work never proved enough, so the stint was increased to two days and as many more as thought necessary by the road committee, and to that was added still another day for work on the King's Highways exclusively.

Nothing was more distasteful than employment for the benefit of his majesty. Superficial improvements could be detected every spring, but one good downpour would obliterate all evidence of the effort. Yet these impossible highways threaded their way to every part of Connecticut—down the Housatonic, the Quinnipiac, the Quinebaug, and Shetucket valleys, along the Sound, cross-state from Voluntown to Norwich and Hartford, from Thompson and Mansfield to Hartford, from Hartford to Waterbury and west to the Hudson, from Hartford into the greenwoods of Cornwall and Canaan, diagonally from Windham County to Fairfield, from New London County to Litchfield.

"Long distance freight movement was absolutely impossible," concluded one observer. "The charge of hauling a cord of wood twenty miles was three dollars. For hauling a barrel of flour one hundred and fifty miles it was five dollars. Either of these charges was sufficient to double the price of the article and set a practical limit to its conveyance. Salt, which cost one cent a pound at the shore, would sometimes cost six cents a pound three hundred miles inland, the difference representing the bare cost of transportation." But impossible as it was, an enormous volume of commerce did pass over the roads—beef, turpentine, lumber, pork, potashes, grain, cider, and a great many cattle, sheep, and horses on the hoof, destined for markets in New London, Boston, or the West Indies. If the shipments couldn't get through in summer, they went by sled in winter.

The journey to port or town might take days, but hardships en route were no deterrent. In winter when a caravan was making up, "friendly word was circulated from farm to farm, spread chiefly at the Sabbath nooning, that . . . at break of day the long ride to market would begin. Often twenty or thirty neighbors would start together on the road to town. The two-horse pung or single-horse pod, shod with steel shoes one inch thick, was closely packed with farm wealth—anything that a New England farm could produce that could be sold in a New England town. Frozen hogs, poultry, and venison; firkins of butter, casks of cheeses—four to a cask—bags of beans, peas, sheep-pelts, deer-hides, skins of mink, fox, and fisher-cat that the boys had trapped, perhaps a splendid bearskin, nuts that the boys had gathered, shoe pegs that they had cut, yarn their sisters had spun, stockings and mittens they had knitted, homespun cloth and linen, a forest of split brooms strapped on behind, birch brooms that the boys had whittled. So closely packed was the sleigh that the driver could not sit; he stood on a little semi-circular step on the back of the sleigh, protected from the cutting mountain winds by the high sleigh back. At times he ran alongside to keep his blood briskly warm."

Peddlers, postmen, and tourists took the same roads in summer. The shore route between Stonington and Greenwich was one of the oldest and one of the most popular. It was the Pequot trail, the Boston Post road, the King's Highway to New York, the road over which Paul Revere, face daubed with war paint, dashed in December, 1773, to carry word of the Boston Tea Party to Philadelphia, the road on which Benjamin Franklin as postmaster general set up milestones—certainly a route worthy of improvement, yet for two centuries it was perhaps the worst road in the whole state.

Madame Sarah Knight, Boston social arbiter and gadabout, "a lady of uncommon literary attainments as well as of great taste and strength of mind," set out over it on horseback October 2, 1704, unaccompanied except for such guides as she could procure en route, and soon discovered that she needed strength of body as well as strength of mind to survive the trip. "Law for me—what in the world brings You here at this time of night?" screamed her first tavern hostess. "I never see a woman on the Rode so Dreadfull late in all the days of my versall life. Who are you? Where are You going? I'me scar'd out of my witts." Then to her sullen guide: "Lawfill heart, John, is it You?—How de do! Where in the world are you going with this woman?"

On her third day out of Boston, Madame Knight crossed the line into Connecticut, and her real troubles began. She "ridd on

very slowly thro' Stoningtown where the Rode was very Stony
and uneven," put up at Saxton's for the night, dismissed her guide,
and went on the next day to New London suffering sorely from the
ride, but suffering more for eighteen-year-old Jemina, sharing the
humped back of "a sorry lean Jade" with her father, who was
doubling as guide. To the pleas of Jemina that "this bare mare
hurts me Dingeely, I'me direfill sore," the old man laughed and
"kik't his Jade o'the side, which made her Jolt ten times harder."

The adventurous Madame crossed the ferry at New London
where "by reason of a very high wind, we mett with great difficulty in getting over—the Boat tos't exceedingly, and our Horses
capper'd at a very surprising Rate." On October 6, she advanced
toward Saybrook to find "the Rodes all along this way are very
bad, Incumbred with Rocks and mountainous passages, which
were very disagreeable to my tired carcass. . . ." Crossing a rude
bridge over a rampaging stream at Lyme, her horse stumbled and
she "narrowly 'scaped falling over into the water." After a safe ferry
ride at Saybrook she paused at an inn for "bait," to be greeted by
a landlady "with her hair about her ears, and hands at full pay
scratching it." Without washing the "scratchers," the hostess
broiled some pickled mutton for her, doused it in head sauce, and
served it up, but since the repast proved to be "only smell," Madame Knight paid the sixpence charge without touching it and
drove on to Killingworth for the night.

Even her guide lost his way the next day in the confusion of
lanes and bypaths about Guilford, but they managed to reach
New Haven the same night, and she stayed there for two months,
resting up and summoning courage to complete the journey to
New York. On December 6, she set out from New Haven on the
most tortuous part of the route, crossed the ferry at Stratford, arrived in Fairfield at seven in the evening for a savory dinner of
fried venison, and the next day with her guide "hasted toward
Rye, walking and leading our Horses neer a mile together, up a
prodigios high Hill; and so Riding till about nine at night, and
there arrived and took up our Lodgings at an ordinary"—where
she had to share an attic bedroom with male customers. She rode
into New York an hour before sunset the next day.

Fifty years later James Birket, a merchant and sea captain from
Antigua, went over the same route, and found no improvement in
either the road surface or the inn fare: "We traveled through a
great deal of Stony uneven road until we got to . . . Stoninton
being 21 miles where we dined upon Salt pork and Turneps with
thick Cyder to drink, here we Cross'd the Mistick river at a wooden

bridge and So proceeded through Groton a very Stoney uneven Country but no high land, only full of Small hills and risings and fallings."

En route to Nyantic, he reported, "We had very Stoney road to the rope ferry which is 6 miles. We got over very well being so narrow that a rope is Stretched across for the Safty of travelers as the tide runs here with great violence." He was rowed across the Connecticut and the Farm River on ferries, and found a "Long wooden Bridge" across the Quinnipiac; then, between New Haven and Byram Bridge, he encountered the same neglected thoroughfare that was always the subject of excoriation: "Most Intollerable bad road," "Most miserable road"—until he "entered the Government of Newyork and presently Found an Alteration in the road and Buildings &. Everything from this Bridge bearing the Marks of Industry."

Still later in the century, Hugh Finley, surveyor of continental post roads, made a tour of inspection along the old Pequot Trail and found sections of it " 'past all conception bad,' so that from daybreak to sunset he was able to make but thirty-three miles. As the road was one continuous bed of rocks, besides being very hilly, it was impossible to ride above four miles an hour and only at that speed, if the rider had a good horse." And this important post road was only a sample of hundreds of miles of similar thoroughfares.

Rhode Island, coveting the Windham County trade, looked upon Connecticut with compassion and even volunteered assistance. Their statesmen reported that the highway across the border was "very rough and greatly out of repair whereby travellers are fatigued and discouraged"; and since it was not likely to be put in good repair by "legal methods" because it lay through such "rugged and uneven country . . . the inhabitants being generally poor and scattered," they came up with a neighborly proposal that their own legislature create a lottery for the assistance of the destitute across the state line—with expectation, of course, that a considerable number of tickets would be sold in Connecticut. But the subsidy from Rhode Islanders never materialized. In 1776, a tourist, headed toward Providence from Norwich in a chaise, got only as far as Pomfret and complained, "The road was so stony and rough, that I could not ride except at a slow walk but very little of the way. I was near two days in going, such was the general state of the roads." And a trader, setting out from Killingly with a load of produce for the Boston market, made such slow progress in a day that he went back home to spend the first night.

There were two colonial post roads, one skirting the Sound, the other running down the Connecticut valley; and the men who carried the mail over them perforce made a career of battling highway impedimenta. The first "post" galloped out of New York on January 1, 1673, bound for Boston by way of Hartford, carrying two port-mantles crammed with letters, sundry goods, and bags, as well as instructions "to keep an eye out for the best roads, best ways through forests, for ferries, fords, etc., to watch keenly for all fugitive servants and deserters, and to be kind to all persons travelling in his company." The round trip took no less than a month, the exact schedule depending on the weather, the height of water at river fords, the stamina of his horse, and the number of distractions found en route. The time was gradually cut down to eight or ten days, but even in 1799, when the post carried the news that George Washington had died on December 14, the intelligence did not reach Boston until December 24.

The postrider was burdened with all manner of restrictions, which were freely disregarded. He frequently pocketed the postage on way-letters picked up and delivered on his route; he made a tidy business of serving as banking agent, carried on a variety of transactions for his own benefit as well as for the benefit of the public, and was not above accepting small gratuities from the travelers whom he was supposed to guide free of charge. A young college graduate who overtook the post between Hartford and Boston in 1790 noted that he had an entourage of "six Dames, neither young nor fair," and the postman turned abruptly surly when he began joking about the "harem."

Competing with the official "post" was a variety of private post-riders who advertised their services in newspapers and carried messages and merchandise "for the good of the Publick." They were expressly forbidden to convey letters, but since their deliveries were much more prompt than the regular mail, they rode hard over the highways transporting "sham bundles of paper or straw, weighing little, . . . used as kite-tails to the letters."

In the larger towns and cities, there were coaches and carriages, but few of them ever ventured on to the King's Highways of Connecticut prior to the Revolution. In 1772, the New York *Journal* advertised the first stage trip between Manhattan and Boston with the prospect of being "at each of those places once a fortnight. . . . Gentlemen and Ladies who choose to encourage this useful, new and expensive Undertaking, may depend upon good Usage . . . If on Trial, the Subscribers find Encouragement they will perform the Stage once a week." But the Subscribers found such impassable roads across Connecticut that there was nothing encouraging about the enterprise. Regular stage service had to be postponed until after the Revolution, when private corporations took over the management of thoroughfares.

Of necessity, many of the King's Highways became military highways during the war and were improved by men under arms—artificers and army engineers. It may have been the example they set, it may have been a new burst of spirit when independence from the Crown was something more than bluff, it may have been pride or just the realization that a good road was essential to satisfy the Yankee instinct for trade, but the late 1780's and 1790's brought on an epidemic of enthusiasm for highway improvement that had never existed before. Suddenly, even the most remote villager, as though he were tired of confinement, wanted an easy route to town. Private turnpikes were succeeding in England; they were the only answer to Connecticut's trade and transportation problems. The era of turnpikes was ushered in with tumult, shouting—and only local misgivings.

The Mohegan Road was the first—the first in New England and the second in America. The road connecting Norwich and New London, through the Mohegan country, was originally laid out in 1670 along the tribal path, and for over a century it was little more than an Indian trail and oxcart route for the loads of farm produce carried to the New London docks. In 1789, a lottery for the benefit of the road was authorized by the legislature and drawn in Norwich, with such eagerness that within two years the funds derived from it had built practically a new highway. The distance was greatly reduced by elimination of windings and sidetracks to private dwellings, so that the trip down the valley could easily be made in four hours instead of the full day formerly required. To the local populace, advantages of this sort seemed well worth paying for, and the General Assembly agreed. It became a turnpike in May, 1792; a tollgate was promptly erected, and until 1849 every tourist and merchant who traveled that route bought his right of way.

What started at Norwich soon spread in every direction, and during the next half-century 121 franchises for pikes were granted. All the highways of consequence in the entire state became toll roads. They varied in length from three or four miles to fifty or sixty and carried such names as the Greenwich, the Greenwoods, the Groton and Stonington, the Pettipague and Guilford, the Saugatuck, Salisbury and Canaan, Stafford Mineral Spring, Connecticut and Rhode Island, or Sugar Hollow. Every road had its name, and every road its individual tax, e.g.: coach, phaeton, chariot, or other four-wheeled carriage drawn by two horses, twenty-five cents; cart, wagon, sled, or sleigh drawn by two oxen or horses, ten cents; chaise or other carriage drawn by one horse, ten cents; man and horse, six cents; oxen, horses, mules, and neat cattle led or driven, one cent; sheep and swine by the dozen, three cents; etc., etc.

Bridges across which turnpikes led were all too frequently separate enterprises, exacting additional toll, and there might be three conflicting bridge companies in one town. Along the Housatonic, the struggle to attract paying customers was so fervent that bridge battles went on for years, and patrols armed with shotguns guarded the crossings day and night. Only when periodic washouts destroyed all the bridges were there truces in the warfare.

Repudiating the crooked Indian trails and meandering town ways, the surveyors of turnpikes, who went about their business seriously, reverenced the straight line with the devotion of geometricians. They disregarded hills, swamps, and private domiciles in their ardor to reach the next town by an undeviating direct course. It was a passion with the pike-builders—an uncompromising passion that brought on endless dispute. The corporation surveyed the route; the town through which it passed was then required to purchase the land on behalf of the private road company and turn over a clear title. If the town raised objections, the dispute was referred to the courts, and almost invariably the courts ruled in favor of the corporation. The Hartford and New Haven Turnpike cut in so close to the rear of Samuel Yale's residence in Meriden that "the house stood like a precipice above the roadway and soon became an eyesore and a source of so much mortification to the town that the citizens bought the house and moved it away." And for damages the corporation paid Mr. Yale a total of fifty-seven dollars.

The Woodstock and Thompson went "straight through all obstacles including the granite hill range of western Thompson." The builders of the Waterbury River Turnpike plunged directly through a cemetery at Salem (Naugatuck) Bridge, and "graves were ruthlessly opened and the bones scattered about." In laying out the Colchester and Chatham, surveyors were so intent on establishing a beeline that, before turning a spade or cutting a tree, they located a high point between towns where they could pick out two church spires, and after reading a compass bearing on the spires, they cut an unbending swath between them.

Conservative Milfordites were determined that the New Haven and Milford Company would follow the winding route of an old road instead of "running the turnpike-road through peoples' land." The Milford objections, however, served only to delay construction. As usual, the county court took the side of the company, and all objections were overruled. But it was Stamford that touched off the furor of the day. When the citizenry learned that one of those "soulless corporations" proposed to straighten a section of the Old Boston Post Road by cutting through the center of town and dividing the cemetery, they rose up en masse. It was an intolerable desecration. One by one the bodies in the graveyard were reverently transferred from their resting places to new graves, as horrified villagers looked on helplessly. There was no criticism of the handling of Stamford's honored dead, for the movers were careful to act in accord with church and state dictates, but that was slim appeasement. "Following the first day's grading operations in the cemetery, large numbers of citizens with many yokes of oxen gathered in the early darkness and labored all night, hauling large rocks into the opening at each end and blocking the entrances. But what man could put in, man could take away, and for three days Stamford piled rocks in by night and the corporation's forces removed them by day, until the money power finally prevailed. Many of the good people . . . were so wrought up by the invasion of their sacred precincts that they never afterwards would pass over that portion of the road."

While one town pleaded for the privilege of having the private turnpike connect with Main Street, the next rebelled at the suggestion. The Straights Turnpike Company, operating between New Haven and Litchfield, ignored the invitation of Waterbury to route the road through the center of town, and forever incurred the wrath of the town fathers by locating it well to one side. The company, however, depended on the town-owned bridge crossing the Naugatuck, and that bridge had a habit of going out with every freshet. The bridge was more important to the townspeople than to the company, but they would ford the river rather than rebuild it for the benefit of the turnpike. Their spleen was inexhaustible. Invariably, the legislature had to intercede before Waterbury would deign to replace it.

Pomfret, on the other hand, waged war with the Boston Turnpike Company in 1797 to keep the road outside its town limits. The distinction of having all the traffic of the "Middle Route" pass through the village was a small attraction compared to the cost of procuring land rights. But Pomfret lost its battles with both the company and the legislature, and had to levy a damaging tax to pay for a privilege it couldn't afford. Five years later, the village lost another hassle to keep the Connecticut and Rhode Island out of its limits. By that time, Pomfret was so near bankruptcy from fighting turnpikes and paying legal fines that it seriously considered selling its new town hall to get out of debt.

The establishment of a turnpike did not necessarily assure a through-way that was an appreciable improvement over the old King's Highways. The stumps were hauled out of the way, and the largest boulders; its width, length, and general features were described in the state charter; but there was ample room for evading anything but the letter of the contract. The mud could be as deep as it had always been, the inclines as sharp, and the ledge outcroppings as frequent. Occasionally, charters had the scent of a political plum, and gates were erected on old roads with scarcely any improvement at all. That was the case with the turnpike between Norwich and Hartford. Both of these settlements were elevated to the status of cities in 1784—thirty-eight years before the same distinction was conferred upon Boston—but the track between them remained in an appalling state of disrepair. Finally, a corporation with the formidable title of "Hartford, New London, Windham and Tolland County Turnpike Society" was organized in 1795, with an extravagant prospectus for a grand highway. The old road was worked over perfunctorily, gates were erected, and the toll poured in—as regularly as the complaints. In winning the franchise, members of the society had too obviously known the right legislators. There was virtually no improvement over the original road, and the interest of the incorporators was limited principally to cashing in on the heavy traffic between the two cities. Both a scandal and a legislative investigation loomed up—and only then did the "Society" begin to meet its obligations.

Financing was often on an amateur basis. The Talcott Mountain Turnpike, which formed part of the route from Hartford to Albany, was so badly managed that the legislature "deemed it necessary to appoint a committee to liquidate the accounts of the company, determine the amount of stock, audit the accounts, and thereafter report yearly to the assembly." The Ousatonic, serving one of the most prosperous sections of the state—the whole Housatonic Valley south of New Milford—had as good prospects of success as any company, but it was always deeply in debt. A third of its right of way had to be abandoned; half of the remainder was transferred to a kind of "holding company," and that too failed; and finally the operators took the easy way out, signed the poor debtor's oath, and abandoned the effort. The Farmington and Bristol, incorporated in 1801, proved to be such a total failure that its charter was "disannulled" in 1819, at a loss to the stockholders of $15,232.10. And the Shetucket, trying to compete with two other lines to Rhode Island, fared almost as badly.

Gate-keepers were subject to all the human frailties of anyone engaged in a boring, underpaid job for which there was no foolproof audit. There was the temptation to admit close friends without charge, or to make little mistakes in counting the sheep and cattle passing through. The toll-takers had to contend perennially with short-tempered patrons who disapproved of turnpikes and didn't have the toll change on them, anyway; bargainers who wanted special rates; people who tried to slip through the gate under cover of darkness or use the "shunpikes," which made a forbidden loop around the barrier; voluble women wanting the services of a blacksmith and wheelwright in addition to a reconsideration of the heavy rates. The gate-keeper was popular with no one. His fellow townsmen ranked him with leeches and highway robbers; to travelers, he symbolized the obstructionist; to the turnpike officials, he was an equivocator intent on putting the company into bankruptcy. Toll-taker Robert Rankin, who kept the Saybrook gate of the Middlesex Turnpike, valued so highly an early retirement hour that finally his superiors, to discourage desertion of his post, ruled that he could pocket anything collected after nine at night. That ended the inclination of the "public to postpone its travelling until after his bedtime."

A few companies actually did make money. The Greenwoods, a franchise of twenty-four miles on the main route from Hartford to Albany—the road over which the migratory traffic to the Susquehanna passed—offered a cherished investment on which the stockholders were still collecting 5 per cent on an original outlay of some $20,000 up to the year of its demise in 1872. The Hartford and New Haven paid slightly over 3 per cent, and that was considered a rich return, for there were too many like the Shetucket that averaged less than 1⅓, and more still that never paid any dividends at all.

Seated on a log along the road outside Naugatuck one day, Victory Tomlinson, "a man so rich that he could be careless with his dress," was mistaken for a tramp and arrested for vagrancy. It wasn't until he was hauled before a justice that the sheriff realized the enormity of his error. Tomlinson, the brief hearing brought out, was no tramp; he owned the entire length of the Waterbury River Turnpike, some sixty miles of it, all the way from Naugatuck north through Waterbury, Thomaston, Litchfield, Torrington, and Winchester to the Massachusetts line. The log he had been sitting on was his private property, and the road he was inspecting belonged to him. Tomlinson paid no vagrancy fine, but he suffered a magnificent loss when the turnpike folded soon afterward.

The turnpike fad was waning fast by 1850, but a few, like the Greenwoods, had a longevity of three-quarters of a century. The Bridgeport and Newton, the Huntington Turnpike, and the Weston survived until March 24, 1886, when Fairfield County declared quits on all turnpikes in the county. The Oxford, extending from the Long Wharf in New Haven through Seymour and Beacon Falls, rounded out nearly ninety years, and anyone traveling between Derby Landing and the center of New Haven paid toll for almost a century—1798 to 1895. It was the last turnpike in Connecticut to pass out of existence. The eight-mile Derby at least held its own in value until the end, for its original capital stock totaled $7520, and after ninety-seven years of service it sold out for $8000.

The competition of the railroads is generally offered as the principal reason for the termination of the nineteenth-century toll road, and the locomotive certainly added to turnpike troubles. The forty-five-year-old Norwich and Woodstock, for instance, running through Lisbon, Canterbury, and Brooklyn, requested disenfranchisement in 1846, on grounds that the Norwich and Worcester Railroad had been undercutting it for a decade, until the income was insufficient to meet expenses of repairs; no dividends had been paid for six years. Although the thirty-eight-mile route had cost only $370 a mile to build—the lowest rate of any turnpike in the state—still it couldn't afford the competition of a railroad.

But the steam engine was not solely to blame. The great majority of the private highways were badly constructed and badly managed. Rarely did they invite enough trade to make them a paying proposition. Even if the advent of the locomotive had been postponed another fifty years, few of the toll roads would have survived.

The toll movement made a significant contribution by promoting straighter through-ways and encouraging the construction of hundreds of bridges and the establishment of safer ferries. It whetted the public appetite for better road surfaces, and even introduced some twenty companies operating plank roads—boardwalks that were to extend as long as thirty-four miles in the case of

the run between Danbury and Westport—but the plank roads
had a life expectancy of only seven years, and before most of the
charters were carried out, the pine planks at the other end had
begun to decay.

The ownership of turnpikes in all cases reverted to the towns
through which they passed. And in the very year that the last of
the toll roads was closed, the start was made on a highway system
under state commissioners. By 1908, "trunk line" or "state aid"
roads replaced what had been the Indian paths, the King's Highways, and the turnpikes. The novel doctrine of McAdam, which
decreed the use of finely crushed rock in place of corduroy logs
and "natural" soil, ushered in the macadam era. Bitumen was
added to the crushed rock, and in the next four decades practically
every mile of the once soggy highways and byways was trans-
formed into a black-top network reaching to the most remote
hamlet and hill.

A mechanical gadget called the automobile put in its appearance during the first year the highway commission was in operation. For fifteen years the public paid little attention to it, except
to single it out for scoffings and try to rule the new menace to
equine traffic off the road. But the automobile won the race with
the horse; and then came motor trucks, calling for still heavier road
construction—a subbase, metal surface, concrete, and asphalt
composition. Wooden bridges, once the wonder of the road, with
their latticed trusses and magnificent timber-arch spans, could no
longer stand the strain. They had to be replaced with steel and
concrete, and in 1915 the state took on all bridge construction
as one of its obligations.

The commission, which had started out as an experiment, developed into the most diversified branch of the government of
Connecticut—concerned with grade crossings and grade separa-
tions, banking for high-speed traffic and snow-plowing, landscap-
ing and rosebushes, roadside picnic benches and monuments dedicated to the Indians—and to the pioneers who had bungled the
road-building so badly. The year 1908 saw a few automobile
registration fees going into the commission's kitty, 1924 saw the
gasoline tax going to the same. During its first year, the highway
commission expended the astronomical figure of $31,643.45 on
new construction, and the public grumbled about it. In 1928,
sixteen and a half million, including $35,000 from the federal
government, was spent by the commission, and no one grumbled,
though even the least conservative were sure it was an all-time

peak. A quarter of a century later the highway budget had reached close to forty million, not counting the millions in federal aid or expenditures for turnpikes and toll facilities.

Under the supervision of the Highway Department was enough hard-top mileage to span the country from Stonington to San Francisco—and if it were stretched out in that direction, it would serve as an excellent substitute for many of the transcontinental routes. Moreover, in place of the Old Boston Post Road is a magnificent expressway skirting the Sound from Greenwich to East Lyme, and northeast across the rest of the state to the Rhode Island line at Killingly.

The state had gone full cycle, for it was slowly returning to the New England toll-road philosophy of 1795, a philosophy inspired by Charles II of England more than a century before, when he decreed that the users of highways should pay for them. The automobile owners were paying for the roads in their registration fees and gasoline taxes, and they were also paying for de luxe transit over a new series of toll pikes.

But through all the generous expansion, Connecticut has retained one vestige of its original ornery spirit of independence. As though the back-country roads were still intended only for local citizens who knew the shortest way to their destination, and trespassing tourists weren't supposed to use them, town and state have economized on crossroads signposts until it is almost as easy for a fur'ner to get lost on the maze of macadam in the 1950's as it was on the rutted hardscrabble of the 1750's.

· 7 ·

TINKERERS

THE MOST CHERISHED SOUVENIR CHRISTOPHER SPENCER HAD IN HIS possession was a short slab of weathered board, six inches wide by ten or twelve long, with some holes in it. It was a certificate of his success as an inventor and a certificate demonstrating the marksmanship of the President of the United States; the seven holes, neatly grouped around an improvised bull's eye, had been drilled at forty yards by Abraham Lincoln.

For the best part of a decade Spencer had devoted all his spare time to the perfection of his breech-loading repeater rifle, and had borrowed time off for his project rather liberally from the New York Central, where he had worked as locomotive repairman, from Cheney Brothers' silk mill in Manchester, and from the Colt Armory in Hartford, where he held the title of machinist. To the inventor, the rifle was a business proposition as much as a boon for the military. He was in the arms manufacturing business, and needed some orders. In March, 1860, he had patented his rifle— an ingenious weapon that could spew as many as twenty-one cartridges a minute, compared with three a minute from the standard muzzle-loader. One flip of a lever opened the breech, automatically ejected the empty, eased a fresh cartridge into the rear of the barrel; and the marksman had only to cock the hammer and squeeze the trigger. There was no fussing with paper-encased bullet and powder charges, or an awkward percussion cap. It was just the weapon the Union troops needed to turn the tide of conflict against the Rebels: Spencer was convinced of it; he had convinced his public-spirited boss at the silk mill, Charles Cheney; and Cheney in turn had convinced his old Hartford neighbor Gideon Welles, Secretary of the Navy; but nobody had succeeded in making an impression on the Bureau of Ordnance, which equipped the Army.

The Navy had placed an order for seven hundred repeaters, and the Cheney Brothers, eager to contribute to the Union cause, had put up most of the capital for creating a half-million-dollar arms manufacturing company. Still the Army bigwigs were content to issue obsolete weapons. General McClellan, commander of the Army of the Potomac, with a board of three officers, had watched a demonstration of the Spencer and forwarded a warm recommendation to a Bureau of Ordnance pigeonhole. A cavalry sergeant gave the rifle a field trial in a Maryland engagement and submitted an enthusiastic report. A lobbyist worked unsuccessfully for six months in Washington, trying to break through the stubborn bureaucracy. Spencer personally journeyed all the way to Tennessee to make an impression on Grant and his generals; they were duly indoctrinated with the merits of the gun. But the inventor was brushed off with the explanation that it was the Bureau of Ordnance, not the field generals, that had the last say about arms equipment; he'd have to go through channels.

The channels were blocked, for crusty old General Ripley, who fought a paper war from his Washington desk as chief of the Bureau, was adamant. Muzzle-loaders had won the Revolution, the War of 1812, and the Mexican War; they were good enough for him. They wasted less ammunition than the newfangled breechloaders. But the mind of Commander in Chief Lincoln was not closed. He had had enough experience on hunting grounds and battlegrounds to know that a man with a gun had either to close in on his enemy or choose an accurate weapon that could make up the distance; the Union troops were not getting "close enough." Privately, he was experimenting on the White House lawn and in the Potomac fields with all kinds of firearms that inventors kept sending him.

Back in Manchester, Spencer suddenly got a rush order for two thousand rifles, not from Ordnance, nor even from Washington; it came from Tennessee. Colonel John Thomas Wilder, a practical frontiersman and tinkerer himself, who was one of the officers to witness Spencer's demonstration before Grant, had proposed to his

"Lightning Brigade" that every man under him make an individual purchase of the marvelous seven-shooter. Unanimously they accepted the proposal, and, waiving all accepted military procedure, put up their thirty-five dollars apiece or signed personal notes bearing the Colonel's endorsement. The Brigade got its rifles, and in a test battle repulsed a charging army of Confederates that outnumbered them five to one. "The Yanks loaded on Sunday for the rest of the week," complained the Southerners.

General Ripley heard the report, but still liked his single-shooters. In exasperation, Charles Cheney then tried a new approach. He went to Speaker of the House James G. Blaine, who arranged the strangest deal in the history of American red-tape-cutting and interservice cooperation: the Navy ordered ten thousand Spencers for delivery to the Army. Half of them arrived in time to alter the outcome of Gettysburg, but they didn't alter Ripley's convictions. So at last the Secretary of the Navy paved the way for Christopher Spencer to give the President of the United States a personal demonstration.

"This evening and yesterday evening," wrote John Hay, Lincoln's assistant secretary, in his diary for August 19, 1863, "an hour was spent by the President in shooting with S———'s new repeating rifle. A wonderful gun, loading with absolutely contemptible simplicity and ease, with seven balls, and firing the whole, readily and deliberately in less than half a minute. The President made some pretty good shots. S———, the inventor, a quiet little Yankee who sold himself in relentless slavery to his idea for six weary years before it was perfect, did some splendid shooting."

Lincoln peppered the bull's-eye; General Ripley was relegated to New England as inspector of coastal fortifications; Spencer went back north with his souvenir, and before the Civil War was over his company had filled orders for more than 200,000 rifles and cavalry carbines.

The difficulties Spencer experienced in trying to convince a clientele of the worth of his product were not unique. There were few among the throng of Connecticut creators of gadgets who did not encounter comparable skepticism and obloquy. Time and again industrial progress and sociological reform did not occur because those who should have been most interested refused to recognize a bright new idea that was being extended to them. With the courage of martyrs, inventors could spend two decades perfecting a device that might help lift humanity out of the doldrums of drudgery, and would have to spend the rest of their lives convincing a hard-shelled world that it was worth trying.

But it was not all unselfish martyrdom. Certainly there was an element of altruism among the inventive forefathers—self-denial, too, and lofty patriotism—yet few sensible Yankees ever undertook a tedious job of their own free will without at least running the risk of earning a tidy reward. They were the best bargainers, opportunists, and gamblers on the continent of North America, but often they miscalculated, and the reward came in humiliation and adversity rather than in worldly goods.

Elias Howe invented a wonderful sewing machine, organized the Howe Company at Bridgeport in 1865, won the gold medal at the Paris Exposition in 1867, and during the last few years of his life was collecting a magnificent compensation of four thousand dollars a year, but he put in longer decades of anguish than Christopher Spencer before his handiwork paid off. He was born into poverty in Massachusetts, where his father was a farmer, gristmiller, and sawyer. While he was very young he managed to get in a few days of schooling each winter, but he was needed on the farm and at the mills. Tinkering with the mill machinery was his one pastime, and whenever there was a repair job, Elias was allowed to work it out, perched on barrels and boxes before he was tall enough to reach the height of a grindstone. By the time he was twelve, however, his father could no longer afford the luxury of his help; he couldn't even keep him in clothes, so the boy was hired out to a neighboring farmer, then as an apprentice in a cotton factory, and later to a Boston watchmaker named Ari Davis.

One day he overheard Davis suggest to an aspiring inventor that the one labor-saving device the world most needed was a good sewing machine. The aspirant walked out of the shop with a snort, and Elias went to work on the idea. Day and night for years he brooded over a device that would duplicate at high speed what fingers did with a needle. He modeled a little machine with a double-pointed needle, its eye drilled in the middle. Into it went months of patient work and all his savings, and it was an utter failure. So he tried a new approach. He was twenty-six and the date was April, 1845, before he finally produced a machine that could actually stitch. Two hundred and fifty stitches a minute it would sew, and he proved it in a public demonstration for which he assembled the five swiftest hand sewers in the industry. There was no question about its success, but he could interest neither seamstresses nor the general public. Nevertheless he took out a patent and sent his machine to England, where the patent rights brought a munificent 250 pounds from a manufacturer of corsets, shoes, and umbrellas. In fact, the manufacturer was so pleased that he induced the inventor to travel to London and develop there a stronger machine for sewing leather. Working for eight months at fifteen dollars a week, he finished his model only to have a quarrel with his boss and be discharged. Stranded with his family, and penniless, he pawned his model and patent papers to get his family back to New England, and later worked his own passage back by serving as cook for steerage passengers. Hopelessly discouraged and shaken, he returned home to find a worse calamity: his wife was dying.

But the fame of his little machine had reached America by way of England, and manufacturers were already producing what he had invented. On borrowed money, he started in all over again, and started, too, one of the longest legal battles for infringement in the annals of American patent law. It went on from 1849 to 1854, but eventually a judgment for royalty was granted him. He died before he was fifty, so that he had only a few years in which to enjoy the acclaim and the little wealth his labors brought him.

Broken in health, weighed down with disappointment and discouragement because of the way his own medical colleagues in Connecticut discredited him, the discoverer of anesthesia, Horace Wells, committed suicide rather than face continued derision. He, too, had been honored abroad, acclaimed at the "great seat of medicine" which Paris was in the 1840's, and awarded an honorary doctorate of medicine there, but Americans chose to belittle him as a crackpot dentist.

Like so many other inventions, the discovery of anesthesia was an accident. On the evening of December 10, 1844, none other than Samuel Colt, inventor of the Colt revolver, disguised as "Dr. Colton," gave an illustrated lecture on "laughing gas" at Hartford. "A GRAND EXHIBITION of the effects produced by inhaling Nitrous Oxide, Exhilarating or Laughing Gas," ballyhooed his flier. "Forty gallons of Gas will be prepared and administered to all in the audience who desire to inhale it. Twelve young men have volunteered to inhale the Gas, to commence the entertainment. Eight strong Men are engaged to occupy the front seats, to protect those under the influence of the Gas from injuring themselves or others. This course is adopted that no apprehension of danger may be entertained. Probably no one will attempt to fight. The Effect of the Gas is to make those who inhale it either Laugh, Sing, Dance, Speak, or Fight &. &., according to the leading trait of their character. They seem to retain consciousness enough to not say or do that which they have occasion to regret. N.B. The Gas will be administered only to gentlemen of the first respectability. The object is to make the entertainment in every respect a genteel affair."

A huge crowd assembled for this "genteel affair," and dentist Horace Wells took an aisle seat. "Dr. Colton" gave a brief lecture on the properties of the gas, and, to reassure his audience, took the first dose himself, "declaiming quite wonderfully afterward." Others quickly came forward for their turn at the experiment, and soon Union Hall was reverberating with hilarious entertainment, as the participants danced, sang, gave amazing gymnastic performances, shadow-boxed tenuous opponents, and presented profound declamations. The audience roared and cheered, but the hit of the show was Sam Cooley, a popular drug clerk from Front Street. He had no sooner fallen under the influence than he spotted an enemy in the audience and went after him with a vengeance, while the fugitive dashed in terror down the aisles, over the settees, across the stage. The audience loved it. Discreetly, the "eight strong men" kept their distance. And suddenly, looking very foolish, the pursuer came to his senses as the effect wore off, and he slid into a seat next to Horace Wells. Sam presently leaned over in astonishment to discover a pool of blood under his foot. He rolled up his trousers and revealed to the dentist a badly gouged leg.

"How did that happen, Sam?" exclaimed the doctor.

"I've no idea," Cooley replied. "It's the first I knew of it. Must have scraped my shin on the back of the settee when I sprung over it."

"Didn't you feel it at all?" asked Dr. Wells.

"Not at all," said Sam. "I just now felt a little smarting of my skin and looked!"

The discovery of anesthesia was made at that moment. The next morning "Dr. Colton" gave a powerful dose of nitrous oxide to Dr. Wells, and another dentist extracted a molar without pain from Wells' jaw. Several colleagues soon adopted the practice, and the following year, Wells requested the privilege of giving a demonstration to a group of doctors and students at the Massachusetts General Hospital. By mistake the gasbag was withdrawn too soon; the patient squirmed and yelled in agony as the tooth was confidently extracted; the audience laughed and jeered. Wells never lived it down; in one exhibition he had become a humbug, and despite the honors of Paris physicians and his acclaim in Europe, in America he was a fake—though others in the medical profession lost little time in entering counterclaims for his discovery. He experimented with chloroform, ether, and combinations of gases, and published a booklet, *The History of the Discovery of the Application of Nitrous Oxide Gas, Ether, and other Vapours to Surgical Operations.* For the exhilarating effects of the vapors, he more and more frequently inhaled them, and while under the influence on January 21, 1848, created a disturbance and was arrested. Smarting from the shame of the new incident and the accumulation of jibes, he slashed his thighs with a razor and died in the pain he had lived to conquer. He was only thirty-three.

The capacity of Connecticut's inventors to accept misery and derision as payment for their efforts seemed unbounded. With tireless devotion they would dedicate half their lives to an innovation and demonstrate its usefulness and workability, only to have their audiences walk away with a sneer or a smirk of disinterest. The greatest hardship inventors faced was not the frustrating years of trial-and-error experimentation; it was the cruel showdown when a finished mechanism was finally ready for market or public exhibition—and it was ignored. Too often the originator gave up in disgust when he discovered that the returns weren't going to be as generous as he had estimated; too often his contribution to science and society was abandoned, while others years later accepted his initial endeavor as theirs, claimed the credit, and pocketed the royalty.

On Collect Pond, just off Broadway in the heart of New York City, John Fitch, son of a poor East Windsor farmer, in 1796 gave a spectacular demonstration of a steamboat driven by a screw propeller. But the crowd that gathered along the shore saw nothing spectacular about the invention of this crackpot—any more than others had seen in his paddle-propelled steamboats on the Delaware. Altogether, he constructed four successful boats driven by steam power, but instead of acclaim, he received cutting criticism for wasting money on experiments that could have no possible economic value. While brooding about steam navigation, he had spent miserable years as a storekeeper, as a maltreated deck hand on a coastwise sailing vessel, as a menial apprentice to a clockmaker, as a brass-shop proprietor in East Windsor, as a peddler of beer and tobacco to the Continental Army, as a surveyor and land speculator in Virginia and Kentucky. In everything he tried he was a failure, and two years after the eventful demonstration on Collect Pond, he went west again to commit suicide.

David Bushnell of Westbrook was the father of the submarine, but to his contemporaries he was the crackbrained fanatic who built "Bushnell's Turtle." As a student he had gotten into an argument with his Yale professors, who wouldn't agree with him that

gunpowder could be exploded under water as a demolition agent
for enemy ships. He was determined to prove them wrong, and out
of stout oak planks built a weird contraption that indeed did look
like two huge turtle shells placed together. It was propelled by
paddle wheels run by a treadle; it had a water gauge to indicate the
boat's depth, a phosphorus-illuminated compass, a foot-operated
valve in the keel to admit water while descending, and hand-
operated pumps to eject the water while ascending. A torpedo
with a clockwork mechanism was attached above the rudder and
ingeniously contrived so that it could be screwed into the hull of a
ship. Bushnell was on the right track, but attempts to blow up
ships during the Revolution in Boston Harbor, in New York Harbor, and in the Delaware River all failed. He needed a crew, more
capital, and a lot of cooperation, but got none of them with
much enthusiasm. His principal reward was ridicule, and his sensitive soul couldn't take any more of it. So he went south incognito,
and spent the last years of his life as a schoolmaster and physician
in Georgia under the name of "Dr. Bush."

Connecticut inventors learned the hard way that recognition, re-
nown, and wealth were not a ready reward, and most of them had
to be content with what personal satisfaction they could gain
from their creativity. If there had been a grander spirit of dedica-
tion to humanity, it might have been different, for most of them
did not conceive of the business of invention as anything more
than a way of making an easier living. They weren't trying to establish their fame for posterity. Their vision did not extend very
far into the future. They were businessmen or mechanics, tinkerers or repairmen, as interested in lightening their own burdens as
the burdens of mankind, trying to improve their own lot, to promote a product that would sell better than another's. Selflessness
wasn't too common a Yankee trait.

The large majority came from the farm, where inventiveness
was first displayed by youngsters or oldsters during long winter
evenings in devising some clever contrivance that would do a distasteful chore quicker and better than an old method—shaping a
lighter cradle for mowing wheat, making a gadget for paring apples, cracking nuts, or shelling corn, building a hand-cranked
blower for winnowing grain, putting together a tougher horse
harness, devising a pump to make water-drawing easier.

Thousands of such makeshift devices were scattered about the
state, unpatented and unacclaimed, referred to disrespectfully in
the neighborhood, freely copied, and improved upon in the copy-
ing. Creating them was an accepted part of farm life, and when

the sons escaped from the farm and found employment in a shop or in industry, they carried their inclinations for gadget-making with them. It was no more than a natural instinct for economy of motion—applying a little God-given ingenuity to save time and labor. A good Yankee was lazy; he hated drudgery and was always on the lookout for a way of saving himself an hour's hard work. Getting his invention into operation could occupy infinitely more time than performing a task in the usual way, but tinkering was much more fun than labor. The great majority of Connecticut inventions were in labor-saving implements and tools, in labor-saving methods of manufacture, in substitutions of simple machine-made products for complicated hand-wrought crafts. Until the twentieth century, rarely did they originate from new chemical formulas or physical theories—except by accident.

Even the first would-be rubber barons came from the farm and the shop to make Connecticut the original center of the nation's rubber industry, and that started with an accident when Charles Goodyear lost his temper in the middle of an argument and accidentally dropped a mass of rubber and sulphur on the top of a red-hot kitchen stove. This was the "laboratory" in which the most important part of the discovery of vulcanizing was made.

For years Connecticut experimenters had been trying to make a serviceable material out of "caoutchouc." During the 1820's peddlers hawked rubber shoes from the Roxbury, Massachusetts, factories along their country routes, and sold quantities of rubberized coats, caps, and coverings, but it was a short-lived trade, for the fabric stuck together, the rubber melted in hot weather and became brittle as a shingle in winter. The Roxbury mill closed and the trade stopped. In 1829, John Howe of Ridgefield, who had become an important physician in New York, hit upon the idea of mixing rubber with other chemicals, drew out a patent, and gave up his medical practice to open a rubber-goods factory in North Salem, New York. But he soon abandoned it with the explanation: "So far as I know I was the first person who attempted to utilize rubber by combining other substances with it, but I did not happen to stumble upon the right substance." Everyone interested in rubber was interested in finding that evasive substance.

Charles Goodyear had spent most of his life in an atmosphere of invention. In New Haven his father was always working out new designs for pitchforks, scythes, and cultivators to manufacture in his farm tool factory and to sell in his hardware store, and Charles had contributed his share of practical notions, dividing his time between factory, store, and farm, and finally taking over a sub-

sidiary establishment in Philadelphia. Passing by the New York
show window of the Roxbury India Rubber Company one day in
1834, he noticed on display an inflated rubber raft with a crude
inflating valve. He went back to his room, fashioned a more serviceable one, and took it to the proprietor with his compliments.
Instead of showing urbane gratitude, the manager laughed off the
little invention, adding that the old valve was as good as the life
preserver—and that was no good; if the inventor had ingenuity to
spare, he should use it on curing Indian rubber, not on making
valves. The challenge became an obsession, and the beginning of
a career as rough as any inventor ever endured—a life of trial and
error, success and failure—mostly failure.

First his father failed miserably, went into bankruptcy because
of too great liberality in extending credit to customers, and went
to prison for his indebtedness. As operator of a subsidiary store,
Charles went to prison too. He was in and out of prison most of
the rest of his life as old family debts caught up with him. And in
prison he worked on his rubber experiments, kneading rubber with
every kind of material he could lay his hands on: magnesia, nitric
acid, copper in solution, bismuth, and always sulphur, about
which one of the foremen of an abandoned rubber factory had
told him. Later came the kitchen-stove accident, in which the
combination of rubber and sulphur charred instead of softening.
If he could stop the charring process at the proper point, the
compound would lose its stickiness. From that observation the
Goodyear Tire and Rubber Company grew, though the founder
still had to face years of ignominious hardship. Daniel Webster
once sent him a bill itemized at $25,000 for successfully defend-
ing one of the Goodyear patents. The company paid the bill,
but it was more than Charles acquired from his own contribution
to rubber-making in his whole lifetime.

Eli Whitney fared little better. For his cotton gin, an invention that was to change the economic and political history of the
world, he received about $90,000, almost enough to pay the legal
fees for some sixty suits on patent infringement. "In one instance," he wrote to Robert Fulton, "I had great difficulty in proving that the machine had ever been used in Georgia, although at
the same moment, there were three separate sets of this machinery
in motion within fifty yards of the building in which the court
sat, and all so near that the rattling of the wheels was distinctly
heard on the steps of the courthouse." The invention was so valuable that he couldn't afford to defend it; no one in the South
dared testify to the most obvious facts. Yet Whitney, a young

tutor just out of Yale, had perfected the first model in two weeks, thinking of it only as a labor-saving device in the same category as the gadgets being made on Connecticut farms, and never dreaming it would bring notoriety, litigation, and an industrial revolution.

Though others would have had him virtually make a career out of defending the rights to his gin, Whitney had too much inventive genius to squander all his time on lawsuits, and he made fully as great a contribution by introducing to Connecticut manufacturing the new idea of interchangeable parts. He applied the idea to gun manufacture in a concern that was to develop into the Winchester Repeating Arms Company, but others soon adapted it to every kind of manufacture from clocks to locomotives. "Filing jigs" were Whitney's first step in the new process—simple devices for shaping hammers or triggers by clamping the rough material between two forms of hardened steel and filing to the contour of the form—but this hand filing was soon replaced by "fixtures," gauges, and machine-operated cutting tools. Scores of them were required for the production of a single gun. It was a complete innovation for manufacturing, containing the germ of assembly-line technique as well as providing a system for making any one part of a mechanism interchangeable with the corresponding part of another, a method so revolutionary in scope that no one at first thought of a patent in connection with it. Where the cotton gin inaugurated an American industrial revolution, the introduction of interchangeable parts created another revolution in mechanical appliance.

Simultaneously with Eli Whitney's operations at Whitneyville, Simeon North, a farmer's son with a love for gadgetry and with a few years of experience in scythe-making at an old mill adjoining the family farm, started making horse pistols at Berlin, and by 1813 he had received a government contract for twenty thousand in which "the component parts of pistols are to correspond so exactly that any limb or part of one Pistol may be fitted to any other Pistol of the twenty thousand." North had so far advanced the interchangeable-parts technique that he contracted to supply them for seven dollars apiece.

Tired of his lecture tours in behalf of laughing gas, and settling down after years of world-wandering, Samuel Colt started manufacturing short arms with a revolving barrel, based on a model he had whittled out of wood on a trip to Singapore. A thousand of his revolvers were carried into the Mexican War, and soon he had an immense armory abuilding at Hartford. And Horace Smith, after an eighteen-year apprenticeship to a Norwich gunsmith, employ-

ment under Eli Whitney, and several years of service at Allen and
Thurber's pistol factory in Norwich, paired off with inventor
Daniel Wesson and went into production of Smith and Wesson
revolvers at Springfield, with orders from Japan, China, England,
Russia, Spain, France, and most of the South American countries, as well as from the United States Army. By Civil War days
the principle of a repeater with interchangeable parts had become
so firmly established it appeared incredible that the Bureau of Ordnance could have been lagging far behind the times in not recog-
nizing the value of the Spencer.

What had proved successful in the manufacture of firearms was
quickly applied to clocks by Eli Terry, Seth Thomas, and Chauncey Jerome. Clockmaking had always been a woodcraft, and with
the public it was to remain in that category for a long time. Terry
was overwhelmed with ridicule by his Plymouth neighbors and fellow craftsmen when they learned that he was working on as many
as twenty clocks at a time. But Terry knew what he was doing; at
the age of fourteen he started his apprenticeship, produced his first
clock in 1793 just after he turned twenty-one, and spent seven
years filling orders for hang-up models, trying to eke out a living by
doing repair work, engraving, and selling spectacles on the side.
By 1800 he had learned of the Whitney technique and was ready
to apply it to his craft, convinced that cheaper and better clocks
could be made by machinery than by hand. Disregarding the storm
of derision, he established his factory at Plymouth, with lathes,
gauges, a circular saw, and machines for cutting teeth in the
wheels—the first clock factory in America. Seven years later he
had a contract for four thousand clocks at $4.00 apiece—while
others were selling them for $15 and $25. In 1814 he perfected his
"pillar scroll-top case," an instrument that at last satisfied the inventor, and he began turning out ten to twelve thousand a year.

Seth Thomas, a carpenter and joiner, who had helped build the
Long Wharf at New Haven, teamed up with Terry in mass production of "hang-up" or "wag-on-the-wall" clocks, and finally
went into business by himself. Chauncey Jerome, graduated from
blacksmithing, farming, and carpentry into the same profession
under Terry, then teamed up with his brother and developed the
"bronze looking-glass clock," which became the top fashion in
timepieces between 1827 and 1837. For a while, he was selling
more clocks than any of his competitors in America, with assembly plants in Virginia and South Carolina as well as Connecticut.

Most of the makers of wooden clocks experimented with brass
works, too, and Jerome made more on his cheap one-day brass

pieces than his wooden ones, but Joseph Ives of Bristol was the real inventor of the rolled brass clock, and it was he who paved the way for the cheap kitchen clock that was to sell for a dollar.

Occasionally the ingenuity of the Connecticut Yankees was channeled into less constructive endeavor. At Killingworth, just prior to the Revolution, Abel Buell had served a normal apprenticeship to a local gold- and silversmith, the reputable Ebenezer Chittenden, but there was something eccentric about the blooming genius that his fellow townsmen did not appreciate: he showed unmistakable signs of affluence without comparable evidence of personal industry—except for his everlasting tinkering. Moreover, lights late at night were seen in his upstairs bedroom. He was suspect, and the subject of interminable small-town gossip, until one of the neighbors at last worked up courage to pry into his affairs. Stealthily a ladder was placed against the house, and while the assembled witnesses below held their breaths, an appointed spy took in the candle-lit bedroom scene. Abel was caught in the act of altering pound notes, and the alarm was given. Indignant people swarmed over his house, and the King's Attorney, Mathew Griswold, was summoned.

But Griswold was a man who respected genius in all its forms, and even in his capacity as prosecutor he recognized it in Abel. Branding, cropping of the ears, and possible life imprisonment were the prescribed penalties, and Griswold followed the letter of the law. "The tip of Buell's ear was cropped off: it was held on his tongue to keep it warm till it was put on the ear again, where it grew on." The branding iron with the "C" for counterfeit was to be held against the criminal's forehead while he said the words "God Save the King." Abel recited them with alacrity, and the iron lightly touched his skull just above the hairline. Off to prison in Norwich Abel went, only to be transferred back to his home town shortly. Behind more friendly bars, he put his genius to work in constructing the first lapidary machine in America. With it he made a handsome gold ring, set with a magnificent stone and surrounded by smaller gems. The ring went to Attorney Griswold; Buell got his pardon and considerately left town for New Haven.

There he was put to work as an assistant in engraving the first map of North America made in the colonies. But Buell was uneasy about his proximity to Killingworth law, and the mapmakers were uneasy about the authenticity of their information on the Gulf of Mexico. As surveyor, Buell headed for Florida. And at his headquarters in Pensacola, he was immediately recognized as a man of genius, given an unofficial assignment of breaking a governor's seal on an envelope and replacing it so that the break could not be detected. He performed the job as cleverly as he had altered the bills in Killingworth, and was quickly arrested for his pains. Escape, however, for a man of his talents, was a minor challenge, and within a few months he was back in New Haven with his sketches. He finished engraving the map, and during the Revolution, when it was impossible to procure British type, he established the first American type foundry, employing some twenty boys; then, getting nearer the kind of employment that had originally brought trouble upon him, he constructed a mint that could turn out 120 copper coins a minute.

By this time the state legislature was so impressed with his capabilities that he was sent to England, ostensibly to procure copper for coining, but actually to filch information on textile machinery. Passing through one British mill town, he became involved in a bridge-building project that had stumped the king's engineers; he ingratiatingly provided them with the solution to their problem and earned a hundred guineas for his dexterity. With an ample supply of copper, a headful of information on weaving, and a smuggled Scotch mill expert, he returned to New Haven to construct one of the first Connecticut cotton mills. And finally in 1825 the ingenious counterfeiter, lapidary, engraver, surveyor, type designer, minter, bridge engineer, and miller died a pauper in the New Haven almshouse.

Innumerable Connecticut inventors, like Buell, could turn their talents to a variety of fields with uncanny adroitness. Dr. John I. Howe, who gave up medicine to experiment with rubber, abandoned rubber to make common pins. As resident physician of the New York Alms House he had seen the inmates devoting most of their time to shaping pins by hand and was appalled by the scene of drudgery. With no pertinent mechanical experience to rely on, he modeled a pinmaking machine that won him a patent in 1832 and a silver medal at the American Institute Fair. He built a better machine for producing "spun head" pins and a still better one for solid-head pins—one of the marvels of the nineteenth century —and even designed a machine for sticking pins into paper folds.

Eli Whitney Blake in turn abandoned farming, cabinetmaking, law, and gun manufacturing with his Uncle Eli to pioneer in the production of domestic hardware. He drew out patents for equipment like door locks and escutcheons, thumb latches, bedstead casters, and cupboard-door fasteners, and took time in 1858 to invent a type of stone crusher that is still used the world over.

Every mile of macadam highway in every industrialized country of the globe is the by-product of his notable invention.

Linus Yale, Jr., watched Linus Yale, Sr., work out the details of such inventions as a threshing machine, a process for pressing millstones, sawmill improvements, and bank locks, but Linus, Jr., wanted to be an artist. He devoted himself to portrait painting for years, but couldn't resist the inherited urge to invent. Much of the nation's material riches is secured behind Yale dial-and-combination locks that the two Linuses invented in principle a century ago, and front doors from Maine to Mexico are guarded with the pin-tumbler mechanism Linus, Jr., borrowed from the Egyptians and started manufacturing quantitatively at Stamford.

Hiram Hayden, like most of the early brass manufacturers, started with brass buttons, but it was Hiram who first thought of spinning disks of sheet metal at high speed over a die to make kettles. His inventions made the Waterbury Brass Company a leading firm in the industry, and during the period of kerosene-lamp illumination a good share of the country was reading under his burners and fittings. Hayden was the acknowledged authority on petroleum illumination, but as a hobby he had to devote time to "inventions" in firearms and photography, and is credited with one of the first successful attempts at producing a positive photograph without the use of the negative.

Practically all of the great Connecticut inventors went from farms or modest shops into their makeshift laboratories. They came up with metallic cartridges and paper shotgun shells for big firms like Remington Arms, turret lathes and machine tools for Pratt and Whitney, new dyes and new designs for the Cheney Brothers Silk Mills, and hundreds of patents and practical ideas for the cotton and woolen mills along the Connecticut rivers and creeks. There were new ways of making cannon, new ways of weaving checks, new ways of making wood screws, bolts, buzz saws, augers and bevel-gear cutters. No facet of interest was too ordinary to claim the attention of the Yankee inventors. They worked on pewter buttons and submarines, straw weaving and steam cars, electroplating and electric streetcars. The inventiveness all stemmed from dexterous use of a jackknife by young and old, claimed a small-town philosopher: "That is what comes of whittling."

The amazing diversity of the inventions and the wide dispersion of the inventors defied all efforts to establish any more plausible reason for such a concentration within the borders of the state.

Little wonders were wrought in small towns and big towns, among both the educated and the unschooled, in industrial centers and in agricultural centers. From Eb Jenks' workshop in Colebrook came the first American-made steel fishhooks and the first elastic steel-wire teeth for cotton and woolen carding. Derby produced the first U.S. hoopskirts and tacks; Meriden the first patented coffee mill, the first airtight fruit jar with a spring-fastened glass top, the first kerosene-oil burners and the first mechanical player piano.

Tom Sanford of Beacon Falls—Coe Town, to him—invented friction matches in 1834, and thought he was getting the best of the bargain when he sold his formula for ten dollars. In 1840 J. B. Williams of Glastonbury put on sale the first American soap made especially for shaving. At Granby, Ensign Bickford produced the first safety fuse for blasting with dynamite. Tired of dragging around their old bull rake, Daley and Treat of Morris devised and put on the market a wheeled horse rake with a hand lever for the rider.

The industry that David Humphreys had started in Seymour paid off in patented local productions ranging from buttonhooks and mohair brushes to machine-made horseshoe nails and corrugated springs for railroad cars. At Bristol a tinkerer named Everett Horton, who liked to go fishing on Sundays, invented the telescopic fishing rod—an instrument that could readily be hidden under his coat without detection by prowling constables.

From Bridgeport came scores of inventions, not the least of which were Alonzo House's steam-propelled horseless carriage in 1866, and the intrusion of the first American trading stamps twenty-five years later. The little town of Marlboro gave birth to a retinue of patent-holders for washing machines and mechanical devices, breadknives and wagon seats. In 1840 two Plantsville blacksmiths discovered a way of manufacturing nuts and bolts without the arduous process of hand threading, and for over a century the industry they founded supplied much of the nation with their product. And from the modest village of Gilman came the first football blocking dummy, invented and assembled by Marty Gilman, who couldn't find enough local boys on whom he could practice his line plunges during summer vacations from college.

One patent-holder among every three thousand citizens is the average ratio for the United States, and in nonindustrial states it runs as low as one in thirty thousand. The Connecticut ratio over the years has averaged one in a thousand, and sometimes as high as one in seven hundred, and that excludes the shy inventors and the careless ones who can't be bothered with the red tape of registration. No authentic Yankee was quite content unless he was creating something, whether it was a toy or a turret lathe, a stage show or a shuttlecock. It goes on and on, though few of the inventors any longer come from the backwoods farms. Now they are university products with titles like Research Chemist, Physicist, and Analyst—uniformed and often anonymous professionals, with enormous salaries, officiating in the laboratories of companies like Bridgeport Brass, General Electric, or Aetna Life. And the problems that agonized their predecessors in the profession are all taken care of by corporation lawyers, vice-presidents, and handy press agents.

· 8 ·

PROSPECTORS

IT WAS CONNECTICUT'S MOST ANOMALOUS EXPERIMENT IN MINING.
Somehow geology got mixed up with penology, metallurgy with
misanthropy, politics with petrology—and the state had engraved
on its records for all time as weird a tale of sadism and botchery as
could be found in any Christian land. The details are still buried
in the depths of Simsbury mine.

In 1705 a group of guileless explorers, combing the hills of Simsbury, came upon a deep cavern hiding a conspicuous vein of tell-
tale green, flecked with golden sparklets. The normal reaction
would have been to stake out a claim and make a clandestine purchase of the rough hillside—quite incidentally incorporating the
cave. It could have been acquired cheaply without too much risk of
arousing suspicion. Instead, the excited prospectors dashed back
to the village and set the whole population on edge with the
public announcement at a town meeting that untold riches had
been discovered in yonder hills. Translated into the minutes of the
meeting, the intelligence read succinctly: "There was a mine either
of silvar or coper found in the town." Official machinery was immediately thrown into high gear: a committee of investigation
was appointed. Then, indeed, the neophytes realized they had
pulled a blooper.

The committee officiously poked about the cavern, their faces

brightening as they chipped off chunks of the verdant rock. A sack
of findings was trundled down the hill, and with less than cautious
excitement, samples were dispatched to Yale and London for assay.
"Fifteen parts pure copper," came back the report shortly, with a
reminder that the yield in the famed Cornish mines was only 8 per
cent. Two years after the original discovery, a company had been
formed and the mines were in operation, the only condition being
that a tenth of the proceeds would have to be returned to the town
in royalty, "two-thirds of which was to go toward maintaining an
able schoolmaster in Simsbury, and one-third to the support of the
Collegiate School at New Haven."

For seventy years the mine was worked, by free labor, by slave
labor, by imported labor. Chambers and channels radiating from
the cavern were dug far back under the hills. Tunnels for drainage
of the constantly seeping and dripping water were chiseled out,
and shafts were cut to the surface for ventilation, light, and easier
conveyance of the ore. The mining was the most distasteful occupation in Connecticut, labor was hard to secure, and profits were
never bountiful, but the copper from Simsbury supplied the scattered smiths and metalworkers all through the northern colonies,
and a surplus was shipped to England.

By 1773, however, labor recruiting had become a serious problem and profits were dwindling. It was then that it occurred to
the resourceful owners that the underground vaults of the failing
mine would make the ideal home for Connecticut malefactors, and
besides furnishing safe confinement, the managers could also
provide useful employment. County jails at the time were over-
crowded with prisoners; there was no general colony prison, and
prospects for an appropriation to construct one grew dimmer with
every legislative session. The proposition was the ideal solution
for a mounting dilemma; without appreciable expenditure and
without delay, the mines could be turned into the needed convict
hold. The idea had popular backing, and the legislature buoyantly
voted a resolution to "constitute the subterraneous caverns and
buildings in the copper mines of Simsbury a public gaol and
workhouse for the use of the colony."

A legislative committee shortly reported that they had "prepared
a well-finished lodging room" of twelve by fifteen feet, and had
placed over the west shaft an iron door at an expenditure of three
hundred and seventy pounds. It was a bargain at any price for the
entertainment of horse thieves, burglars, and counterfeiters. The
unsavory reputation of employment in the Simsbury depths was
already widespread, and to point it up the title "Newgate" was bor-

rowed from the infamous brother institution in London and attached to the new oubliette.

Armed with a pick and shovel, the first customer, John Hinson, descended into the pit on December 2, 1773, under the watchful eye of mine-keeper overseer Captain John Viets. But Hinson suffered from lack of female companionship. He found the remote corridors so lonely, the working and living conditions so unsatisfactory, that he declined to stay for long. With the assistance of a strong-armed feminine ally of the free world, he ascended one of the unbarred ore shafts in a bucket on the eighteenth night of his entombment and disappeared into another Connecticut underworld in the arms of his confederate.

For two months Captain Viets guarded an empty, unproductive prison, until three more prisoner-miners were placed in his custody late in February. They were so zealously guarded that they were unable to make good their escape until April. Another particularly restless fellow remained in confinement only four days. Connecticut culprits all seemed to have loyal accomplices in Simsbury ready to heft them out of the unguarded air shafts, and eager to foil the best efforts of Captain Viets to maintain a hospitable institution.

At their first opportunity the legislators expressed dissatisfaction with the good captain and his administrative methods. With a war against Great Britain spawning, a reliable supply of copper as well as an adequate depository for political prisoners were needed at once, and the lawmakers now more than ever were convinced that Newgate was the place for them. The management was changed, firmer security measures were imposed, the escape hatches capped, and by 1775 the dungeons were ready for tattling Tories, spies, and traitors to the cause of liberty.

The commander in chief of the Continental forces himself issued from Cambridge the first letter of commitment under the new order: "Gentlemen:" he wrote to the flabbergasted chief jailer, "the prisoners which will be delivered you with this, having been tried by a court-martial and deemed to be such flagrant and atrocious villains that they cannot by any means be set at large or confined in any place near their camp, were sentenced to Simsbury, in Connecticut. You will, therefore, be pleased to have them secured in your jail, or in such other manner as to you shall deem necessary, so that they cannot possibly make their escape. The charges of their imprisonment will be at the Continental expense. I am, etc., George Washington."

With this document the copper mines of Simsbury became the

Continental penitentiary, and the offenders whom Washington had singled out entered one of the most imposing prison fortifications in the civilized world. The only entrance was through the quarters of the sentries. Past a double column of guards, the manacled prisoners straggled to a trap door that led to a floor below, where the kitchen was located. It took the strength of two men to hoist the second trap door at the foot of the stairs, which was fitted with iron bolts and bars. A six-foot, perpendicular ladder extended from this opening into what was known as "Hell," but this led only to a grated hatchway locked over a narrow shaft sunk through solid rock, large enough for only one man to pass at a time. The "bottomless pit" was below—thirty-eight feet below, and that only a landing, for prisoners were marched from that point down wet, slanting shelves another forty feet until they reached their quarters, a platform of boards with a few more fixed overhead to carry off the dripping water.

Here were deposited the political prisoners, deserters from the Continental army, and Tory marauders of the Revolution. But they were not all renegades of this character, for in the same quarters were men of social distinction and learning, physicians, lawyers, and one passionate minister of the gospel, Simeon Baxter, who labeled himself "a Licentiate in Divinity and Voluntary Chaplain to those Prisoners in the Apartment called Orcus."

Equipping the prisoners with picks and shovels for purposes of mining ore was soon discovered to be ill-advised. The tools were more gainfully employed in excavating a route toward freedom. As a source of gravely needed copper the mines were abandoned, tools were taken away, and the inmates were put to work in the production of boots and shoes, nails and barrels. But even the removal of the implements did not forestall one major attempt at prison break. Henry Wooster, a Long Islander caught on a retaliatory whaleboat mission of pillage, armed himself with a nail rod stolen from the workshop, and for months picked away at a narrow drain, in an attempt to enlarge it enough to crawl through. Bit by bit he chiseled at the masonry in which the iron bars were set, until at last they could be wrenched free. Then, flat on his stomach in the wet filth, he squeezed his way down the narrow passageway, chipping out the sides as he went, a few inches each night. Light was coming from the exit; he had nearly reached his destination one morning when the signal was passed to him from behind that he was due back for roll call. Hurriedly he worked his way back, feet foremost, to discover to his horror that during the night a stone had fallen from the roof, completely blocking his passage. It was too light outside to attempt a desperate frontal break. For a long moment he considered his inevitable fate: the lashing from the guards, as many as fifty stripes, shackles, fetters, death perhaps. With a superhuman thrust he succeeded in dislodging the rock and moved it an inch backward with his feet. Then painfully he edged it along until it fell into a hollow in the drain. He squeezed over it and reached the cavern, haggard and bloody, just in time to report for twelve-hour duty. A few nights later, the Long Islander led his companions down the drain for the last time to freedom.

The drain was repaired so that it could never be used again as an escape route, and as the war wore on, the success, security, and horror of Newgate became legendary. The strength of the solid rock and the tightness of iron grills clearly indicated that the prison could be manned without professional soldiers. They were sorely needed on other fronts. So there was a change in personnel. The tough martinets were replaced by a couple of dozen boys, and the hardened officers by gentle superiors who could afford sympathy for their tortured clientele below. Discipline was relaxed; even wives were permitted occasionally to visit their husbands in the filthy cells. And the change promoted the notorious break of May 17, 1781.

That night, after the convicts had been chained in the dungeons, a woman appeared with a plea to be allowed to see her husband. She was admitted without guard and promptly went about her compassionate mission. Some hours later she called to the guards that she was ready to depart. Two sleepy boys started to hoist the trap, and at that moment they were helped by a violent thrust from strong arms below. Up from the maw of "Hell" stormed the entire complement of prisoners, including thirty desperadoes, and in the skirmish that followed, the guards were overpowered, several wounded, one killed. The trap door was lowered over the heads of the survivors.

The prisoners were beyond recall when the legislature, which happened to be in session at the time, heard of the downfall of Newgate. In their investigation they were unsparing in their insults directed at the state committee as well as the prison personnel. "A small lad, just fit to drive a plow with a very gentle team," they scoffed at one guard. "A young man more fit to carry fish to market than to keep guard at Newgate."

Once more Newgate became the impregnable prison fortress everyone had assumed it to be. All sentiment was cast aside, all feeling for prison suffering, all humanitarianism. Connecticut and the Continental Congress had a penitentiary that could match the worst known to mankind. Prisoners were subject to a grueling twelve-hour workday, from four in the morning to four in the afternoon. Whether at work or at sleep they were chained to their places, handcuffed, fettered, and collared. The inhumanity extended to them was observed by one contemporaneous visitor who called while the unfortunates were being fed: "Going again into the workshop or smithery I found the attendants of the prison delivering pickled pork for the dinner of the prisoners. Pieces were given separately to the parties at each forge. They were thrown upon the floor, and left to be washed and boiled in the water used for cooling the iron wrought at the forges."

Another visitor watched convicts kneading the community supply of bread by trampling the dough with unwashed feet in a huge trough. For greater economy of space, prisoners were dovetailed into the sleeping bunks, with each man's feet resting on the straw pillow of his neighbor. For the benefit of a public that occasionally expressed reservations about the salutary effect of the diet and underground exposure on the health of prisoners, it was reported that "the convicts enjoyed good health and that certain cutaneous diseases were cured by the confinement."

Eyewitnesses, however, dared to mention the "foul vermin, reeking filth and horrible stench, hard fare and cruel punishments," a climate in which "the clothing of the prisoners grows mouldy and rotten, and falls away from their bodies, while their limbs grow stiff with rheumatism." They saw prisoners so heavily ironed with handcuffs and fetters that they could move about only by "a sort of jump or hop," others chained in pairs to wheelbarrows, and men in the smithy wearing iron collars hung on chains from the roof.

"At a place called Symsbury," wrote the British traveler Thomas Anburey in September, 1781, "are some copper mines . . . which are converted to a state dungeon, where formerly such offenders as the General Assembly did not chuse to punish with death were sent, shewing the humanity and mildness of the law: but not, in my opinion. They would have shewn it more considerably by hanging up the unfortunate wretch: for in the course of a few months, after lingering out a miserable existence, the dissolution of nature puts a period to their pain. . . ."

What started out as a venture in mining had indeed taken a strange course, and after the war, when Newgate once more became a state institution, the regimen was not altered appreciably. More accommodations were erected aboveground, and there the treadmills and sweatshops worked overtime until 1827. It was then that the Prison Discipline Society reported that conditions in the buildings aboveground were so deplorable that most of the 127 prisoners had volunteered to return to underground quarters, where they could "curse, swear and fight, and do other unutterable abominations, without having it known to anyone." The report concluded, "There probably has not been on earth a stronger emblem of the pit than the sleeping rooms of that prison, so filthy, so crowded, so inclined to evil, so unrestrained."

But the principal reason for the transfer of the Newgate libertines to Wethersfield was the expense of maintaining the old underground fortress. Between 1790 and 1826 the state had poured over $200,000 into its support and upkeep. And as though even Simsbury preferred to disown the awful blot on its history, "Copper Hill" was transferred intact into the towns of Granby and East Granby.

Three years after the bastion was evacuated, the Phoenix Mining Company attempted to erase the stigma of retributive penology by once more introducing profitable copper mining, and the Connecticut Mining Company later tried the same. Enormous sums were spent on erecting new smelting furnaces, but the scandal was not to be so easily varnished. As one apologist satirically explained, "The ore, although rich in copper, was, like most of the prisoners confined there, of a *refractory* character, and could not be economically utilized." Over the decades far more money went into effort to keep the mine occupied or operative than ever came out in marketable metal.

Newgate gave copper mining an inglorious reputation; it was a celebrated and sometimes lucrative undertaking, but its economic importance was dwarfed by the iron industry of Litchfield County —"Salisbury iron," as it was known for miles north and south of the village of Salisbury. The lack of iron was one of the deficiencies most keenly felt among the colonies, and in 1665 John Winthrop, Jr., helped to set up a forge and "a mill for rolling balls of iron" near New Haven. Some half-dozen attempts were made to establish crude furnaces and forges, and in 1728 Joseph Higley took out the first American patent for a process of making steel, but until the deposits of rich brown hematite were discovered in 1732 at Salisbury, a mile from the New York line, the colony was sorely handicapped.

Catching a touch of claustrophobia from the civilization that was crowding in upon him at Windsor, Daniel Bissell took off in 1731 to the northwest wilderness of the colony and staked out one of those hundred-acres-more-or-less grants on a wooded prominence in the Salisbury country. No sooner had he taken possession than he began to realize that he had struck a poor bargain in plowable land. His whole farm site was ribbed with an ironlike rock. But a few indiscreet inquiries among men of learning brought to light the fact that he had planted his log cabin on the richest source of iron ore then known in the new world. Suddenly Ore Hill became the most coveted piece of property in Connecticut, and swindlers were trying to convince him that his deed to the land wasn't clear, that he was expropriating "lands appropriated by the Colony to Yale College."

In the excitement Bissell's discovery stirred up, Ore Hill changed hands several times in indecorous deals, more deposits were found on Davis and Chatfield hills, and a rude forge went into operation in 1734 at Lakeville. During the next century Salisbury blossomed into the Birmingham of America. The flare of furnaces and the glow of forges brightened the landscape and the prosperity of the upper Housatonic valley. Ore Hill opened a future for a new nation as well as for northwestern Connecticut, for without the hematite of Salisbury, George Washington could never have kept his artillery supplied with enough mortars and ordnance to ward off the armies of George III.

The first of the Taconic iron dukes was Samuel Forbes, a giant of a man, described by one appraiser as the possessor of "the ugliest face that ever covered a human soul . . . He was of a size, of a power of muscle and a power of will to match his dreadful face." And to his wife were attributed unfeminine qualities to match those of her husband. Samuel came down from Canaan in 1762 and shouldered into the Salisbury enterprise; he acquired another young giant of an operator in Ethan Allen as one of his dozen partners, and at Lakeville set up the first real furnace in the valley. Turning out a high grade of hollow ware—caldrons, kettles, pots, and kitchen utensils—the company flourished for two years before the partnership began to break up over disagreements. Ethan, who had no liking for a partner named George Caldwell, was one of the first to go, leaving behind him on the magistrate's blotter the descriptive charge "that the said Ethan Allen did, in a tumultuous and offensive manner, with threatening words and angry looks, strip himself even to his naked body, and with force and arms, without law or right, did assail and actually strike the person of George Caldwell of Salisbury, aforesaid, in the presence and to the disturbance of His Majesty's good subjects."

Ethan had other worlds to conquer with the Green Mountain Boys up north, and soon set out for Vermont; "Squire" Forbes carried on as ironmaster, and there was more reshuffling in the partnership until Governor Trumbull came to the rescue on the eve of the Revolution, took over the whole property in the name of the state, and put Colonel Joshua Porter of the local militia in charge over ironmaster Forbes.

As many as a thousand heavy cannon were cast in the Salisbury molds during the next four years—nine-, twelve-, eighteen-, and thirty-two-pounders—with an equal number of threes, fours, and sixes. Countless tons of the iron went into swivels, shot and ball, grapeshot, grenades, and miscellaneous castings. There were few forts or warships that did not fend off the enemy with cannon, shot, and shell from Ore Hill. On orders from the Continental Congress, a force of sixty men kept the indispensable supplies flowing from Salisbury. General Knox, as quartermaster of the Continental forces, frequently called there, and under the scrutiny of notables like Alexander Hamilton, Jonathan Trumbull, John Jay, and Robert Morris, the guns were tested and exercised on the local proving grounds at Bostwick Hill. The *Constellation*, the *Constitution*, the New York Battery, were all outfitted with castings from Salisbury and Lakeville.

The Revolution gave Salisbury the impetus for its industrial boom, and long after mines to the west offered formidable competition, Ore Hill, the Davis and Chatfield mines, and a dozen private back-yard openings continued to produce ore for the toughest, most malleable metal in America. Blast furnaces were scattered across Litchfield County—as many as fifty of them, centered about Salisbury, Lime Rock, Sharon, Kent, Bull's Bridge, New Preston, Cornwall, Canaan, and Falls Village. Iron became the circulating medium, and promissory notes were more frequently made payable in iron than in money. In oxcarts and in the leather saddlebags of horses the rich ore was lugged up hill and down from the open ore beds to the nearest furnace. Ore Hill and Davis Hill gradually disappeared. At night the sky around Salisbury glowed as if it were reflecting an eternal inferno; by day the sky was yellowed by the smudge from the furnaces and the enormous charcoal pits; day and night the whole area was haunted by the ominous grunts of the furnace bellows and the unearthly screech of revolving water wheels.

The usual pattern for a furnace was a cubical tower of solid masonry, rising to the height of a three-story structure from a base of ten-foot supporting arches. The massive proportions were always deceptive until one surveyed the top surface—some twenty-five or thirty feet square. Enclosed in the masonry was a bulbous-shaped cavern lined with firebrick as smooth as a mason could fashion it. This was the furnace proper, and the only access to it was from the cupola on top where the ore, lime flux, and charcoal were turned in, or the outlets at the bottom where slag and molten iron were released. The searing golden fluid flowed down clay channels to prepared molds—for kettles or cannon, anchors or andirons. The overshot water wheel at the side furnished power for the enormous bellows, which forced an even blast of air into the interior and kept the furnace white hot. The bellows were the key to the whole operation, for if ever the blast of air petered out, the fires soon died, the iron in the interior solidified, and the furnace was doomed. The only remedy for such an exigency was to tear down the whole structure and start over again.

Finding exactly the right location for a blast furnace was the most difficult part of the enterprise: it had to be near water power, and it had to be adjacent to a side hill, for the loads of ore and charcoal were delivered directly on top of the tower, and the furnace had to be near enough to the side hill to allow for the construction of a bridge to the top. Over the bridge passed a steady procession of charcoal vans piled high with flaring bushel baskets, and of horses with their saddle-bags of ore. The "top man" had the job of keeping the traffic unsnarled as well as of keeping the inferno below him properly "charged." From the cupola belched flame and acrid smoke, and in this cloud the top man worked, alternately pouring in bags of ore or lime and baskets of charcoal, occasionally pausing to settle the interior with a long iron flail. Sudden death always lingered beside him, for the slightest miscalculation in the combustion processes could cause a mighty explosion that would send him and his fellow laborers to kingdom come.

It required about 130 bushels of charcoal to smelt a ton of ore; and, in a supplementary industry, the choppers and charcoal burners were kept busy for miles around beside their "pits"—oak and walnut logs slowly smoldering under mounds of dirt sometimes forty feet high. The forests in the vicinity of Salisbury, forests all over Litchfield County, up into Massachusetts, and over into New York disappeared even faster than Ore Hill and the other mountains of iron dirt.

"Squire" Forbes gave up cannon production for nail production. Old partnerships and combines broke up and new owners moved in. Joseph Pettee became the ranking ironmaster of Salisbury, and Holley and Coffing the king company. Into the clutches of Holley and Coffing between 1799 and 1810 gradually fell the ownership of the Lakeside furnace, Ore Hill, Lime Rock, the Davis mine, most of the smaller mines and water rights—and at once Holley and Coffing began to have labor trouble. Yankees weren't amenable to working as day laborers for big operators. So, in a huff, the new company imported several hundred colliers from Switzerland and Lithuania, built a whole town for them on the crest of Mount Riga three miles north of Salisbury, and installed a new furnace village at a cool altitude of two thousand feet, well out of range of the critical Salisburians. Actually it was not an impractical move, for although the new furnace was five miles and a vertical thousand feet from the nearest ore beds, the heights of Mount Riga offered what appeared to be an unlimited supply of wood for charcoal, an ideal water supply from Forge Pond near the summit, and downhill transportation all the way to the Hudson. With the backing of Holley and Coffing, who provided an annual payroll of some $150,000, Mount Riga soon grew into the gayest, wealthiest village in the district.

Ironmaster Joseph Pettee lived in a spacious house with wainscoted rooms, a gracious staircase, and a ballroom, his front windows overlooking the summit lake. Around it scores of workmen's houses, a school for eighty pupils, and a trading center sprang up. In distinction the village far surpassed its foster town at the foot of the mountain, and trade in the general store was so brisk that four clerks were kept on the jump. When the women of Salisbury wanted to purchase a silk dress or a fine hat, they climbed Mount Riga to acquire it.

Along the plunging Wochocastigook for half a mile the furnaces and forges blazed around the clock. Everything that was needed for the industry was close at hand—everything except iron ore, so the ore that was laboriously dug from the beds of the surrounding countryside was more laboriously dragged up the mountain. Holley and Coffing had connections in high places, too. Shortly the United States Navy was placing its orders for anchors and chains there, and foreign dignitaries frequently called to talk business with the ironmaster.

The great occasion of the year came late in the fall, when deputations of admirals, captains, and commanders ascended the mountain for the annual inspection ceremonies. In their honor there were gala dances, dinners, and parties at Pettee's pretentious mansion, and then the whole town gathered in its finest array for the inspection formalities around an enormous iron tripod standing close to a hundred feet high in the center of town. One by one the great anchors ordered by the Navy were drawn to the tripod, and, dangling from the chains, the tons of iron were hoisted to the apex. On the sharp order from Pettee, anchor and chain were dropped with a thunderous clang. If they survived the shock, an admiral came forward to place the naval stamp of approval on casting and chain.

The Mount Riga fires did not go out until 1847, and then it was a stoppage in the line from the bellows to the fire of the big furnace that was the immediate cause. While men worked frantically and futilely to unplug the inlet, the interior slowly solidified. The furnace died. But it was really the iron horse which Mount Riga had helped to create that spelled doom to the mountain community. On rails, coal and ore could be transported at a fraction of the cost at which oxen and pack horses could lug the loads up the mountain, but the iron horse would not venture the climb. Gradually the families moved off the mountain, the village disintegrated, and only the furnace turrets, the mountains of slag, and Pettee's great mansion were left as memorials of the mountaintop industry.

But a few of the other furnaces in the Housatonic valley did not surrender so readily. Kent had three blast furnaces and was annually producing over three thousand tons of iron during the middle years of the nineteenth century. From the Taconic hills still came the rifle iron for the arsenals at Springfield and Harpers Ferry. At Sharon, Benjamin Hotchkiss went into production of the explosive shell he had invented for rifled guns. His munitions business reached a peak there during the Civil War, before it was moved to Bridgeport. As late as 1880, 38,000 tons of iron were being produced from Salisbury ore. Most of it went into wheels for railroad trains, which required the toughest, most indestructible metal that could be wrought. Ore Hill had been reduced to a soggy hollow, but the nation's commerce was still rolling on Salisbury iron in 1923, when the pumps could no longer keep ahead of the water, and the mine was finally abandoned. A lake flowed in to mark the site of the mountain that had been brought low.

Besides iron and copper, Connecticut is credited with having nearly every mineral known to science—in quantity and quality not quite rich enough for commercial exploitation. There are manganese and mica, coal and cobalt, granite and garnet, lead and lignite. There is gold in the hills and bog iron in the valleys. More than half a century ago, a single town—Woodbury—boasted of a remarkable collection of thirty-one minerals in its immediate vicinity: "iron, ocher, Fuller's-earth, agates, prehnite, epidote, chalcedony, purple quartz, plumbago, magnetic iron pyrites, al-

bite, white copperas, dyalogyte, triplite, gypsum, kyanite, meso-
type, andalusite, spar, hornblende, botryoidal chalidocrase, garnet, dolomite, bitumen, opal, chrichtonite, mispickel, yellow
copper pyrites, coal, mica and spathic."

For a few of the multitude of minerals, prospectors even claimed
original discovery, and hastily attached local names to them. One
afternoon in 1877 the Reverend John Dickinson, a pastor with a
passion for geology, went for a stroll from his parsonage in Redding across Fillow's field to the Branchville ledges. He filled his
pockets with odd rocks, rocks that he was so confident were new to
mineralogy that he sent off samples to both Columbia and Yale
for analysis. Presently a scholarly representative of Yale descended
upon him to join in the investigation of Branchville strata. Before
the two were through chipping away at a vein and writing articles
for scientific journals, they had laid claim to seven new minerals,
including "dickinsonite," "reddingite," "fairfieldite," and "fillow-
ite."

The most fertile field of mineralogy is the Housatonic valley,
but a geological enthusiast from almost any section of the state
would rise up to defend his favorite locale. To support his contention, he could point out the lead and copper veins in the hills of
Plymouth, magnetic sand at Killingworth and Voluntown, the
coal mines of Durham, bog ore at Stafford and Hebron, the copper of Wallingford, legends of quantities of pure lead in Harwin-
ton's Lead Mine Brook, the ancient ironworks in Lyme, the feldspar and brownstone quarries of Portland, the back-yard mica
mines of Middlesex County, even the private gold mine in a pasture outside of New Haven where a hard-working Italian labored
for years with a crude windlass earning some three dollars a day
from his effort. And one defender would be sure to point out the
real mecca for mineralogists halfway up the Connecticut River at
the Strickland quarry, reputed to yield a greater variety of minerals
than any other one spot—beryl, garnet, quartz, and quantities of
uncommon specimens. On the other hand, the wide Housatonic
valley has the lead in variety as well as its past record of productivity: the iron of Salisbury, the bismuth of Monroe, the coal of
Southbury, the silver and garnet of Roxbury, not to mention
marble, lime, asbestos, feldspar, and a score of others.

The one mineral that created the greatest extraterritorial pageantry was the brownstone from the Portland quarries. In endless
processions of barges, the blocks were ferried down the Connecticut during the late nineteenth century—a major item of traffic on
the river. Vast tonnages of the stone were transported to cities

along the northeast seaboard, but principally it went to New York, to alter the façade of the big American metropolis. For a generation Manhattan proudly put up a distinguished Connecticut front, its millionaires and socialites residing behind the famous veneer from Portland, as well as from Hudson River quarries. It encouraged a whole new school of structural style, and modern architects are still reluctant to forgive the beneficent neighbors to the east for letting so much of the stuff out of state. Downtown sentimentalists raise mild objection as demolition crews move from one block to another trying to destroy Connecticut's most famed architectural export, although they demonstrate no eagerness to acquire more of it; but there is little danger of further incursions, for most of the Portland quarries are now as dead as the dinosaurs whose tracks the quarry men kept turning up in their blastings.

Somewhere there is probably a "Brownstone Street" to commemorate Portland's contributions. Connecticut, at least, has reverently retained a few town names acquired from what was unearthed in their confines—towns like Marbledale, Ore Hill, and Cobalt. At Marbledale it was Philo Tomlinson who started quarrying and sawing the white outcroppings along the East Aspetuck River, and he was among those who were credited with invention of the modern marble slicer—a toothless gang saw of soft iron fed with sand and water and driven by water power. Within a few years after his invention, Marbledale was trying to vie with Vermont as capital of the industry. Fifteen quarries opened up along the East Aspetuck, and some twenty mills were using neighbor Philo's cutting invention. The neat slabs were hauled by oxcart cross-country to the Hudson for shipment to builders throughout the east. Then further competition came from East Canaan to the north, where a new saw with diamonds brazed into the blade went into operation; in fact the competition soon reached all the way from Danbury to Canada, where a marble wall roughly parallels the New York state line. To many an important building the Taconics contributed trim and columns, but eventually Vermont won out in the race for supremacy.

Like Marbledale, Cobalt held claim to its name far longer than its industry in cobalt persisted, for that sprang up and died within a few years during the middle 1700's. Governor Winthrop first discovered the uncommon mineral in 1661, but little was done with it for exactly a century. Then a German chemist, Dr. John Sebastian Stephanney, acquired the mine and, cloaking his operations in secrecy, proceeded to dig out vast quantities of ore, which went into the production of a gorgeous blue paint. In casks the ore was shipped to his native country; twenty tons of it went to China for use in glazing porcelain; a thousand tons went to England where, belatedly, discovery was made that it contained too large a percentage of nickel to be used practicably for either paint or glazing.

With hopes as high as those of Dr. Stephanney, many a would-be industrialist launched upon a mining project, and occasionally one would pay off. The whole trap formation stretching from East and West Rocks at New Haven north to Massachusetts is pock-marked and honeycombed with diggings made by eighteenth-century prospectors for precious metals. It was with dreams of finding quick wealth in the unexplored terrain that adventurers came to the new world, and it took more than two centuries to convince the men of Connecticut that it wasn't there. Disappointed prospectors were more than generous in leaving trails of mystery and tales of ungarnered fortune behind them. At Sandy Hook there are still scouts who need little persuasion to take up shovels and picks with the intention of verifying the story that British soldiers during the Revolution were getting out casks of ore which yielded seventy-two cents in gold and eleven in silver for every pound of pay dirt shipped to England for processing.

"I have visited and examined your leased mineral lands in the township of Durham, Conn.," reported a learned mineralogist early in the 1900's, "and find surface indications of coal-seams superior to those I found in North Carolina . . . even better than the surface indications at Chatfield, Va., where at a depth of 700 feet, coal 30 feet in thickness based on hard granite, was struck, which led to a vast coal trade." The glowing promises of a prospectus soon followed the prognostications of the prospector, and thousands of dollars were invested in the fifteen-hundred-acre tract in Durham and Wallingford, but the quality of the product never quite matched the cheaper coal of West Virginia and Pennsylvania.

For years the quartz quarries near Ridgefield did pay dividends. The huge dust-covered crushing plant, over 160 feet long and three stories high, dwarfed most of the barns in the area. To it the horse-drawn dump carts led in a steady three-mile line from the company's quarries. Included in the works was a kiln where the stone was "calcined," a "chasing machine," rubbing tubs, and furnaces. In showers of dust, the silicon was crushed and ground into fine powder and shipped out to a ready market for soap, paint, and pottery glaze. And similar products went out from the feldspar quarries of Redding and Newtown.

Roxbury had so many lusty mining booms during the eighteenth and nineteenth centuries that at least one good boom should be expected during the twentieth. The iron ore of Mine Hill, 550 feet above the Shepaug River, was first prospected in 1724, but major operations were postponed for thirty-five years until a German goldsmith named Feuchter appeared, formed a company, plied the public with invitations to purchase his silver-tinted stock, and went to work. It was silver rather than iron he was seeking, and indeed quantities of white flakes scattered through the iron ore would be enough to convince less gullible investors that Roxbury had a bonanza. Mine Hill contained such wealth, according to Feuchter, that special security measures had to be taken. He and his well-paid crew worked in secret, occasionally exhibiting silver-plated bars for the benefit of wary stockholders, and for the benefit of those who hadn't yet had the foresight to make investments. It all turned out to be a monstrous fraud, and Feuchter was ridden out of town; but on that ride, a trunk full of silver bars accidentally fell open, leaving the inhospitable Roxburyites still in a doubt as to how Feuchter would assay in a real test of his capacity as metallurgist and thief.

In 1837 the mine was again opened, but this time the treasure hunt was for iron rather than silver. Two excellent furnaces were erected, but no sooner were they in operation than it was discovered that the ore was impregnated with dangerous combustive gases. Lives were lost and furnaces damaged in violent explosions before a scheme was invented for cooking gases out of the ore prior to its deposit in the smelters. The ore of Mine Hill proved superior even to the Salisbury type and was eventually used by the Bridgeport Silver Steel Company for production of steel surgical instruments.

Enlightened Litchfield fell prey to the most magnificent get-rich-quick fraud ever perpetrated within the state. Her cautious citizenry put up almost a million and a half, P. T. Barnum anteing ten thousand, in a local gold-mining venture that prospectuses compared to "Aladdin and his Wonderful Lamp." And all that came of it was the uncovering of a few perfect garnets, some handsome quartz, nickel, and a little copper ore.

Indefatigably men have dug for copper at Whigville, Hamden, New Britain, Cheshire, Torrington, Bristol; and some earned enough from the effort to pay for the broken shovels. A little industrial mining returned to the state under the pressures of World War II, when capital losses did not have to be reckoned as such, but, for the most part, mining is not for Connecticut of the twentieth century. Building lime and agricultural lime can be procured in plenty, brick clays, traprock for highway construction, feldspar from Portland, and granite from Roxbury. Students at the Columbia School of Mines occasionally scout Mine Hill as a practice area, and amateur geologists roam the hills picking up nuggets, but capitalists are content to let the crumbling stacks of Salisbury, the ruins of Newgate, and the scattering of picturesque ponds once unprofitably excavated in search of lucre, stand as memorials to enterprise that belonged to another century.

· 9 ·

TRADERS

THE INSURANCE CATHEDRALS OF HARTFORD STAND NOT ONLY AS MAG-
nificent symbols of the American religion of security, but also as
GHQ for the world's best-indoctrinated army of salesmen—policy
salesmen with a mission, the gracious approach, and a magnanimity
of purpose. From Connecticut's capital radiate thousands of these
campaigners—probably more salesmen than any other one industry in any other one city of the country sends forth, and to a
man far outranking their predecessors in the profession.

Connecticut may not have been the birthplace of the insistency of modern salesmanship, but it was the birthplace of the
Yankee tradesman, and out of respect for pioneers who devoted
their lives to development of the craft of hawking, it is only appropriate that the same locale should take a lead in the refined art
of selling.

At an early date the state was bountifully blessed with a tribe
of canny salesmen—chapmen so disarming, so felicitous, so persistent, so voluble, that only their most incredulous client failed
to be convinced that they were entrusted with an unselfish charge
to help lift the burden of mankind. In the seaports and river towns,
the shipmasters were the salesmen incognito, negotiating with a
show of rectitude for goods and produce that would be bartered
for a neat profit on some distant wharf. Inland, the peddlers were

the farmers and mechanics with surplus stock setting out on horse-back for the next town or the next state in search of a bargain and a buyer. Most of the mongering was on a small scale, con-ducted to supplement a scant living, but some of the shipmasters came back from the Orient, Africa, or the Carolinas with hand-some returns, and a few of the wagon hawkers boasted so loudly of opulence acquired on trips to the Alleghenies, Quebec, or Cape Cod that their stories could not be entirely discredited.

Salesmanship got its start in Connecticut when a farmer had a calf or a colt, a few extra barrels of cider, or a hundredweight of corn that neither he nor his neighbors needed, and he went afield to find a market. He came back with a plow, a clock, or a second-hand saw. The great handicap to local trade was lack of cash. It seldom existed, or it existed in such stint that much of the small-town trade in the seventeenth and eighteenth centuries was built upon an economy of swapping. Early trading centers and the rural store were organized on the same basis, but these were clearing houses for anything from butter to beaver pelts, so the element of salesmanship had little scope here. Over the counter farmer or trapper accepted what was offered, along with the complimentary mug of rum, or he sullenly took his goods to the next establish-ment where he thought he might do better. There was higgling and haggling, but the storekeeper had the upper hand and the last word; usually he maintained a fair standard of honesty. He was a professional, who, like the minister or the doctor, placed him-self at the service of the public in attempting to supply the wants of his clientele. Pressure selling was beneath his dignity, and he bitterly resented the intrusion and competition of transient ped-dlers. For generations he fought against their ethics, their prac-tices, their very existence, but it was not a winning battle. The elusive chapmen kept coming on. Everyone with any productive genius seemed to have something to peddle.

Peddlers had been going from door to door with an assortment of wares for a long time before the town of Berlin introduced a new economic order and the new psychology of salesmanship. In 1740 tinsmiths William and Edward Pattison arrived from Ireland with a quantity of tinned sheet iron and some new ideas. They set up shop on the outskirts of Berlin, translated Irish dexterity into Yankee ingenuity, and started cutting, shaping, and soldering a handsome line of shiny tin dinner plates, tin cups and saucers, tin teapots, lanterns, candlesticks, and candle sconces. The wares were displayed attractively on their shelves, along with a side line of tin milk pans, pots, and pails—an irresistible exhibition for any

housewife tired of swabbing the crude wooden plates and heavy
bowls that were standard culinary equipment. Here at last was a
lightweight, eye-catching substitute for the cumbersome old vessels. They sold almost as fast as the Pattisons could produce them.
Their cellar bulged with the vegetables and potatoes taken in exchange; their pantry was a veritable storehouse of cheeses, barrels
of grain, biscuits, and corned beef that represented gross income.
Berlin was pleased with the Pattisons and proud of its new pursuit.

One of their neighbors, the erudite Emma Hart (Willard),
shared so keenly the feminine excitement over a single tin platter
displayed among the bridal gifts at a wedding reception that she
felt called upon to compose their first rhymed advertisement:

> Oh, what's that lordly dish so rare
> That glitters forth in splendorous glare?
> Tell me, Miss Norton, is it silver?
> Is it from China or Brazil?
> Then altogether on they ran.
> Quoth the good dame, 'It's a tin pan,
> The first made in the Colony,
> The maker, Pattison's just by,
> From Ireland on the last ship o'er.
> You all can buy. He'll soon make more.'

The Pattisons did make more, and sold it in such quantity that
after a time the local trade slacked off as households became well
supplied with the durable luxury. So the manufacturers took to
the road, carrying knapsacks and satchels of their craftsmanship
from door to door into neighboring towns—insisting now on cash
sales. Invariably they returned to their shop with empty carriers
and money in their pockets. They tramped to Wethersfield, to
New Britain, to Southington, to Westfield and Middletown. Everywhere the reception was the same. There seemed to be no limit
to the market. The fad for tinware spread faster than the demand
could be filled. They took on apprentices and taught them their
craft—the craft of salesmanship as well as tinning. Shipments of
tinned sheet iron from England became a major import, and the
Pattisons soon had several dozen boys hammering out merchandise
at their work benches. They had the beginning of an industry, and
needed almost as many men on the road filling orders and opening
up new territory as they had at the shops. In two decades the Irish
peddlers had personified the first Yankee peddler.

But as the days of the Revolution approached, tin became almost as scarce as tea, so the inventive Pattisons substituted a miscellany of other household notions, sending forth agents with saddle baskets filled with scissors, thimbles, brass buttons, pins, combs, and such tinware as the diminishing supply afforded. The assortment of goods brought even larger returns, and reports of the success were not long in circulating. What the Pattisons had started so speculatively became within a few months a state-wide occupation—without tin and without scruples. Trunks and shoulder packs were the carryalls, and never into such small space was so much merchandise telescoped. "Shining coffee pots were crammed with spools of thread, papers of pins, cards of horn buttons, and cakes of shaving soap—and bolts of gaudy riband could be drawn from the pepper-boxes and sausage stuffers." Revealing the secret hiding places of calicoes, iron spoons, linen handkerchiefs and shoelaces to gaping housewives was all part of the skillfully worked out stunt of sales promotion. And Yankee youths were wonderful in the act.

Every town harbored some ne'er-do-well who could do well indeed as a glib and gracious chapman in territory where he was not known. Impersonation, guile, and deception were treasured traits that paid off, and while muskets and sixteen-inchers were booming on Revolutionary War battlefronts, the peddler's trade was booming on the home front. "On my way home from the army some time since," wrote a subaltern of the Continental Army from the Golden Ball Tavern at Middletown in September, 1777, "I fell in with four well dressed men, two of which were in uniform, all with swords and cockades. I supposed they were officers of the continental army, going on business like myself. We traveled to the next inn, where we stopped for refreshment, and met half a dozen more of these meek soldiers, for, on attending to their discourse, I soon found they were all itinerant traders. I fell into conversation with one of them, who informed me he had made five thousand pounds since the last year, by trade. I supposed he must have been a large importer of merchandize from abroad, but, on inquiry, found he had never risked a shilling afloat, but had been buying and selling from state to state, and from town to town; he began with a hogshead of rum, (which he purchased with his tools and credit, having been formerly an exceeding good house carpenter): he sold this out by the small quantity to the troops at King's bridge last campaign, and by his industry this way had acquired the above sum. This information led me to make inquiry into the other characters, all of which I found of the same class. Some had more, some less than my informant.

"I arrived soon after at my own farm, and my hired man had commenced trader, and quitted my farm. I went after him, and . . . asked him why he wore a cockade: he said it answered for a pass, and he should have a uniform coat as soon as he could find a tailor, which were scarce, as they had all turned traders. I pulled out my cockade, and got me a plain coat, and am now on my way to join my regiment, having completed the business I came on.

"Mr. Printer," pleaded the subaltern, "I think it would not be amiss to take up all these new created gentry, form them into a regiment, send them to camp, and let them work at their old trades: they would be useful then; they are a curse now."

The audacity of the peddling misanthropes frequently brought them into trouble with the patriotic citizenry. At the expense of one of them, Lyme took the hint from Boston and arranged a tea party of its own on March 16, 1774, when one William Lawson arrived in town with a hundred-pound sack of tea "which he was peddling about the country." He claimed that he had purchased it in Newport, but everyone else knew he had procured it from a sly customs officer. "Whereupon a number of the sons of liberty assembled in the evening, kindled a fire, and committed it to the flames, where it was all consumed, and the ashes buried on the spot."

By the end of the Revolution, when raw material for tinning was once more available, the stage was set for prosperity among both tinsmiths and salesmen—though prosperity existed in few other professions. Where saddle horses and saddle baskets had previously been used, wagons now came into vogue. Piled high with tin and miscellaneous hardware, pots and pails hanging from the sides and underneath, the wagons of the peddlers set out from Berlin and adjacent towns to the far corners of the country, while drays and ships kept way stations filled with Connecticut goods that the peddlers could pick up when their supplies ran low.

One could hear them approaching a mile away with the clanging and clattering of metal against the sides of the wagon, like a whole percussion orchestra out of tune. Through Connecticut, Massachusetts, and New York the hawkers traveled, alternately walking beside their teams and riding the high seats. They rapped on the back doors of every farmhouse en route. Through the village they cried their wares in high-pitched dissonance. In city market places they gathered swarms of chattering women about them. They headed far south along the Atlantic seaboard to the Carolinas and Georgia, across Pennsylvania or New York to the Great Lakes, down through Ohio and Kentucky toward the Mississippi. Far into the hinterland, wherever there was a new thriving settlement the hucksters followed, undeterred by impossible roads and inhospitable country.

"The manner in which this ware is disposed of puts to flight all calculation," wrote Yale's itinerant president, Timothy Dwight. "A young man is furnished by the prospector with a horse and a cart covered with a box, containing as many tin vessels as the horse can conveniently draw. This vehicle within a few years has, indeed, been exchanged for a wagon; and then the load is doubled. Thus prepared he sets out on an expedition for the winter. A multitude of these young men direct themselves to the Southern States; and in their excursions travel wherever they can find settlements. Each of them walks, and rides, through the vast distance, till he reaches Richmond, Newbern, Charleston, or Savannah; and usually carries with him to the place of his destination no small part of the gain, which he acquired upon the road. . . . He wanders into the interior country; calls at every door on his way, and with an address and pertinacity not easily resisted, compels no small number of inhabitants to buy. . . . This business is said to yield both the owner and his agent valuable returns; and the profit to be greater than that which is made by the sale of any other merchandise of equal value. . . . Every inhabited part of the United States is visited by these men. I have seen them on the peninsula of Cape Cod, and in the neighborhood of Lake Erie; distant from each other more than six hundred miles. They make their way to Detroit, four hundred miles farther, to Canada, to Kentucky, and, if I mistake not, to New Orleans and St. Louis."

The usual procedure was to start out with a load of tin worth three or four hundred dollars, sell it en route, and replenish supplies at seaports or warehouses previously agreed upon, depositing at these way stations scrap copper, deer pelts, and other miscellany taken in exchange. Then when a destination was reached at the end of six or eight months, the empty wagon and horses were auctioned off too, and the peddler set out for home by ship or coach as best he could.

By 1815 ten thousand boxes of tin plates were being manufactured in Berlin. The Pattisons' original modest establishment had expanded into a dozen factories, each employing twenty, thirty, even sixty tinsmiths and traders. Where loads worth a few hundred dollars formerly had set out on an expedition, vans now carried cargoes valued at several thousand, and they had become "peripatetic department stores," with everything from hats, shoes, and cotton goods to vest buttons and children's books—and of course, the tin pans, tin plates, tin pails, and tin porringers.

The peddlers carried a few commendable Connecticut mores with them into the southlands and the frontier to the west, but in general they were not good ambassadors. They were mongers and merchandisers; opulence was their objective. There were crooks and swindlers among them, and the smooth garrulity lost its appeal when clients discovered later that shoes didn't wear, that the tin rusted, that there was no court of appeal when the glib guarantees of quality did not hold up. In their cadging they lost as many friends to Connecticut as they won.

British traveler John Bernard discovered that the Southern trader regarded the Northern peddler "in the light of a visitation," and looked upon a "Connecticut chap as a commercial Scythian, a Tartar of the North whose sole business in life is to make inroads on his peace and profit. He ranks him in the list of plagues next to the yellow fever, and before locusts, taxation, and a wet spring; indeed some go so far as to suppose that the shower of Yankees was the crowning pestilence which made Pharaoh give up the Israelites. . . . There is no getting rid of them. None of the usual similes of a burr, or sticking-plaster, give any idea of the pedlar's tenacity; he has the grip of a crab, with the suction of a mosquito; you can't deny, you can't insult, you can't fatigue him; you can only dismiss him with a purchase. . . . A tornado could not create greater havoc in the ease and enjoyment of a Carolinian evening than the buzzing and humming of such a wasp."

Dwight added more temperately that "many of the young men employed in this business part at an early age with both modesty and principle. Their sobriety is exchanged for cunning; their honesty for imposition; and their decent behavior for coarse impudence. Mere wanderers, accustomed to no order, control, or worship, . . . the only source of their pleasure, or their reputation is gain. No course of life tends more rapidly or more effectually to eradicate every moral feeling."

President Dwight liked to dine off the tin plates he found in the private homes and hostelries on his travels, but he never developed an enthusiasm for their vendors, and he had still less in common with the unprincipled coastal and intercontinental peddlers he met in river ports and seaports. In character, the ship peddlers differed little from the wagon peddlers. Their trade was likely to be wholesale rather than retail, the scope of their ventures was sometimes prodigious, their intrigue and duplicity on a far greater scale, but a smart, experienced land hawker who chose to take to the sea was an assured success.

Whether a ship was destined for Barbados, Boston, or Bristol, England, the master had to be as adept at bartering as at navigation. On Connecticut jetties he haggled with farmers over the worth of horses and bundles of pipe staves; he haggled again with plantation agents in the West Indies over the high price of sugar, molasses, and rum; but the real genius of peddling skippers came to the fore on trips to Great Britain, where hides, salt fish, and beaver pelts were bartered for ammunition, hoes, hatchets, shoes, nails, pins, paper, fishhooks, knives, looking glasses, pewter, bottles, ladles, bells, thimbles, brass kettles, and jew's-harps.

The skipper knew his hardware as well as he knew the points of the compass; he was shrewd, persistent, and persuasive; and he constantly had to make calculated guesses on how reckless he could be as a smuggler. In 1764 a whole British squadron was sent to cruise the New England coast in an effort to suppress smuggling and enforce peddling regulations. The *Cygnet* was anchored at New London, where the most evasive and most perverse coastal peddlers were known to harbor. But instead of the *Cygnet's* bringing New London to its knees, New London turned its social charm on crew and officers alike. In the three winters the ship was stationed there, smuggling ostensibly ceased while the ship's company made merry in port. Six of the crew deserted and were kept in hiding by cooperative citizens until after the ship had sailed; the purser married a New London girl and established a family there. Three miles offshore, another officer went over the side the night before the ship was to return to England, and would have perished from exposure and exhaustion had he not luckily made rendezvous with a rescue party as he was about to go under. He went ashore to become one of the most prominent shipmasters and coastal peddlers in the port.

By the time Timothy Dwight was making his critical excursions, the Revolution was over, shipping was hampered by French and English disagreements, but the disposition of venturesome intercontinental peddlers had not altered. When trade in West Indies rum did not pay off, they took surreptitious side trips to Africa to deal in slaves. Often it was a circuitous run, with a cargo of Connecticut lumber and foodstuffs going to a destination like the Azores or Madeira; the vessel would deliver its legitimate produce, then slip down the African coast "to the market" and return to the West Indies with a hold full of steaming, languishing blacks. At Barbados, Antigua, or Jamaica the human cargo was peddled for sugar, molasses, rum, or salt, and a month later the ship glided into Norwich or New London with an air of respectability—and perhaps only a dozen hand-picked Africans, on consignment. No less a figure than the Reverend Ezra Stiles, president of Yale, bribed a coastal peddler with a barrel of rum to select a particularly fine specimen for him. The learned and pious Stiles got his slave.

Newspapers were frequent participants in the game of Negro trading, running advertisements to suit their clientele:

> To be sold a Mulatto Slave, about 21 years old, is healthy, strong and active; well acquainted with all kinds of farming business, and can work at the Shoe Maker's trade. For further particulars, enquire of Edward Barker, of Branford, or the Printers hereof. November 25, 1778.

> Wanted to purchase immediately, Two negro or Mulatto Boys or men, from 14 to 24 years of age. Also wanted a second hand Sulkey. Inquire of the printers. New Haven, May 9, 1779.

> To be sold,—At the Subscriber's in Goshen, a young, lusty, and very likely Negro Wench, that can cook, wash, and spin either flax or wool. July 27, 1780.

But much of the slave peddling in Connecticut was as clandestine as it was self-righteous. The slavers at least had a latent conscience, "were usually ashamed of their vocation, and in some instances denied being engaged in it, though not a few mariners amassed large fortunes in the traffic." Prior to the Revolution they could always count on support from the British secretary of state for the colonies, who maintained that "we cannot allow the colonies . . . to discourage . . . a trade so beneficial to the nation." Industrialists and laboring classes, however, had other ideas of expediency: they saw that slaves were not only a threat to free white labor, but also unprofitable in the long range. In 1774 the legislature passed an act that "no Indian, Negro or Mulatto Slave, shall, at any Time hereafter be brought or imported into this Colony, by Sea or Land, from any Place or places whatsoever, to be disposed of, left, or sold within this Colony."

The slavers had had their big day, though the law was freely violated for three-quarters of a century, while shipmasters continued to amass wealth in the service of the South. The era did not end until 1848, when a final act was passed declaring that no person should be held in slavery within the state and no slave might be brought into Connecticut. After that the intercontinental peddlers turned their attention to more legitimate trade in other parts of the globe. They set out on round-the-world ventures dealing in an incredible assortment of wares ranging from silk to sealskins, from calico to copper. Dockhouses were rich with the wares of China, India, South America, and the Mediterranean. In clipper ships, captains set sail for California with loads of Yankee notions as varied as those of the old carts lumbering out of Berlin, and with Yankee chapmen to hawk them in San Francisco and in the gold-diggers' camps. Captain Holmes of Groton doubled Cape Horn eighty-three times—more trips than any man afloat had made.

The land peddlers, meantime, had lost none of their energy, and they made their greatest inroads between 1815 and 1850. The tin town had started a system of marketing that spread to every kind of industry. Single establishments in Berlin were sending out caravans of wagons and were carrying brassware and embossed buttons, clocks, and copper in addition to the old line of tin, hats, shoes, axes, combs, and common pins. The tin business spread to Meriden, Bristol, and Wallingford, and there industrialists attempted to improve upon the product by making a new alloy called britannia, four parts lead and one part tin. It took a better polish than pewter, and the country peddlers had a field day proving it. Farmington turned to industry and was producing quantities of fine linen, hats, leather goods, muskets, buttons, clocks, articles of silver and gold, candles, furniture, and the inevitable tin. These goods were piled high on Farmington wagons that headed South to canvass the same territory Berlin had found so rewarding.

Eli Terry had long been a familiar figure riding over the countryside on horseback with four bulky clocks balanced on his horse, "one forward of the saddle on which he rode, one behind, and one each side of his portmanteau," and Terry clocks were so popular and so successful that imitators sprang up in every other village, with their retinue of peddlers. Terry was an artist, with an artist's love for his creation, and to see his time-piece installed in the home of a family to which he took a fancy, he would accept in payment a few pewter heirlooms, a good book, or a chunk of pork. But where Terry was an artist, his imitators were likely to be shoddy mechanics, all ready, nevertheless, to issue the usual safely worded guarantee "Warranted if Well

Used." One peddler gave the ironclad pledge that he would return in two weeks, and if the clock were not running he would
replace it. At the end of his route he always kept one clock un-
sold, and, true to his promise, he retraced his steps, methodically
replacing the last silent clock he had dispensed with his spare, the
next with that rejected piece, and so on along his itinerary until
every worthless clock had been replaced with another that would
never run.

From Danbury came hats, gorgeously styled beaver hats, hats
worthy of sale only in exclusive metropolitan shops; yet they gathered dust smudges in saddlebags and wagon boxes as they were
peddled from door to door without semblance of dignity. From
New Haven salesmen went out as representatives of L. Candee
and Company carrying baskets of foot rubbers. They were a new
invention, and indeed the salesmen had a hard time convincing
customers that here was an article that would shed water, an
overshoe in which one could wade and walk without getting wet
feet. From Hazardville trekked gaudily painted red wagons peddling explosives to mines, quarries, or rock-bound farms, and the
driver was treated with such cold hospitality that he usually had to
bed down with his horses in church sheds—while nervous ladies
of the congregation put in a rough night expecting at any moment
the explosion that would topple the spire.

The youth who wanted to try his wings on salesmanship and
who was unable to find a more suitable product could always go
into drugs. He bought his pills in quantity, his liniments and
nostrums by the gallon, packaged them with his own trade name
and his own lists of remedies, and was sure to find a market as
broad as his patter. Often he took on the title of "Doctor" and
went through the countryside affecting miraculous psychological
cures of ailments that had stumped local medicine men for years.
Samuel Lee's Miraculous Windham pills and New London pills
for biliousness cured the livers of countless languid New Englanders. Then there were door-to-door salesmen who specialized in
books and pamphlets, women's hats and headgear, dry goods and
linen, perfumes and spices, musical instruments, cheap jewelry,
furniture.

The blast of a horn or the roll of drums heralded the arrival
in town of particularly zealous chapmen. Their comings brought
sparkle to the dull lives of remote farm families—news, gossip,
and a vast quantity of worldly misinformation. They were loved
and derided, respected and rejected. In contemporaneous literature the peddler was the eccentric pundit, on the stage he was the

witty clown. "He wer hatched in a crack—in foresty rocks," one ancient portrayal read, "whar nutmaigs am made outen maple, an whar wimmen paints clock faces an' pints shoe-paigs, an the men invents rat-traps, mantraps an' new-fangled doctrines for the aid ov the devil."

Pungent in his speech, affable and ingratiating in his manner, familiar and bantering in his approach, he always had a way with women. His argument was not always delicate and his intentions not always honorable, but he was adept at talking housewives into offering comfortable lodging for the night—often to the regret of eligible daughters or gullible mothers.

The peddlers may never have sold wooden nutmegs, but they certainly sold worthless worm-eaten ones, Polyglot Bibles all in the English language, pumpkin seeds chipped from white oak, cigars filled with oak leaves and wrapped in dyed cornhusks, cayenne pepper compounded from mahogany sawdust. It is altogether probable that the nutmegs were of wood, and that stories of the swindle were aired over and over again around the hearths of the commercial inns where peddlers congregated to lengthen each other's lies and to give new altitude to yarns about their successes.

Salesmen knew where more of their kind gathered as instinctively as contemporaneous tramps knew the charitable households. Up and down the state were scores of taverns, like the Uncle Ben Wakeman House in Fairfield, known and advertised as rendezvous for salesmen. The taverns thrived on the trade. At a crossroads east of Danbury so many horse-traders and peddlers "on the dodge" were entertained by conniving tavern-keepers that the place took on the name of Dodgingtown.

The peddlers' days of triumph came with the country fairs, the church field days on the green, the weekly markets. For these occasions all the sharp-tongued venders in the area swarmed in, opened their wares, hawked, and hollered, casting ribald gibes at one another and at their audience, furnishing free burlesque, and selling quantities of lotions and luxuries, trinkets and tinware.

So various and voluminous was the trade of itinerants, it would appear that the village stores were entirely robbed of their rightful concessions. And they were deprived of a vast volume of sales. The complaints of storekeepers were loud and chronic. They grumbled to the public, to themselves, to the legislature. The storekeepers had one gambit that the road hawkers couldn't touch —the honored custom of long credit. That alone could have kept them in business. But the jealous keepers of country stores played a large part in eliminating their competitors. Through legislative representatives, they saw that the itinerants were all but taxed out of existence, and hauled off their beats when they failed to carry proper papers. Yankee peddlers, too, began to be outnumbered by immigrant Jewish peddlers, and voluntarily withdrew to avoid being placed in the same social category. New transportation facilities, the coming of the railroad, canals, and steamships altered the economy under which the peddlers had thrived. Manufacturers at last discovered that they could market their goods in Boston, New York, Hartford, Philadelphia, London without having to bother with traveling door-knockers. And the public lost some of its naïveté; housewives declined to be taken in by the glib nonsense of male admirers offering bargains in five-dollar clocks for thirty, or cheap soap for ten cents when two bars could be purchased over the counter for a nickel.

The great army of peddlers had done themselves out of their profession by Civil War days, and many of them exchanged the ambulatory occupation for more sedentary proprietorships of country stores—in Connecticut and in upstate New York or out on the prairies. Thomas Danforth of Rocky Hill, pewterer and general supplier of peddlers, dismayed by the slacking off of house-to-house selling, organized the first chain-store system in the country and set up outlets in Philadelphia, Atlanta, and Savannah—as well as Rocky Hill. Charles Thompson, never a very successful wagon hawker, opened a mail-order business at Bridgewater, offering free dolls in exchange for soap coupons. In a few months he had so much business that no soap manufacturer could fill his orders, so he established his own soap factory. Bridgewater with its scattered population of a few hundred was suddenly supporting a first-class post office. Assuming that he might get several hundred lanterns if he placed an order for five carloads of them, he was astonished to receive a bill of lading for the entire order. In all Bridgewater there was no place to store five carloads of lanterns. He strung them up, lighted so many at night that the town glowed brighter than Times Square. For scores of miles spectators came to see the spectacle of illumination—and to buy lanterns. He sold every last one of them.

Scotsman Neil Alexander, whose original capital came from a gold ring found on the deck of the ship on which he had crossed the Atlantic, gave up a fabulously successful career as peddler to go into real estate and agriculture, and founded a little Scotch community of Alexander children and grandchildren at Alexander Lake in Killingly on a thirty-five-hundred acre plantation. Amos

Bronson Alcott of Wolcott, who had packed a trunkload of tin-ware on his back all the way to Virginia but had never taken to the trade, gave up peddling for pedagogy and became a founder of progressive education at Concord, Massachusetts.

With a canny business instinct, other less notable peddlers had picked out likely sites for crossroads stores on their long ventures. "Sam Slick" backed up his dilapidated cart to an ancient building near the village green and moved in, married the farmer's daughter he had once ogled on his trips, and settled down to become the town merchant and mentor. Here was a calling worthy of a man who had seen the world and benefited from some of its riches.

During the last decades of the 1800's, the pastor had lost some of his preeminence as the counselor in all things material as well as spiritual. The storekeeper—the ex-peddler—filled the gap. It was to him that parishioners went with problems of finance, problems of petty jurisprudence, problems of political weight. This redeemed man of the world came to be recognized as the banker and business confidant, the postmaster and patriarch. His emporium acquired more luster than the fanciest peddler's wagon had ever known.

There were never enough seats to entertain the corps of village philosophers who assembled at the store in relays from morning to closing time. About the stove in winter or on the porch in summer, in the redolence of molasses, vinegar, whisky, and kerosene, the battles of the century were waged, won, and lost; here justice was meted out, political caucuses held, the moral status of many a lass decided; here gossip was invented and elaborated upon, personal adventures aired and recounted, the tallest tales kept alive in the lurid English of New England. "Everyone spoke the language to which he was accustomed, however profane or indecent it might be," commented onetime storekeeper Wilbur Cross in his autobiography. "Never before nor since have I heard so many double negatives for emphasis; never before so many allusions to sexual and other functions of the human body, or to the hencoop or barnyard. It was the raciest speech God or Satan ever put into the mouth of man." Governor Cross saw his country store at Gurleyville as the "Yankee House of Commons" and "a microcosm of the whole United States."

General-store peddling did not disappear as did the itinerant peddlers. Many of the crossroads emporiums still exist quite as they were in the 1890's and the 1920's, though the patriarch-proprietor has lost much of his prestige. His shelves are now decorated

with row on row of tin cans instead of tin cups and tin plates; the
counter displaying stiff flanks of dried fish is replaced with a glass-
insulated freeze locker, and the barrels of crackers, salt, sugar, and
cereal by sanitary packages in such pretty wrappings that they sell
themselves without the effort of a peddler.

For years after the army of road chapmen capitulated, the
migratory druggists went their rural rounds selling liniments and
salves, hardware stores on wagons and trucks made annual pilgrimages, and peddlers of farm produce kept up their routes. But
Connecticut peddling for the most part is a lost art and a lost profession—except for the insurance salesman, the Fuller Brush man,
the Watkins man, the Bible salesman, the vegetable wagon, and
the long queue of gray-flanneled hucksters who daily file aboard
commuter specials at Westport, Darien, and Stamford bound for
Manhattan to peddle wares to the world at large.

· 10 ·

PEDAGOGUES

IF THE FARMERS OF LEBANON HAD BEEN MORE INTERESTED IN EDU-
cation than in apples two centuries ago, the halls of Dartmouth
might now grace the rolling hills of Connecticut rather than the
mountains of New Hampshire. Columbia—then part of the town
of Lebanon—was one of the state's thriving centers for apple-grow-
ers and cider-millers, and to these industrialists, who did not take
kindly to student orchard raids, is attributed the present location
of the Big Green. Wheelock's boys were all but driven out of town.

Nevertheless, it was Connecticut and that stern son of Windham and Yale, Eleazer Wheelock, that actually gave birth to Dartmouth College. The Reverend Wheelock had hardly settled in the
parsonage of the North Society of Lebanon when he issued an invitation to the enlightened Indians of New England to move in with
him. He was convinced that America's first duty and the ministry's
highest calling was conversion of the red man to Christianity—convinced, too, that properly indoctrinated Indians would make the
most eligible gospel-bearers to their own kind.

Sampson Occum, a young warrior who had recently "emerged
from pagan darkness" in the hands of Norwich apostles, accepted
Wheelock's bid, and Dartmouth was in the making. During the ensuing months Sampson responded to Pastor Wheelock's tutelage
like an eager sophister. He lived with the Wheelock brood, dined

with them, shared their morning and evening devotions, sat in the family pew on Sunday, and in a few years knew enough Latin, Greek, and Holy Writ to go forth on his own as an itinerant missionary.

Lebanon's educator lined up more benches in his study, and soon there were rows of white boys as well as Indians in the academy. Joshua Moor, a Windham compatriot, became both advocate and generous benefactor, and in his honor the institution was named "Moor's Indian Charity School." Occasionally the first alumnus was recalled to civilization and placed on exhibition at the school, in Hartford, in Boston, and in New York, where he always "preached to good acceptance . . . though for many years he was without polite conversation and destitute of a library." To London Occum went in 1766 as the principal exhibit in a fund-raising campaign for the Charity School. In England he preached to such "good acceptance" that funds poured in—particularly through the largess of the Earl of Dartmouth.

It was then that the Lebanon orchardists began to make their complaints, and when an offer came to Dr. Wheelock to move his institution up the Connecticut River to a more fitting frontier, he accepted. Incorporated under the new name of Dartmouth College, the entire student body, accompanied by a delegation of the citizens of Wheelock's native Windham, tramped north in the spring of 1770 to the log-cabin settlement in the wilderness: "The number of souls with him was about seventy. . . . The frame of a college, eighty feet in length and two stories in height, was soon after raised, and partially covered: a hall and two or three rooms in it, were considerably advanced when the autumnal storms advanced. . . . Upon a circular area of about six acres, the pines were felled, and in all directions covered the ground to the height of about five feet. Paths of communication were cut through them. . . . The snow lay four feet in depth between four and five months. Sometimes standing in the open air, at the head of his numerous family, Dr. Wheelock presented to God their morning and evening prayers: the surrounding forests, for the first time, reverberated the solemn sounds of supplication and praise."

Lebanon lost its Dartmouth, but so much fame encumbered the founder that he could not take all of it with him to New Hampshire. For years, many a Connecticut lad trudged north to Hanover for an education, rather than south to New Haven—gradually crowding out the Indians. It was clearly a displaced Connecticut college, as the roster of the early Dartmouth sons showed, and for a brief time the institutional orphan was all but restored to its original parentage when "New Connecticut, alias Vermont" temporarily annexed the town of Hanover in 1778.

"After planting a colony, the English first built an inn," observed the contemporary Chateaubriand, "the Germans built a beer hall, the Spaniards built a chapel, but the Americans built a schoolhouse." If he had stretched the analogy further, the French savant might well have added that Connecticut colonists first built a college. In whatever direction the men of Connecticut expanded, one of their first concerns was higher education. John Davenport was scheming to start a facsimile of Harvard at New Haven in 1641, only a few years after the first ivy had been planted at Cambridge, and New Haven would have had its college fifty years earlier than it did, had it not been for the protests from Massachusetts.

A lot was set aside and six hundred pounds subscribed, but Boston argued that all the resources of New England were scarcely enough to subsidize one institution. Instead of promoting a competing college, the supporters of Harvard pleaded, why not institute a voluntary tax of perhaps a half-bushel of corn from each family to promote the existing school? So while corn-fed Harvard prospered, Connecticut cooperated, and Yale remained a dream until 1701. During all those years the cooperation was seldom hearty; the urge to establish a college on home territory grew ever stronger; and when Connecticut at last gathered enough courage to ignore the dissuasion of Massachusetts and establish its own halls of learning, Yale became a model that emigrants tried to duplicate in their travels north, south, or west.

Migrants pressed into Berkshire County, Massachusetts, and helped to organize Williams in 1793, with Ebenezer Fitch of Norwich as its first president. They did the same at Amherst, with Heman Humphrey of West Simsbury at the helm. Thirty New Haven families—a whole congregation, complete with pastor, deacons, and records—moved to Newark and created there the College of New Jersey, which later became Princeton. Scores of Litchfield county families migrated to Vermont's Champlain Valley, and, across the hills from Dartmouth, established Middlebury College before there was a road down the valley. The settlers at Middlebury couldn't agree on the site for a church or even on a town center, but they agreed on the site for a college.

Samuel Kirkland of Norwich, disciple of Eleazer Wheelock, missionary and negotiator among the Senecas and Oneidas, in 1789 was awarded jointly by the Indians and the State of New York a tract of land two miles square in Oneida County as a recognition of his public services during the Revolution. Settlers from Connecticut were swarming over the area. Their children needed a college. His gift of land had come from the people, so he gave it back to them: "A serious consideration of the importance of education, and an early improvement and cultivation of the human mind . . . has induced and determined me to contribute of the ability wherewith my heavenly Benefactor hath blessed me, toward laying the foundation and support of a school . . . contiguous to the Oneida nation of Indians, for the mutual benefit of the young and flourishing settlements, and the various tribes of confederate Indians; earnestly wishing that . . . it may prove an eminent means of diffusing knowledge, enlarging the bounds of human happiness, aiding the reign of virtue, and the kingdom of the blessed Redeemer." The Hamilton Oneida Academy became Hamilton College in 1812, named for one of the charter trustees, Alexander Hamilton.

Yale men were in the vanguard that pushed into the Northwest Territory to promote Western Reserve College, and for years there was an annual interchange of instructors between New Haven and Cleveland. Marietta and Beloit were planned and put into operation by Connecticut emigrants. Oberlin followed the same pattern, and then her sons, imbued with "the life of simplicity, especial devotion to church and school, and earnest labor in the missionary cause," in turn founded Olivet in Michigan, Tabor and Grinnell in Iowa, Ripon in Wisconsin, Drury in Missouri, Carleton in Minnesota.

Norwich University, like Dartmouth, started in Connecticut—at Middletown—but the legislature was loath to grant a charter to the "American Literary, Scientific and Military Academy." A former West Point superintendent, Captain Alden Partridge, headed the enterprise, and Middletonians were sufficiently impressed with his objectives to provide two permanent stone structures. Still the charter was not forthcoming, and the Academy went north to Vermont to become the first engineering institute in the United States. But all was not lost, for at the time the Methodist Episcopal Church was looking for a college site. The buildings and grounds were a bargain at $33,000, and Wesleyan University had a better plant for a start than any other New England institution of the century.

Living in a perpetual state of alarm that somehow their theology might be lost in the expanses of the New World, Connecticut cultivated a brave philosophy that education for the ministry must be within reach of every new settlement. Perpetuating the cultural traditions of Emmanuel College was a God-given responsibility. Relentlessly, generously, presumptuously, the propagandists went about the business of converting every foreign wilderness into an educational Eden. In remote Connecticut villages there were pioneer experiments in the training of apprentices, in medical and law schools, in singing schools and art schools, in teaching the deaf and dumb, in foreign-language schools, in bringing enlightenment to natives of far-off lands.

At Cornwall, of all places, a Foreign Mission School was started in 1818 for educating Hawaiians, and two years later six "Owyheean youth" were enrolled there, along with nineteen American Indians. Pining for his islands, Henry Obookiah, "an Idolater designed for a Pagan Priest," died in the chill Cornwall climate and was buried in the local graveyard under the inscription, "By the grace of God, and by the prayers and instructions of pious friends, he became a Christian. He was eminent for piety and missionary zeal. When almost prepared to return to his native isle to preach the Gospel, God took him to himself. In his last sickness, he wept and prayed for Owyhee, but was submissive." Plainfield Academy imported a score of Chickasaw Indians from Texas in 1848 to imbibe New England learning, and later went farther afield by playing educational host to South American Indians.

In all this enthusiasm for educating foreigners and for establishing institutions of learning on the frontiers, the home front was often sadly neglected. Educators were so busy carrying moral philosophy and Latin syntax to Vermont and Ohio that English grammar and long division were given less-than-perfunctory attention at the village school. After the first auspicious start, for almost two centuries what little "system" existed at the elementary level was fumbling, erratic, and misguided. Here and there enough enlightenment emanated from the crossroads shack, known nostalgically as the little red schoolhouse, to have it pictured as a seat of learning, and there were devoted masters and mistresses who conveyed the first glimmer of understanding to recalcitrant farm boys, but for the most part the district schools were the disgrace of Connecticut.

The one-room building itself, often located on a barren spot of worthless land, was carelessly knocked together more to comply with the law than to offer shelter. Seats were of unfinished plank, from which the tender bottoms of the younger generation gradually removed the slivers. Frequently there were no desks—and no books except what the teacher possessed. Blackboards were unknown. The warmth from the hearth fire was never enough to take the chill off the room in winter, and when the stove came later, students were exposed alternately to oven temperatures or a breath of the Arctic. When the minister served as teacher, the instruction was competent, though the pedagogy was likely to be primitive; when a Yale undergraduate filled in, or when a neophyte took over, anything could happen. Keeping some semblance of order among a heterogeneous score of students, ranging in age from six to twenty, was the principal challenge of the instructor, and he used his rod, his lash, or his finger-pinchers with dexterity and indiscrimination.

Connecticut's greatest educator, Henry Barnard, "victim of a miserable district school," hatched a plot of escape at the age of thirteen, and would have gone to sea if a kindly father hadn't interceded on the eve of his secret departure. Henry Ward Beecher, long after he had allowed himself time to develop nostalgia, if there had been any, wrote: "It was our misfortune, in boyhood, to go to a District School. A little, square pine building, blazing in the sun, stood upon the highway, without a tree for shade or shadow near it; without bush, yard, fence or circumstance to take off its bare, cold, hard hateful look. Before the door, in winter, was a pile of wood for fuel; and there, in summer, were all the chips of the winter's wood. . . . Certainly we were never sent for any such absurd purpose as an education. . . . We were read and spelled twice a day, unless something happened to prevent, which *did* happen about every other day. For the rest of the time we were busy in keeping still. And a time we always had of it. . . . O, dear! can there be anything worse . . . than going to a winter district-school? Yes. Going to a summer district-school! There is no comparison. The last is the Miltonic depth below the deepest depth. . . . The benches were slabs with legs in them. The desks were slabs at an angle, cut, hacked, scratched, each year's edition of jack-knife literature overlaying its predecessor. . . . As for learning, the sum of all that we ever got in district-school would scarcely cover the first ten letters of the alphabet. . . . We abhor the thought of a school. We do not go into them if we can avoid it. Our boyhood experience has pervaded our memory with such images as breed a private repugnance to district-schools, which we fear we shall not lay aside until we lay aside everything into the grave."

Of course there were almost as many testimonials to the contrary. Abraham Lincoln's friend, Julian Sturtevant, went west like Beecher in 1830 and became the first instructor and later President of Illinois College, but he fondly recalled his school days at Warren: "As I compare the school experience of the first eleven years of my life with what I should have enjoyed in the costly and much lauded public schools of the present day, I must frankly confess that I greatly prefer the schools of seventy years ago to those now found in most of our large cities. I do not believe it would have been better to have substituted for the rude and simple arrangement of the Connecticut district school of 1815, a little arithmetic, a little geography, a little diluted and simplified physical science, and a little of almost everything else administered in the manner of modern times." However, Julian quit Warren at the age of eleven to make a preliminary trip to the Northwest Territory, and after that commuted between Talmadge, Ohio, and Yale in a one-horse wagon. It may have been on the eight-hundred-mile pilgrimages behind his nag that his affection for district school was restored.

The controversy among former inmates raged on and on. It never was resolved. But certainly the circumstantial evidence was on the side of Barnard and Beecher. Connecticut district schools were perhaps a little worse than they were elsewhere because of Connecticut parsimony. At the start, affairs went reasonably well. The Assembly had charged local authorities with the responsibility of establishing schools and of belaboring parents in an endeavor "not to suffer so much barbarism in any of the families as to have a single child or apprentice unable to read the holy word of God, and the laws of the colony; and to bring them up to some lawful calling or employment." In every town of fifty families "reading and wrighting" was to be taught, and in every town of a hundred families a grammar school was to be established. Then year after year, as towns protested and freely disregarded the mandate, the law was modified, strengthened, weakened.

Sometimes the legal minimum for a school year was three months, sometimes six, sometimes eleven. There was open confusion over the "who" and "where" of attendance, for the "district" or "society" might be a town, a part of a town, or segments of several towns. Almost any able-bodied male willing to work for $14.50 a month was qualified to serve as schoolmaster, or money could be saved by employing a woman for $5.75. The attempt to have a Latin school in every county seat was abandoned. Norwich was indicted by the Grand Jury in 1700 for "failing to maintain a school to instruct," although there were forty societies within the town area. Everywhere the eternal dispute was over financial support. Originally wages were "to be paid either by the parents or masters of children, or by the inhabitants in general." The latitude was all too sweeping. Towns declined to make appropriations; families neglected to make their contributions toward tuition. Property taxes of varying amounts were tried, lowered, and abandoned.

Then the final gimmick that killed the effectiveness of the "society" system was the subsidy of $1,200,000 received from the sale of the state's reserve of western lands in Ohio. The first interest of $60,000 was paid off in 1799 and was distributed among the school districts. Thereafter, for many years, penurious parents and penny-wise politicians accepted the tradition that the allotment from the "School Fund" was all that any economy-minded town ought to spend on education. In many towns it was doled out so parsimoniously that it would pay for only a month or two in winter and a few weeks in summer. As soon as the money was exhausted, the teacher was dismissed and the doors locked for the year. The little red schoolhouse lost its paint, and many a sixteen-year-old boy never got as far as fractions.

Education had fallen so low that one teacher complained that the schoolroom had been converted into a sewing circle. "I have finished my teaching at Middlefield," she sighed. "Sewing was one of the branches to be taught, and I soon learned it was an adroit way for the mothers to get the family sewing done. Small children would appear, boys as well as girls, with difficult parts of dresses to be made, also trousers both large and small. Of course the teacher was expected to know how to do all kinds of sewing, and little girls and boys could not put in pockets and make buttonholes, and that was a way to get the work done by the teacher. One day my table was loaded with fourteen pairs of trousers! I took garments home and worked morning and evenings on them, instead of my own sewing. I understand they are very sorry I will not teach longer."

This was the situation that lawyer Henry Barnard found when he pushed through the Assembly in 1838 a bill to provide a state board of commissioners "for the better supervision of common schools." Momentarily the representatives were so appalled by his description of elementary education that he was quickly made the first commissioner. Deplorable schoolhouses, complete lack of equipment, untrained teachers, no uniformity in management, intersociety jealousy, and an estimated total of five thousand growing children who had never been to school at all were among his observations. Barnard went to work with such vigor that he was legislated out of office within four years, but four years were long enough to gall towns and societies into action. He went on to become the commissioner of education in Rhode Island, Chancellor

of the University of Wisconsin, President of St. John's, the first
United States Commissioner of Education; but, bowed with
honors, he returned to Connecticut long enough to inaugurate the
New Britain Normal School and start the state on its long, up-
hill road toward establishing an exemplary educational system—
though school districts were not abandoned until 1909, nor state
aid put on a per student basis until 1945.

Youth was not as completely deprived of exposure to culture
during the long blight as circumstances betokened. Other educational influences helped fill the gap—maternal tutoring and pastoral tutoring, library associations, Congregational catechisms,
hornbooks, apprenticeships, and Bible reading. A good example
was the little agricultural community of Franklin, where the farmers were so scattered over the hills that there was "no place which
may be considered as a village." The district schooling was deplorable. So remote was Franklin, it would be the last town where
one would look for erudition. But it had a Congregational church
and an indefatigable pastor, Samuel Nott, who occupied the pulpit and the parsonage for an unbroken period of seventy years,
1782 to 1852. During his first half-century as minister he fitted
forty youngsters for college, besides giving theological training to
half a dozen more, and general instruction to youths who became
"physicians, merchants, mechanics and farmers." Altogether he estimated that he had taught close to three hundred, and teaching
was only a spare-time hobby.

Meticulous, patient, good humored, always ready with wise
counsel, he kept in touch with his students long after they had
left his study, through little paternalistic notes: "Whenever you
write, write slowly. Compose carefully. Do all things as well as you
can. You will then soon be able to do better. You may easily,
with the blessing of God, make a very useful member of society.
Seek for no promotion, but be careful to deserve any that is in the
power of the town to give. You must be careful to improve the
instruction you have received, and fill up your leisure hours to the
best advantage. You must, in addition to the books you now own,
buy Webster's Dictionary, Morse's Eastern and Western Gazeteer.
These, with the Bible . . . will in some measure be sufficient for
you."

While the parson was busy with the boys in his study, Mrs. Nott
and her daughters were busy with the girls in the front room.
Social culture, refinement, and parlor manners were on the educational bill of fare for the weaker sex. "They drilled and rehearsed
their pupils in the minute but important particulars of entering a

room full of people and passing the ordinary civilities of a social hour," recalled one Franklinite. "They taught fancy work, the nicer ways of household management, cooking, mending, making. All this touched a great many homes, and gave a new spring of life to the younger generation. A Christian refinement came in and sweetened the intercourse of life. Ideas of personal improvement, social and domestic accomplishments were planted in noble natures whose true nobility would otherwise have remained undiscovered, and those ideas repeated themselves at a later day in many a refined home in Franklin."

Every community did not have a Nott family, but the ministers of any town could be counted on to supplement the lean diet of the "society" school. And the astonishing evidence of success in this hodgepodge of exposure to the three R's was seen in the census of 1840. In the total white population of 301,856, only 526 over the age of twenty years were unable to read and write.

Sad as was the decadence of the public schools, some good came of it, for model private schools, free of any taint of snobbery, sprang up on Connecticut hilltops in most unexpected townships. They were called "academies," as Benjamin Franklin had proposed in an essay published in 1749, and were open to both boys and girls from the surrounding countryside, or even from distant states: Greenfield Hill, conducted by Timothy Dwight for over a decade before he was summoned to Yale; Staples Academy at Fairfield; Plainfield, the first academy in Windham County; Woodstock Academy; Berlin; Bacon, at Colchester; Stratford; a school for instruction in Latin, Greek, and English at Wallingford; Danbury; Goshen.

"Many academies are maintained by private funds," noted Webster, whose spellers and grammars were used in all of them. "In these are taught primary branches and geography, grammar, languages, and higher mathematics. . . . Among the academies of first reputation are one in Plainfield and the Bacon Academy."

That was in 1806, and still the academies multiplied as the terms at the district school grew shorter and were attended only by children from poorer families who couldn't afford the tuition—a famous academy at Wilton, others at Greenfield, Tolland, Brooklyn, and Saybrook. The Connecticut Literary Institute opened its doors at Suffield in 1835; the Betts Academy at Stamford three years later; Black Hall at Lyme. Frederick Gunn, who had been excommunicated from Washington for his views on abolition, returned in 1847 to re-establish Gunnery. In 1854, Norwich, which had once been in trouble with the courts over its forty-odd inoperative district schools, received a gift of $160,000 for the erection of Norwich Free Academy. Benefactions brought institutions to many other towns; any community with social or cultural aspirations had to have its academy.

"I do give all the remainder of my estate, both real, personal, and mixed of any kind . . . to the Inhabitants of the First Society in Colchester for the purpose of supporting and maintaining a school . . . near the meeting house . . . for the instruction of Youth in Reading, and writing English, in Arithmetic, Mathimaticks, and the Languages, or such other branches of Learning as said Inhabitants shall direct," . . . Pierpoint Bacon, wrote into his will. Such documents, representing small fortunes, more and more frequently appeared under exclamatory headlines in local papers.

"Stingy Old Bacon," the townspeople of Colchester had called him. Everyone knew that he was laying up a tidy fortune from his selfish, tireless labor on a huge farm three miles south of the church, but no one knew that he had decided long before to donate whatever he could accumulate toward an academy. Weekly he drove his team over the eighteen rugged miles to New London with a rich load of farm produce, frugally carrying his lunch, and returning mysteriously long after dark by lantern light. Frequently he brought a newly purchased Negro with him, and that did not set well with the townsfolk either—not so much because of objections to slavery: they objected to any man's hoarding the wealth he was hoarding in both money and Negro manpower.

For Colchester, he had a vast number of slaves, so many that a little schoolhouse especially for Negro children had been built. He treated the slaves well, worked shoulder to shoulder with them in the field, fought their causes until the names of Bacon and Colchester were known far to the south. "Wherever I go," reported Epaphroditus Champion, Connecticut congressman to Washington in 1807, "east or west, north or south, everybody, even the negroes, are inquiring about 'Cowlchester,' Connecticut and the way to get to it."

Despite all this notoriety Bacon was bringing to Colchester, despite the fame of his family in both England and America, he was not socially accepted. When he went to church he was not privileged to sit in the front pews reserved for those "of age and dignity of descent," nor in the next pews designated for families whose sires had held "places of public trust." Stretching an ecclesiastical point, they allowed him to sit among "those of pious disposition and behavior, and of estate." So "Stingy Old Bacon" gave his hard-earned thousands to Bacon Academy. Every state in the union prior to the Civil War sent sons there. In the 1830's it had over two hundred students and half a dozen instructors, was famed for its liberal education from Montpelier to Mobile. And Lydia Sigourney penned a proud tribute to the farmer who gave it:

> *What throngs have drank the waters of the spring*
> *That thou didst open here!*
> > *We see them come*
> *Back through the mists of time.*
> > *Where now is sport,*
> *They played, with merry shout, and flying ball,*
> *And trundled hoop, or o'er the frozen flood*
> *Glided with steel armed feet.*
> > *As these now bend*
> *O'er Livy's lore, or Homer's glowing page,*
> *Or the long task of figures, without end,—*
> *They bent, perchance to hide vexation's tear.—*
> *They rose to men.*
> > *Some from the pulpit spake*
> *The holy word of warning; some assayed,*
> *Of Jurisprudence the unmeasured toil,—*
> *Some tending in the couch of wan disease,*
> *Parried the spoiler's shaft. To giddy youth,*
> *Some from the teacher's chair, wise precepts dealt.*
> *Some, 'mid the statesman's perils rode to fame,*
> *And others tested the marts of trade*
> *The value of the wisdom gathered here.*
> *All were thy debtors.*

Generation after generation of distinguished graduates went forth from Bacon, and what occurred at Colchester was repeated in like measure at the scores of other academies.

Contrary to custom in other parts of the globe, women had to be educated in Connecticut, as well as men, and when a coeducational academy was not within reach, a female institute blossomed. Sarah Pierce opened the first United States school for girls at Litchfield in 1792 and in forty years graduated over fifteen hundred pupils. At Norwich was the Goodrich School; at the capital, Hartford Female Seminary; at Farmington, Miss Porter's; at Bridgeport, Golden Hill Seminary; Grove Hall at New Haven; the Female Seminary at Windsor; St. Margaret's at Waterbury. Emma Hart Willard of Berlin took her Connecticut conception of a college curriculum to Vermont and then Troy, New York, and was the nation's pioneer in promoting higher education for women. The singing and dancing, the embroidery and painting that went on in the female seminaries, along with a smattering of linguistics and algebra, often inspired smart lampoons from the Latin and Greek students in the boys' academies, but they survived the slander graciously—in fact, Miss Porter's survived the fad of public high schools that overwhelmed academies and seminaries alike before 1900, and is still going strong.

But no Connecticut institution of learning, at any level, found completely smooth going over the years. New ideas and new jealousies, financial squabbles and ideological squabbles were always intruding. Even Yale did not always prove to be a tower of strength in the face of hostilities. When the Assembly tried to settle the struggle over a permanent location for the Collegiate School and authorized its removal from Saybrook to New Haven in 1717, the citizens of Saybrook displayed their spleen by destroying the carts in which the books were to be transferred, breaking down every bridge between the towns, and pillaging papers and valuable documents. The scrimmage was a foreboding of some of the scenes that were to follow—pitched battles over religious doctrines, bread-and-butter wars over the indigestible salt pork served at the commons, senior-freshman riots, brutal assaults upon the presidential residence. To cope with the mob of unruly students, the president had to have the combined qualities of a field general, an experienced diplomat, and a flawless scholar in every recognized field of human knowledge. He had to teach and preach, handle finances and wield a big stick, and defend his every move before both parents and politicians. And there were few such men in Connecticut.

When New Haven was invaded by the British in 1779, President Naphtali Daggett even felt called upon to lead his students into the field in defense of their alma mater. He was a good scholar and a fair disciplinarian, but he was not cut out for a competent combat officer—"inclining to be corpulent," as one admirer described him, "slow in gait, somewhat clumsy in his movements, with a drawling, unanimated delivery."

Armed with a musket, he sallied forth, but the students were more agile in the retreat than he was, and as a captive he was subjected to more indignities than any college president was entitled to. In his own words, he complained that the enemy discharged "not less than 15 or 20 balls at me alone. . . . The fury of infernals glowing in their faces, they called me a damned old Rebel.

. . . One made a pass at me with his bayonet. . . . I continued pleading and begging for my life with the utmost importunity, using every argument in my power to mollify them, and induce them to desist. . . . One of them gave me four gashes on my head with the edge of his bayonet, . . . the other gave me three slight pricks. . . . But what is a thousand times worse is the blows and bruises they gave me on my bowels. . . . Their avarice further led them to rob me of my Pocket handkerchief. . . . I was insulted in the most shocking manner by the ruffian soldiers. . . . One would strike me on the back with a heavy walking staff and kick me behind with his foot. At length, by the supporting power of God, I arrived at the green in New Haven. But my life was almost spent, the world around me several times appeared as dark as midnight. I obtained leave of an officer to be carried into the widow Lyman's and laid upon a bed."

Yale survived, but the good president never fully recovered. And the British were not the only ones to cause a commotion in New Haven. Tutor Clap bore witness to one occasion when "a number of persons gathered together near the college, and there . . . fired a great number of guns to create disturbance and terror . . . and brake the College windows and fences, and several of them had gowns on, with a design to bring a scandal upon the College. . . . I and the Tutors walked among and near the rioters, and could not see any scholars."

Not until Timothy Dwight took the reins in 1795 was Yale really tamed. Up to that time even its continued existence was often in doubt. Dwight rallied the student body, modernized the curriculum, and started the college off on the road to respectability and to its status as a great university, anticipating the day when it would have schools of engineering, medicine, divinity, law, fine arts, music, forestry, nursing, and drama. It was at Yale in 1861 that the first American Ph.D. was conferred.

The kind of spirit originally expended in the planting of colleges across the nation was applied to the creation of better education at home after the middle of the nineteenth century. From a small Methodist college, Wesleyan expanded into one of the foremost New England liberal-arts institutions. Washington College, renamed Trinity, gave Hartford the distinguished institution it had long sought to complement its famed Theological Seminary. In slow, easy strides, Storrs Agricultural School developed into a college, and finally into an enormous state university with fifteen different schools all far larger than the original Storrs.

New Britain became Teachers College of Connecticut, and acquired sister normal schools at Danbury, New Haven, and Willimantic. The Coast Guard Academy and Connecticut College for Women came to New London. Excellent Catholic colleges and over 125 parochial schools found warm hospitality in what had once been a Congregational state.

In less than a decade new institutions like Hillyer, Bridgeport, Fairfield, and Quinnipiac acquired academic status that older ones had achieved only after a century of struggle, and a half-dozen junior colleges sprang up as quickly. More secondary schools—private and public—spawned than there were towns in the state—and among them many of the old names survived in nationally famous preparatory schools like Avon, Kent, Hopkins Grammar, Pomfret, Hotchkiss, Choate, Gunnery, Taft, Loomis. Within commuting distance were business colleges, denominational seminaries, music-and-art schools, or vocational-technical schools in any field for which a youngster had a leaning.

The "barbarism" that bothered the lawgivers three centuries ago still may not be entirely beaten, but if building bricks, multi-million-dollar appropriations, football fields, and yardage in sheepskin can lick it, Connecticut is well on the way toward winning the struggle.

neously sang out a jingle to the familiar folk tune of "Lucy
Locket Lost Her Pocket":

> *Yankee Doodle came to town*
> *Riding on a pony.*
> *Stuck a feather in his hat*
> *And called it macaroni.*

It caught on as no other ditty in American history before or after
ever caught on. It lasted through the French and Indian War. It
was adopted as the rallying song for fife and drum corps of the
Revolution. The Blue marched to it in the Civil War. World Wars
I and II carried it around the globe. The nonsense song, originally
intended as a jest at a dozen gawky farm boys, became a national
classic. It helped to disperse the tradition of Yankeeism across the
northern half of the country and make "Yankee" synonymous
with "American." In times of stress, it even helped keep the
United States united.

"Yankee Doodle" was far removed from any partnership with
Art, but it was apt to represent Connecticut's distinction in artistic
attainment for a great many decades. Yankee ingenuity did not
flow in the direction of sublime artistry. There were too many inhibitions and prohibitions to discourage it. From the sensitive
soul could come a well-organized sermon but not a symphony, a
witty proverb but not a great poem, a graceful church steeple but
no noble sculpture. The Connecticut creative artist was droll,
whimsical, original, but he shied away from the pretty and the
elegant as he would from idolatry. He leaned toward painting colorful tavern signs instead of charming landscapes; he carved quaint
designs on gravestones rather than experimenting with Venuses
and Apollos; he wrought shapely tin kitchen utensils when he
might have done an icon; wrote almanacs in place of novels; fashioned handsome clock cases and carved "Hartford chests" rather
than haloed reliefs for adorning the meetinghouse; at Clintonville
manufactured millions of Christmas cards, "sparking cards," and
valentines instead of producing a memorable nativity scene. He
was naïve, dexterous, and cunning; in his effort, he demonstrated that he had genuine talent to attain heights far greater than
"Yankee Doodle," if his conscience had only let him give full play
to his feeling.

The field of music perhaps best illustrated the handicaps under
which he worked. While Handel was writing his magificent ora-
torios, while Bach was composing his immortal works, and Purcell

was giving luster to English folk and religious music, the Connecticut Puritans were still lustily singing the five orthodox tunes— "Old Hundred," "York," "Hackney," "Windsor," and "Martyrs." Regardless of feet, meter, or accent, all the psalms in the long repertoire were squeezed into the five tunes—and even those, without accompaniment, were never chanted the same way twice, for a confident bass always managed to reach the "Amen" sooner than a timid soprano. It went on for eighty years. "Old Hundred," as sung in Lisbon, might not be recognized as the same tune sung in Saybrook, and each accused the other of taking liberties with the divine pattern. The variations were endless, but as long as a church kept within the established bounds of musical propriety, it mattered little. About the five tunes gathered an aura as sacred as the Scriptures, and anyone who proposed innovations for the psalter was a messenger of Satan.

At taverns and around the home hearths of libertines, merry folk songs and lugubrious ballads, brought over from the old country and amended in generation-to-generation transit, were sung for entertainment, but when the same voices were raised at the meetinghouse, it was only to echo in melody what a dour deacon had first "lined out" phrase by phrase. A careful reading of the Old Testament showed to the satisfaction of most that the ancient Jews made a more joyful noise unto the Lord than they were making, but the conservative could find equally convincing Biblical injunctions against Sabbath music.

In defiance of tradition, however, a new enthusiasm for music sprang up about 1720. Singing schools were started, and choirs took seats in the church galleries. Against firm opposition, revised editions of psalmbooks found a place in church pews, but the "lining" continued for decades among congregations where obstinate dogmatists had established a stronghold. From them emanated endless excuses for not singing in unison or part— claims "that it was a new way to sing by note; that it was less melodious than the old way; that there were so many tunes, no one could learn them; that churches were disturbed and good men grieved; that it was popish; that it would introduce instruments; that the names of the notes were blasphemous; that the old way was good enough; that it was a contrivance to get money. They asked seriously whether men forty years old and more could learn to sing by note, or ought to try."

Similar arguments kept coming for another half-century. Then, in 1770, from Boston was issued *The New England Psalm-singer: or American Chorister*, the work of a revolutionary William Billings. His daring collection contained 120 tunes, with a few anthems for good measure. His bounding enthusiasm for the new music was best expressed in the description of his own fugue, which he maintained had "twenty times the power of the old slow tunes; each part straining for the mastery and victory. . . . Now the solemn bass demands their attention—next the manly tenor —, now, the lofty counter—now, the volatile treble. Now here— now there, now here again. O ecstatic! Rush on, you sons of harmony."

Even in Connecticut, sons of harmony rushed to him. He introduced the pitch pipe into congregation singing, and the tuning fork soon followed, so that at least the introductory notes of a hymn were not entirely speculative. He encouraged the use of a viol, and that made way for exactly the instrumentation that the die-hards had fought most doggedly: flutes, hautboys, clarinets, and bassoons. In a few years the whole band used for parades and training-day ceremonies moved into the gallery. The organ came later.

In the frigid climate there could be slim incentive for any kind of musical creativity. What few musicians of talent there were expended their energies in trying to break the opposition toward their art—in teaching, writing, and arguing. Andrew Law of Cheshire composed fugues and songs, but not enough to bring him notoriety beyond his own generation. Along with his partner Timothy Olmstead, he was too preoccupied with editing his periodical, *Art of Singing*, giving singing lessons, conducting choirs, and defending himself against hostile attacks of those who thought him sinful for giving the air of a tune to women rather than men.

Thomas Hastings of Washington wrote hymns, composed tunes, taught, and edited a journal, but Puritan restraint so rigidly shackled the musician in him that he could not be persuaded that a symphony should be anything more than an exercise for professionals to study: certainly it should not be offered to the untutored public; and as for chamber compositions—"Parlor music when not intended for the mere exercise of talent, should be adapted to promote moral principles, refined sentiments, and sympathetic emotions." Dudley Buck of Hartford became an eminent musician and composer; he studied in Leipzig, Dresden, and Paris under the European masters of the mid-nineteenth century, and returned to his native city as organist and teacher, but Hartford couldn't hold him. His great fame as organist, conductor, and composer of cantatas, pastorals, and marches came to him in Chicago, New York, and Boston.

Few of the artists brought distinction upon themselves as composers, but they did eventually succeed in bringing music to Connecticut. Little by little they wrenched control of aesthetics from the deacons, and even got some of the deacons into their choral groups. Music schools spread from large towns to small towns; the discipline of singing grew into a fad. In 1854 an aging songster recalled a lively youth when he had responded to the waving arms and stamping feet of his teacher Timothy Olmstead, and extravagantly referred to him as "the Mozart of America." "Had he been born in Germany," conjectured the student, "surrounded by the authentic models of his art, and with opportunity for its cultivation, he would have achieved a fame like Handel and Mozart; but born in America, with no antecedents in the art he loved, unable to travel . . . dependant almost entirely upon the suggestions of his own genius, he nevertheless produced the only musical compositions in America worthy of consideration up to this era. . . . It is greatly to be feared that the reputation and the compositions of Olmstead will be forgotten in the great advance which has been made in music in the United States during the last twenty five years."

Olmstead's admirer was right. The "Mozart of America" was forgotten, but he and a long line of similar music teachers did establish a cultural birthright that is not forgotten. They were the leaders of hundreds of quartets and choral societies, glees and choirs. Organizations like Hartford's Euterpian Society and the Jubal Society made up in less than a decade what the five-tune psalms and "lining" held back for over a century. In 1839 the interest in private instruction led to the inauguration of the first music school for teachers in America.

Orramel Whittlesey, piano manufacturer and composer, had been persuaded to take on a few pianoforte students, and one blustery winter evening a pair of his pupils eagerly appeared for their lessons despite the weather. The storm turned into a blizzard by the time the lessons were over, and gallantry decreed that he put them up in his guest room. Music Vale Seminary at Salem grew out of that night of playing host. He gave up piano manufacturing and started a boarding school, with class instruction in notation, harmony, thorough bass, composition, counterpoint, fugue, and private instruction in voice culture, piano, organ, harp, and guitar. Pupils flocked to Music Vale from the Deep South and Middle West, from Canada and the West Indies. The school increased to over a hundred, and the state board of education authorized the granting of a degree in pedagogy. "Strict! You have no idea what Yankee strictness means," wrote one of his pupils to her parents in Kentucky. "There is no shirking the rules!"

The young ladies were treated like Prussian privates, and reveled in it: up at five o'clock in the morning for an hour's practice before breakfast, never a spoken word to another pupil during exercises, practice periods of four solid hours both morning and afternoon, with classes in between. Twice a week all students performed before the assembled faculty and undergraduate body, and once a month the advanced musicians demonstrated their accomplishment in a public concert at the Seminary Theatre. Neither Norwich nor New London had a hall that could compare with Salem's. In fine carriages during the summer, and sleighs during the winter, enthusiasts from these two cities and the surrounding towns drove fifteen and twenty miles to hear the "Moonlight Sonata," "The Last Rose of Summer" (played with the left hand only), Rubinstein's "Melody in F," "The Spinning Song," "Home Sweet Home," and "The Last Hope."

Undeterred by the confusion of activity at the normal school, Superintendent Whittlesey still found time to be Composer Whittlesey, and published an assortment of sentimental pieces on the order of the popular numbers his students performed—"The Harp of the Wild Wind," "Music Vale Quick Step," "The Dying Soldier of Buena Vista"—and a complete opera, *Ralvo, or the Pirate of the Gulf.*

The Civil War brought a slow end to the school. Girls from the Carolinas and Kentucky weren't interested in coming North for their musical education after Bull Run and Gettysburg. The buildings were burned in 1868 and replaced, but the professor was growing old, and conservatories were beginning to flourish in other parts of the country. The new seminary was not the same. Music Vale was the embodiment of Whittlesey, and, with his death in 1876, Connecticut's most noble experiment in pioneer musical training died too. No great lasting compositions came from the Seminary, but what was started there paved the way for creativity elsewhere. The contribution of the state to music was in education rather than masterworks.

For a quarter of a century Asa Hopkins labored at Fluteville in the interests of instrumental music, turning out flutes by the gross, flageolets, clarinets, fifes, guitars, drumsticks, and castanets, but by 1852 he appeared to have satisfied the demands of pipers and percussionists, and his company folded. From 1899 to 1925 the Norfolk Music Festival flourished under the Carl Stoeckels, and composers of the stature of Coleridge Taylor, Jean Sibelius, and

Horatio Parker received commissions to compose and conduct their works at the Festival. A local voice teacher in Meriden gave Rosa and Carmella Ponselle their start toward the Metropolitan. At Falls Village the former conductor of the Chicago Symphony established the Jacques Gordon Musical Foundation and opened a summer school for young musicians of talent; now, every summer Sunday afternoon, the Berkshire String Quartet brings superior music to Music Mountain. Summer "Pops" concerts have come both to the Yale Bowl and to the Fairfield University campus. But Connecticut annals have to be sifted patiently to find many great moments in music history.

In drama, the artist encountered even colder coercion than the limitation of five-tune psalm singing. Any form of make-believe, except perhaps the minstrel show, was a worldly compromise with the devil, and inflexible church fathers assiduously fought against the intrusion of legitimate theater for three centuries after Shakespeare had come to the rest of the English-speaking world. Down to the 1900's there were still deacons who openly conspired against playwrights, actors, impresarios, the stage, the theater, or any association with the dramatic arts. George Pierce Baker and his twentieth-century Yale Workshop weren't entirely immune from the fiery darts of the dogmatists.

In 1778 the Reverend Andrew Eliot, who had just returned to Fairfield from the annual Election Day festivities at Hartford, voiced his indignation over what he had just witnessed at the capital: "Could you think of it? On Monday evening in election week, in Hartford, the capitol of the state, in the court house, the place where the Fathers of the Senate meet, at the most public time and in the most public manner, was acted 'Tancred and Sigismunda,' by the Junior Sophister Class of Yale College, who had been forbidden to act the same in Glastonbury . . . and who embraced the opportunity of vacation and secured the court house for the purpose. To this succeeded a farce of their own composing in which Generals Burgoyne and Prescot were introduced. To keep up the characters of their generals, especially Prescot, they were obliged (I believe not to their sorrow) to indulge in very indecent and profane language. . . . When diversions are innocent in themselves, and are not carried to excess—when they are not attended with too great expense, and do not lead to levity, dissipation and vice—they are allowable and salutary. But when to the variety of amusements peculiar to the country (the moderate use of which is prejudicial) are added stage plays, it appears to me an alarming circumstance."

The indignation of Dr. Eliot was mild compared to some of the sentiments of laymen about the colony, for pastors often were far more liberal than their constituents, but the expression from Fairfield clearly represented the views of the great majority in 1778, as it did in 1678, and as it would for a controlling church plutocracy in 1878. Nevertheless insidious forces were at work during much of this period—notably the enlightened of Hartford and the needlers at Yale. There were undergraduate zealots at New Haven gravely concerned about the salvation of souls, but there were also brave spirits who liked nothing better than to tease their elders with stage satire and buffoonery at every opportunity. As in any student body in any age, they were a trial to the patience of their parents and their pedagogues. Perennially they made their young voices heard; perennially they were slapped down.

Following examples set by New York, Philadelphia, Boston, and a few cities in the South, worldly Hartford permitted the "Old American Dramatic Company" to move into the city in 1794. On July 31 the group opened with a comedy and a farce: A *Child of Nature* and *Love-a-la-Mode*. For eight weeks they held their own against gathering opposition from the clergy, offering two or three plays and farces at each performance. But by September the brickbats were getting thicker, the audiences thinner, so Old American and Hartford parted company.

Profiting from their experience of the first season, the sponsors toned down the emphasis on theatrics, and in 1795 actually constructed a rough auditorium, discreetly labeled "The School for Morality." To the public they spelled out their high-minded motives in advance: "It will be a great source of instruction and amusement. . . . The theatre is well constructed on chaste principles—vice is drawn in colors that will disgust, and virtue painted with all its alluring charms. It is hoped it will meet the approbation and encouragement of the citizens and of the neighboring towns."

The ruse was so successful that both Joseph Jefferson and John Hodgkinson, two of the foremost actors of the day, were engaged for the third season. Hodgkinson was on stage for the opening night of July 11, 1796, to play *The Provoked Husband and Purse,* as he had played it up and down the Atlantic coast to national plaudit.

"Hodgkinson is a wonder," wrote the prominent critic John Bernard. "In the whole range of the living drama there is no variety of character he could not perceive and embody. . . . To the abundant mind of Shakespeare his own turned as a moon that could catch and reflect a large amount of its radiance. . . . I doubt if such a number and such greatness of requisites were ever before united in one mortal man."

The "Hartford Wits" and many of their disciples agreed, but the response was not large enough to warrant retaining the notable Hodgkinson in Connecticut. The keenest supporter of American theater, William Dunlap, commented that Hartford had imitated Boston "most unwisely" in trying to establish a theater. "What may be good in a large and populous city," he said, "may be an evil if not under the supervision of the government and other strict regulations, where the population is sparse. . . . It immediately appeared that the receipts could not support such a company of comedians."

The Hartford Theatre remained open for part of a summer with an ever thinning audience. Hodgkinson visited the city again in 1797 and in 1799, but after that "there was a long respite from stage plays." The laws of economy would have brought an end to the venture, but before the creditors moved in, the theater was firmly closed by the laws of Connecticut.

Twenty years later Mr. and Mrs. George Bartley, renowned in Drury Lane and Haymarket, were persuaded to pay a visit to America. En route from New York to Boston they stopped overnight at a Hartford hotel; immediately the two top-flight personalities of the London stage were recognized and—quite unaware of the laws that prohibited theatrics—were induced to remain for a few days and perform in the Connecticut capital. A hotel assembly room was engaged for the event, notices were stealthily distributed, and every seat sold, "but no sooner was the announcement made than the rigid and puritanical part of the community set up an outcry against these repeated innovations, and Mr. Ebenezer Huntington, the State's Attorney, resolved to put into execution a dormant act of the legislature against the performances."

In devious diplomacy, the sponsors carefully insulated the Bartleys from any knowledge of the "outcry," the standing law, or the Attorney's threats. A crowd that would have warmed the heart of any company assembled. As the curtain was going up on Mrs. Bartley's dramatic reading from Milton and Shakespeare, a formal warning was delivered to the hotel proprietor stating that the couple would be prosecuted for their "unlawful practices." But the proprietor was making too good a thing out of the enterprise not to favor the cause of art. He pocketed the notice, and "the performance went off with great eclat."

Preferring not to contend with the audience as well as the actors, the protectors of Connecticut law and order postponed attempting an arrest until midnight, but they had to reckon with a first line of defense—a squad of drama advocates who remained at the hotel to ward off just such an outrage. The agents were intercepted and held off with a pledge to produce Mr. Bartley the next day, as well as with a down payment on a bond of $500. It snowed all that night and all the next day. Stagecoach travel was impossible. The Bartleys were royally entertained and persuaded to put on another performance, since they could not proceed to Boston. Still not a hint of their hassle with the law was passed to them. Self-appointed guards wrestled with the police and kept them off the stage. The second night had a larger attendance than the first; then, as soon as the blizzard had blown itself out, the Bartleys were encouraged to be on their way. They made a safe escape from the clutches of Connecticut guardsmen and learned of their predicament only by accident long afterward. There were in the state such ardent patrons of art that they were ready to risk incarceration for its promotion.

The one great actor that grew out of this antagonism was William Gillette, who spanned the years from 1853 to 1937. Booth Tarkington attended a revival of his *Sherlock Holmes* in 1930, when the old stager was seventy-seven, and conceded: "I would rather see you play Sherlock Holmes than be a child again on Christmas morning." From 1899 to 1915, Sherlock and Gillette were synonymous. He created the famous detective for the stage, played the role almost nightly between 1899 and 1903, revived it frequently during the next two decades, made the play one of the spectacular successes of theatrical history, and converted it into a movie in 1915. Gillette's forte was in portraying a man of extraordinary calmness in a situation that would break the nerves of a normal person; twenty years after his death, the Sherlock Holmes popularly visualized is as much William Gillette as the sleuth Conan Doyle depicted.

He pioneered in introducing naturalness to the stage, in underplaying his part, in daring to abandon the ranting and recitative that were as old as the Greeks. In his directing he brought a new kind of realism to the theater by introducing stage effects and lighting never used before. His invention was the off-stage hoofbeat, his was the fade-out. But virtually his whole professional life was outside Connecticut. He escaped when he was twenty and, except for brief visits, did not return until 1919. Then, in a glorious second childhood, he built his castle on the Connecticut above Hadlyme and constructed there a defiant make-believe world, traversed by a big toy steam engine and another electric one running over and under the hills on miles of narrow-gauge railroad track. The state that had so many antagonisms to the art he cultivated now maintains the castle as a public shrine. And as convincing proof that the dictate of Calvinism is outmoded, many a Broadway show crosses the New York line for a trial run in New Haven, summer theaters flourish in a dozen resort centers, and in 1955 Stratford opened a million-dollar American Shakespeare Festival Theatre, a home at last for the bard of Avon in New England.

Among all Connecticut's men of art, the painters fared best. They pocketed their pride, and went forth with brush and canvas to peddle their art in much the same fashion as the peddlers of Berlin hawked their tin. Up and down New England they traveled, rapping at the doors of the aristocracy or those who had leanings in that direction, offering bargains in "sittings," often carrying an assortment of rich, ready-made, headless busts on canvas, which needed only the insertion of a face to memorialize the family patriarch or his wife. It was a form of commercial art that only the Yankees could have exploited in the grand manner: "If the gentleman can't afford the large portrait, then there is the medium-sized, or the miniature parchment—such a fine strong face, it's a duty to your children." The bargains and the sales patter were too good to decline. Scarcely a family of repute did not acquire at least one or two of these anonymous "old masters."

Quaint, stilted, naïve, and charming, the portraits graced the walls of thousands of parlors. In fact, the returns to the artist for a single sitting were so modest that he could make a respectable living only in mass production, and out of that mass were bound to come a few masterpieces. The reputation of a painter who composed a good likeness in a community spread rapidly and led to innumerable commissions, possibly a temporary studio. At Hanover it led to the painting of an enormous mural—a New Englander's conception of the walls and temples of Jerusalem as seen from on high—all crowded into the arched recess behind the pulpit of the Congregational church.

When Hartford was still little more than a village, it was supporting two portrait studios, three engravers, and six sign-painters, but most of the artists shut up shop in the summer and took to the road. The road led to New Hampshire and western Massachusetts, to Vermont, the Genesee Valley, Pennsylvania, and Ohio. And occasionally they paused for a few days to sketch Mount Washington, Lake Champlain, or Niagara Falls. More often they persuaded an affluent householder that dignity of his home called for a mural or overmantel landscape. From underneath the layers of wallpaper and cheap paint, these picturesque effusions in design are still being uncovered.

Ralph Earl was an exemplar of the school of itinerants. Before the Revolution he had made a name for himself in doing both small and life-size portraits; he engraved the first historical prints published in America, was the first to incorporate representations of the homes and holdings of his sitters into the portrait pattern, and for a sick friend painted the first known American landscape: too ill to lift his head from a pillow, the invalid craved a picture of the view from his window on the wall opposite the bed. John Copley was his idol, and to the Copley style he gave the rustic touch.

In 1777 Timothy Dwight sat to Earl and became one of his admirers. Then the artist spent four years in London studying with Benjamin West, became a member of the Royal Academy, and returned to the United States to paint the likeness of a long list of distinguished Connecticut citizens, governors, and men of affairs. He suffered the indignities reserved for artists of any age— poverty, humiliation, distrust. He was imprisoned for indebtedness in 1787, and earned his release only through the intercession of Alexander Hamilton, who induced his wife and others to sit for him in his cell. Once free, he became the itinerant of itinerants, followed the route of Connecticut emigrants north and west, leaving along the way uncounted anonymous portraits—often wooden figures without articulation, but always with a spark of originality. Family groups and children were included in his subjects, and a whimsical primitiveness crept into the more striking characterizations. Like other artists, he stopped at Niagara to record the falls, and few landscapes of the period excited greater admiration.

Far removed socially from the generation of itinerants was the Governor's son, John Trumbull, soldier, diplomat, architect, man of affairs, and author, as well as painter. He could afford to be aloof and egocentric, maintain his own studio, and draw commissions through the reputation of his family as well as through his own talent. He could afford to profess modesty. "I find myself so imperfect in my profession," he wrote Yale's President Stiles, who wanted a portrait of Governor Trumbull for the college library, "that I would not willingly expose one of my productions to the public Eye in a place at once so honorable, and so much an object of the Attention of foreigners as well as our own Countrymen—and tho' what I now do might please my friends and myself at present: yet we should be mortified a few years hence to see so poor a monument of so good a man, so conspicuously exposed." Trumbull studied in France as well as England, and returned to America to do miniatures and murals, panels and portraits, historical, mythological, allegorical, and religious subjects, designs for medals and badges, charts and maps. He was one of the most versatile and talented artists of his day, ranked by his contemporaries second only to Gilbert Stuart. In fact, his fame became a fad, and close to a thousand forgeries signed with a spurious "J.T." have been identified. No other American painter has been so amply complimented.

The most dangerous pitfall to be avoided by Connecticut artists was choosing a profane subject, or profaning a suitable subject by presenting it improperly clothed. In a country where even the names of the weekdays were naughty words because of their profane origin, and numbers were used in their place for a century, artists did well to select their subject material with the utmost discretion. The successful ones happily complied. Timothy Dwight particularly commended Trumbull in "Greenfield Village" for his finesse:

> On the bright canvas, see the pencil trace,
> Unrivall'd forms of glory and of grace!
> No scenes of lewdness and no deeds of shame: . . .
> Deeds where fond Virtue loves to gaze and smile:
> Such forms, such deeds on Raphael's tablets shine,
> And such, O Trumbull! glow alike on thine.

And lest some unenlightened reader miss his point, the poet added a prosaic footnote to the stanzas: "It is not a little injurious to the honor of human nature that the elegant arts of Poetry, Painting, and Music have, in Europe, been so often prostituted to the celebration of vile characters, to the display of subjects and sentiments gross and pernicious, and to the commemoration of facts which deeply stain the name of man."

Regardless of their wisdom in the choice of subjects, no other Connecticut artist experienced anything so fabulous in praise or compensation as did Trumbull, and there were a great many competitors. In the century following the Revolution, towns in every section of the state produced their painters or sculptors of some distinction. From Lebanon came Elkanah Tisdale, remembered for his fine portrait of General Knox; from Litchfield, Anson Dickinson and Daniel Dickenson; from Windham, Samuel Waldo, a perfectionist and teacher who charged his pupils,

"When you paint a coat sleeve, paint it as carefully as you paint an eye;" from Woodstock, Samuel Morse, the first president of the National Academy of Design; from Kensington, Edwin Percival; from Mansfield Center, water-colorist Thomas Cummings; from Middletown, Henry Shumway, who did a notable portrait of Henry Clay and received acclaim for his oil miniatures on ivory; from South Manchester, Seth Cheney, who ranked among the French for his crayon drawings. New Haven spawned a remarkable group, such as Nathanael Jocelyn, who gave up a remunerative living as engraver of bank notes to paint and teach; Henry Flagg, famed for his marine views and animals; George Flagg, known for his popular "Landing of the Pilgrims." And on the side, most of them served apprenticeships as itinerants.

Among the Hudson River School were John Frederick Kensett of Cheshire, who tramped through England, Switzerland, the Rhine country, and the Italian Lake district, and spent two winters in Rome. Then, with an established European reputation, he returned to New England to do his "Mount Washington from North Conway," "High Bank on the Genesee River," "Sunset on the Adirondacks," "Afternoon on the Connecticut Shore," "Hudson River from Fort Putnam," and dozens of others hanging in dark museum corners.

But of all the landscapists, George Henry Durrie of New Haven emerged as the best interpreter of the Connecticut scene. Many of his paintings were used as subjects for Currier and Ives prints. Hills, farms, barnyards, snowscapes—best represented in "Home for Thanksgiving"—were his forte. What Whittier did in stanzas, Durrie did in oil and water color.

It was one of the inconsistencies of the Yankees to give painters such free scope while artists in other fields were hidebound. Connecticut's interest invited artists from outside to form "colonies" in the 1890's at Mystic and Old Lyme, and later at places like Kent, Westport, and Silvermine. It encouraged, too, the establishment of schools and galleries: the Yale School of Fine Arts, founded in 1866; the Hartford Art School; the Slater Memorial Gallery at Norwich Free Academy; the Wadsworth Atheneum in Hartford; the Lyman Allen Museum at New London; historical art collections at Hartford, New Haven, Waterbury, and many other cities. The Connecticut painters went through all the stages of artists in other states; primitivism gave way to an appetite for style, which in turn gave way to romantic vapors of expressionism; then came the impact of French impressionism, and finally the international aspect, with at least an effort to retain local character.

The graphic arts prospered also, although printers leaned on Massachusetts for their inspiration. Before the Revolution, Isaiah Thomas imported to his plant in Worcester fonts of the handsome types designed by artist William Caslon of London, and Thomas set the standard in printing for all of New England. His typography was freely aped, and sometimes improved upon, in printing shops of New London and Hartford. Even during the long Victorian era, the demand for fine, conservative printing stood up in a few quarters against the popularity of the pretty and the ornate. The shelves of Connecticut imprints offer the testimony. In the twentieth century little establishments like Hawthorn House at Windham, or big establishments like Condé Nast in Greenwich, carried on the tradition.

Starting in 1909 as a modest printing plant specializing in dress patterns, the Condé Nast Press within two decades developed into one of the country's finest commercial printers. An obscure little publication called *Vogue* became the leading feminine fashion magazine of the world. *Vanity Fair* was added in 1913, *House and Garden* two years later, and soon Condé Nast was printing some of America's most popular monthlies. In typography they fell short of the Isaiah Thomas standard, but it was a new century calling for representation in half-tone and color, for publication in quantity never known before. Nast was a pioneer of the elite in graphic arts. To subscribers and newsstands all over the globe, slick magazines went out from Greenwich in the multimillions, but the Nast presses also manufactured art reproductions and brochures that would readily have gladdened the heart of old Isaiah.

Like the musicians and the dramatists, the literati were all too frequently drowned out by the clergy. However, the Congregational Church did set a very high standard for the written as well as the spoken word—the standard of the logician and pedagogue; there was no place for imaginative writing unless it could be a vehicle for the expression of some moral platitude. If the Church fathers had had their way, the shelves of the elect would have been crowded with tomes of sermons and little else, for they were published and distributed by the ton.

Just before 1800, a group of Yale intellectuals—satirists, poets, critics, and essayists—converged on the capital to form a loosely-organized literary society, popularly dubbed "The Hartford Wits," and for a short generation they set a cultural tone for the laity; but with the passing of the "Wits," as one critic notes, "Connecticut could not lay claim to any authors of real genius until the days of Mark Twain and Charles Dudley Warner"—and they had no state kinship.

The literature of early Connecticut was, indeed, a "distinguished blank," broken only by a few interesting diaries; the first book of poems, *Poetical Meditations: Being an Improvement of Some Vacant Hours*, written by Governor Roger Wolcott in the Calvinist tradition; and the philosophy and mysticism of Jonathan Edwards, under titles that were essays in themselves: A *Careful and Strict Enquiry into the Modern Prevailing Notions of that Freedom of Will which is Supposed to be Essential to Moral Agency, Virtue and Vice, Reward and Punishment, Praise and Blame.*

With his forceful expression, cold logic, and occasional splendor of imagination, Edwards—Connecticut bred, but transplanted to Massachusetts—stirred the "Great Awakening," opened many eyes to the light of eternity as he saw it, and in the process wrote what might be called a literature indigenous to the Connecticut Valley. But the state had to wait for the "Hartford Wits" to create the first secular literature. None of the dozen "Wits" was a journalist or professional writer. They were lawyers, diplomats, educators: men like Colonel David Humphreys, who had been an aide to Washington; Lemuel Hopkins, the American authority on tuberculosis; Joel Barlow, an ex-chaplain, law student, and publisher; Richard Alsop of Middletown, a bookstore proprietor; John Trumbull, jurist and poet; and Yale's Timothy Dwight.

Jointly they published *The Anarchiad, The Political Greenhouse*, and *The Echo*—all political satires, the sting of which was felt from Philadelphia to Boston. Individually, Barlow wrote *Hasty Pudding*, a realistic portrayal of New England home life, and *The Columbiad*, revealing the past and future of America in a ponderous epic. Trumbull burlesqued the Tories in *McFingal*, a brilliant epic patterned after Samuel Butler's *Hudibras*. Dwight compared Revolutionary heroes with Old Testament warriors in *The Conquest of Canaan*, and gave a delightful description of New England village life in *Greenfield Hill*. Out of the group rose no Addison or Steele, but they formed the first literary circle in America, allowed the state its one claim to a literature of its own, and, more than that, created the first national literature.

Connecticut gave birth and board to a long succession of authors during the next century, but to few of them could she lay full claim. There was no Concord or Cambridge with which distinguished men of letters were identified during their entire careers. The Beechers of Litchfield, including Harriet Beecher Stowe, went west. Jared Sparks moved on to become editor of the *North American Review* and president of Harvard. John Fiske was born in Hartford, but he became distinguished as a philosopher and historian in Cambridge. Bronson Alcott, the transcendentalist, was born in Wolcott, but he is identified with Concord, and his daughter wrote *Little Women* there. Mark Twain moved to Hartford, but never got over his homesickness for Mississippi. Charles Dudley Warner wrote *Being a Boy* in the same city, but he came there to be near Mark Twain, and if the great humorist had chosen Philadelphia or Cleveland for his residence, Warner undoubtedly would have joined him.

A few secondary authors who were idolized during their day did remain. Norwich may claim sentimentalist Lydia Sigourney, Kensington its poet James Gates Percival, New London its John Brainard; but one looks in vain for a first-rate native whose work lasted very far beyond his own generation. "Recent Connecticut writers have dealt with a civilized and urbanized community or with subjects not peculiar to the state. Thus the true, the old Connecticut has entered into literature, but faintly, incidentally, inconclusively."

The artists needed a medium more tangible than words for their best effort. Where artistry and craftsmanship merged, the Yankees were most adept, and possibly because of an inbred concern with being economical, they were freest and most imaginative when they could use native materials.

They were practical and utilitarian, but they saw no reason why a useful structure or a useful object shouldn't be attractive also. A glacial boulder with a name and dates carved on it would have served the purpose in marking a grave, but they chose instead to make a tablet of quaint beauty, well proportioned, with good letters, neat scrolling, and chimerical figures. They designed the pages of a book or a flier in the same way. Into home-wrought latches, hinges, and andirons went both whimsy and practicality. An undecorated wooden chest of pine would have been as serviceable as a fancy one with carved panels, and would appear to be more in keeping with the severity of their principles, yet amateur joiners devoted spare time over months or years to make at least this one item of furniture unaffected, graceful, beautiful. And quality in craftsmanship became artistry when a conscientious builder constructed a house, a church, or a town hall. The early Connecticut architects left an enduring artistic legacy.

The homes were more frank than beautiful, but in their hundred-year evolution, many did acquire charm and distinction. From the story-and-a-half structure with a thatched roof and a chimney at one end, the typical domicile expanded to a building twice as long, with the chimney in the center and with a shake roof. The chimney was always the pivotal point. Then a lean-to was added in the rear, continuing the original roof line and creating the "salt box." By 1700 the lean-to became an integral part of the structure, and the "salt box," with its long, steep unconventional roof, was the traditional Connecticut home. But inside there was almost as much attic as there was living space; it was as wasteful as it was picturesque, and during the next fifty years the blunt house of two full stories took its place—the chimney still in the middle. As families grew, and as they could afford more imposing edifices, a second chimney was added, with a hall and stairway between the two massive stone stacks. Until the Greek revival of about 1830 this was the standard fashion, and the halls, staircases, and parlors offered choice opportunity for clever joiners and skillful carpenters to exercise their individuality of taste.

In the Connecticut valley—and only there—the idea of the second-story framed overhang was common, and this extension of a foot or two invited the use of ornamental pendants, drops, and brackets. Contrary to supposition, the overhang was never intended or employed as a protective device for scalding Indians or for close-range shooting; it was an artistic expedient (borrowed from Europe) for breaking the lines of the façade, giving the front a horizontal shadow that the flat façades of massive homes in the Shetucket and Willimantic valleys sorely needed for relief.

Every part of these structures—except the shingles and the wainscoting—was of solid oak. The frame was of hewn oak, fastened with mortise-and-tenon joints and secured with oak pins. The double floors were of oak plank, hand cut on up-and-down pit saws. Even the hand-split laths and clapboards were of oak. And the toughness of this medium for building made the accomplishment of the artisans the more remarkable.

The original windowpanes were small and diamond shaped, and that feature alone gave relief to the somber bulk. Genuine artistry was seen in the fluted doorframes, delicate and intricately wrought detail in mantels, stairways with spiral or twisted balusters, and the corner cupboard in the parlor—called a "bowfat," "boffet," or "buffit," depending on local lingo—with fluted pilasters at the sides, a semicircular back, and a shell-like termination at the top in carved ribs and flutes. If the architects erred, it was on the safe side of simplicity and plainness. Never was their work over-ornate or in bad taste. From Salisbury to Stonington, from

· 12 ·

CONSERVATORS

"THIS YEAR, ON SATURDAY, THE FIFTEENTH DAY OF AUGUST, WAS SUCH a mighty storm of Wind and Rain, as none now living in these parts, either English or Indian, have seen the like, being like unto those Hirricanes or Tussins that writers mention sometimes in the Indies. It began in the morning a little before day, and grew not by degrees, but came with great violence in the beginning, to the great amazement of many; It blew down sundry houses, and many more in extream danger. It caused the Sea to swell in some places . . . twenty foot right up and down, and made many of the Indians to climb into Trees for their safety: It blew down all the Corn to the ground and never rose more . . . and had the wind continued without shifting, in likelihood it would have drowned some part of the Country. It blew down many hundred thousands of trees, turning up the stronger by the roots, and breaking the high Pine Trees and such like in the midst, and the tall young Oaks, and Walnut Trees of good bigness were wound as a Wyth by it; very strange and fearful to behold: It began in the Southeast, and veered sundry ways. . . . It continued not in extremity above five or six hours, ere the violence of it began to abate; the marks of it will remain . . . many years in those parts where it was forest. . . ."

It might have been called Abigail, Ada, or Adeline, but the first recorded New England hurricane in 1635 answered the description of sister blows that swooped across Long Island Sound in 1815 and in 1938; it was a reasonable facsimile of Carol and Edna of 1954, or Diane of 1955. Connecticut has been subjected to the buffetings of big winds and big rains for a long time; losing "trees of good bigness" is not an affliction peculiar to the twentieth century.

The destruction of the estate and effects of man has grown ever larger as more and more expendibles have been fixed in the path of the onslaught. In 1635, the settlers were just arriving, and the loss was insignificant. In 1938, the destruction of beach property ran into the hundreds of thousands, with incalculable losses inland to forests, shade trees, and "scenery"; in 1954, damage to shore resorts alone totalled over twelve million; Diane cost almost a quarter of a billion in flood damage. On the eighteenth and nineteenth of August, 1955, an average sixteen inches of rain fell over the state, with twenty recorded in some areas. Brooks to the north turned into mighty rivers, rivers into tidal waves. Bridges, dams, and streamside mills by the score were swept away. Two hundred and fifty factories in the Naugatuck valley were temporarily paralyzed, with appalling destruction in Waterbury, Winsted, Naugatuck, Ansonia, and Torrington. Mill towns along the Quinebaug suffered almost as severely. Then two months later another flood struck, inundating thirty-nine communities, a majority of which had escaped the first. For a few days Stamford and Norwalk appeared to have been ravaged. When the toll from the two storms was counted, close to 100 persons were dead, 86,000 were unemployed, 11,000 families were homeless, 1000 more were without shelter, and 20,000 homes had been damaged.

Even if the state had been given forewarning of a month or a year, much of the property destruction could not have been averted. Civilization had been crowding close to the shores and riverbanks for three centuries; it was too late to reroute economic history. Contending with periodic cataclysms of nature was one of the challenges of modern existence—the price that had to be paid for living in twentieth-century Connecticut or anywhere else in the path of convulsive tides, winds, and torrents.

But generations of shortsighted Yankees had also invited disaster. For quick financial gain they had raised hob with nature, robbed the hillsides of trees and soil necessary to absorb and hold back downpours, removed the windbreaks, created gullies that would facilitate swift runoff, and then built homes or factories along the watercourses without making counterprovision for the disruption. They disturbed resources not only in their own state, but also moved back to the headwaters of rivers in Massachusetts, New Hampshire, and Vermont to do the same. The mountains and meadows along the Connecticut River valley for four hundred miles were stripped by Yankees, their cousins, and their heirs. Spring floods and summer freshets were often serious before the tampering with nature was started; later they were disastrous. And since much of the watershed of New England had to pass through Connecticut en route to the Sound, the state became the beneficiary of the errors made over an area many times larger than her own.

Rivers everywhere went on the rampage in 1815. A freshet in March, 1823, carried a Norwich Methodist church down the Thames and into Long Island Sound with lights still flickering from the windows. The years 1826, 1840 brought major floods; 1862 saw the highest water that had ever been known. And catastrophic local floods and winds were interspersed between the general ones. On October 13, 1846, the fifteen-hundred-foot railroad bridge across the Connecticut at Windsor Locks was blown bodily off its piers into the river. On March 28, 1877, Edwin Pinney rode ahead of a wall of water, descending upon Stafford Springs faster than Paul Revere ever traveled, to warn the town. Freight cars were lifted from the tracks and lodged on the roofs of houses; even a church was swept away, with a couple who had too confidently sought sanctuary there. On August 9 the following year occurred the "Wallingford Disaster," when thirty-four were killed and a hundred injured, and property damage mounted into the hundreds of thousands in the wake of a giant tornado.

Over the years Connecticut towns spent more money in replacing bridges after freshets than in original construction. Time and again, one dam at a factory town along the Quinebaug, the Shetucket, or the Housatonic would go out, and under the impact of a gathering mountain of water and debris, the next dam on the stream and the next were carried away. Spring thaws, melting snow, and monstrous floes of ice repeatedly swept out bridges and dams on the Connecticut, leaving broken barns, drowned cattle, and rich lands buried in silt along the flooded shores.

The great flood of November, 1927, was hardest in Vermont, but the waters that gathered to the north picked up a toll of $600,000 while passing through Connecticut; and the all-time record for a Connecticut River flood was set in March, 1936, when summer temperatures and heavy rains caused phenomenal runoffs and disastrous ice jams that cost the state close to twelve million dollars. "Do you know," cautioned an East Windsor tobacco-grower, overwhelmed by the magnitude of that receding flood but trying to curb a neighbor's extravagant appraisal of destruction to his acres, "they tell me all the water that came down the river didn't raise the ocean an inch?"

It was the 1936 flood, occurring in the WPA era, that at last crystallized in New England the concept of interstate flood control, and made everyone and his neighbor an enthusiast for conservation of resources that were being flushed into Long Island Sound. The governors of the affected states got together with federal engineers to plan headwater reservoirs that would help to take the place of natural forest-slope reservoirs long since destroyed by overeager Yankees.

Still the damage shouldn't all be blamed on them, for the Yankees took their first lessons in soil conservation from the Indians and followed aboriginal practices for years. They began in ignorance of the most primitive laws of agriculture, and continued until the predicament they had created called for a truce.

Long before the white man came, the forests were subjected to wanton abuse. The Indians annually set fire to their hunting lands, kindling great conflagrations that crept across the valleys and over the hills. They had even less conception of the value of leaf mold and lumber than their white successors; but destruction of the woodlands was not their aim. They wanted only to burn the leaves and underbrush to produce broader visibility for stalking deer or hostile humans—and to establish a protective clearance against surprise raids around their encampments. For them it was a very practical ecology. Most of the giant monarchs survived the fires, but in the upper Housatonic valley, the destruction went so far that the first Dutch settlers of Salisbury complained that the country "wore rather an unpleasant aspect." Hills were denuded, swamps and flatlands were covered with a grotesque stand of dead, blackened trunks. "In every fall of the year," they explained, "the face of the township was burnt over to destroy the old grass and other vegetation, and that there might be a fresh and tender crop the ensuing year. Fires . . . to ring deer were made in a circular form, and all the deer included were driven by the fire to one place where the huntsmen could easily kill them. A ring for this purpose was made in the northeast part of the town, and the fire ran with such rapidity that an Indian lad was shut within, overtaken by the fire, and burnt to death. These burnings, with the ponds, mountains and clefts of rocks, made the face of nature appear forbidding."

The white settlers continued the practice, for burning the woods was the quickest way of clearing land for cultivation—and incidentally getting the same kind of area protection the Indians sought. In 1665 John Killburne agreed to burn all the woods along the Connecticut River for ten miles between Wethersfield and Middletown for six shillings "at such a time or times as may be most convenient for the advantage of the town," and Enoch Buck contracted to do the burning to the north. In fact, the discontinuance of the practice was solemnly deplored a century later when the forests were no longer "passable." "While the red men possessed the country, and every autumn set fire to the fallen leaves," an explorer recounted, "the forests presented a most noble and enchanting appearance. The annual firings prevented the growth of shrubs and underbrush, and destroying the lower branches of the trees, the eye roved with delight, from ridge to ridge and from hill to hill; which, like the divisions of an immense temple, were crowded with innumerable pillars, the branches of whose shafts interlocking, formed the arch work of support to that leafy roof which covered and crowned the whole. But since the white man took possession, the annual fires have been checked, and the woodlands are now filled with shrubs and young trees, obstructing the vision on every side, and converting these once beautiful forests into a rude and tasteless wilderness."

Connecticut had three general areas where the soil was naturally adapted to cultivation—the long narrow strip parallel to Long Island Sound between Stonington and Greenwich, the Connecticut valley north of Middletown, and the old valley between Hartford and New Haven. Elsewhere the good soil was spotty. There were plenty of these spots, but farmers who were ingenious in every other way failed to distinguish between the unfit and the fertile. They were blind to the most obvious conception of soil conservation. A field was ruthlessly robbed as long as it would bear a crop—planted and replanted to the same grain or vegetable —and then abandoned. By 1850 there were deserted farms scattered all through the interior; neatly walled lots that had once grown a fine potato yield were overgrown with sumac, and cattle were browsing on eroded hillside meadows where it no longer paid to plant corn.

All of Connecticut up to that time had an agrarian economy, and soil conservation was the farmer's problem. Rarely did the legislature lift a voice to interfere. What a farmer did with the land was his individual concern, not the concern of politicians and society. He blundered along in trial and error, and the errors were more common than the successes. Benjamin Franklin had done a little effective educating. David Humphreys popularized the raising of merino sheep, in addresses before agricultural groups supported the cause of raising purebred stock, and tried to promote an intelligent use of manure and fertilizers. Governor Oliver Wolcott went so far as to propose a subsidy for fairs and cattle shows. But altogether they made little impression on hard-headed farm folk, too set in their ways for change.

"When our forefathers settled here," observed Jared Eliot, physician and pastor, in 1760, "they entered a Land which probably never had been Ploughed since the Creation; the Land being new, they depended upon the natural Fertility of the Ground, which served their purposes very well, and when they had worn out one piece they cleared another, without any concern to amend the Land . . . whereas in England they would think a Man a bad Husband, if he should pretend to sow Wheat on Land without any Dressing."

Dr. Eliot talked in past tense to avoid offending a majority who were still operating their farms and woodlands exactly as had their forefathers. And of all the spokesmen for conservation of field and forest, he probably had the strongest appeal. Eliot knew his people, wrote for them as though he were indoctrinating them in the ABC's of agriculture, and prudently made his approach through the Bible.

"The only old Rules of Husbandry that I have met with," he ventured, "I find in the Bible: and there not professedly taught, but only for Illustration and by way of Comparison: Yet this serves to shew us what was the Practice of Farmers in those days." He quoted Proverbs 27 : 26—"The lambs are for thy clothing, and the goats are the price of the field"—and then gave his eighteenth-century application, noting in down-to-earth lingo that goats "are excellent to subdue rough uncultivated Land: they are in their nature abundantly fitted to serve that useful Purpose; they destroy Bushes, Briars, and Weeds: By their Tread, their Dung and Urine, which is very hot, they sweeten the Ground to that degree, as in a little time the Land subdued by them, will thereby be doubled in its Value or Price." From Ecclesiastes he quoted, "In the morning sow thy seed, and in the evening withhold not thine hand," to demonstrate the wisdom of planting when the soil was moist. From I Kings 19 : 19, he brought in Elisha's "ploughing with twelve yoke of oxen," as the text for an essay on improvement of cultivation methods and increased ox-power for plows.

The approach easily fixed the divine stamp of approval upon soil conservation and better farming. He was eloquent on the subject of manure—"yard-dung," sheep, cattle, and fowl manure—and wrote learnedly of the value of ashes, peat, and lime. He tried to start a "green pastures" movement by creating an appetite for mutton—"I have observed that where Sheep are well kept, and remain upon the Land Night and Day, the Land will grow better." He expounded on the subjects of seed and swine, weeds and wire-grass; talked about the drainage of swamps, the cultivation of turnips and timothy, clover and cabbage. Eliot was the most practical conservator of his day, and without doubt he rescued many an acre from abandonment, gave a few farmers greater pride in their profession, and indirectly was responsible for keeping a little of Connecticut's land and water from washing down-state.

A "Society for Promoting Agriculture" was started at Wallingford in 1794, and farmers' clubs in other communities occasionally appeared. Ostensibly they met to discuss seeds and fertilizers, but their discussions were likely to veer to politics; the farm folk controlled government, and maintenance of political unity or the *status quo* was of more importance than crop production and conservation. County societies established September fairs, made a dramatic splurge of their accomplishments in magnificent cattle parades and bunting-bedecked exhibition stalls, and in a small way helped to promote better farming practices. In Derby a seminary for the future farmers of Connecticut was founded in 1825, but youngsters were too busy learning the conservative ways of their fathers to bring success to such an educational enterprise.

Theodore S. Gold, a practical agronomist with a missionary spirit, in 1845 opened a trade academy in West Cornwall—the Cream Hill School—and kept it alive for twenty-four years, sometimes with an enrollment of four students, occasionally with as many as twenty.

Cream Hill offered a curriculum in soil tillage, tree culture, stock raising, and compost. Simultaneously Gold inaugurated a chain of clubs under his "Berkshire Plan," to minister "to the wants of the farmer as a human being by improving his powers of conversation, to give him an understanding of the troubles of others, and to create in him a pride in his calling." The clubs worked valiantly—and unsuccessfully—to stem the steady flow of farmers to the West and to factories; also they failed to put across any notion of effective conservation. In 1847 Yale opened the first American agricultural experiment station; courses in farm chemistry were introduced at Trinity and Wesleyan, as well as Yale, yet the boys who benefited most from this instruction did not return to the farms. A state agricultural society was incorporated in 1852, and this was followed more than a decade later by a State Board of Agriculture, with Theodore Gold as secretary.

Yet all these activities did not convert the ordinary dirt farmer into a scientist. With him still rested the ultimate responsibility for reviving spent soil or preventing floods in the lowlands. Moreover, he controlled the vote that might stimulate progress in that direction. The constitution of Connecticut gave every town, regardless of its size, at least one legislative representative. Even in the villages where factories were becoming more important than farms, the old guard dominated politically. These slowly deteriorating rural towns outnumbered the progressives, and their influence on the lower house obstructed any attempts to bring in a new order. The conservators didn't have a chance. As late as 1880 the fourteen-year-old State Board of Agriculture complained that "most farmers tilled the soil in a dull, blind way, knowing little of the nature of the soil or its wants, so that they overfed good ground and starved the poor, reducing the whole to a state of unproductivity."

However, the Civil War did bring an awakening to the value of farm and forest in long-range state economy. Despite the long period of lassitude, Connecticut pioneered in the establishment of an independent State Agricultural Experiment Station in 1875, devoted to research in plant breeding, pest control, and soil chemistry; and Storrs Agricultural School was chartered with state and federal support six years later. These efforts were concerned primarily with introducing better stock and better field growth on the individual farms, but the Board of Agriculture, as the official conservation agency, was beginning to see a broader horizon. The board published an informal "Handbook" in 1901, and incorporated in it reports of the Connecticut scene, ranging from hygienic milk production to historic monuments, reservoirs to tobacco wrapping, population statistics to pomology.

"Dear reader, kindly receive my well meant efforts," petitioned the editor, "and overlook the omission of the thousand and one familiar scenes and events which are clear to the mind and eye of every son and daughter of Connecticut, wherever they have wandered from the old home, and alike to the children and grandchildren, who have heard the tale on their mother's lap—memories that can never be effaced. To such is this effort dedicated, that the memory of the past may be the inspiration of the future. . . ."

The editors apologetically pointed out that agriculture in the state had been directed in the past "partly by soil and climate, but more especially by some *accidental circumstances*"; that its evolution had been "at a limping gait, but . . . the new century is full of promise for the Connecticut farmer. . . . The methods of the past demanding the severest and most constant toil are left behind, but they dedicated and fostered a social, civil and religious sturdiness of character that has made Connecticut the synonym for integrity, intelligence and progress, and is today her guarantee of future prosperity."

The agronomists had never asked for the controlling interest in state conservation and had never recognized their possession of it, but their representatives in the State Board of Agriculture at last gained an intelligent and far-reaching perspective. They knew that collectively the individual farms and the way they were managed affected the whole future of Connecticut society.

Theodore Gold, who had started Cream Hill half a century before, and during all those years had tried in one way or another to introduce that perspective—the relation of a potato field, a sheep pasture, or a wood lot to conservation of natural resources—finally spoke his piece in the *Connecticut Quarterly*. He expressed his grief over the indiscriminate clearing and cultivation of woodland that should have been allowed to remain in forest—"hillsides too steep for profitable culture, where rains wash away all fertility from uncovered soil—or even the soil itself."

"The effect of forests upon the conservation of water supply, both of rain and snow, of modifying destructive winds is better shown where reforesting has produced favorable results," Gold prophetically asserted. "The destruction of the forests about the headwaters of our rivers has resulted in failure of the even flow of water, in both extreme low water and disastrous freshets. . . . Civilized man takes possession of a country covered with primeval forests, and by wanton waste unsettles the balance of water fall and its safe delivery to the ocean. Mountain torrents scour and sear the lands about the headwaters of rivers and deposit silt and gravel lower down and about the mouth, obstructing navigation with sand bars and choking harbors."

It was a new, upstart thought for most of the Connecticut public at the beginning of the twentieth century. Europe had been dictatorially preaching and practicing forest conservation for decades, and New York had already set an example in America

by marking off reserves in the Adirondacks, but Connecticut
farmers continued to treat their wood lots as though they were a
nuisance and a handicap to the real purposes of agriculture. Gold
charged into them with feeling: "The lumberman by his slashing,
leaves an inviting field for fire, the careless hunter furnishes the
spark, or the thriftless squatter sets the fire to clear up pasture for
his cow, and thousands of acres of this priceless absorbent, accumulated by nature through past centuries, all the time doing its
silent work, goes up in smoke, leaving the hillsides, the watersheds
of the country, as bare as barn roofs, bare not only of all organic
material as soil, but also deprived of all young forest growth and
seeds that would otherwise, by nature's provision speedily reclothe
these mountains with their natural forest cover. This fearful waste
of these bounties of Providence is followed by inevitable con-
sequences. Devastating freshets . . . succeeded by the drying up
of springs, and of the fountain streams that feed our rivers, these
are facts that cannot be disputed."

The ardent conservationist emphasized that the problem was of
interstate and national significance, that the denuding of Vermont
and New Hampshire hillsides could bring ruin to the Connecticut
River valley: "The even flow at the mouth is dependent upon an
even supply at the source. . . . In the forest the snow lies level
and melts slowly, often from beneath, the forest bed absorbing the
moisture. In open ground it thaws rapidly by sun and rain . . .
and it flows in destructive torrents. . . . Again the forests have
much influence in restraining the violence of winds—a wind
blowing over a forest is checked in its velocity and modified in
its temperature. Trees on the mountain side or even in the narrow
valleys often delay currents of air or divert them from their
course, so that the growth of all kinds materially modifies the local
climate, an influence extending to unexpected places."

Acknowledging that he didn't expect immediate results from his
declamation, Gold had to admit that the government "has little
power to control matters," that "everyone must use his influence
with the general government to do for the whole country what is
necessary and proper, and by a general diffusion of knowledge
prevent these great outrages upon posterity. It must be repeated
by the press and from the platform, discussed everywhere by lum-
bermen and sanitarians, become a part of education from the district school to the university, to counteract the national disregard
for forests, the result of generations engaged in their destruction."

The critical situation was brought home to Hartford on Decem-
mer 7, 1899, when it was announced that all of her six reservoirs

were empty except the distribution center, which had a supply that might last eight and a half days. It was brought home by reports that annually 27,000 acres of forests were being devastated by fire. And the floods periodically roaring down the Connecticut and the Quinebaug brought it nearer home.

But in the romantic years near the turn of the century, the popular conception of conservation turned evasively to municipal parks rather than headwaters or private timberlands. Sweeping areas of green lawn adjacent to a riverbank, with pretty pavilions, settees, foot bridges, winding walks, and fountains, were the fashion. Central Park in New York had set the pattern, and Bushnell Park at Hartford followed it; by 1900 Hartford had acquired a whole family of parks, and Bridgeport almost as many seaside acres of public ground. The village green, originally set aside for common pasturage, militia parades, and church sociables, was as old a Connecticut institution as the church; but as towns expanded into cities, a comparable expansion in open space was needed, and usually there was a civic-minded benefactor with the conscience and financial wherewithal to provide it.

Hyde Park, Regents, and Battersea were the "lungs of London," an enthusiast reminded his fellow citizens. Connecticut cities should have them too: "The life current of a large city rushes forth from its heart in a feverish circulation, through narrow streets and alleys, arteries often choked with filth and foul with smoke and dust, through crowded tenement districts, and into dirty factories and close shops and warehouses. Unless it can come forth occasionally into some reservoir of fresh air to be purified and invigorated, the city will drag on at best a sickly life. 'God made the country; man made the town,' and unless man can succeed in blowing into the nostrils of his creature the breath of the fields or the sea, the pure fresh air of the country, he cannot put life into the thing of his creation."

No self-respecting town or city could get along without its "lung"; the grounds of huge estates were vacated by their owners and opened to the public; there were formal keep-off-the-grass memorial parks, athletic fields, woodsy parks, arboretums; and for a few years, before rubber tires took the constituency on longer jaunts into the open country, they were crowded. The park fad helped the cause of conservation, too. Any move that focused public attention on landscape and green countryside was likely to lead to broader interests.

With very little opposition, a state forester was added to the staff of the Experiment Station in 1901. Two years later, with less

To Harry F. Farnum of South Windsor the state is more deeply indebted than to any other one man for its current policies on the improvement and judicious use of land resources. He fathered the present conservation act and lobbied it through the legislature almost single-handed. Born and raised on a farm, Harry left it for bigger things. But after wide travel and experience in affairs that weren't as big as he had calculated, he returned in 1917 to purchase a tobacco farm near East Windsor Hill. The soil was losing its productivity and needed a change of use, he soon discovered. Pure-bred Ayrshires were his answer, so he shifted from tobacco to cattle and became the foremost champion of soil conservation. He was among the first in a new generation to rely extensively upon grass rather than corn for silage; he adopted the green-pastures doctrine, and reforested areas that had proved subject to erosion; he practiced the elements of contour farming, installed an irrigation system, even resorted to the use of ornamental rose hedges for self-repairing, self-perpetuating farm fences. In 1941 he went to Hartford as representative from South Windsor. What he had learned at East Windsor Hill he drilled into his fellow legislators for seven years, until they finally incorporated in an act the essence of his practical experience. Harry Farnum died in 1950, but all he stood for lives on in greener pastures, growing woodlands, and more intelligent farming in every section of the state.

Another hurricane may blow in next year, another flood wash down the Housatonic, the Shetucket, or the Connecticut; and the toll may be heavy. It would be less if we had listened to the Jared Eliots, the Theodore Golds, the Harry Farnums earlier and more attentively.

· 13 ·

MERRYMAKERS

BETWEEN THE MORALISTS AND THE MERRYMAKERS RAGED INCESSANT
war during the early generations, but the party boys and girls
managed to kick up their heels with much broader abandon than
their great-great-grandchildren prefer to believe. Old and young
made whoopee at soirees as gay as any hinted at in the Old
Testament; they rocked with laughter over practical jokes and
salty repartee; at carnival banquets they gorged themselves on the
fat of the land; they consumed primed beverages with the aplomb
of sons and daughters of Bacchus; disregarding ministerial scold-
ings, they attended dull dancing classes in the morning and
demonstrated what they had learned in rollicking hoedowns at
night. They danced and danced and danced.

Nor did the deportment of youth readily meet Puritan standards
of propriety. Diarist Julia Cowles was shocked over the way the
girls of sedate Farmington carried on. "It wounded my delicacy,"
she remarked disdainfully, "to see girls of 17 encircled in the arms
of lads. . . . Could not sweet Charity lend them assistance?" Then
at Hartford, as far back as May Day of 1660, occurred the love-
making scandal of Sarah Tuttle and Jacob Murline in broad daylight, with witnesses to recount the event: "They sat together,
his arm being about her, and her arm upon his shoulder and about
his neck, and hee kissed her and shee kissed him, and they kissed

one another, continuing in this position about half an hour."

But according to the pulpit, it was at the dances where chastity was put to the test. "What harm is there in mere dancing?" questioned the Reverend Guernsey of Derby. "The truth is, there is no such thing as mere dancing. . . . Evil is its leading and invariable consequence; it cannot be repeated without guilt; . . . go to the vilest haunt of pollution; go where virtue is derided and scoffed at; go where the lowest lust is unbridled; where vice in its most degraded, disgusting form reigns triumphant; and amid all the signs of wretchedness and woe, you will find the night-consuming dance."

There was no common agreement, however, among the pastors on just how evil was the dance. Theocrat John Cotton, back in 1625, did not wholly condemn dancing—"yea, though mixed." From his poring over the Scriptures he had discovered two kinds: "the one religious, the other civil," and concluded that he should bear witness only against "lascivious dancing to wanton ditties and in amorous gestures and wanton dalliances." More than half a century later Increase Mather started the endless series of tracts on the subject when he published "An Arrow Against Profane and Promiscuous Dancing, drawne out of the Quiver of the Scriptures," but Mather's arrow was directed, too, at dancing that aroused the passions.

While the squabble went on and on at the elevation of the pulpit, the people of Connecticut declined to be lured away from the fun. Nominally they eliminated the "wanton dalliances," and adopted terpsichorean exercise as their favored pastime. They had their nuptial balls and anniversary balls, private balls in house kitchens and public ones at the tavern, balls to express the spirit of Thanksgiving and of the Fourth of July, election balls in honor of a new governor, and, incongruously enough, ordination balls in honor of newly appointed pastors. Everybody danced—almost everybody—the young tots doing their ring-around in the corner, the old folks stomping out an awkward fling in the center of the floor, the teen- and twenty-agers cutting up around them in contra-dances, reels, and jigs.

Newspapers rarely took heed of local social events, but one editor stopped his press to insert the succinct announcement: "A great wedding dance took place at New London at the house of Nathaniel Shaw Esq. June 12, 1769, the day after the marriage of his son Daniel Shaw and Grace Coit; 92 gentlemen and ladies attended, and danced 92 jigs, 52 contra-dances, 45 minuets and 17 hornpipes, and retired at 45 minutes past midnight."

In the cities wedding festivities began early and lasted late—
often they were prolonged for two or three days. In the villages
they were simple evening affairs that broke up at a respectable
retirement hour, but there was always time for a little hoofing and
scuffing.

If there were need for rationalization, dancing was regarded as
an educational activity. As one defender put it, "The balls were
considered as the school of good manners in opposition to clown-
ishness and rowdyism. The young men met together and appointed
managers of the ball, usually four or six in number, who provided
a room and refreshments, engaged music, sometimes sent out
cards, sometimes assigned to the several gentlemen the duty of
waiting on the several ladies, or assigning partners, preserved order,
paid the bills by collecting the assessments on the gentlemen who
attended." All a very genteel and educational experience.

Nor was this branch of education allowed to flourish untutored.
Fathers and mothers rarely relied on local instructors for their
children. They were satisfied with nothing but professionals with
the latest steps, the dainty manner, and the ultimate in sophistica-
tion. Norwich, a conservative town, set a typical standard. There
Griffith's Dancing School was opened at a prominent home on
the town plot in October, 1787. As in other schooling, classes were
held in the morning. Farm youngsters neglected mathematics for
minuets, then appeared at a designated evening every fortnight for
a public examination in the form of a "scholars' ball." The
school was so popular that it outgrew the private home, and ten
years later dance master Devereux was tutoring enormous classes
at the courthouse and at Kinney's Hotel in Chelsea.

"Dancing-schools were peculiarly nomadic in their character,"
apologized a disciple, "the instructor (generally a Frenchman)
circulating through a wide district and giving lessons for a few
weeks at particular points. Reels, jigs, and contra-dances were
most in vogue; the hornpipe and rigadoon were attempted by a
select few; cotillions were growing in favor; the minuet much
admired."

Attendance at dancing school was sometimes more regular than
attendance at district school; and, considering the place that reels
and rigadoons were accorded in the educational scheme, it was
only natural that marriages, holidays, elections, and ordinations
had to be celebrated with the fine art of dance.

Still all of the clergy wouldn't countenance dances in their
honor, and a few never gave up delivering periodic diatribes
against the evils to which minuets and hornpipes led. As soon as

a dancing school was announced at East Haddam, Pastor William Lyman was ready. "I wish not to appear, or be thought a sour reprover of innocent mirth, nor a foe to all the harmless propensities of youthful sprightliness and vivacity," he apologized, "but there are limits beyond which even the most sprightly age may not pass without guilt. . . . It is of but little consequence by what name those schools of refinement are distinguished. They may be politely termed 'Manners Schools', or 'Schools of Morals and Good Manners', but I apprehend the more ancient and vulgar appellation of Dancing Schools is the most proper." He insisted that "these scenes of diversion," rooted out seriousness, were a foe to the economy of time and money, the dignity of character and peace of mind. "Can you pray in sincerity," he pleaded to guardians of the young, " 'Lead us not into temptation but deliver us from evil', and then place your children in this whirlpool of danger?"

The School of Morals and Good Manners was not successful at East Haddam that year. Increasingly through the years, like sermons played on the consciences of Protestant churchgoers, until by the 1890's dancing had become one of the recognized New England sins, and the "whirlpool of danger" had been flushed from most God-fearing villages. Only in the worldly cities and big booming towns, where there was a growing foreign population, could balls be conducted with reasonable impunity.

In his catalogue of Yankee amusements, Timothy Dwight ranked dancing second only to "visiting," and then added "music, conversation, walking, riding, sailing, shooting at the mark, draughts, chess, and unhappily in some of the larger towns cards and dramatic exhibitions." Drama was placed last, for the Yale president looked upon theatrics with righteous indignation. He was so outspoken against plays in any form that his students adopted them as their favorite means of tormenting him. When his plot against them became too thick, they carried their acts beyond his reach to a distant town during the holidays. The show had to go on.

Abetting the craft of Yale undergraduates were small traveling troupes that paused briefly at crossroads taverns to put on their "drolls"—plays like *Pickle Herring*, *Harlequin*, and *Scaramouche*. And although the performers usually posed as "ministers of piety and virtue," the acts were commonly vulgar if not indecent, and before the show was through, uncooperative magistrates frequently arrived on the scene to ride the troupe out of town.

Hartford was the principal place where theater was given half a chance, but even there it was a kind of sporting event intended for the consumption of men. On bills, women were specifically invited, but only the most unladylike or the emancipated dared put in an appearance. When Hartford opened its "School for Morality" in 1795, the widely circulated playhouse "rules" gave some hint of the orderly house the management *hoped* to maintain: "Tickets and places for Boxes to be had at the Box Office Keeper and at Bliss's Tavern opposite State House. — As door keepers will be prohibited in the future in the strictest manner from taking money at the door, it is hoped that every visitor to the theatre will furnish themselves with tickets. — Ladies and Gentlemen are requested to send servants by five at the farthest, to keep their places in the Boxes. — N.B. Ladies who choose to sit in the Pit are respectfully informed there is a Partition ruled off for their accommodation. — Doors open at 6, performance starts at 7. — Boxes one dollar. Pit three-quarters. Gallery half dollar. — Positively no smoking allowed. — Young Gentlemen up to 14 years old, and young Ladies up to 12 will be admitted half-price. — *Good order at all times will be the rule.*"

Hartford's theater—even with the School-of-Morality label—was very short-lived, and it wasn't until the 1840's that showmanship was revived on a popular scale, after a thousand citizens of the central part of the state, including "many of its respectable people," united in a revolutionary front to declare that it was "ridiculous for Connecticut to outlaw theatrical entertainments which were not only condoned, but encouraged in every other state of the Union, and in all civilized nations of the world."

It was the age of minstrelsy that changed opinions. Even the conservatives could invent few objections to the innocent and irresistible antics of blackface comedians. So for nearly sixty years the craze for Negro minstrels as the favorite form of stage show swept over Connecticut and the country. The companies brought to the public and the parlor organ all the old favorite songs and many new ones that in time were to become old favorites too, like "Old Folks at Home," "Dixie," "Home, Sweet Home," "Marching Through Georgia," "Tenting on the Old Camp Ground." The state was surrounded by notable companies which formed in cities like Providence, Boston, and New York; was invaded annually by them, and did its full share in creating new ones.

The catchy tunes, the infectious African rhythms, the garrulous humor, the colorful parades were what captured and held the fancy of the public. Into the center of town during the noon hour burst the lilting band and the regal splendor of a minstrel parade to advertise the evening show. Headed by a small boy carrying the brilliant banner with the name of the company gaudily embroidered on it, the procession romped down Main Street. A pair of Dalmatians, or the largest, fiercest dogs available, tagged the emblem bearer; then came the minstrel band piping a popular tune in march rhythm, with black comedians clattering the bones alongside and making passes at vulnerable bystanders. Two by two, or three abreast, depending on the size of the company, the troupe followed, spaced to cover the street and give the appearance of a much larger force than there actually was. All were in blackface, all carried canes, all wore an exaggerated style of top hat in black silk or tan, evening dress with low-cut vests, broad tails, great lapels, and, regardless of the summer temperature, broadcloth capes lined in crimson satin. It was a thrilling show, as effective as a circus parade in drawing an audience, and it never overadvertised; it didn't need to.

The curtains parted for the big evening performance with the blackface orchestra arranged in tiers behind the half-circle of empty downstage stools. To a rollicking medley, the cast marched to their places; the interlocutor—always in whiteface—halted the music, introduced the end men and soloists with flourishes from the orchestra, and gave the order that opened all minstrel shows: "Gentlemen, be seated." The fun started, and the barrage of stock, long-winded jokes in Negro dialect poured forth for an hour, prompted by the interlocutor and end men and interrupted by soloists, choruses, and ballad singers. Slightly risqué, slightly ribald efforts were interspersed with sentimental songs that brought floods of tears to the audience. It was from the minstrel stage that the public first heard "Darling Nellie Gray," "Dixie," "Silver Threads Among the Gold," "Dear Mother, I Come Home," "Do You Think of Me at Home." And before the tears were dry or the laughter dead, the interlocutor was starting a new exchange with the end men—a drab, woeful yarn if the song had been light, a hilarious burst of banter if the song had been sad. Before the first part ended, the emotions of the audience had been plucked raw by the continuous play between tearful sentimentality and bubbling hilarity.

The minstrel show always had two parts: the jokes, choruses, and songs of the first, ending with a "walk-around" procession into the wings; the solos and specialty acts of the second, when the real stars were given their chance to perform. There were banjo and bones solos, Negro songs, duets and quartets, dancing, sketches, and variety acts—altogether worth every penny the box office or local drugstore had extorted from the spectators. On the generous bill was something to please everybody, and it was that generosity that accounted for the extraordinarily long vogue of minstrelsy.

Native sons of Connecticut added little to legitimate drama. To minstrelsy they added much. Names like singer M. B. Leavitt, comedian Billy Conway, song-and-dance man Willie Guy, and "Hank" Mudge, champion clog dancer of the United States, were the rage of the era. Eddie Horan of Hartford, dancer and producer, was one of the great names with the George Primrose Company. William A. Porter, also a native of Hartford, opened in New York with the Christy Minstrels, which billed themselves as the first company in the business and gave the name of "Christies" to all minstrel organizations in England. Porter played in New York for almost a decade and then, like so many of his brethren, got itchy feet; he wandered off to California and Australia.

From Derby came Horace Weston, a colored man, musician and dancer, one of the world's greatest banjoists. He was a member of Georgia Minstrels and left them to go to Europe in 1878 with *Uncle Tom's Cabin*. He played the principal continental cities and was a sensation. J. Henry Murphy, a well-known minstrel tenor, got his start with Mead's Minstrels in his native New London. The pride of Putnam was Harry Morse, famed for both his minstrel acts and his "rube" characters. Two generations remembered his title roles in *Country Sport, Gay Old Boy*, and *Jack, the Giant Killer*.

Larry and Billy Freeze of Rockville had the distinction of being "the champion tambourine spinners of the world." Their brother John operated Rockville's Opera House, and for him the two seasonally put on amateur home-town minstrel shows with a double tambourine-spinning act. As soon as it was perfected they went big time with Newton's Varieties in Hartford; in other companies, they were featured in Barnum and Bailey's circus, and toured Russia, Austria, England, France, Holland, and Hungary, winding up with an eighteen weeks' engagement in Paris.

But the greatest name of all was Lew Dockstader—George Alfred Clapp, to his fellow townsmen in Hartford. "Lew knew what the public wanted, when they wanted it and then gave it to them," commented a contemporary. "The fame of Dockstader will live forever"—and his name *was* a household word for decades. His phenomenal success began with his appearance as an amateur at his home city in 1873. Three years later he owned Newton's Varieties, changed the name to Adelphi, and with a fat wallet in his pocket moved on to San Francisco within a few months to open the New Adelphi there. He toured the country most of his life doing spectacular shows—what no other blackface monologuist had ever attempted, a different specialty every season, each one an expensive scenic extravaganza requiring a full stage.

Sooner or later every minstrel of repute served time with the circus, which was gradually outdoing minstrelsy in glamour and parade during the last decades of the century. And in the circus, too, Connecticut furnished the star performer in P. T. Barnum.

Exhibitions of animals—the forerunners of the circus—were given a much warmer welcome than other forms of entertainment, for their managers could point out that they illustrated "the beasts of the Bible and inspired children with a love for the study of natural history." Periodically in the tavern barn were confined walruses and camels, lions and leopards, a moose billed as possessing "a face like a mouse, ears like an ass, neck and back like a camel, head parts like a horse, tail like a rabbit and feet like a heiffer." And to illustrate the "pygard," which the children of God were permitted to eat according to the fourteenth chapter of Deuteronomy, appeared a beast with the "likeness of a camel, bear, mule, goat, and common bullock."

The first real circus, providing entertainment value as well as biblical education, was Rickett's, which toured the state in August, 1795, and this was accepted without too much disapproval on grounds that George Washington had just sat through a performance in Philadelphia. Besides the display of Noah's Ark animals, Rickett's had a show of feats in horsemanship—twelve acts, with a few clown and tumbling numbers thrown in. That was all. There was no big top; it was held in the open behind canvas side walls, although people who could afford the price of a dollar might get seats under a canopy in the rear.

Every few years after that, wagon circuses traveling behind spans of decorated horses and led by a red band wagon paraded from town to town more like gypsies than proud showmen. For the most part they were menageries—Macomber's Menagerie, Howe's Menagerie, Hopkins' Menagerie. The first elephant was exhibited in 1826, the first hippopotamus in 1850—"the only one in the United States"—and the first man in a lion cage the same year. With the animals occasionally were subdued specimens of various Indian tribes, before whom the public was encouraged to display no terror.

P. T. Barnum of Bridgeport witnessed these spectacles and liked what he saw. He saw, too, how much the public liked to be "humbugged," and how much more profitable humbugging was as a profession than store clerking and bartending. He would outdo them all. A wizened old vituperative Negress, Joice Heth, caught his eye, and he quickly persuaded her to go into business with him, posing as George Washington's childhood nurse, aged 160. She was coached in a few details of Washington family lore so that she could answer questions by convincing rote, and, supported by faked, yellowed documents proving her sale by Augustine Washington, the two were off to the ring. "She has been a member of the Baptist Church for upwards of one hundred years," explained her manager to those who valued an exhibition in terms of Christian fidelity, "and seems to take great satisfaction in the conversation of ministers who visit her." At Niblo's Garden in New York she drew thousands to "receptions" during August of 1835.

Barnum opened a museum of wild animals, experimented with acrobatic troupes and minstrels, discovered Tom Thumb in 1838, and soon took the midget on a tour of Europe. In 1850 he brought the Swedish prima donna, Jenny Lind, at the height of her fame, to the United States, and overnight made her America's first sweetheart. And the next June he was ready to introduce Barnum's circus to his native state.

"P. T. Barnum's Asiatic Caravan, Museum and Circus," screamed the playbill. "On Talcott Lot. June 23-24, 1851. Hartford, Conn. — Largest Menagerie in United States. — General Tom Thumb smallest Lilliputian in the world will ride baby elephant 3½ ft. high. The General will sing and dance. — Mr. Nelles, man without arms, will load and fire pistol with his toes. — Other feats of skill. — Six beautiful lions from native jungle. — Mr. Pierce will enter cage of Lions. — A Museum of Wonders, wax statuary, etc. — On entering, a fine Brass Band in a band Chariot drawn by 8 horses will play airs. — Doors open from 2 to 5, 7 to 10. — Admission 25 cents to all. — Circus has 110 horses, 90 men."

After that first magnificent show there was no dearth of circuses in Connecticut for a century. Except in years of economic or political stress, they came every season, as regular as tobacco planting and shad runs—sometimes as many as a half-dozen competing shows to a single town. Barnum opened his great circus at Brooklyn in 1871 and soon made the transition from a wagon show to a railroad show, including the "Only Mastodon on Earth." And Barnum had plenty of competitors: Carnivals of Fun, United Monster Shows, The World's Greatest Railroad Shows.

Few of the competitors could match what Barnum had to offer, but the mob took them all in. The parade and the advance publicity, with its brash misrepresentation of actuality, brought them. An oldster who had never seen a circus, and wanted to, told of the crowds he had to cope with at Danbury in 1873: "There were three tents—two small and one very large one. The former enclose the menagerie and museum—the latter the arena. . . . When I got inside the large tent I was surprised. A sea of faces spread out before and around me. The tier seats are crowded, the ring seats are crowded, the gang-ways are crowded. It is a mass of suffocation, fun and sweat. I don't think I ever saw so large an attendance at a prayer meeting, and I have been to many of them. . . . I had an excellent view of the tent, and once in a while, of the ridge pole or the giant who stood nearly opposite. I knew there was something going on in the ring, but if I had been prostrated on my dying couch, I could not have told what it was. But I knew whenever a different act commenced, because the folks in front of me stood up on the seats, and the folks behind me put their children on my head, and their umbrellas down my back. . . . But all things have an end, and the dreary afternoon performance was not an exception. The last act was performed; the clown finally convulsed the audience; the children in the rear were pulled out of my hair, and I was permitted to fall over, roll around, and eventually get to my feet. With the crowd gone, I stole back to the tent and took one fond, piercing glance at what I had not yet seen— the ring."

Buffalo Bill toured the state in 1884 with his famous Wild West Shows, and reappeared for years with his freaks, giants, midgets, tattooed men and women, Siamese twins, fat women, strong men, and living skeletons. Ringling camped at Watertown on July 14, 1889, with "110 Horses and Ponies, 3 Elephants, 2 Camels, 3 Lions, 2 Leopards, 1 American Panther, a Kangaroo, Emu, Hyena, Zebu, Stork and cage of Monkeys." The circus tent was "100 x 145 feet."

The year 1903 brought to Connecticut "The World's Greatest Shows with the Spectacle Jerusalem and the Crusades"; 1908, "Barnum and Bailey's Greatest Show on Earth with the Spectacle of Joan of Arc." And the spectacles multiplied year after year: "Cleopatra," "Solomon and the Queen of Sheba," "The Wizard Prince of Arabia," "Cinderella," "Aladdin and His Wonderful Lamp." By 1919, in the effort to outspectacle the spectacular, Barnum and Bailey had merged with Ringling Brothers to provide the "Combined Shows Featuring the World's Greatest Shows and the Greatest Show on Earth." And if Cecil de Mille hadn't taken the lead about then in dictating the dimensions for grandeur, the circus would have reached into the celestial.

But the greatest American circus spectacle of all time was a tragic one, and it had to occur in the state where the biggest of big-top men was born—at Hartford, on July 6, 1944. That was the day when the worst heat wave in twenty-five years was already scorching the city, but it did not deter six thousand from crowding into the Ringling Brothers–Barnum and Bailey tent. The performance was well under way, with the wild-animal acts just concluded and the aerialists taking their positions. A small flame appeared along the side wall near the main entrance. There was no panic at first; the crowd started to move quickly toward exits, but suddenly pandemonium broke loose as the paraffin-soaked canvas blazed up like a gasoline torch. Within seconds, the entire tent was a flaming mass and death trap. Falling sheets of fiery canvas enveloped the helpless throng. Underfoot, scores were trampled in the frenzied anguish. One hundred and sixty-eight were killed, 654 gravely injured; and a half-hour after the first blaze was sighted, all that remained of "The Greatest Show on Earth" was a confusion of twisted metal poles, and the vehicles, animals, and personnel that were out of reach of the flash fire. It was the beginning of a succession of tragedies and reverses that finally spelled an end to the traveling circus in 1956.

During the period that the circus was maturing, another kind of "educational" entertainment was concurrently growing around towns little and big in the form of agricultural fairs. Country fairs, patterned after the English parish festivities, were almost as old as the Connecticut colony, dating back to 1643. But these benefit sales, with the display of home crafts, bore little resemblance to the big autumn exhibitions that began to spread over Connecticut in the 1830's and 1840's. Towns and groups of towns, counties, the state, and finally groups of states, in a competitive effort to encourage achievement in better farm and industrial products, went into the business. And the sponsors, eager to draw a crowd, took tips from the traveling circus, from crafty peddlers, from city marketplaces, even from the Colosseum of Rome.

There was an exhibition tent for mince pies and cucumber relish, for the piles of warted winter squash and golden ears of corn, for baskets of scarlet apples and the quilt Aunt Agnes worked on from November to March; there were pens for prize hogs, stalls for prize bulls or horses, and the corner of a field set aside for display of the latest in plows and threshing machines; but there had to be something more exciting than these familiarities to hold the interest of country folk and keep them coming back for two or three days. The scattered exhibition booths expanded into a compact "midway," each concession commanded by a garrulous hawker. A race track with a grandstand was erected behind a permanent exhibition hall, and over the years were added fireworks and Ferris wheels, merry-go-rounds and minstrels, lotteries and carnival side shows, and the biggest attraction of all, the balloon ascension. The balloon act, which nobody wanted to miss, was delayed until almost dusk to make sure that the public remained on the grounds to the end. In breathless awe they watched the inflation process, the sudden rise, and then the death-defying parachute drops—once, twice, three times—and the deflated balloon in a smudge of gas and smoke, slowly settling.

The Danbury Fair was a good example. It got its start, according to one humorist, when "Fill Carter, old Sol Carter's son by his first wife," about 1820 built a high board fence and then constructed a mysterious structure inside it. "Some said it was a chicken house. Some said it was a barn. Some said it was a conservatory, and some said, 'What the dickens is it for?' It had an air-shaft, and a cupalow and an attic, and several stalls something like a hoss barn."

Regardless of exactly how Danbury's fair came into existence, exhibitions had been held in the town for more than three decades before the Fairfield County Agricultural Society was constituted in the 1850's, "for the improvement and encouragement of agriculture, domestic manufacture, industry and economy, and the holding of annual cattle shows and fairs in some town of Fairfield County during the month of October." The idea was to auction off the show to the town that offered the largest cash inducement. Danbury got it in 1857, 1858, and 1860; Bridgeport in 1861; Stamford in 1853 and 1854, Norwalk between times and from 1862 to 1868. After that Danbury had it for keeps; two local businessmen purchased a pasture, dubbed it Pleasure Park, and erected a tent in the middle. No other town in Fairfield County could outbid them.

Annually for a week or more, Danbury became the temporary home for scores of back-state farm families. Father, mother, and the children drove down in the lumber wagon, piled high with their tent, and precious pies and preserves destined to get blue ribbons, enough food staples to last seven days, and the fat, smelly sow in a pen at the rear. The prize animals were tethered behind.

At Pleasure Park the youngsters often learned more about the ways
of the world than they learned about agriculture, but mother
didn't always find out. City folk came "up to Connecticut" by
train for a lark; in carriages, and later in flivvers, the curious from
the big Fairfield County cities came for the carnival. Teen-agers
got lost in the crowd, found new city companions, were carried
away with the fairyland of festive music and Ferris wheels, and
went back to the farm at the end of the week with new horizons
and sometimes new moral codes. Danbury was a merry, merry
occasion. Recollections of it warmed many a winter evening, and
plans for the next year filled many a dull summer day.

World War II stopped the Fair, as it did other Connecticut
fairs, but it reopened in 1946 with an assortment of twentieth-
century attractions, midget auto races, speedboat races on a newly
constructed waterway, a machinery hall, and a renewed carnival
spirit. It is still a big event of the year for the county—representing the survival of "one of the most important and one of the most
spectacular of all economic and social associations."

More than two score other agricultural fairs there are in Connecticut—county fairs, 4–H fairs, Grange fairs, Future Farmers'
fairs—but most of them have been reduced to a day or two. Danbury goes on for nine days in much the same spirit it has known
for over a century.

It was not always spectacle that the merrymakers of Connecticut sought for their amusements. They found almost as much sheer
pleasure in events they cooked up for themselves. Before the days
of motor cars and skis, old and young looked forward to "sliding
down hill" as the most exciting community revelry of the year.
"In the winter the whole town went crazy about coasting," recalled a New Canaan addict. "Crowds of people came out for
coasting parties on moonlight nights. . . . In those days the hills
were safe, but there were plenty of spills and occasional broken
arms. Everyone aspired to have a winning sled, a pung, or double
rip. . . . With the money they had earned picking blueberries in
the summer, the boys paid for the iron work on the sleds. One
winter when the coasting was especially fine, the Johnsons made
a huge double rip for their own use. The board was so long it had
to be sprung up in the middle by means of a tie-rod, running its
entire length. The whole shop—30 men—could pile aboard at one
time. It roared down the long steep slopes at a terrific clip. . . .
We always started from St. Mark's Church. There were prayer
meetings on Wednesday nights which everybody had to attend.

One memorable night the Methodists and the Congregationalists had a joint prayer meeting at the Congregational Church, which let out early so that everybody could go coasting. Sometimes they coasted from St. Mark's down the hill to Main Street and on to Maple Street, or they might turn down East Avenue and with a little push go clear across the pond when the ice was good." Every town with a similar incline could boast of parties just as spirited; and the skating and sleigh-riding jaunts were no less exhilarating.

Communities in different parts of the state developed specialties in entertainment. Norwich had its tradition of Thanksgiving barrel burnings. On poles as high as the mainmast of a schooner, barrels were threaded to the top, with hundreds more artfully stacked about the main support to create draft for a mighty conflagration. Competing teams vied with each other to build the barrel monuments on a hill above the city and touched them off on Thanksgiving evening. Thousands gathered at vantage points from all over New London County to witness the show, to deplore the waste and thrill to it. The custom went way back into the 1700's. In 1792 a mob of boys, who had pilfered the barrels from Norwich merchants, decided to delight the audience with a preliminary attraction, the firing of a supercharged cannon. "The explosion," reported the press with a reverence for gruesome detail, "burst the swivel into a multitude of pieces, the largest of which, weighing about seven pounds, passed through the body of the deceased, carrying with it his heart, and was afterward found in the street 30 or 40 rods from the place where it was fired." The newspapers once more used the incident to campaign against the barbarous practice of barrel burning: "While the serious lament the unhappy accident, they entertain a hope that good may come of evil, that the savage practice of making bonfires on the evening of Thanksgiving may be exchanged for some other mode of rejoicing, more consistent with the genuine spirit of Christianity." But the plea was ineffective. Similar editorials were still being written in the twentieth century. The practice didn't stop until staves were almost extinct.

Greenwich had its traditional skimmington parties after every wedding. Old and young turned out with drums and guns to serenade the groom, who in response to the din was invited to serve his admirers quantities of hard cider and wedding cake. A cannon left over from the Revolution saw service for years at these parties, and all went well until 1850, when a groom objected to being serenaded, and appeared at his door with a gun of his own to threaten anyone who dared haul the cannon within range. Three bold assaults were made before the cannon was finally fired, and the incident deserved stanzas of far better verse than it got:

> *All gathered at night with fife and drum*
> *At the appointed place with busy hum;*
> *Each one cheered his brother's courage up*
> *Some cheered their own with drink from the cup.*
>
> . . . .
>
> *What a noise that cannon did make,*
> *Everything got a terrible shake.*
> *A score of glass lights, all ranged in rows,*
> *Came to the earth with terrible blows,*
> *Doors open, stoves jump two feet high*
> *Not minding the leap more than a fly;*
> *Success gives courage to Skimeton;*
> *The gun is drawn back at a stiff run.*

The affair was eventually settled in court, but the groom never regained his standing in the community, and Greenwich saw the last of its skimmington raids.

The red-letter days for revelry in the river towns came when a new vessel was making a maiden voyage up or downstream. Ancient cannon were dragged to the water front for salutes, the wharves were decked with patriotic bunting, and as the scheduled hour for the appearance of the boat approached, villagers for miles around assembled at the pier dressed in their Sunday best or in clownish costume as a welcoming committee. Flags and pennants flourished wildly as the vessel came into view, the crack of torpedoes and firecrackers punctuated hoarse cheers from the crowd, and when hawsers were at last cast over the piles, there were solemn speeches, band music, and prayers.

"Fusillades of musketry from both sides of the river," wild "huzzahing," and repeated thirteen-gun salutes greeted the *Barnet* on her unsuccessful attempt to conquer the Connecticut all the way to Barnet, Vermont. She was held in ports along the route night after night while passengers and crew were feted with elaborate banquets and inebriant parties. But the *Barnet* never saw Barnet. Farther than Bellows Falls she could not go. Someone had miscalculated the width of the locks there. But even as she drifted back to her grave in Hartford, the crowds on the banks cheered

her like a triumphant heroine. The river won over every challenger, and the principal contribution of expensive efforts to
reach the Connecticut headwaters seemed to be the provision of
a great deal of celebrating for landlubbers along the route.

Toward the end of the century Hartford had its swank Wheel
Club dedicated to the purpose of "maintaining a library, reading
room, rooms for proper social amusement and for the promotion
of the interests of bicycling as a recreation and exercise." The
members were as regimented as the state militia, with a captain, lieutenant, color-bearer and bugler—"who shall receive and
transmit the orders of the Captain while wheeling." "No member
shall parade with the Club unless he is in Club uniform," prescribed
the constitution. "In mounting, no man shall mount until the man
immediately in front of him has mounted safely. During Club runs,
no participant shall pass the Captain or pace-makers without
special permission." There were races, too, which made big news
for the social as well as the sports columns.

To citizens of the Thames valley, steamboat excursions down
the river to Block Island, Watch Hill, or Eastern Point provided
the gayest day of the summer for over a century. Past Poque-
tanuck Cove, the Mohegan reservation at Trading Cove, the handsome clubhouses at Kitemaug, past the summer resort at Gales
Ferry and the headquarters for the Yale and Harvard crews, the
Navy Yard, through the bridge at New London, which boasted "the
second longest draw in the world and the largest in the United
States," and then out toward the Sound and the Atlantic. Arms
waved tirelessly from the deck for most of the fifteen miles downriver, as if to convey to the groups of inveterate arm-wavers along
the shore some token of the thrill of being afloat.

Macadam roads, car cylinders, movies, and radio brought a
slow end to the simple pleasures, to the quilting bees and husking
bees, to the boat excursions and adult bicycle clubs, to the coasting and minstrel shows. The tempo of living changed, and standards changed. Native son P. T. Barnum did more than any other
to alter the Connecticut inhibitions against professional amusements; the development of his circus paralleled a new hospitality
toward theatrics. He helped prepare the way for acceptance of
small-town plays and big-town vaudeville. And soon the voice of
the patient clergy was drowned in the clamor echoing from road-
houses, public dance halls, drive-ins, TV, and the rasping soprano
of cocktail lounges. The merrymakers had won the long war with
the Connecticut moralists.

· 14 ·

THE BIG OPERATORS

"AT MY BOARDING-HOUSE, I FIND THE PLATED WARE TO BE OF CON-
necticut manufacture. The clock that tells me the time from the
mantlepiece; the watch my friend carries; the hat he wears; his
pocket knife, are all from Connecticut. At the office I write with
a Connecticut pen, and when I need an official envelope I find
that the original package from which I take it bears a Connecticut mark. If I make an error and wish to erase it, I do so with a
steel eraser made in Connecticut. . . . My desk has a Connecticut lock and key. . . . I am attracted to a shop window . . . and
read on an ugly looking machete 'Hartford, Conn., U.S.A.' A
Winchester, or a Marlin rifle, or a Colt's revolver, all made in Connecticut, I find in another window; and in still another a supply of
fixed ammunition from New Haven and Bridgeport. Axes, hammers, augers, all kinds of builders' hardware, are in a shop close by
—all made in Connecticut. Foulards, cottons, woolens, worsteds,
rubber goods of all kinds, are near by—they are standard makes
from Connecticut. The gas and electric fixtures that show them off
are of our manufacture. . . . Do I want a button? Made in Connecticut. 'Hand me a pen.' The box tells me it is from Waterbury,
Connecticut, U.S.A. That automobile rushing by came from Connecticut. That bicycle, those tires, those novel call and door bells
—all from Connecticut. Typewriters on every side from our little

state. . . . From open doors and windows the sound of music . . . emanates from a Connecticut-made graphophone or phonograph. . . . And last let me say that where my trousers are put away at night, they go into a hanger of the best kind—made in Connecticut."

That was the report of clerk William Countryman, written from Washington in 1902 to the folks back home, in an effort to relieve his own nostalgia. On paper he could prove that Connecticut was all around him; he couldn't get very far away from his home state. The homesick lad buttoned himself into a Connecticut-made nightshirt and, lulled by a smug sense of satisfaction, slept as peacefully as he would have in Hartford.

Before 1650 John Winthrop, Jr., had made a sharp appraisal of the colony he had helped secure, and concluded that its future lay in commerce and industry—not in agriculture as everyone else contended. He set an example by promoting ironworks, leadworks, and saltworks, and did his best to encourage others to go into big-scale manufacturing. But no one paid much heed to his counsel. People were too busy with their plowing and harrowing, too preoccupied with making contraptions, too involved in dreams of lands somewhere else—lands that would produce an easier living. Almost universally, they nurtured obsessions for contriving "a machine which would create a monopoly and make a future," but it was a long time before they realized that Connecticut was the place to put the obsession into practice, and a longer time before the obsessions paid off—almost two centuries.

The Irish immigrants at Berlin showed the Yankees what a big operation was like in tinware. The Terrys and Thomases demonstrated it with clocks. Dr. Howe tried it with common pins, and the Waterbury craftsmen proved Winthrop was right with brass buttons. But it all came very slowly. Nails were being shipped to Great Britain before 1716; jealous London hatters complained in 1732 about the competition of Connecticut hats; a silk factory was opened at Mansfield in 1759; Norwich started a paper mill in 1768, Hartford the first New England woolen mill in 1788, Manchester a cotton mill in 1794. David Humphreys, home from his diplomatic exploits in Spain and Portugal, revived the Winthrop philosophy in 1806, and created the first real factory town at Seymour, ready to produce paper, woolens, tools, and hardware under an original educational and apprenticeship system of his own projection. The idea was catching on, yet only an insignificant fraction of the potential water power and man power was going into manufacturing.

About 1765 the legislature was persuaded that the textile industry with the most promising future was silk. Half an ounce of mulberry seed was sent to every parish in the colony, and for a few years a bounty was offered on mulberry trees and raw silk. It was one of the early efforts of government to help subsidize an industry. Silkworms, raised in New Haven, on Long Island, and in Philadelphia, developed an appetite for mulberry leaves grown in every town between Narragansett Bay and the Hudson. Two hundred sixty-five pounds of silk were raised in 1793. The output had increased to over a ton and a half by 1830—a lot of silk for a small state. A second factory was opened in Mansfield "with swifts for winding hard silk; 32 spindles for doubling; seven dozen of spindles for throwing; 32 spindles for soft silk winding; and 2 broad and one fringe silk looms . . . machinery enough to keep 30 broad silk looms and fifty hands in operation. . . . A larger quantity of silk is manufactured here than in any other place in the United States," reported John Barber in 1836. If the mulberry trees hadn't been destroyed by blight a decade later, native silk might have remained the mainstay of Mansfield.

Up north at Barkhamsted, Lambert Hitchcock opened a chair factory in 1818, using the "interchangeable parts" idea that Eli Whitney was promulgating for machinery. Knocked down, the chairs went by the van load to Hartford, whence they were shipped to Charleston, South Carolina, and Savannah, Georgia. In three years his business grew to such proportions that a little town had sprung up around his factory, and Hitchcock decided that he should go in for quality as well as quantity. He gave up shipping the parts and concentrated on finished, decorated furniture, building up his line year after year with uprights and rockers; "pillowtops" and "turtlebacks"; chairs stenciled with pears and plums, grapes and roses, fountains and "horns of plenty"; chairs with rush, solid wood, and cane seats; "Boston rockers" with rolling seats and rolling crests; "Cape Cods" or cradle settees; highback armchairs with rockers; and children's models of all descriptions for fifty cents up. "By Industry We Thrive!" he advertised. "Rest for the Weary!" People all over America rested in his chairs, and then handed them down as heirlooms for grandchildren and great-grands to lounge in. The warranted chair with the "L. Hitchcock" label proved to be almost as imperishable as it was attractive and comfortable—so admired that its production called for a twentieth-century revival—"every stencil, every last measurement, every turning, every step in the preparations of materials taken directly from Mr. Hitchcock's own work records."

During the Revolution, when good British hats were hard to come by, Zadoc Benedict started experimenting with beaver toppers at his home in Danbury. Alone, he found that he could average about one a day, and the demand for his product was greater than he could supply. He took on a journeyman and two apprentices, and the four turned out three handsome beavers a day. Although the hatter's trade was widespread in New England and New York, Danbury liked to maintain that its artisans made the first hats "this side of the Atlantic." If they weren't the first, they were certainly the best, and the trade grew prodigiously. Over twenty thousand were produced in 1800. All of Danbury turned to men's hatmaking, and in addition to the New York market, two stores were opened in Charleston, South Carolina. By the 1830's five hundred men and women were employed in thirty-nine different shops and factories. Annually they were producing over a quarter of a million pieces of headgear, valued wholesale at a little better than two dollars a hat. And that was only the beginning. Nowhere in America was there a community ready to challenge the priority of Danbury in the field of men's headwear. One town was beginning to hit a stride in mass production that would have pleased even John Winthrop, Jr.

The examples set by Danbury, Barkhamsted, and Mansfield were soon being duplicated in scores of towns. "Sharon and Watertown made mousetraps by the hundred thousand. Brooklyn manufactured ten thousand pairs of spectacles a year. Woodbridge made five hundred dozen iron candlesticks. North Haven and Wallingford made razor strops by the thousand dozen. Chester manufactured thousands of dozens of inkstands; Manchester made ink to fill them, as well as blacking and shaving soap. . . . Prospect had thirty people employed in the manufacture of friction matches. . . . Ledyard and Redding made sieves by the thousand dozen."

The little village of Collinsville, with only five hundred inhabitants, went into the ax business, and stowed into barrels seven or eight hundred helves and heads a day to ship to Central and South America, to the country stores and trading posts of backwoods New England, New York, and Canada. Never before had anyone conceived of ax production as an industry. A railsplitter in need of a new ax had fashioned it himself or had taken his order to a blacksmith, standing by to give instructions on exactly the right weight, shape, temper, and edge. But in 1876 the Collins brothers—Samuel and David—got the quantity-production bug, opened the first ax factory in the world, and used "Lehigh coal fires" in their forges for the first time in America—

"an undertaking of great audacity." The "Yankee chopping ax" was their specialty—an instrument weighing exactly three pounds, with a thin, wide bitt and a three-quarter-inch poll, but axes and hatchets of every size and shape came from their shops—the "Maine," the "New Jersey," the "Kentucky," the "Baltimore," the "Long Island," the "Turpentine," "Boxing," "Post," "Fireman's," "Butcher's," "Ship Carpenter's." No less than a hundred models were made there. A little enterprise grew into an enormous enterprise, producing nearly five thousand axes and tools a day— tools with razor-sharp edges and points, anything from a broad-blade to machete. The Collinses, indeed, became big operators, and to this day anywhere in the world that cane or jungle bush is cut by hand, chances are that the flashing blade bears a Collins label.

East Hampton moved into the big-operator category as a manufacturer of bells—so many kinds of bells the whole town tinkled and rang with them: sleigh bells, hand bells, cowbells, house bells, school bells, church bells, toy chimes for children; during the 1890's, when no dandy of distinction would be seen in public without a chestnut bell in his lapel, East Hampton was the provider. And, oddly enough, New Britain got its start as a manufacturing center through filching some of the trade in bells from East Hampton. The specialty in New Britain was sleigh bells, supplied by the gross to peddlers traveling across the land. It wasn't until 1850 that New Britain was divorced from the town of Berlin and became an independent community, but by then the bells had rung in the new day when New Britain was to be a manufacturing center for steel and hardware, carpenters' tools, electric ranges, ball bearings, locks and lathes, washing machines, and paper goods.

Farmington, one of the foremost industrial towns of the nine-teenth century, at one time was manufacturing fifteen thousand yards of linen a year, as well as hats, clocks, candles, and carriages. In 1807 Tiffany's established a cotton mill at Danielson, but moved on to found a jewelry firm in New York City, never antici-pating that Danielson would develop into the state's largest cotton manufacturing center.

Then in just the right chronological order, while all this industry was burgeoning, the railroad came to give an additional impetus the little operators needed. There were plenty of roads—such as they were; there were steamboat, sail, or tow services to any destination on any navigable stream; but the locomotive was a large enough symbol of industrial progress to inspire businessmen with grandiose ideas. The monster engines belched sparks, smoke, and wood ashes over the country side, set fires in the forests, made hideous noises; and between the smoke and the noise they aroused Connecticut to a destiny manifest. Something of the divine will was seen in this heaven-sent symbol. "We must not forget," cautioned an editor, "that the railroad is but one step in the ascending staircase on which the race are mounting, guided and cheered by heavenly voices. The resources of infinite grace and wisdom are not exhausted, and we only mark the beginning of wonders which shall co-operate with the divine purpose in the redemption of man, and the restoration of a ruined world.

"The procession of heavy cars," continued the admonishment, "winding among the hills after the panting engine, a seeming realization of the dragon, fabled in the middle ages, whose breath was flame, and whose course was as a rushing tempest, always interests and quickens by its illustration of power and skill. The eye never wearies of watching a railroad train as it whirls on its appointed track, seemingly instinct with life, running with merry wantonness its matchless race unwearied, and screaming madly in the pride of its power. But when we remember that it is the product of human intelligence, and a token of divine love, and reflect on its promise for the future, the spectacle is invested with moral grandeur, giving us courage for the conflict today, and prophesying of a good time to come, when creation shall rejoice in the liberty of the sons of God."

To many a well-grounded businessman it appeared that the traveling steam engine was a preview of traffic in the New Jerusalem, let down especially to encourage him to strive for bigger and better industrial ventures. This was his reaction in spite of the fact that there were already two thousand miles of railroad track along the Atlantic seaboard, and trains had been operating for ten years before his Connecticut conservatism allowed the locomotive to cross the state line.

The first road was chartered in 1832, but it was not completed for five years. It ran from Providence to Stonington, traversing only about five miles of Connecticut soil. Almost simultaneously other rails were being laid in other parts of state—the Norwich and Worcester, the Housatonic between Canaan and Bridgeport, the Hartford and New Haven, the New Haven and Springfield. The fever for railroads struck almost as contagiously as had the turnpike fever forty years earlier.

But when the first symptoms of that fever appeared, no one had any idea that the rails would be anything more than a convenient supplement to water and stage traffic. The two major purposes were to connect upstate towns with the Sound and to eliminate the treacherous ocean passage in open water around Point Judith. There was a luxurious steamer voyage down the protected waters of Long Island Sound from Stonington to New York, but the short stretch between the mouth of the Narragansett Bay and Stonington was always unwelcome. The first railroad took care of that; then as one line was extended into the interior it invited another. Every backwoods hamlet wanted a railroad station. No one had any clear conception of what the railroad would develop into. The legislature visualized a service similar to that of a toll road or a canal; when a company was granted a franchise it was made responsible for the construction of an iron thoroughfare, and empowered in turn to grant individuals or companies who furnished their own rolling stock the right to travel on it—for a price. With a charter went the authority "to erect toll houses, establish gates, appoint toll gatherers, and demand toll upon the road," as well as jurisdiction over "the transportation of persons and property, the construction of wheels, the form of cars and carriages, the weight of load and all other matters." Specifically, the charter stated that the railroad was for the use of any person who should comply with the rules and regulations. The magnificent experiment in transportation was several decades old before there was any definitive shakedown in the rules and regulations.

With names like *Lion, Planet, Comet,* the trains roared over the rails at a breath-taking twelve and fifteen miles an hour, the engineers exposed to the elements out in front, a brakeman on each car sitting approximately where coachmen had held harness reins for years, the passengers riding in luxury behind the glazed windows of converted stagecoach bodies. The Norwich and Worcester line had the finest appointments, with a separate compartment for unattended ladies—"carpeted, and in every respect beautifully finished with wide and convenient sofas, dressing table, wash stand and other arrangements for the comfort of passengers." And among all the Connecticut railroads, the elite Norwich and Worcester was the only line that found it necessary to introduce an undemocratic distinction between first- and second-class passengers. Elsewhere, as one commentator explained, "the passenger carriages are not distinguished, as in Europe, by different modes of providing for the ease and comfort of the traveller. There are no first, second, and third classes. All are first class, or rather," he added guardedly, "of the *same* class."

Half the old stagecoach routes were soon replaced by competing rails crisscrossing the state in every direction: the New York and New Haven; the New Haven and New London; the New London and Stonington—completing the link, except for a few ferry passages, between Boston and New York; the New London, Willimantic, and Palmer; the New Haven and Northampton; the Naugatuck, between Winsted and Devon; and one circuitous route across the middle of the state covered by the Hartford, Providence, and Fishkill.

Changes came very rapidly. A cab was soon provided for the engineers; the "London omnibus" style of coach was substituted for the stage type; stoves, kerosene lights, and cushioned seats were added for the comfort of passengers; the brakemen were discarded when more reliable couplings were invented; bridges across the Thames and Connecticut allowed for the abandonment of ferry connections; and late in the century the dozens of railroad companies began to consolidate for a less competitive and more efficient transit service.

The key rail lines were established by 1850 or soon afterward. Addition of spurs and connections continued for another forty years, but at mid-century they had served the purpose of stirring industrialists to a realization of what course the future of Connecticut was bound to take. Cities that had been centers for agricultural trade became manufacturing centers. Quiet rural villages were aroused by factory whistles as well as train whistles. Where falls for water power didn't exist, dams were erected. Every village along the tributaries of the Quinebaug, the Shetucket, the Willimantic, the Connecticut, the Farmington, the Naugatuck, and the Housatonic drew a mill-town clientele. Led by French Canadians and Irish, the opportunity-seeking immigrants crowded into bright new tenement houses. Row on barren row, these corporation dwelling houses radiated out from the mill, every house like every other, hundreds of them in towns like Pomfret, Jewett City, Taftville, Danielson, Rockville, Winsted, and New Milford. The unwary public was being endowed with standardization in everything from living quarters and lunch hours to wages and water closets—equal treatment, equal benefits, equal opportunity, yet an entirely different democracy from what New England had known. And the new industrial order turned the tide of emigration. For decades the census had shown that the population of the United States had been increasing seven times faster than the population of Connecticut under its agricultural economy, but after 1850 Connecticut began to settle down. From a slow increase of 4 or 5 per cent, it jumped almost to 20 in a single ten-year period.

Industry did not immediately replace agriculture, for the hay crop alone in 1845 was valued at over four million dollars, against an appraisal of some three million for the two most extensive manufactures—cotton and wool—but there would soon be more textiles than timothy. Up to 1818 there were only thirty-eight manufacturing companies large enough to warrant incorporation, and most of these were capitalized for less than a hundred thousand dollars. The four leading enterprises were clocks, brassware, firearms, and silverware. By 1850 scores of companies were capitalized at over a million, and the little factories making boots and shoes, woolen and cotton goods, arms and metalware were expanding their employment rolls into the hundreds. The railroad made the difference. By rail came quantities of the raw materials; by rail went forth the carloads of factory fabrication.

But the train couldn't take all the credit; for the loads would have been light if inventors, craftsmen, and visionaries hadn't first had an idea. Over and over again the factory towns demonstrated that their busy railroad sidings were due to one man's planting of an industry before someone else in Massachusetts or Pennsylvania or New Jersey thought of it. Geography wasn't responsible. There was no good reason why the brass industry could not have developed at Watertown, Massachusetts, or Waterville, Maine, as readily as at Waterbury, Connecticut. The raw materials were not in the state; the major market was not there. Even English brass workers had to be imported—smuggled ashore in wooden casks from ships anchored well off the coast. Other towns within a few miles had superior water power. The region was originally considered so uninviting that when it was purchased from the Indians the town proprietors estimated that it could never accommodate more than thirty families. But Henry Grilley and his brothers settled there in 1790 and started casting pewter buttons. Twelve years later Abel and Levi Porter joined them in manufacturing buttons out of sheet brass—the first use of fused copper and zinc in America and the first brass-rolling operation in America. All their raw material was junk—copper from old stills, kettles, ship sheathing—scrap that could have been much more easily assembled near a larger population center. Yet from their persistence in contending with handicaps, their energy, initiative, and application, the brass industry grew. Waterbury buttons, peddled up and down the land, were known from the Gulf of Mexico to the Gulf of Saint Lawrence. Their success invited competition, and new companies formed at Waterbury. They produced brass kettles; brass pins; brass for clocks; brass wire, grates, fenders, fire engine nozzles, hinges, hooks and eyes, daguerreotype plates, tubing, lamps. Most of the rolled and finished brass for the nation was soon coming from the Naugatuck valley. Ten notable firms entered the business before 1865. The Waterbury Brass Company, which bought Hiram Hayden's process for spinning brass kettles, showed capital stock of $40,000 in 1846. Later the same year it was increased to $50,000; in 1848 it rose to $75,000; in 1850 to $104,000; two years later that amount was doubled; in 1853 the stock stood at $250,000; in 1857, $300,000; in 1860, $400,-000. And these early companies later became the parents of great corporations like American Brass, Anaconda, Kennecott, and Chase.

Over in Fairfield County, Danbury kept growing and growing for no good geographical reason. It turned into the hat city of America, producing more men's head coverings than any other one city. It followed or created the styles in hats for over a century and a half—from beaver or wool to silk and felt. Toward the end of the century four and a half million were being shipped out of the city annually. Fur and hair from beaver, otter, nutria, muskrat, mink, and rabbits were imported by carload and shipload from France, Scotland, Australia, New Zealand, Russia, Siberia, and hats with a Danbury label were worn in every part of the world—in Europe and Mexico, as far away as South Africa, Japan, and the East Indies.

South Manchester, under the Cheney Brothers, became the center for silk manufacture; New Britain for hardware; Meriden for silver; Hartford for insurance and airplane motors; Willimantic for thread—the first spool-wound linen thread in America; Stamford for locks; New Haven for firearms and clocks, Groton for submarines; Naugatuck for Goodyear rubber—more rubber footwear than was produced in any other mill in the world. A few cities, rather than concentrating on one product, went into many, altering the emphasis with an altering economy and sociology. From whaling, Bridgeport ventured into pewterware, carriages, saddles, furniture, and shirts; for a time it was the sewing machine capital, then the carriage capital; for a quarter of a century it manufactured automobiles—the high-quality Locomobile; the first Gramophones were produced there, and Bridgeport parented the Columbia Phonograph Company. Then as factory after factory found a home in the city, the Bridgeport trade-mark was found on ammunition and firearms, automatic machinery, nuts, bolts and screws, brass products, brake linings, corsets, chairs, hardware, electrical supplies, plumbing fixtures, rubber goods, scissors, typewriters, toys. Its five hundred factories represented more diversified industry than any other city in America. The manufacturing area of Bridgeport merged with the manufacturing area of Fairfield, where the production of chemicals and cans, aluminum castings and structural steel, fabrics and refined silver was making another mighty industrial domain out of a community that steadfastly remained agricultural for over two centuries.

The river towns that went into textiles—cotton and wool—were destined to have more fluctuation of fortune than big Bridgeport or even the little communities that slumbered into agricultural oblivion. Their market was in New York or in far-off places subject to the irregular pulse of national economy. In good times, the mills ran in two shifts; in bad, they often didn't run at all. Wars, financial crises, business booms had a way of affecting what people wore, and when city people weren't buying new cotton prints or new woolen jackets, the country people didn't always eat.

In cotton manufacturing, Connecticut was "an imitator rather than an innovator." Rhode Island got the jump on its neighbor state. From Pawtucket the impetus spread to Waltham and Lowell; New London and Windham Counties caught the spirit at second hand, but adopted it with lusty enthusiasm. Jewett City, Sterling, Plainfield, Thompson, Willimantic, Killingly, and Norwich were the big centers, but any town with enough water flowing through it to turn a wheel abetted them. In most of the towns it was a small-scale operation at first. The home looms were fast disappearing by the 1830's, and the weaving previously done in the kitchen merely became a community venture under a tough capitalist. Pomfret adopted a policy of hiring whole families with five or six children to tend the machines. The head of the house earned a dollar for a twelve-hour day, his wife thirty-five cents, and children under twelve, twenty-one cents. And if anyone complained about the wage system, the millowner could retort benevolently that the family never had it so good: the farm had yielded an annual income of only two hundred dollars, but with the whole family employed in the factory the income was five or six hundred.

Nevertheless, the scores of little factories with a dozen employees steadily grew. The Thames Manufacturing Company in Norwich and the Windham Manufacturing Company in Willimantic graduated into the big-operator class, and were soon turning out over a million yards of cotton cloth a year. And the woolen factories were doing about as well. Precedents set by David Humphreys at Seymour and the Scholfields at Montville were freely copied in

Middletown, Winsted, Rockville, Talcottville. From a start with a few hundred spindles, tended by a score of women and children, the industry expanded until Connecticut proudly boasted that its output in woolen goods was exceeded by that of only three other states.

And Connecticut could produce the unexpected, too—make a great industry out of almost any stock or staple to which its human ingenuity was applied—even oysters and insurance. New Haven was famous for oysters long before it was very widely acclaimed for its learning. "The principal oyster beds," explained Pease and Niles in 1819 (before mentioning that Yale was also located in the city), "are in the Quinipiak, where it has been estimated that several hundred thousand bushels are taken annually. . . . Large quantities are opened and conveyed in kegs into different parts of the interior . . . into Vermont, and some sections of New Hampshire and New York." Row on row of oystermen's huts thatched with seaweed lined the water front at Milford during the eighteen hundreds. Then the industry moved down the coast toward New York, and the Fairfield-Bridgeport-Stratford region became the oyster capital. "With nearly 70,000 acres of land devoted to the great enterprise, employing at times 600 men and half a thousand vessels of various sizes and shapes, the dark depths off the coast of Connecticut are not only making large fortunes for the promoters, but paying heavy revenue into the state exchequer," reported an overseer in 1902.

The oyster farmers had been in the business since 1845 when the first offshore cultivation was started; then the legislature had come to their aid by establishing "natural beds" in the Housatonic River, and in a single year over half a million bushels of "seed" oysters were taken from the beds merely for planting on the acres of private growers in the Sound. With cool Connecticut efficiency, the ownership of every one of the seventy thousand submerged acres was recorded in state records, exactly as were inland acres. Taxes were levied and collected in the same manner as town taxes, and even an oyster policeman guarded the real estate.

By 1900 the traffic in oysters was reckoned in thousands of tons, and the proudest moment in the history of the Connecticut oyster came when barrels of them were shipped to London for the coronation banquet of King Edward VII of the British Empire. But industry on the riverbanks and water fronts was everlastingly at odds with industry in the Sound. Starfish gorged on the bivalves, eel grass closed in on the beds, gales buried them in drifting sand.

Textile dyes, refuse, and sewage were not the right diet for oysters. Yet fifty thousand underwater acres are still planted with seed oysters, and the tons shipped to market are ample evidence that the battle with nature and inland industry is not yet lost.

The insurance business prospered inversely. The marine or fire companies that sprang up in port towns around the turn of the eighteenth century were, for the most part, very short-lived. Generally the "company" was merely a group of underwriters who agreed to share losses from fire, piracy, or shipwreck with the owner of a vessel, and in return for the risks, the insurers would share in the profits of the voyage—if there were any. The first bona fide organization incorporated in the state was at Norwich, not Hartford. In May, 1795, the Mutual Assurance Company of the city of Norwich came into existence, and thanks to its policy of good Connecticut caution, it has never closed its doors. For over a century and a half it limited its clientele to owners of property known personally to its officers. Norwich Mutual chose to remain a small operation and let Hartford take the big risks.

Hartford Fire Insurance Company, incorporated in 1810, and Aetna, born nine years later, took the risks in stride. Their stockholders were outstanding businessmen of principle as well as prowess, and all went well until seven hundred buildings were leveled in the great Manhattan conflagration of December, 1834, with a loss of twenty million—an overwhelming disaster to that generation.

Sketchy news of the fire arrived by post rider as a bitter cold dawn broke over the Connecticut valley the next morning. There was no detailed information about the area burned, and the Hartford Fire Insurance Company possessed no street maps on which to trace their interests even if the information had been available. The only honorable thing to do was for the president of the company himself to go to New York and get the facts. Eliphalet Terry was the man. He knew that the company had policies on buildings that must have stood in the burned district, and "if ever fire insurance was to demonstrate its worth to society, this was the opportunity. He called on the Hartford bankers, secured a blanket promise that they would honor any and all drafts he might make on behalf of his company and, as security for this promise, pledged his private fortune. With the thermometer registering below zero, he started for New York in a sleigh. On his arrival he found that most of the insurance companies of New York were already bankrupt. Sufferers from the fire were in consternation and despair, and property owners outside the burned districts had

concluded that fire insurance had failed in its mission. . . .
Calmly he announced that he would pay in full all claims against
the company." He did. And almost immediately the company was
overwhelmed with new policies.

Eliphalet Terry's mission to New York did more to establish
insurance firmly at Hartford than any propaganda of the era.
Eleven years later both Aetna and Hartford repeated the performance when New York was again swept by a disastrous fire, and in
1871, when one hundred forty million dollars' worth of Chicago
went up in flames, the president of Phoenix wired Governor
Marshall Jewell, who happened to be in Detroit and who happened to be a Phoenix director, to act for the company. "On
the morning of October 13th Governor Jewell stood on the bank
of the river overlooking three thousand flame-swept acres from
which a mighty city had vanished. Around him was a surging,
sullen, half-crazed, despairing crowd, which seemed to feel that
even the foundations of the earth were crumbling. . . . Mounted
on a dry-goods box . . . he announced that the Phoenix would
pay all losses in full, and offered to draw his check on the spot for
any claim. . . . Immediately the *Tribune* dropped from its window
a huge placard, announcing that the Phoenix of Hartford had
begun to pay its losses. As the news spread from one to another,
the multitude cheered, and cried, and laughed by turns." The
establishment of Hartford as the insurance capital of America
did not come by accident. In response to a Yankee business policy
of bold leadership and integrity, the people of the nation themselves established it there.

The wonders of Connecticut industry took a trip across the
Atlantic in 1900 for the great Paris Exposition. There the products
of the mill towns and the factory cities could be seen in perspective and compared with the productions of the rest of the
world. Upon Pratt & Whitney was conferred a Grand Prize;
textiles of Rockville won "highest awards"; there were honors for
electrical machinery, for Yale & Town hardware, for Stanley levels.
The sensational Des Jardins Type Justifying Machine won three
diplomas, a gold medal, a silver medal, and an honorable mention.
Frenchmen critically ogled Connecticut-made tacks and typewriters, Columbia bicycles and Quinnipiac beer, wood veneers and
varnishes, Heublein cocktails and Veeder Cyclometers. A cross
section of Connecticut products was on spectacular display in
the scores of exhibits, but the one that caught the Frenchman's
eyes was the door catch: "The idea of buttons in the door to release the spring lock fairly took foreigners' breaths away," noted

a curator. "They are so used to clumsy keys that our improvements seem magical. . . . French people marvel at the cleverness of American locks. The Yale pattern is practically unknown. Other countries are equally surprised at this particular example of Yankee ingenuity." At Paris the Connecticut tinkerers and manufacturers received their due acclaim.

The state is twenty-fifth in population and forty-sixth in area, but it has accepted the philosophy of John Winthrop. Always responsive to the call of patriotism, Connecticut was dubbed the "Arsenal of Democracy" during World War I when 80 per cent of her manufacturing went directly or indirectly into production of rifles, machine guns, clothing and other articles used by the armed forces. In World War II the "Arsenal" received government contracts totaling over eight billion dollars and facility contracts in excess of another half billion.

The state still produces more than half the nation's hats, firearms, fabricated brass products, ball bearings, typewriters, springs, and counting devices; only one other state exceeds her productivity in machine tools, cutlery, needles, pins, hooks and eyes, snaps and zippers; it ranks first in the production of aircraft engines, firearms, felt hats, nonferrous metal products, silverware, clocks, hardware, insulated wire and cable, office and store machines, tools, and mechanical transmission. And the agriculturists who have turned farms into factories continue to maintain the government surpluses by coaxing their hens to lay twenty-five million dozen eggs every year.

Yankee notions in plentitude there are, but the big operators have made a big business out of them. Any nostalgic native of Connecticut, dislocated in some far corner of the earth, will find his state all around him, and more consolation than William Countryman found at Washington in 1902. Over his head will be roaring an airplane motor representing what is now the state's biggest industry, and stuck in his lapel, he'll be wearing the Yankee emblem—a common pin.

· 15 ·

OUTLANDERS

THE YANKEE HERITAGE REMAINS, BUT YEARS AGO THE SONS OF THOSE who created it began to lose their predominance. To the poor and oppressed of Europe, to political orphans and land-hungry peasants, Connecticut held its doors open wide and sent forth scouts to summon others. They poured in by the thousands—Italians, Irish, French Canadians, Germans, Poles, Jews, Scandinavians, Greeks, Slavs, Assyrians. They came singly and they came in huge families, with their cousins and uncles close behind. For a generation or two they diligently served their Yankee masters in the factories and on the farm, until they too caught the spirit of American democracy and went out on their own to establish family businesses and assert their Connecticut-given rights.

The state couldn't continue indefinitely to be a refuge without losing its old identity. In the back country the big square houses looked about the same, but by the 1920's and 1930's most of them were occupied by newcomers. The principal tillers of soil were the sons of Italy, Poland, and Russia; the tobacco producers were Jews and Russians; on the payrolls of the textile factories were French Canadians, more Italians and Poles, Irish and Lithuanians; in machine factories were expert mechanics from Germany, Austria, and Scandinavia; in wholesale and retail trades Jews, Italians, Greeks, and Armenians predominated. Personal services fell to the Slavs, Italians, and Negroes. Segments of a city like New Britain were a cosmopolitan confusion of foreign tongues, foreign ways, and foreign living standards. Two-thirds of the inhabitants of the state were foreign born or of foreign-born parentage. And among all the forty-eight states, only Rhode Island and Massachusetts had a larger proportion of foreign blood.

In 1938 a WPA study on immigration pointed out that in banking and finance, in the professions and in the higher political offices, the old Yankee families still furnished the leadership, but a generation later, even that statement would have to be modified. The sons and grandsons of immigrants from continental Europe were moving into the high places. Connecticut had crossbred a new kind of Yankee.

The transformation began less than a century back. As late as 1850 nearly 90 per cent of the state's inhabitants were of British descent, and fifty years before that, the percentage was close to 100. There are die-hards who grieve over the change, sentimentalists who sadly recount what might have been if the original Hooker dream of an exclusive club for conforming Calvinists had only been carried out. But neither the die-hards nor the sentimentalists, when faced with the facts, would deny that each foreign group has added versatility and vitality to the growth of Connecticut. The original Yankees unwittingly sketched the blueprints for exactly what transpired. Their invention created industry; their industry created the demand for labor; and their democracy gave the same rewards and privileges to proven worth in labor as it did to proprietorship. The immigrants earned their place.

"It does not matter from whence he come. A man of the right sort can be born anywhere, and if he breathes Yankee air, he inhales the Yankee soul." That was a fair expression of the Connecticut attitude toward early outlanders, whether they were immigrants fresh from Ireland or escapees from the tyranny of the Turks. It took a few generations for the aristocrats to accept the philosophy, and it came hard for the straighter-laced Puritans, but after a while almost everyone warmed to the realization that he had no God-given priority on the rocky Connecticut soil: he was close to being a foreigner himself in a strange land. Year in and year out, the philosophy was put to the test, for there was no such thing as a stable population in any community. The welcome mat, a cheerful greeting, and a dozen fresh eggs always had to be kept handy for newcomers. And they turned into surprisingly loyal neighbors.

All in all, the Connecticut citizenry went about playing host much as they entered into any enterprise—slow to commitment, cautious, shrewd, looking for a slight advantage, keeping a discerning eye out for a sign of fallibility, and through it all, maintaining an amiable front and a hospitable patter. It was fortunate that they had a great deal of early practice on fellow Britishers and embraced the spirit of charity toward immigrants during the adolescent years of Connecticut history, for they were soon to be overrun with hordes from overseas, representing all the brotherhoods of the old country.

The English who kept swelling the Connecticut ranks even after the divorce from Great Britain weren't regarded as foreigners. Often they were kin, and treated as such. The colonists had little experience in absorbing diverse groups. Along the New York border were a few hardheaded Dutchmen who were reluctant to give up their estates. In the 1650's a scattering of Spanish and Portuguese Jews, fleeing the Inquisition, took asylum in the port towns. Indentured Irish servants or slaves frequently arrived as part of the household effects of well-to-do English settlers, and periodically a brave Irish family drifted into the colony of its own volition. From Acadia came French-Canadian deportees just before the Revolution, even a few Czechs appeared at New London in incongruous array during the later Colonial days, and an insignificant number of German deserters from the Hessian army elected to stay on after the war. But until the 1820's or 1830's, free and white foreigners were rare enough in any community to be the subject of considerable attention.

The first real aliens to arrive in large numbers were greeted as errant children, for they represented an utterly different class from the European and Canadian refugees. They were Africans, and they came not as voluntary immigrants in search of American freedom. They arrived in bond—hundreds of them. In the heyday of Connecticut slavery, before the separation from Great Britain, there were six and a half thousand, a modest representation compared to the black population of southern states, but enough to supply most of the families of repute and affluence with at least one dark vassal.

A tavern-keeper without his African flunkies was not regarded as very enterprising. Every farm or shop of standing had its black servant to do the menial chores. To professional men they were indispensable—either male or female slaves to do the odd jobs about the estate or office. Gospel ministers, lawyers, doctors, college

professors particularly counted on their servile darkies. They were
a recognized part of the presidential household at Yale. George
Whitefield, the noted English divine, recommended the acquisition of slaves to his congregation. Governor Gurdon Saltonstall,
himself a minister of the gospel, maintained that under Connecticut law "no man shall put away or make free his negro or
mulatto slave. . . . Such persons as are born of negro bondwomen
are themselves in like condition, that is, born in servitude."

At Hanover, Captains John and Matthew Perkins each had
what was called "a house-full of slaves." John enumerated his
African servants: "Tamar, Ziba, Jehu, Selah, etc. to the number of
fifteen, the best valued at fifty pounds. Probably no larger number
than this could be found in any one family in the county," commented his assessor. But if John Perkins had the largest count
in New London County, Godfrey Malbone, an Oxford graduate
living at Brooklyn a few miles north of Hanover, in Windham
county, far out-classed him. His inventory was in the fifties and
sixties.

Still the attitude toward this by-product of the West Indian
trade was not entirely uncharitable. On the farms the slaves often
dined with the family; they had respectable quarters, lived under
the same protective laws as their white masters, and, like the masters, were required to attend church—in the African corner; though
sometimes their seats were "hidden from the rest of the congregation by a tall board partition." They were catechized at family
prayers and at special Sabbath noon-hour sessions. Accorded privileges unknown in many other parts of America, they occasionally
served as family jesters, fiddle players, and entertainers; were allowed mock franchise in a political system of their own; attended
Negro balls in pomp and borrowed splendor; and when recruiters
for the Continental Army arrived in town "neither the selectmen
nor the commanding officers questioned the color; white and black
if able bodied, went into the roll together, accepted as the representatives or substitutes of their employers."

In churchgoing, amusements, and politics they mimed their
masters, and at towns like Durham, Derby, and Norwich they had
Election Day ceremonies even more colorful and entertaining than
the splendid inaugurals at Hartford and New Haven—an entertaining farce for the white audiences, and a curious make-believe
for the colored participants. By proxy, a supreme state governor
was annually elected—a Negro "of imposing presence, strength,
firmness, and volubility; who was quick to decide, ready to command and able to flog." And as arbiter for his people, he took his

position with grim seriousness, imposing fines and penalties for immoral conduct or grave infractions.

With consummate dignity the governor was inducted into office, and the whole black population for miles around formed an election parade "in which the borrowed horses, saddles and trappings of their masters figured prominently. The Black King, as he was dubbed, was escorted through the streets of the town while the din of fiddles, fifes, drums and brass horns filled the air with an unearthly noise which the blacks themselves modestly described as a 'martial sound.' . . . Puffing and swelling with pride, moving with a slow majestic pace, as if the universe were looking on, the great mogul in a triumphal procession never assumed an air of more perfect self importance." The festivities concluded with a feast as magnificent as the parade—and usually a drunken riot.

However, there were many exceptions to this spirit of amused cordiality toward Negro compatriots. Quakeress Abby Kelley, who worked widely within the state for the antislavery cause, was denounced as "that woman Jezabel who calleth herself a prophetess to teach and seduce my servants." An old letter written by Governor Oliver Wolcott was exhumed and quoted widely: "I wish that Congress would prefer the white people of this country to the black. After they have taken care of the former they may amuse themselves with the other people."

An attempt to create a Negro college in New Haven was condemned. At Puritan Canterbury the greatest clash took place. There Prudence Crandall opened a school for girls in 1831; and it prospered until she admitted a colored girl. It couldn't happen in little Canterbury, but it did. At town meetings she was unanimously and vehemently denounced; her pupils were barred from making purchases at the village store. Spurred on by elders, a crowd of boys maintained a continual uproar outside the school while classes were in progress, and pelted instructor and girls alike with decayed fruit and bad eggs. Miss Crandall was arrested for violation of a new evasive state law prohibiting the instruction of out-of-state children, and the case went from the County Court to the Superior Court to the Supreme Court of Errors before it was dismissed. Congregational officers refused to allow the pupils within the walls of the church; Miss Crandall's barn was set afire; and finally, three years after the school was opened, on the night of September 9, 1834, a crowd of enraged citizens broke into the school, smashed every window and door, and barbarously demolished the structure. That ended Connecticut's first educational experiment in desegregation, but the town fathers met once more in solemn conclave to resolve "that the Government of the United States, the nation with all its institutions, of right belongs to the white men. . . ."

The one stormy incident in Canterbury did more in the end to invoke a widespread charity toward Connecticut Negroes than all the pamphlet-writing and public debating of the emancipation proponents. The reaction against Canterbury gave the colored race a new status and helped to bring an end to slavery in the state.

Hospitality toward other early immigrants was more amicable. Always there was a little condescension and a little aloofness, but once the foreigners had proved their worth, they were accepted as openly as old-timers. Contrary to all rules of chemistry, the Irish got on fine with the Yankees. The two had a common distrust of John Bull, a common passion for tinkering, a common respect for hard work. Those were about the only ties they did have, and the differences were large enough to encourage their keeping out of each other's way in matters ideological. To one another they were as jovial as brethren, and the few flare-ups that did occur were of short duration.

Thomas Tisdall was as good a model as any. He had come over as a British army paymaster, taken to Connecticut ways, and changed camps in 1778, just after he came of age. "Without money, without friends; in not only a strange, but a foreign land; having had but small advantages as to education, and exposed to the illiberal prejudices against his countrymen, he had no resources but a firm constitution, a sound mind, and a consciousness of his own worth." He went to Hartford, modestly took on any odd job that came his way, became a prominent businessman, and a beloved citizen. "A consciousness of the rectitude of his life raised him far above the jesuitical arts of hypocrisy," one of his Congregational friends circumventively explained. "He wished to appear precisely what he was, no more, no less. . . . Mr. Tisdall never attained any distinguished public employment, but he was one of those few who can be conspicuous in a private station, and exalted in the humblest situation. . . . Although not possessed of shining talents, few have had more good sense, or a juster view of life. . . . He was, in the strictest sense, an honest man. . . . It raised him to the rank of one of the most distinguished citizens of this town."

Sturdy Irishmen with the quality of Tisdall helped fight Yankee wars, as ardent in their demands for liberty as the natives. They bought lands they had helped free, made good woodsmen and

superior factory hands; they were the builders of Connecticut
bridges, canals, roads, and dams; they pushed the wheelbarrows
and drove the spikes for the first railroads, and after the potato
famine of 1846 and 1847 their cousins came by the shipload to
form the backbone of industry.

The demand for cheap, hardy laborers in the construction of
transportation facilities brought the Irish; the demand for cheap,
competent mill hands in the textile factories brought the French
Canadians. Their migration to the Quinebaug and Shetucket
River valleys started as a trickle in the 1830's and continued for
eighty years in ever increasing numbers. They took over the spinning and weaving jobs during a period when millowners were
desperate for help. Toward the middle of the century long black
wagons, known as "slavers," toured up and down the countryside,
luring men, women, and children—principally teen-age girls—to
the factory towns, offering free transportation in the bargain. But
the French Canadians needed no such lure. Quebec farms were
yielding scarcely a marginal existence, and as word reached them
that New England was paying hard cash—as much as two or three
dollars a week—for easy mill employment, the families flocked
south.

Unquestionably they were "exploited," but for years they were
more than happy with the new life they found in the neat tenements. It was luxurious compared to what they left behind. The
transformation of Lord's Bridge, halfway up the Shetucket, into a
French-Canadian community was a fair example. For three generations the Lords had operated their remote farm, gristmill, and
tavern on the edge of the river. Then one day in the 1850's, Governor Sprague of Rhode Island made the crossing at Lord's. He
was an industrialist in search of a new base of operations, and he
paused on the bridge for a long time, watching the unharnessed
water and surveying the shore lines. He began making inquiries
about the availability of land, purchased three hundred acres, and
returned later with engineers and plans for a cotton mill nearly a
thousand feet long, sixty-eight wide, and five stories high, all to be
powered by six giant water wheels.

"Suddenly the blasting of rocks and the roar of machinery
commenced," an awed spectator chronicled. "Hills were upset,
channels were dug, the river tortured out of its willfulness, and
amid mountainous heaps of cotton-bags, the rural scene disappeared, and Baltic village leaped into existence. In the course of
five years, more than a hundred buildings, comprising neat and

comfortable houses, several shops, a church, and a schoolhouse, grouped around the largest mill on the western continent, had taken possession."

Into villages like Baltic the French Canadians swarmed, bringing their patois, their Quebec culture, and their Catholicism with them. In Canada for generations they had been struggling to preserve the vestiges of a French tradition against the threat of Anglo-Saxon absorption. That struggle had been built into their character, and it was not given up in their new homes. More than any of the other immigrating nationalities, they were determined to keep the old customs. For necessary shop talk they learned English, but for home conversation they retained their French patois, and the priest, invariably accompanying them, made sure that they kept their distance from Congregationalism.

While the French Canadians were establishing themselves in eastern Connecticut, Germans were moving into New Haven, Bridgeport, Hartford, and Meriden. Recurrent crop failures and economic depressions, the revolutions of 1830 and 1848, the wars of 1862, 1866, and 1870, were more than enough to give them a lust for the life of freedom and plenty in America.

The conversation recorded in Germany by a Bavarian schoolteacher, who emigrated to Connecticut, vividly told the story of their quest. Nor could the break then be made directly; Bavarians started for America under the pretext of going to "Polen."

"Where are you people going?" a sympathic bystander addressed the leader of a migrant throng of seventy peasants.

"To Polen."

"So you are going to Polen, and where do you come from?"

"We come from the Munchweiler County which belongs to the Duchess von der Leyen."

"No, but why did your mistress let you go away?"

"Well, even if she did not want us to, what could she do? The people are so poor that they can lose nothing either way and she cannot put them all in jail."

"No, that cannot be done, but tell me, is your mistress so hard with her subjects?"

"Yes, she is, probably without her will and knowing."

"Why so?"

"She has instituted a new government and a new minister, and since that time the condition has become worse and worse every day."

"Tell me why. . . ."

"Just imagine the Munchweiler County is about two hours long and one and a half hour wide. Within this area are seven villages, that are occupied by about three hundred families. These people have fourteen herds of cattle as hogs, cows, etc. Now take off the meadows, fields and the mistress' possessions, and how much is there left?"

"Not very much."

"Now think of the injustice of these ministers. They keep in this little spot thirteen hundred sheep grazing all the time for the benefit of the administration, and of course what is left for the poor peasant does not amount to very much. Besides this, he has to give one-tenth of all his harvests to the administration. . . ."

"It wonders me that the people don't do anything for their relief."

"Yes, what can they do? One petition after the other has been submitted, and I myself have worked hard for the cause of the people without avail. . . . The peasants cannot go to court with their mistress, as they have no means and are too stupid themselves. So they finally get discouraged and do the same as we are doing . . . Look here, I leave with these seventy people our dear homesteads, our parents, children, our fatherland to go into the new world not knowing where and what we shall find. Do you think, sir, we are doing this just for the love of adventures?"

"Yes, but my dear people, do you believe Polen to be so good a country?"

"It is certainly better than the country we are leaving."

"Oh, I don't know, it is a cold and rough country."

"Dear sir, the German can make a living anywhere, providing he has his freedom. Of course, we are not already there and really don't know what we are going to do."

"Possibly it would be a good idea to go to America?"

"Yes, we may go there."

"That would be a good plan, as America is a fine country."

Over and over again, during the nineteenth century and into the twentieth, the story was the same for hundreds of thousands of emigrants—a story of political oppression, overpopulation, lack of opportunity in the home country, poverty. Whether they came from Bavaria or Bessarabia, Italy or Ireland, they were almost invariably escaping the same circumstances. Such extravagant hopes for relief and deliverance had never before been concentrated on one nation. And the immigrants found America and Connecticut foreign beyond their wildest conception of a foreign country. There was nothing like it in all Europe—the open spaces, the strange system of government, the white churches and noisy factories, the concern over personal morals and deportment that were of no concern where they came from, the unaccountable confusion of warm welcome and opportunism.

The town tavern was the first point of call at a chosen destination. In the old country an inn landlord was a mercenary scoundrel, schooled to calculate at a glance what a guest was likely to add to his revenue, sly, impersonal, churlish to any except the well heeled. In New England he was a receptionist who seemed to rule with a firm hand the "barnacles" on the front porch, the "rounders" at the bar, the villagers who flocked around to greet an outlander. The same price for accommodations stood for everyone, and if the foreigner chose not to make use of the accommodations, the innkeeper gave orders, and the immigrant with his queerly dressed brood of children took off to his backwoods home in a long, bewildering parade of townsfolk, one member of the new family allocated to a cart or carriage. Language barriers were somehow broken, and for days, while the foreigners were being sized up by the curious, they were showered with furniture and fruitcake, harrows and hard cider.

But woe unto the alien who happened to drift into a Connecticut town on the Sabbath, when trade and travel were illegal. "A multitude of peace officers under the various titles of beadles, constables and street-keepers, were posted all day in the streets and avenues to enforce maintenance of that quietude which the statutes enjoined," observed a newcomer more sophisticated than the average, who made the mistake of riding into New Haven on Sunday. "It was their business to take care that no person appeared without-doors during 'meeting time' and on the entry of a traveller into the town, immediately to stop him, lead his horse to stable, and himself to a meeting house. . . . From the growing spirit of commerce in the country at large and the unlucky situation of Connecticut, which renders it the thoroughfare for business, it was found, however, to be every day, or every seventh day, a more difficult task to carry these regulations into effect. . . . Not on the most urgent plea of necessity might an arrival be permitted to clink his profane hoof upon the Sabbatical stones of New Haven. . . . The deathlike dullness and absolute privation of sound which prevailed throughout the day can hardly be imagined. Under the influence of the mournful contrast to the pleasurable tranquility or the light-hearted, innocent gayety of a European Sunday, I really conceived myself abstracted from the world, or rather like the personage who wandered into a petrified city and in the midst of human habitation beheld no sign of life."

With amazing rapidity, however, the foreigners learned to comply politely with the strange Connecticut customs. Rarely was there resistance to the law of the land. But as the nineteenth century advanced there was less actual participation in the customs. The aliens learned to remain aloof and silent when there were conflicts of conscience, and before the conservative Yankees realized what was happening, they were making more and more allowances for their new neighbors. Slowly, subtly, New England laws were altered to take into account the differing convictions of a growing foreign population. The outlanders changed the life of Connecticut more than the invention of all its inventors, the sermons of all its Congregational pastors, the lessons of all its schoolmasters.

In the last quarter of the nineteenth century the invasion was accelerated with a new kind of community aggression: industry from outside was openly solicited. Stamford set a typical pattern. For years the town had been turning out an amazing assortment of products ranging from wool to wire, shoes to spices, carriages to camphor. The "good times" for Stamford began in the 1840's, when Irish immigrants deserted their wheelbarrows along the railroad tracks and took more rewarding jobs as local mill hands and gardeners. But visionaries of Stamford weren't content with "good times"; they wanted better times. In 1879 the Gillespie Brothers, representing a group of tradesmen, published the first "Borough Directory." It looked like a directory, with the lists of industries, streets, names and addresses; but in addition to giving this standard information, it presented a frankly chamber-of-commerce form of advertising, urging New Yorkers to make Stamford their summer resort. It explained that nineteen trains ran every weekday to Manhattan, described the stylish equipages that awaited at the depot for the evening commuters' train, recited the virtues of the steamer *Meta* plying between Stamford and the Battery, pictured the beauty of Stamford parks and its macadamized streets and flagstone walks "laid in all directions by property owners"; it gave details on improvements in gas and water supply, its low-priced commodities, the convenience of its livery stables and hack systems. Accounts of successful industries demonstrated that Collender's billiard tables "were being shipped to every civilized country in the world," that the Advocate cooking store "was making a name for itself," that Yale post-office locks "are in demand by postmasters all over the country." Then it launched into the real purpose of the "Directory"—its bid for New York business capital. "Along the banks of the canal," the bulletin read, "and at the waterside are acres of land where factories could be easily located and tenements for workmen be easily put up. This land can be purchased low if for factory purposes."

The invitation paid off. New York industrialists came for the resort season and stayed on. Their business houses and manufacturing plants soon followed—with the inevitable influx of European workers. Until the 1890's Stamford was a village growing into a big town. After that it boomed into a manufacturing center crowded with factories producing brass and bearings, lacquers and typewriters, deodorants and dry shavers, X-ray tubes and radios, artificial rubber and artificial leather, pianos and printing, boats and blouses. And the example set by Stamford was duplicated in progressive communities throughout Connecticut. No longer did the town fathers wait for the local inventor to build a factory for production of his gadget. There was a quicker way to prosperity by finding an outside capitalist to set up shop. Wherever there was a home for a new factory, there were soon avenues of new tenements for immigrant workers.

The great influx of many nationalities to the state came during the three decades from 1880 to 1910. The Poles, mostly peasants from small farm villages, were distributed widely over the counties of Middlesex, New London, Tolland, and Hartford, as factory employees and farmers. Northern Italians and southern Italians, as different as the people of two nations, poured into the New Haven area, creating compact colonies, converting fine residential areas into slums, and turning the waste lands around New Haven into what President Taft described in 1921 as "productive gardens, magnificent vineyards, fields and orchards rich in fruits and vegetables, which supply the city, thereby releasing it from the burden of importation from Long Island and from the markets of New York, and creating in itself a new source of wealth beyond the fondest expectations of anyone." Quickly the Italians became the largest single foreign group in the state, and besides serving as the bulwark of truck farming and factories, they predominated in wholesale and retail food business, as restaurant-owners, cooks, waiters, barbers, cobblers, tailors, and musicians.

Although a few Jews came in the colonial period, they were not an important group numerically until 1891, when farm colonies were started in Chesterfield and Colchester. The largest concentrations soon shifted to Hartford and New Haven—Jews fleeing persecution and pogroms of Russia, Poland, Germany, Austria-Hungary—and in the two Connecticut cities they made a place for themselves as free and enterprising citizens in trade and com-

merce, retailing and jobbing, law, medicine, dentistry, manufacturing, or as tailors, peddlers, paper-hangers, painters, carpenters.

The Swedes were the most easily assimilated of all the European
peoples, scattered over the state as toolmakers and builders, gardeners and skilled mechanics. The Czechs and Slovaks headed for
the industries of Bridgeport and other Fairfield County cities.
Lithuanians became important employees of the metal industries
in Waterbury, Hartford, and New Britain. The oyster fisheries,
textile plants, light metals, and small shops of Norwalk and Bridgeport absorbed the Magyars. As unskilled factory workers, the
Ukrainians concentrated in Ansonia, Derby, Shelton, and Seymour.
The vast Sikorsky plant at Stratford induced many of the mechan-
ically-trained Russians to settle there. Danish and Norwegian
skilled mechanics, toolmakers, dairymen, and truck farmers found
homes around Hartford, New Haven, and Bridgeport.

Greeks went to the same three cities, as well as Stamford. Hundreds of them had operated coffee houses in Europe and naturally
gravitated to the same kind of trade in Connecticut, as owners of
restaurants, candy shops, fruit stores, and ice cream parlors. Skilled
metalworkers from Switzerland took up residence principally in
Torrington and Waterbury, Finns spread over Windham County
on the best farms they could buy. And as assiduously as the Finns
adhered to farms of their own, the Armenians clung to little self-
established business enterprises, virtually monopolizing the rug
trade around New Haven, Hartford, New Britain, Bridgeport, and
Thompsonville.

Each of these nationalities added something to the stature of the
state. If they found difficulty in reasserting their native culture—
and they almost always did—they at least added color, character,
and a cosmopolitanism to the community. They gave a new perspective to the neighbors in both the big cities and the small towns
—an awareness of the conservatism and confinement in which the
old guard had too often taken satisfaction. Enlightenment came in
small things which led to larger. The neighbors were invited to
try out the sweat house which invariably adjoined the Finnish
farm, and in the exhilarating banter that followed came an understanding of Finnish folkways or an appreciation of the suffering
under Russian domination. The Italian family down the street
was given a cold shoulder until the flavor of the homemade wine
or the emotion of the homemade music were sampled. A stere-
opticon lecture on Swiss scenery, a Saturday evening at a Polish
dance, attendance at a French-Canadian wake, a workout with a
prewar German turnverein aroused enough curiosity to inspire

further investigation of a foreign culture. To stimulate the cause of internationalism, native festivals were promoted here and there, such as the annual Scottish celebration at Greenwich, where members of bagpipe bands vied for prizes and contested for honors at tossing the caber, dancing flings and reels; or the Ukrainian festival at New Britain put on by Russian immigrants with choruses, peasant costumes, and presentation of native dramas.

In much less than a century Connecticut made a complete swing. Those to whom the welcome had once been extended became the hosts. Foreign names of every European nationality were written across the metropolitan store fronts and rural mailboxes. The Greek Orthodox church was just one block over from the old Congregational meetinghouse, and "Popery," denounced so vehemently by Puritan prophets, was busier on Sunday morning than Protestantism. A kosher market was next door to the A.&P., which had formerly been the village general store. Even in the small-town post office, the postmaster pushed newspapers in a half-dozen languages through the window. And at Grange meetings there were asides in Yiddish, Polish, French, and Slav dialects. Connecticut, which had long before tried so hard to restrict itself to the language of Congregationalism, was a melting pot as heterogeneous as Brooklyn or San Francisco. Descendants of the old families had become a distinct minority group, and the Poles and Slavs, the Italians and Irish, the French Canadians and Czechs were developing into a new breed of Yankees as assertive as the Yankees of English origin. Eventually, a homogeneity would be found among them—perhaps.

· 16 ·

HOSTS

GEORGE WASHINGTON SLEPT THERE, LAFAYETTE SLEPT THERE, AND SO did Ben Franklin and Daniel Webster. Until Duncan Hines came on duty as the patron of approved beds and board, the benediction of one of that quartet stood for more than a century as the manifesto of fine hostelry. Washington put up at Porter Tavern in Union City, Naugatuck, and the tavern keeper never let the fact be forgotten; he spent the night at Sheldon's in Litchfield with similar results; was entertained profitably at Sun Tavern in Fairfield on October 16, 1789, at Eaton's in Plainfield, Caulkins' in East Lyme; stopped for supper at Clark Tavern in Milford, ordered bread and milk, and when the serving was placed before him with a pewter spoon—all that the management could afford —he ordered the *garçon* to go to the minister's and borrow a silver one. On the reputation the visitor established for him, Clark could soon afford silver spoons.

The General dined at Leffingwell Inn, Norwich; breakfasted with Martha at Webb's Tavern, Stamford, in 1775; planned the Yorktown campaign with Rochambeau and De Ternay at Hospitality Hall in Wethersfield during May, 1781—and in his honor the bedchamber where he slept still retains the original wallpaper. An epidemic of "Washington Taverns" broke out in the wake of every tour made by the Father of the Country. On back roads and across village greens, up and down the Connecticut valleys, are ancient public-house portals he is alleged to have entered— and, if he didn't, Lafayette, Franklin, or Webster were soon granted the honor. Nothing brought quick fame to a tavern like one of these notable visitors.

Tavern keepers were the official Connecticut hosts, appointed by the civil authorities, and licensed at the discretion of the Court of Common Pleas. They were men of at least local distinction; they had to be, in order to retain their prerogatives. Often the host was a member of the legislature, more often commanding officer of the town militia; occasionally he held a combination of titles like selectman, road surveyor, tax collector, constable, and town moderator. John Adams portrayed him "as happy and as big, as proud, as conceited as any nobleman in England, always calm and good-natured and lazy, but the contemplation of his farm and his sons, his house and pasture and cows, his sound judgment (as he thinks) and his great holiness, as well as that of his wife, keep him as erect in his thoughts as a noble or a prince." Collectively, the innkeepers were Connecticut's committee on hospitality. They set a good standard, and they had no advertising agents other than their satisfied customers—or the famous ones they may have conjured up.

Entertaining tourists, transients, commercial men, and village revelers was a big business then, considering the population; it is an enormous business now, worth some fifty million a year in out-of-state traffic alone—thanks not entirely either to George Washington or Duncan Hines. And, whereas the state anted not a shilling in 1800 to promote the tourist trade, over $100,000 is budgeted annually in these plush mid-twentieth-century days just to beckon visitors from Vermont or Florida or Nevada and other far-flung places. In affairs as diverse as agriculture and education, industry and road construction, the government took on the post of opulent philanthropist, and the recreation business is no exception to its largess. The Development Commission with its corps of professional advertisers and invitation-senders is the host supreme, making life easier for the successors to the innkeepers: the managers of tourist courts and resort hotels, the owners of roadside restaurants, and the housewives with a spare bedroom. If Thomas Hooker had suffered a premonition that the state he was helping to found would one day go into the ephemeral business of playing host so enthusiastically, he might have proved a more reluctant host himself.

For many a decade the New England tavern keepers ably per-

formed a noble function, unique in the annals of hostelry. For all
comers the tavern was the reception center and its keeper the professional town greeter. If anyone could be credited with establishing a legacy of camaraderie toward outlanders, it was he. He was
host to the passengers of every stagecoach, and to the occupants
of most of the phaetons, shays, curricles, chariots, whiskies, lan-
daus, wagons, and carts that passed through town until the Civil
War. He knew the first names of all the draymen who made bi-
monthly trips to downstate trading posts. He knew the youngsters
in his own town and those in neighboring towns, for it was in his
ballroom that they congregated on Friday evenings to play forfeits,
rim-the-thimble, grind the boule, cut-and-tailor, woo-a-widow.

No situation, however foreign, fazed him—or his wife. Their
business was to know all the answers, and they readily gave an
answer though it might occasionally veer from the truth. And they
were as adept at performing personal services. Both husband and
wife assiduously shied away from admitting ignorance on how
to carry out any request, whether it was for mixing a rare potion
at the bar or for preparing a favorite dish. The assignment was
accepted with a nod of confidence, and if the end product inspired
complaint, they were ready with a gracious explanation of how the
drink or dish was "ordinarily served in these parts."

At a remote tavern, before tea was a common American beverage, two English gentlemen paused for their customary afternoon
refreshment, trustingly handed the landlady a half-pound tin of
their favorite herb, and requested that tea be served them. Grandmother took the tin to the kitchen, puzzled over the contents for
a time, then turned the whole half-pound into a pot. She soaked
and boiled the leaves, threw out the water, and served the residue
as "a dish of greens, most carefully prepared, with a small piece
of boiled pork resting daintily in the middle."

Room accommodations also missed the standard of perfection,
though experienced itinerants were inured to the lack of privacy.
For Washingtons and Daniel Websters a reputable tavern had
one fine chamber, heated, well furnished, provided with a feather
mattress, and even decorated with expensive wallpaper that began
to come into vogue after about 1750; but the rest of the chambers
were as bare as barracks, often with three or four beds to a room,
and each bed expected to accommodate up to four guests. Lone
women travelers were forever complaining about being assigned
a bed in the same room with strange men. And a guest who retired early could anticipate being aroused a dozen times during the
night when the landlord intruded, candle in hand, to escort new

bedfellows or roommates to the common dormitory. Then at an early hour the interruptions started all over again, as prospective stagecoach passengers were aroused for three- or four-o'clock departures.

Teamsters were wise in foregoing bedroom privileges. For fifty cents a night, including meals, they were permitted to roll up in their own blankets on the floor of the parlor or taproom. On a big night as many as thirty snoring guests would be encamped around the hearths of the common rooms, and to them all the landlord was as affable as he was to the refined company occupying the chambers above.

But any such modest shortcomings as crowded beds and indifferent provender were more than compensated for at the bar. Service there was qualitative as well as quantitative—not too much beer or cider: those were "small drink"; the tavern clientele preferred flips and punches with a substantial base of brandy, whisky, or Barbados rum. Around the bar gathered wedding parties and funeral parties, student groups and "bees," vestry meetings and ministerial ordinations, stragglers from Methodist camp meetings, and the biennial assemblies of the "milish," who always topped off their regimental training with a few social hours. All were fortified in the spirit of unbounded hospitality. Until the 1840's, when talk about the benefits of abstinence became a fad, everybody drank. For the more sedate ladies, the landlord produced his best wines or hard cider, and if there were an infant in arms, he prepared a nightcap of mulled hard cider, widely approved for its soothing properties—"a beverage which would kill a modern babe."

Ministers of the gospel set the example when they stowed in their cellars a winter's supply of from twenty to forty barrels of cider. But for ordinations, the ministers commonly took their celebrations to the tavern, and one jolly group of twenty-four ran up a bill—exclusive of rum and bitters—for twenty bowls of punch, twelve bottles of wine, five mugs of flip, two mugs and three bowls of toddy. And they also ran up a record for hang-overs, for on the same bill appeared a charge for twenty-four dinners, and quite relevantly only three breakfasts.

Parties of this nature, however, never seemed to compromise the reputation of an inn. Samuel Goodrich, famed for his instructive stories for the young, commented that the tavern at Ridgefield, as an institution, "ranked second only to the church," and he accorded its keeper a recommendation almost fit for a pastor, picturing him as "a hearty old gentleman who united in his single person the varied functions of publican, postmaster, representative, justice of the peace, and I know not what else. He besides had a thrifty wife, whose praise was in all the land. She loved her customers, especially members of Congress, Governors, and others in authority, who wore powder and white-top boots and who migrated to and fro, in the lofty leisure of their coaches. She was indeed a woman of mark."

Until the village store came of age, the tavern as a place of congregation was indeed second only to the church. It was the exhibition hall and temporary lodging for all secular events that could not fittingly be held at the meetinghouse. Usually it contained the second-largest assembly room in town, and with a slight rearrangement of chairs and benches the room was successively a dance hall, theater, courtroom, convention auditorium, and music chamber where "consorts" were given. The tavern was described as: "The resort at once of judge and jury, of the clergy and laity, of the politician and the merchant; where the selectmen came to talk over the affairs of the town, and higher officials to discuss the higher interests of the province; where royal governors and distinguished strangers were entertained alike with the humblest wayfarer and the meanest citizen; where were held the carousels of roistering officers, and the midnight plottings of muttering stern-lipped patriots; where, in fine, the swaggering ensign . . . the frowning Puritan, the obnoxious Quaker, the Huguenot refugee, and the savage Indian chief from the neighboring forest might perchance jostle each other in the common taproom."

Besides exhibitions of biblical beasts in the back shed of the inn, there were demonstrations of cassowaries and other rare birds, learned pigs, learned horses, deformed beasts and persons, pictures, "prospects," statues, clocks, puppets, mechanical contrivances, lightning rods, and electrical machines. With the sanction of the Church and the community, lotteries were drawn in the parlor—lotteries for roads, bridges, charities, debts, and educational endowments. The lodges of Freemasons met there, literary clubs, projected corporations and companies. Many of the first insurance offices were in taverns, as well as the original business exchanges, and the upper rooms doubled as a jail when occasion demanded. Activities often spilled over onto the village green in front, where, for instance, were held the first balloon ascensions, advertised grandly as "archimedial Phaetons," "Vertical Aerial Coaches," "Patent Foederal Balloons."—"Persons of a timid nature will find nothing to terrify them in the ascent."

The four holidays—Election in May, the Fourth of July, Thanks-

giving, and Training Day—always brought excitement and a throng
to the porches and parlors. Christmas and Easter were all but ignored "owing to the old grudge against Episcopacy," but the pompous parades for Election Day formed at the inn, the participants
in Thanksgiving turkey shoots gathered there, and the best vantage
point for Fourth of July speeches and fireworks was the tavern
porch.

For local hilarity no other holiday quite matched Training Day.
From the pre-Revolution period until the Civil War it was a
riotous spectacle. "The marching of the troops, and the discharge
of gunpowder, which invariably closed the exercises, were glorious
and inspiring mementos of heroic achievements, upon many a
bloody battlefield," recalled a participant. "The music of the drum
and fife resounded on every side. A match between two rival drum-
mers always drew an admiring crowd, and was in fact one of the
chief excitements of the great day."

According to the lawbooks, the purpose of Training Day was to
keep reserve forces in trim for battle, but over most of the decades
war was too remote to make drill a matter of urgency. There was
more clowning and cutting up for the amusement of onlookers
than there was serious military practice. To the brisk orders, "Put
your right hand on the firelock," "Put your left hand on the firelock," "Poise arms," "Blow off the loose corns," "Shoulder! hoo,"
any awkward gyration might be expected.

The day started off in a light spirit with privates en masse making the rounds of officers' residences, where they received their reward in the form of well-laced mugs; nips were in order during interruptions of drill; at noon there was a scramble for the tavern
bar; and by mid-afternoon few in the sweating brigades felt any
pain in their maneuvering, marching, and wheeling. Usually the
exercises degenerated into a field day, with races and wrestling
matches, contests in marksmanship, quoits, and cricket. The whole
show was designed for the entertainment of the crowds that used
the inn porch as a grandstand.

As early as 1704, Madam Knight took note of the confused objective of these military exercises. "On training days," she wrote,
"the Youth divert themselves by Shooting at the Target, as they
call it, (though it very much resembles a pillory) where hee that
hitts nearest the white has some yards of red ribbon presented
him, which being tied to his hattband, the two ends streaming
down his back, he is Led away in Triumph, with great applause as
the winners of Olympiack Games." A century and a half later,
neither the color nor the confusion had changed appreciably.

Townsfolk, however, didn't have to wait for a celebration or a holiday to gather at the tavern. The "barnacles" were always there, exchanging the latest gossip, everlastingly whittling, and swapping yarns. All in all, the Yankees displayed a fairly satisfactory sense of humor there, though it tended somewhat toward the sadistic: the best stories were always at someone's expense. They were as corny as they were abrasive, and with every rehearsal became more so. Something new was added with each recounting, and the raconteur could count on an hilarious response so long as there was one person present to whom the tale was novel. Ministers of the gospel brought back fetching sagas from their conferences, legislators from political conclaves, farmers from their trading expeditions; and the one inexhaustible source was the peddler, who deemed it his social function to circulate wit, and, whenever possible, to cast a particularly pungent narrative with characters known vaguely and unaffectionately to his audience.

Excessive drinking was the perennially favorite subject, particularly after the adversaries of alcohol began to muster in the 1850's. There was the story of the Danburian tippler, for instance, who had signed the pledge eighty-three times, declared himself the champion, and was looking around for anyone to challenge his record.

Yarns about the shortcomings of invulnerable pastors were almost as popular. Professional storyteller Samuel Goodrich perpetuated the account of a fidgety pastor who was all but dismissed from his pastorate because of an inclination to smile and titter at the wrong moment, and any minister with too much artificial cheer was likely to have the tale affixed to him. Charged with unseemly conduct, Goodrich's pulpiteer was finally brought before a clerical board, to whom he gave his explanation:

"Well, gentlemen," said he, "the fact charged against me is true. . . . A few months after I was licensed to preach, I was in a country town, and on a Sabbath morning was about to enter upon the services of the church. Back of the pulpit was a window, which looked out upon a field of clover, then in full bloom, for it was summer. As I rose to commence the reading of the Scriptures, I cast a glance into the field, and there I saw a man performing the most extraordinary evolutions—jumping, whirling, slapping in all directions, and with a ferocious agony of exertion. At first I thought he was mad; but suddenly the truth burst upon me—he had buttoned up a bumble-bee in his pantaloons! I am constitutionally nervous, gentlemen, and the shock of this scene upon my risible sensibilities was so great, that I could hardly get through the services. Several times I was upon the point of bursting into a laugh. Even to this day, the remembrance of this scene—through the temptation of the devil—often comes upon me as I am ascending the pulpit. This, I admit, is a weakness, but I trust it will rather excite your sympathy and your prayers than your reproaches."

That was a typical nineteenth-century classic, and its renovations at the tavern bar or among the porch "barnacles" were multifarious. The more people that could be the butt of a joke the better. For well over a century the town of Windham was unable to live down its exhibition of hysteria brought on one night during the French and Indian Wars when water was drained from a nearby pond and the army of frogs inhabiting it expressed their resentment in an earth-shaking chorus of croaks. The resounding complaints from the frogs were mistaken for Indian war cries, and the town, quite understandably, panicked.

The most coherent story of what actually happened was told, with a dash of cold water, years after the event by an eyewitness, one Sinda, a Negro maid, in the household of Windham's Squire, Colonel Eliphalet Dyer: "Well it was June, I think, and the weather was very hot," she recalled, "and Master had drawn off the Pond to fix the dam. When he came home he did not think of nothin'—by and by when it became cool, there began to be a rumble, rumble, rumble in the air, and it grew louder and louder and louder, and seemed to be like drums beating in the air. Well, it was in the old French War, when our men had gone to Belle Isle or Canada to fight the French and Indians, and some guessed it was the Injuns having a powwow or war dance on Chewink Plain, and we should be killed in the morning. But Master and Colonel Elderkin and Mr. Gray mounted their horses and rode to the top of Mullein Hill, and as the pond was a little over there beyond, they found out what it was—and the scare was over."

But the ribbing at the expense of Windhamites was far from over. Out of all the excitement and confusion, no two people could agree exactly on what had occurred; each preferred to embroider his own details, and the extended details were rushed by post chaise and peddler from tavern to tavern, where they were further stretched.

"Antiquity relates that the elephant fears the mouse," wrote the Reverend Isaac Stiles of Woodstock to Colonel Dyer; "a hero trembles in the crowing of a cock—but pray whence is it that the croaking of a bull-frog should so Belthazzarize a lawyer? . . . I hope, sir, from the Dyerful reports from the Frog Pond, you'll gain some instruction."

By the time Samuel Peters got the story, he could picture terrified townsfolk streaming naked from their beds, armed to the teeth and making passes at one another with their weapons, until it was discovered that the enemy was comprised of millions of frogs migrating overland from a dried-up millpond to the Willimantic River—a battalion of amphibians blocking the road "forty yards wide for a distance of four miles."

Britisher Thomas Anburey on his journey through New England picked up approximately the same version but discredited the width of the highway, and generally sympathized with the citizenry for their distress on grounds that American frogs were terrifying and hideous reptiles with "thirty different voices among them, some of which resemble the bellowing of a bull."

An anonymous poetaster jumped to the conclusion that there had been a mighty battle between vengeful man and barking bullfrogs and the attacking frogs capitulated only because their enemy used bean poles:

> Those lusty frogs they fought like dogs,
>   For which I do commend them,
> But lost the day, for want, I say,
>   Of weapons to defend them.

"There was no evidence that the frogs had engaged in battle," countered Ellen Larned, Windham County's own historian. "They filled the air with cries of distress . . . continuous and thunderlike. . . . Those who went to the pond found the frogs in great apparent agitation and commotion. . . . There had been no draught, and the pond was abundantly supplied with water. . . . A din, a roar, an indescribable hubbub and tumult seemed to fill the Heavens and shake the earth beneath their feet. The night was still, cloudy, and intensely dark. Sky, village and surrounding country were shrouded in thickest blackness, and thus the terrified listeners were thrown wholly upon conjecture and imagination. . . . The astounding clamour continuing till the breaking of day. . . . Some mysterious malarial malady, some deadly épizoötic, had probably broken out among them."

In 1874, nearly a century and a quarter after the event, a historian deduced that "Few incidents occurring in America have been so widely circulated. Let a son of Windham penetrate to the uttermost parts of the earth, he will find that the story of the Frogfright had preceded him."

Attached inseparably to the drawn-out storytelling—with both the narrator and his audience—was the inevitable Yankee practice of whittling. No man ever appeared at the tavern or before a group anywhere else without his indispensable weapon. An active pocket-knife removed the stigma of idleness, and while the yarns were un-raveled, whistles, candlesticks, kites, spoons, spatulas, and faultless replicas of wooden nutmegs took shape. It was doodling of an elemental and creative order. There were always little heaps of shavings for the landlord to sweep away—and storekeepers, black-smiths, housewives, and even the janitors of legislative chambers had the same chore. The talents of any craftsman and engineer first came to light under the spell of a glistening blade. Whittling led to the shaping of useful gadgets, to invention, and to the modeling of inspired short cuts in industry. Storytelling, shingles, and penknives were fundamental to the predestination of Con-necticut. "Why are our axes, knives, hoes, spades, plows, the best in the world?" asked Samuel Goodrich. "Because—in part at least —we learn, in early life, the alphabet of mechanics theoretical and practical—whittling. Because nearly every head and hand is trained to it, . . . we gain a greater proportion of prizes for use-ful invention, than any other people."

Taverns themselves supplied a liberal share of topics for gossip, for with all the comings and goings, accidents and misfortunes were inevitable—missing funds, missing persons, missing reputa-tions. Things got out of control occasionally in the taproom, and the cajolery of the past master at diplomacy, mine host, couldn't stay a brawl or solve the mystery of what went on in his upper rooms. In his effort to be gracious, he too was taken in by thieves and impostors, swindlers and innocent-looking fugitives, or was unable to detect their wiles until it was too late.

At Coventry, Captain Vaille of Vaille's Inn spent a delightful evening with a personable itinerant, saw him to bed in his finest room, only to find the next morning that his guest had flown after "rifling the house of a calico gown, a camlet cloak, three pair of shirts, six dollars from a fellow traveler"; and not only that, he had somehow managed to tiptoe down the stairs during the night with every item of furniture in his room, including the four-poster. "It is to be hoped for the honor of human nature," ran the broadcast in the next week's newspaper, "that people will be vigilant in ex-posing this crime, as well as detecting future villanies; and that tavern keepers, in this western part of the state especially, would not put too implicit confidence in strangers, for they know not at what hour of the night their effects and beds may by the thief be taken away."

At Canton, the ghastly phantom of a headless horseman rode for years along one shadowy stretch of highway to memorialize the disappearance of a French paymaster during the Revolution. He left Hartford for Saratoga with two saddlebags of gold earmarked for French officers in the Continental Army. He was traced as far as Horsford Tavern, and no farther. The innkeeper always vowed that he had departed "safe and sound," but, a Canton historian adds, "It was probably heavenward, for no evidence of lateral travel was ever found."

The towns began to lose their official and affable tavern hosts in the middle 1800's. Along with turnpikes and stagecoaches, the wayside inns were victims of steam cars and steamboats, and most of them reverted to the big, rambling farmsteads that they had been in the first place. If the tavern were near enough to a railroad station, business continued to flourish, but the office of landlord had lost its prestige. Temperance agitators had altered appetites for alcohol, and the church parties found a more decorous atmosphere in the meetinghouse basement and town hall.

More and more the tavern keeper depended on excursionists and vacation people from the city. He ran a livery to meet the trains; or, to fill in the gap until horsecars and trolleys came, some enterprising teamster rigged up an omnibus to transport guests and salesmen from one tavern to the next. Norwich had its "Hourly" running between Bean Hill and Norwich Landing, and the driver always intended to maintain an on-the-hour schedule, but there were so many stops and waits en route for the convenience of passengers that he never made more than two trips a day. He was loved and lauded for his "accommodatingness," and was finally ascribed a few immortal lines in place of an epitaph:

> The old lady's man was the "Hourly" man—
> If you can't start now, he'll wait till you can.
> He carried them slow, but he carried them sure
> 'Twixt their uptown homes and the Landing store,
> With a gay calabash, and half of a pair
> Of thorough-broke colts (rather worse for wear),
> Whose prominent points showed a wanting of hay,
> Scarse made up by "baitings" of grass by the way.

In omnibuses and private carriages, on puffing trains and steamboats came delegations of the first summer tourists, and as they took up residence, Connecticut hosts rose to the occasion by delivering raspberries and radishes to their back doors, spending vast sums on community fireworks displays, and crowding them with social invitations. Along the Sound on choice promontories between Stonington and Stamford the new kind of immigrants erected filigreed chalets, called "bungalows," and sighed with the ecstasy of discovery: "Imagine a great leviathan, stranded upon a pebbly beach, around which remnants of former forest grew, with green grass almost to the water's edge, and a bay of sapphire stretching before you for a mile, where it is merged into the darker waters of the Sound. Consider, then, the rock upon which the bungalow is built as that leviathan; upon its gray back stands the house twenty feet above the water. The winds buffet it, and the angry waves thunder in impotent fury against its rocky base, the hurricanes lash it with the spray of the surf in vain. From the windows of the house you can look out on stormy days, as you might from the windows of a lighthouse, observing the tremendous workings of the sea and wind. In stormy weather, one hears musical notes swelling like an organ through the wind-harps swinging in the breeze. Then as they madly turn, they blare as the wind increases, a strange weird accompaniment to the shrieking demons of the sea. . . ."

On the shores of estuaries, along the Thames, the Connecticut, the Housatonic, similar cottages appeared, and Connecticut entrepreneurs demonstrated what good hosts they could be by starting steamer runs for excursionists. Inland farm families appropriated adjacent scenic points, and on lumber wagons piled high with homemade sailcloth tents, vegetables, and babies, went to the seaside and riverside for a week of luxury camping, clamming, fishing, and excursioning.

To hilltops—long since gone back to scrub growth—ardent nature fans beat paths and erected ramshackle huts for summer occupancy, in what was then "rarefied atmosphere." The owners were the envy of the countryside. Professor William Blake, who knew the great scenic spots of the world from his travels as scientist and mining engineer, chose Hamden's Mill Rock as his Shangri-la, "a rugged and picturesque spur of East Rock, which site affords most extensive and delightful views of New Haven Harbor, Long Island Sound and the surrounding country." Sight-seers tramped for miles to take in the spectacle of his magnificent stone hut and a whole village of striped tents he put up each summer for his family and guests.

One by one the hundreds of inland lakes were discovered too, and dainty cottages with landings, clumsy rowboats, strings of hammocks, and towering flagpoles graced the shores. Gradually a few of the tavern owners, whose business on the highways had petered out, tested their skill as landlords of spacious shore-front boarding houses.

Upland towns capitalized on their pastoral charm, advertised it in the big cities, and became hosts to a growing throng. For years Stafford Springs was the society center for ladies of wealth who could boast of a fashionable ailment. They came to take the waters, celebrated from Vermont to Virginia—medicinal waters that the Indians had first made famous as an eyewash and a tonic "for livening the spirits." Various doctors had analyzed the waters over the years, and discovered "a solution of iron, sustained by carbonic acid gas, a portion of marine salt, some earthy substances, and what has been called natron, or a native alkili." Stafford was declared to possess "one of the most efficacious chalybeate springs in the United States."

As early as 1765 Stafford water acquired national notoriety when it was credited with "an effectual cure of a most obstinate cutaneous complaint which had completely baffled all medicinal skill, and resisted all other applications." Jasper Hyde made the most of it. He erected a palatial three-story hotel with porches fore and aft, wide enough to accommodate scores of rocking chairs and hammocks; he built elegant bathhouses alongside the Willimantic River, served the water unsparingly in his cut-glass goblets, and drew halt and ailing socialites from every part of the country. Stafford Springs was a famous resort for over a century.

Villages like Litchfield, Salisbury, Thompsonville, and Pomfret didn't require medicinal springs as an aid to their hospitality. The scenery and the salubrious air were enough. Pomfret, which had all but bankrupted itself in trying to keep strangers outside its precincts in the 1700's, was entertaining the most distinguished summer clientele in the state a century later. Aristocrats of Philadelphia, Providence, New York, and Boston began elbowing into Pomfret shortly after the Civil War to establish pretentious estates with names like "Glen Elsinore," "Rathlin," "Hamlet Lodge," "Dunworth," "Pen-y-bryn," "Ingleside," "Wyndlawn," "Oberthal," and "Hoelfeld." There was a great deal of snob appeal in Pomfret. A spokesman for the town shrewdly apologized for a story circulating in the 1890's that "prominent and fashionable strangers on seeking admittance to one of these quiet little Pomfret establishments, have sometimes stood aghast on calmly being asked for their credentials." Without denying the accusation, the spokesman assured the public that "hitherto Pomfret's leaders have erred on the safe side. To such as have any claim for recognition, they are hospitality itself."

As special attractions, there were the Pomfret Club with tennis and croquet, bowling and archery; Pomfret Hall for dances, musicales, plays, and operettas; Pomfret Library Association; the Pontefract boat house on the Quinebaug; Roseland Park; and Tyrone Hill Tower. Owners of the sumptuous residences boasted of their acreage in rose gardens, their greenhouses and stables, "ivy-clad portals," "a lawn as velvety as that of Magdalen College quadrangle and an avenue of trees as beautiful as Addison's walk on Christ Church Meadows," rustic bridges and arbors, stained glass windows by Tiffany, "a small but picturesque rubblestone tower with thatched roof and overhanging vines."

The "seasons" at Pomfret were short, as one townsman haughtily explained—"at their heights, only in June and September; the interim will most likely have been spent at the seaside by the gayer city folk." In 1896, newcomers trying to crash the taut curtain of society were told that "the main and only thoroughfare of Pomfret street is already filled. Future residents must, therefore, take to the hills."

The tourist lure of the Farmington valley was the tower on Talcott Mountain north of Simsbury. In 1810 Daniel Wadsworth, foremost citizen and benefactor of Hartford, decided that Talcott was the most beautiful spot in the state of Connecticut. The sheer cliff and the modest lake at the bottom gave it a Rhineland flavor, and all it needed was a Rhenish tower and a villa to complete the illusion. His hillside residence, "Monte Video," and a fifty-five-foot hexagonal tower on the summit of the promontory were his answer. It was the first mountaintop tower built in the United States for public use, and the incredible sum of $175,000 went into Wadsworth's establishment. During the next decades no European visitor had seen America until he had climbed the eighty steps of the spiral stairway to view the sweep of the Connecticut and Farmington valleys; and soon most of New England felt the same. Every celebrity from Daniel Webster to Buffalo Bill made the climb and usually penned a poem or an ecstatic paragraph about the experience. John Whittier soaked up the view and wrote his "Monte-Video":

> *I love to gaze from thy towered brow*
> *On the gloom and grandeur and beauty below,*

When the wind is rocking thy dwarfish pines,
And thy ruffled lake in the sunlight shines. . . .

Besides entertaining the renowned, Wadsworth was host to most
of the picnickers and naturalists within a range of fifty miles.

The tower was blown down thirty years after it was erected, so
Mr. Wadsworth, a few years before his death, built another, ten
feet higher. This burned in 1864, and was soon replaced by its new
owner, D. W. Bartlett, Washington correspondent for the Springfield *Republican*. Bartlett incorporated landings, outlooks at different levels, a refreshment stand, and an adjacent summit hotel.
People came to Talcott by the thousands. Whole towns arrived
en masse for community field days. It was the Eiffel Tower of
Connecticut. In October, 1877, a genial enthusiast left the note:
"To Mr. Bartlett, who has robbed the historical command, 'Away
with him to the tower!' of all its terrors.—MARK TWAIN."

The tower and the estate were sold by Bartlett to millionaire
Robert Hoe, famed printing press manufacturer, on the assumption that the new owner would develop the mountaintop into a
broader recreation ground for the public, but Hoe had other ideas.
The gates were closed, the tower entrances locked; it was strictly
a private possession. But Bartlett was too good a host to endure
the discomfort of the No Trespassing signs. To the southeast in
1889 he built a substitute Talcott Tower, this time with a seventy-
foot height—an establishment with all the refinements of a hilltop
picnic ground, including pavilions, tête-à-tête arbors and bowling
alleys, and he even persuaded the N.E.R.R. to make a special stop
at the foot of the hill for Hartford revelers. Until long after the
excursionists began to express a preference for motor cars and mileage rather than summit views, Bartlett Tower stood as a monument to the era of Rhenish romanticism.

Sophisticated towns caught a touch of nostalgia for the past
during the years just before World War I and demonstrated it by
playing host to one another, and to former residents in Old Home
Week celebrations, dressing up in colonial and Victorian costumes
to show their loyalty to ancestors; they chipped in generously for
extravagant displays of fireworks, with special set pieces depicting
local historical scenes, and they produced elaborate pageants dedicated to invoking nostalgia. Darien, for example, subscribed over
ten thousand dollars for its 1913 pageant. Five hundred adults and
children were cast as Indians, early settlers, English and colonial
soldiers, Tories, cowboys, clergymen, sailors, and commuters. In a

natural amphitheater between the Gorham estate and the Good Wives' River, thousands from Connecticut and New York witnessed the spectacle—nine episodes including "Men of Wethersfield," "The War with Norwalk," "The Mill at the Landing," "Raid on the Middlesex Church," "The Coming of the Railroad."

But these attempts to recall the past, colorful and exciting as they were, somehow missed the mark in appealing to youngsters and newcomers. They weren't colorful or exciting enough. The effort was short-lived. To the new generation romanticism of the past was slow and stale; the realism of the immediate future, with speed on the broader highways, invitations to other places, the lure of less homely entertainment in the big cities, and thrilling talk of participating in a great war to end wars, was more important than re-establishing contact with bygones. The future was to be on a grander scale than anything of the past.

State government caught the grand-scale spirit, and went into the profession of playing host in a big way by acquiring scores of state parks and forests for public use, operating camps and beaches, stocking streams for guest fishermen, and leasing thousands of acres for guest hunters. The great castle of actor William Gillette at Hadlyme became a shrine and picnic area under the Park and Forest Commission; and the forty-two-room Harkness mansion at Goshen Point was made into a public museum containing the fine collection of Brasher wild-life paintings, while the shore front was converted into a park and beach for the disabled. State bodies like the Highway Department, the Development Commission, the Board of Fisheries and Game, the Park and Forest Commission no longer were organized primarily as law-enforcement agencies; they were professional hosts extending warm invitations rather than issuing cool restrictive warnings.

The old wayside tavern—still advertised as "colonial" regardless of its age or inheritance—is the one institution where the present is most likely to cross paths with the past. The candlelight is mellow, the host is gracious, the porridge is delicious—and expensive—but no colonial landlord would recognize the place as the hearty, raucous, unsanitary tavern he operated; nor would he ever be able to hear the warning tally-ho above the screeching of the traffic racing under the neon sign.

· 17 ·

ESCAPISTS

IT WAS PARTLY RESTLESSNESS, PARTLY THE URGE TO FIND GREENER
pastures—pastures that never would be quite the right shade, in
any location. Good immigrants made just as good emigrants. They
couldn't stay put. Claustrophobia was a chronic affliction. The restraints of society could not be endured perennially. So the Yankee
pioneer was off to the woods again as soon as too many people
began crowding in on him—and his conception of a crowd might
be a dozen neighbors. The patterned life was not for him.

So quickly did the pattern form itself that families often moved
four or five times in a single generation—from Windsor to Woodstock; to western Massachusetts; to Vermont; to the Genesee valley, the Susquehanna, or Ohio. In each place a modest homestead
was erected, lands were cleared, church membership and a good
reputation established; then word of a better prospect farther to
the north or west filtered in, and the restless spirit won out. Perhaps a daughter was left behind in the village graveyard, and a
married son stayed at the old farm to carry on; the others waved
their farewells and tramped away behind a burdened oxcart.
Prompted by the urge to escape an irksome constraint, or dissatis-
fied with the climate, they plunged deeper and deeper into the
hinterland.

"I remember well the tide of emigration through Connecticut, on its way to the West during the summer of 1817," wrote Samuel Goodrich, who, with other New Englanders, experienced the famine of 1816, when severe frosts occurred in every month of the year. "Thousands feared or felt that New England was destined, henceforth, to become a part of the frigid zone. . . . A sort of stampede took place from cold, desolate, worn-out New England. . . . Some persons went in covered wagons—frequently a family consisting of father, mother, and nine small children, with one at the breast—some on foot and some crowded together under the cover, with kettles, gridirons, feather-beds, crockery, and the family Bible, Watts' Psalms and Hymns, and Webster's Spelling Book. . . . Others started in ox-carts, and trudged on at the rate of ten miles a day. In several instances I saw families on foot—the father and boys taking turns in dragging along an improvised hand-wagon, loaded with the wreck of the household goods—occasionally giving the mother and babe a ride. Many of these persons were in a state of poverty, and begged their way as they went."

The population of Connecticut was just over a quarter of a million in the early 1800's, but already close to three times that number had migrated. For every individual who remained, three had gone over the hill. In many a town, people moved away faster than others moved in. The turnover was constant. Hundreds poured into Connecticut annually from Europe or from other regions to fill the lots and farmhouses left vacant, but the majority of the émigrés were native. Establishing a big family was a social duty and an economic necessity. Households with ten or a dozen children were normal. Youngsters were encouraged to marry early and produce offspring in like number. A seventy-five-year-old grandfather with a head for arithmetic could count fifty or sixty grandchildren, and his dividend in great-grandchildren easily totaled three or four hundred. Mr. and Mrs. Breed, who had eleven children spaced in age from twelve to thirty, in 1650 had begotten a tribe of almost half a thousand by 1725. The thousands, multiplied many times, accounted for the migrant throng.

Always they left Connecticut for more productive land and more productive opportunity, ignoring the opportunities that existed where they were, ignoring counsel for less extravagant exploitation of the soil. If there had been a little skill in management, there was plenty of land in Connecticut, and plenty of opportunity. The quest was a disguise for restlessness, wanderlust, and the desire for social latitude. Thomas Hooker furnished a variety of feeble excuses for shifting his congregation from Cambridge to Hartford in 1636, and gave himself away with the remark: "The minds of the people are strongly inclined to plant themselves there." The Harvard meadows weren't broad enough to contain the kind of independence the Massachusetts itinerants craved; nor were the Connecticut meadows to be any broader.

Within four or five years after the first Massachusetts emigrants had arrived on the Connecticut River and Long Island Sound, segments were roving farther inland and to offshore islands. They sought escape on river tributaries, on the Shetucket, the Thames, the Housatonic, and in remote woodlands to the northeast; by 1660 eleven independent villages had taken over the best sites on Long Island, while others were exploring hideouts like Fishers and Shelter Islands. Thirty families pulled out of New Haven and went to Newark; in fact, New Jersey openly recruited New England settlers, to the dismay of New Haven leaders, though New Haven, like other Connecticut settlements, continued to swell prodigiously from the influx of newcomers and the growing families. Amateur economists estimated in 1680 that the colony had already reached its saturation point. With a population of some twelve thousand all the good land had been occupied and "what remaynes must be subdued, and gained out of the fire as it were, by hard blows and for smal recompence." Migration was the only answer they knew. People had to move on.

King Philip's War and the series of European conflicts between 1675 and 1713 had strong repercussions among the American colonies in curtailing migration, but, despite the wars, delegations of pioneers were always in transit. A typical group from Fairfield created the town of Fairfield, New Jersey, in 1697. And as soon as there was a temporary lull in the efforts of Europeans to egg on the Indians to plunder New England frontiers, the expansion began in earnest. The proprietors of new towns in western Massachusetts were Bay State men, but most of the families who made up the communities had old Connecticut addresses. From villages like Canterbury, Suffield, Enfield, Wethersfield, West Hartford, and Granby, scores of families took up residence in the Berkshire wilderness. Pittsfield, Massachusetts, was a portion of "crowded" Wethersfield transplanted; Williamstown was a composite of half a dozen Connecticut River towns. But the escapists of the early 1700's did not all stop in the Berkshires; many went farther west, to Putnam County in New York, and as far afield as South Carolina and Georgia.

The French and Indian War again called a halt to any substantial migration, but that war, like others to follow, was indirectly responsible for promoting a new outbreak of chronic wanderlust,

for in the long overland marches across New England and New
York, Yankee soldiers, always with an eye for a land bargain in a
new country, made discoveries all along their routes. And on the
way back from the conquest of Quebec in 1759, they made circuitous detours of exploration, tramping far off the prescribed war-
paths in search of possible homesites.

Governor Wentworth of New Hampshire, claiming most of the
vast area between Maine and New York, was more than cooperative in offering townships on a come-and-take-it basis—provided
the lands were immediately occupied and a proportionate acreage
cleared within a reasonable number of seasons. Such bargains no
enterprising Connecticut Yankee could resist. Citizens from Lebanon, Plainfield, and Lyme packed up, moved north with their be-
longings and their town names to constitute Lebanon, New
Hampshire; Plainfield, New Hampshire; and Lyme, New Hampshire. During the one year 1761 eighteen townships were granted
on the east side of the Connecticut River, sixty on the west. In the
decade and a half between 1761 and 1776 seventy-four towns were
planted in the disputed territory of Vermont, settled almost entirely by restless Connecticut migrants, and many more towns
would have been established had it not been for the enigma over
the actual jurisdiction of Vermont—whether it belonged to New
Hampshire or New York or Massachusetts, or was to be an independent republic.

The men from Connecticut eventually took matters into their
own hands, and with brazen aplomb in January, 1777, declared the
New Hampshire Grants "forever hereafter to be considered as a
free and independent jurisdiction or state; and forever hereafter
to be called, known and distinguished by the name of New Connecticut, alias Vermont." But there were no aliases for the home-
town names they appropriated for new Green Mountain communities, such as Windsor, Stamford, Plymouth, Pomfret, Norwich,
Hartford, Salisbury, New Haven, Canaan, Chester, Bristol, Berlin,
Colchester, Cornwall, Woodstock, Windham, Manchester, Guilford, Fairfield.

The Green Mountain Boys for the most part were ex-Connecti-
cut boys. The Allen brothers—Ira, Ethan, Heman, and Zimri—
with some of their Salisbury neighbors, bought up vast areas, including whole towns, in land speculation. The discontented, the
religious deviates, the rustic individualists, the impatient, and the
unpopular were the first to leave a Connecticut community, and
Vermont was big enough to absorb them. Brother Joseph Marshall,
a blunt and indiscreet Separatist, was dismissed from his Canter-

bury pastorate, and moved at once to more congenial surroundings and a more receptive audience in Vermont. Arlington became the refuge for unpopular Connecticut Episcopalians. Men who had small chance of acquiring political notoriety in their native state moved to the Green Mountains and became prominent government spokesmen. But even in this sanctuary for dissenters the predominant faith was Congregational, the laws were those of Hartford and New Haven. When the organization of a town was finally shaken down, it was a model of Connecticut propriety.

Vermont permanently adopted its "alias" as a state title to avoid confusion with another New Connecticut that was being shaped out of Pennsylvania wilderness. Although no protest had been raised when William Penn was granted a charter that overlapped the western bounds of Connecticut, a few land-hungry die-hards had never forgotten that Charles II in 1662 had reserved for the colony a strip extending all the way to the Pacific Ocean. In 1750 a group of Simsbury citizens brought the issue into the open for the first time in almost ninety years by petitioning the Assembly for a town grant west of New York. Immediately it started a flurry of other petitions—too many for the legislature to continue to ignore. In every tavern taproom and blacksmith shop, free, fertile land in the valleys of the Delaware and Susquehanna became the current topic of conversation. The 1753 session of the legislature was greeted with six petitions, including one bearing over 150 signatures of residents in Windham, Farmington, Canterbury, Plainfield, and Voluntown. They requested the right to purchase from the Indians a tract sixteen miles square, covering the Wyoming valley on the northeast branch of the Susquehanna River.

From Suffield came another petition for Pennsylvania land, signed by 68, complaining that their town was "grown full of Inhabitants so that a great many must unavoidably move to Sum other Place"; from Norwich came a similar demand, plaintively setting forth how burdened they were with "Great & Expensive Family's & being Confined to very Small Inhiritances." From Stonington and Greenwich, from an assortment of individuals seeking compensation for services in the French and Indian War, came others; but by the middle of the summer of 1753 most of these petitioners had merged into one group who called themselves the Susquehanna Company, and in articles of association, drawn up at a meeting in Windham, agreed on a common purpose "to Spread Christianity as also to promote our own Temporal Interest."

Simultaneously a "Journeying Committee" of seven was sent out to appraise the Wyoming country; negotiations with the Indians were started; and Eliphalet Dyer of Windham was dispatched to London to determine the policy of the Crown. Dyer was described by John Adams as "long-winded and roundabout, obscure and cloudy, very talkative and very tedious, yet an honest, worthy man who means well and judges well." Perhaps he was too obscure or too honest in London, for his mission was a total failure. And it marked only the beginning of grim conflict over western lands between Great Britain and Connecticut, between the Indians and armed settlers, between the Pennsylvanians and impetuous leaders of the Susquehanna Company. Undaunted by either Eliphalet Dyer's rebuff or the massacre of their vanguard, the spreaders of Christianity and promoters of temporal interests went ahead with their plans, though the impatient men of Windham, who had already sold their farms, had to put in months and years of embarrassed waiting.

Because of the long delays, a second group, the Delaware Company, got the jump on them, and in 1760, holding a charter approved by the Connecticut legislature, laid out three townships along a ten-mile stretch of the Delaware River, reaching eight miles inland. In the middle township eighty lots were marked off and the proprietors announced that thirty cabins, three log houses, a sawmill, and a gristmill had been erected; twenty men had already taken up residence, and a hundred families would join them the following spring. Lots of two hundred acres were available to any and all.

From the big talk it appeared that half of land-hungry Connecticut was ready to move to Pennsylvania. And in 1762 a colony of two hundred actually trekked west to the Wyoming valley—an area seventy miles long and covering two degrees of longitude. Nothing but hostility and the sorriest hardship awaited them. The Pennsylvanians had whetted their tempers, and the Indians had sharpened their tomahawks. The next year a few survivors of the frightful massacre plodded back to Windham, and for six years the valley lay desolate. But once stubborn Yankees were touched with emigrant fever, there was no permanent cure. In 1769 and 1770 they tried again, only to be driven out by the Pennsylvanians. Still they would not yield the territory to which Charles II had given them a clear title more than a century before. Fortified with larger numbers and legislative support they surged back, and in 1774 the Connecticut Assembly, in a bold move, asserted its right to New Connecticut in Pennsylvania by converting the entire Delaware and Susquehanna regions into a single Connecticut town, naming it Westmoreland, and, for purposes of jurisdiction, attaching it to Litchfield County. Its two thousand inhabitants were to have all the rights and privileges of any town within the established limits of the colony, including four representatives in the General Assembly.

The year 1774 marked the high point of pre-Revolution excitement in the evacuation of Connecticut proper for New Connecticut in the west. Silas Deane of Wethersfield, ardent supporter of expansion and eager crusader for independence from Great Britain, visualized an extension of Connecticut all the way to the Mississippi—within the limits of its original charter. In a burst of enthusiasm, he painted a glowing future: "Supposing from the Westernmost boundaries of New York to the Mississippi it is Eight Hundred Mile & the width Seventy, there Will not be Two Hundred Acres of Land to Each person in this Colony and allowing our increase to be justly Estimated, We shall from Connecticut alone soon people the whole of it in less than one Century. . . . Looking forward, we stand amaz'd at ourselves, or rather what We must inevitably be, & that very soon."

Other fugitives from land-poor Connecticut villages preferred the more temperate climate of the deep South and found their spokesman in Phineas Lyman of Suffield. Phineas had distinguished himself in the French and Indian War, had been promoted to major general in the provincial troops, and felt that he was as entitled as anyone to a territorial grant in recognition of his services. He spent the best part of a decade traveling back and forth to London, and "after experiencing great difficulties and delay, . . . he succeeded in obtaining a grant of an extensive tract of land upon the Mississippi in the vicinity of Natchez." The word was not long in getting about. "Military Adventurers," his company was styled, and overland through Tennessee, down the Ohio in flatboats, down the Atlantic coast, through the Caribbean and Gulf of Mexico traveled over four hundred families in 1773 and 1774, all bound for Phineas Lyman's colony in Mississippi. But, somewhere in the processing of his petition in behalf of the "Military Adventurers," something had gone wrong. The thronging families converged on the mouth of the Mississippi only to learn from the governor of West Florida that the deal was off; no lands were available.

However, the "Adventurers" had gone too far to be halted by such gubernatorial dictation. Defiantly the emigrants, representing practically every town on the Connecticut River, swarmed up the Mississippi as if it were theirs, and near the old French town of

Natchez established a typical New England village, complete with Congregational pastor and town meeting. And the squatters were doomed to a fate almost as decimating as the Susquehanna catastrophe, though here it was pestilence that struck. A few Connecticut family names still survive in the Natchez region, but most of the colony was wiped out during that first year. Lyman sent his son back to Suffield for the rest of his family, but his wife died on the voyage south, and he died before the sons and daughters arrived. Without their intrepid leader, the colony had small chance of survival; and then the Revolution broke in the north to prevent replacements from filling the empty cabins.

Locally the departure of so many citizens from Connecticut village folds was loudly bemoaned, but by philosophical contemporaries the mobility of the state was extolled as a noble attribute. "What is a more interesting and sublime object," questioned the idealist, "than to observe the progress of civilization—its rapid inroads upon the domains of the wilderness, driving back its primitive inhabitants . . . the growth of towns—the sudden rise of villages, and the general extension of social improvements? . . . The enterprise of the people of Connecticut has disclosed itself in various channels, but more conspicuously by the spirit of traffic and emigration. . . . The current of emigration from this State has swelled to a torrent. Obstacles that seemed insuperable barriers to the inroads of civilization have been converted into fruitful fields by the bold and active enterprise, and the hardy and persevering industry of Connecticut emigrants. . . . It may very well be said that the 'wilderness has blossomed like the rose' and become as fruitful as the gardens of Hesperides. . . . The spirit of traffic has long formed a trait of the character of the people of this State. Enterprise, directed into this channel, has produced the most important results. It has led thousands of our citizens abroad. Prompted by a spirit of pecuniary adventure, they are to be found in every clime and among every people; no hazards have deterred, no obstacles discouraged, and no disasters impaired the boldness. . . ."

The Revolution, like previous wars, did bring a temporary cure to the wanderlust. A few escapists made the most of a good opportunity to return to England, a scattering of optimists carried out their plans to move south or west, and fifteen more towns were incorporated in Vermont, but any great migration was halted. Between the Green Mountains and Lake Champlain settlements were evacuated, and another Indian massacre all but wiped out Wyoming valley, leaving the vast precinct of Westmoreland virtually deserted. But even before Cornwallis surrendered his sword at Yorktown, new schemes were afoot, and with the end of hostilities, the pioneer rush away from Connecticut started on a scale unknown before.

No longer were there royal or parliamentary restraints from Great Britain; settlement of charter titles to overlapping territory was a more tangible problem for states and a federal government to resolve, without the necessity of looking to a vacillating monarch. Frontiers were now in the Alleghenies and beyond them. The road leading west from Windham toward Buffalo was heavy with traffic; the military highways paralleling the Connecticut River into New Hampshire and Vermont were appropriated for the great exodus. Back to the deserted towns along Lake Champlain and in the Wyoming valley went the Revolutionary evacuees, and a few who had chosen to wait out the war in their frontier villages moved farther north and west when they saw the onrush of newcomers. Everywhere in the path of the movement, law and order were in a state of disruption. Yankees were moving on for a second or third time, and often on the roads into the wilderness they met up with old neighbors they had known long before the Revolution in peaceful Connecticut villages. Once more they became neighbors in towns five hundred miles from their original homes. The treasury of the new United States was too empty to repay its war veterans in cash, but there was plenty of land to give instead; beyond the western boundaries of the seaboard states the federal government became the real estate agent and the protector against Indian depredations.

"On to the Genesee!" was the byword at taverns, Sabbath houses, and kitchen gatherings. From practically every village in the state, the adventurers and farm folk went in thousands to plant Congregational meetinghouses and Connecticut village greens through western New York all the way from Binghamton to Buffalo. "Out to the wilderness by way of the Mohawk from Albany, up the valleys from the Susquehanna, settlers poured into every western county by single families, by twos and threes, and by whole colonies. . . . Connecticut must have been beggared of inhabitants, so fast did hundreds of her families make their way into New York." Land speculators had one of their magnificent moments in history. Oliver Phelps of Suffield, with Nathaniel Gorham, was credited with purchasing two million, two hundred thousand acres, "probably the greatest land purchase, or speculation, ever made by two individuals in the United States." Subdivided, sold, and resold, it provided little empires for families like

the Wadsworths of Durham and Hartford, whose estate was meas-
ured by miles rather than rods in Geneseo and Avon.

What happened at Whitestown was being repeated throughout
the fertile valleys. Hugh White of Middletown in 1784 was among
the first to penetrate beyond the Mohawk Flats into the "gloomy
abode of wild beasts and savage men." "For the first four years
after the commencement of this settlement," reported his biographer a quarter of a century later, "its progress was rather slow and
discouraging; yet in 1788 it contained nearly 200 inhabitants. . . .
This township . . . comprised then almost all the western section of that state, which in 1810 contained 280,319 inhabitants;
being about 20,000 more than the whole population of Connecticut; so that Judge White . . . lived to see the dreary wilderness,
into which he was the first man to penetrate, and which once bore
his name, contain a greater population than his native state."

Timothy Dwight toured the region a few years later and estimated that three-fifths of the population of New York was of New
England origin. "It is questionable," he exclaimed, "whether mankind has ever seen so large a tract changed so suddenly from a wilderness into a well-inhabited, and well-cultivated country, as that
which extends on the Western road from the German Flats to the
Genesee River. . . . The mass of the population forms . . . a
most important accession to the State of New York; continually
increasing both in numbers and value."

Dwight marveled at how Connecticut traditions and New England traditions predominated in the Genesee country: "They are
ardent, enterprising, resolute, patient, active, industrious and persevering. Many of them are sober, orderly, moral, and friends of
learning and good government. Many of them are intelligent, ingenious, acute, versatile, ready when disappointed in one kind of
business to slide into another, and fitted to conduct the second, or
even a third, or fourth with much the same facility and success, as
if they had been bred to nothing else. A considerable number . . .
are pious. Others, amounting to a considerable number, are restless, fond of changing their places of residence to a sickly excess:
uneasy in regular established society; clamorous about political
measures, haunting places of public resort; talkative, especially on
political subjects; negligent of their own business, and regardless
of Religion. These are the foresters, . . . the pioneers who march
in front of the army of substantial farmers, destined finally to
colonize the country. The number diminishes as colonization pro-
gresses, driven on by farmers who purchase their farms."

Windham was the first stopping point on the "Great Road"

leading west to Albany, to the Genesee, and places beyond, and
during those years, the town saw more traffic than it was to witness
again for over a century. The traffic grew heavier as other roads
added to it. One observer at Albany during the winter of 1795 in
three days counted twelve hundred sleighs "bearing sturdy New
England people as settlers to the Genesee Valley."

Bright dreams of a New Connecticut in Pennsylvania faded as
they had in Vermont, although Ethan Allen had even volunteered
to bring his Green Mountain Boys to the rescue. "Crowd your settlements," he had advised the Susquehanna leaders, "add to your
numbers and strength, procure firearms and ammunition, be united
among yourselves. . . . Nor will I give up my interest to usurpers,
without trying it out by force of arms." The Company followed
his advice literally. Connecticut crowded into the Wyoming valley in defiance of threats from the peace-loving Quakers, and
time and again armed conflict appeared imminent; but in 1799
both sides finally accepted a compromise, and 1745 land certifi-
cates were reluctantly issued to the Connecticut settlers for a total
of almost 300,000 acres they had occupied. The emigrants from
Windham and its satellite towns gave up Yankee citizenship for
allegiance to the Penns.

With the general cession of western lands to the federal government at the end of the Revolution, most of the states relinquished
ancient claims to extensions reaching toward the Mississippi, but
not Connecticut. Tenaciously the state held on to a tract extending halfway across Ohio—its Western Reserve, some 3,300,000
acres—a little empire almost 1,000,000 acres larger than Connecticut itself.

Late in the afternoon of August 5, 1795, it went up for auction
to the highest bidder. "One million dollars!" bid Elkanah Watson,
and a flurry of other million-dollar bids came simultaneously.
Silas Pepoon raised it to one million, one hundred thirty thousand.
John Livingston outbid him by several thousand, then withdrew
his offer. "One million, two hundred thousand!" proposed Oliver
Phelps of Genesee fame, who already owned more land than any
other private individual in North America. "Going, going—sold to
Oliver Phelps for one million two hundred thousand." The hammer rang down on the largest, quickest land transaction in the
history of Connecticut. Oliver Phelps and his associates fell into
possession of Western Reserve. They were organized into the Connecticut Land Company; the proceeds from the sale went into
a permanent endowment fund for education; explorers set out to
survey the new acquisition; and a tide of emigrants started to flow

into Ohio. Western Reserve became New Connecticut the Third.

Veterans of the Revolution formed the majority of the migration—many of them Connecticut natives who had paused for a few years in western Massachusetts, Vermont, or New York. Proprietors from the Bay State often took the lead, but Connecticut usually had more representatives than any other state in the wagon trains and raft flotillas that slowly labored west. Marietta was the first town to be settled, led by the tireless minister from Killingly, Manasseh Cutler, who had taken a parish in Salem, Massachusetts. Under his leadership a huge tract was purchased in southeastern Ohio and shares distributed among the proprietors, with 640 acres reserved for schools, another 640 for religious institutions, and two whole townships for a college. Formation of a Congregational church was the first order of business upon arrival of the new pioneers, and in a few months a typical New England town was taking shape on the shores of the Ohio. Marietta was the model for scores of similar towns. Greenwich, Connecticut, planted another Greenwich in Ohio, Plymouth a new Plymouth; General Moses Cleaveland of Canterbury laid out Cleveland. By 1800 there were settlements in over a third of the 103 townships of the Reserve; by 1812 New England villages were scattered over half of Ohio.

All of the emigrants were not as enthusiastic about New Connecticut in the west as was the Reverend Dr. Cutler. One of his townsmen, Theophilus Knight, set out skeptically with a group of young Killingly scouts in March, 1788, to make first-hand observations on whether the terrain over the Alleghenies was what the promoters cracked it up to be—whether it was actually any better than the farm land of Windham County.

In a rambling letter, he reported: "I then, according to my roving disposition, left friends to travel into the Western country. There were eight of us young men that set out and had four horses and a wagon, and put our clothes, farming tools, provisions into it, and off we set and had a merry journey through the country . . . Sometimes we were as merry as people need to be. Sometimes we met with disagreeable things, bad luck, bad traveling, etc., etc., but upon the whole, we did pretty well. . . . I think that the best and most fertile country for so large a tract of land that I saw in my travels was the state of Pennsylvania. That is a level, fine country, but I did not find the inhabitants so agreeable as our New England people. The women do a great deal of the farming work. I used to see great splay-footed Dutch girls . . . spreading dung, carting wood, swingling flax. . . . The ladies did

not strike my fancy at all, but, however, I do not consider myself
under any obligations to have any concern for them. So I traveled
through the country without any great anxiety about the matter.
. . . I was about thirty miles beyond any of the states, up the
Muskingum river, where I saw a good deal of good land and a
good deal of poor broken land that I did not like very well. I was
there in the city of Marietta two seasons, so that I saw something
of the climate and liked it very well, and many other things, but
upon the whole look on every side, I thought that the country was
not so much better than any other that it would pay a man for
carrying a large family to such a wild wilderness country as that,
and inhabited with savages and wild beasts of the forest. . . ."
Theophilus was among the minority who elected, upon his return,
to remain in the rugged hills of Killingly.

Most of the speculating in western lands was kept on a remarkably high business level in the hands of public-spirited gentlemen
like Oliver Phelps, Nathaniel Gorham, and prominent political
leaders of the state, but with the contagion in land fever running
wild, there were bound to be unscrupulous dealers—and a great
many sorely deluded dupes. Yankee bargainers had uncanny intui-
tion for scenting sharpers, but their lust for land sometimes let
them in for a fast swindle.

Virginia land laws were loose enough to permit remarkably careless transactions, and over Connecticut, as well as over the rest of
New England, flocked a corps of glib real estate salesmen from Virginia late in the 1790's, carrying plausible maps, title bonds, and
an irresistible patter. In the Connecticut River towns alone, two
scalawags, Bogart and Walmsley, sold a million Virginia and West
Virginia acres, sight unseen—presumably the fallowest, most productive acres on the continent, crossed by fine roads and settled by
congenial people. Then purchasers gradually began to compare
notes, soberly question not only the worth of the land but also the
validity of the title.

Judge Erastus Granger of Suffield, who had had a good bit of
experience in land speculation on his own, was finally employed
by the purchasers to make a trip of appraisal into the Southland.
Across the Potomac, into the Shenandoah valley, and over the
mountains to the west he went. He was so delighted with the first
introduction to Virginia hospitality that he wrote back to one
eager speculator: "I have every reason to be satisfied with the treatment. . . . People are liberal in their sentiments; courteous in
their manner and sincere in their attachment. I really wish, my
friend, I could see you settled here; real worth and merit are re-

spected by all classes of people. . . . Nothing would prevent your election to any office you chose. . . . Provisions are in abundance; planters wealthy. . . . It is the healthiest part of the country I have ever seen; the limestone water and whiskey agree with me."

Optimistically the Judge left the civility and the limestone water behind him, ventured into the lands in question, and soon had reason to retract his first observations. Everywhere he went, he was treated with suspicion and contempt as he interviewed county surveyors and magistrates. He plied them with astonishing quantities of whisky, and in return was occasionally given a chance to check their books; he found them quite unintelligible. Up and down, over trackless mountain barricades, he traveled for over two thousand miles. A "main road" between Warm Springs and Randolph, mentioned by Bogart and Walmsley, turned out to be a blind path with a few blazed trees over a cliff; the congenial settlers were "lawless bandetti," fugitives "from the face of the law," using the impenetrable highlands as their asylum. One fifty-thousand-acre plot was in an area where there was "no vacant or unoccupied land." The survey of an estate of 114,000 acres began "at a poplar tree of Westfalls Mill Run," and he could find no one who might estimate within four or five miles where that poplar tree was.

The reports Judge Granger sent back to anxious absentee landowners were indeed cheerless: "If Milton had described the fight between Michael and the rebel angels to have been upon this planet, I should have concluded that the action took place upon your land on the Big Sandy river, and that the mountains and hills with which they fought had never been leveled, but ever since have remained in the same rough and deformed state as they did at the end of the battle.——My clothes are torn off my back, and I am ill from the effects of this trip, besides losing seven toenails. ——The greater part of the people of this valley are the most indolent and unprincipled set of beings I ever saw. . . . I know not on whom I can place confidence; there is no way of gaining their confidence save by plying them well with whiskey.——The fact is, the land was never surveyed, nor was there ever a chain carried upon it.——The hunters tell me that it is a shocking place; rugged mountains, frightful precipices, ridges of land covered with laurel, quite impassible, and here and there a solitary wolf howling his midnight yell and looking aghast at the deformities of nature. . . . I am convinced that no part of it will ever permit of its being settled." A travel-worn Judge returned to Connecticut; Bogart and

Walmsley went to jail; and the would-be emigrants to Virginia stayed home.

Others were more fortunate in their invasion of the South. To Mobile, Alabama, with a Connecticut retinue, went Lewis Judson of Stratford in the 1790's to establish the distinguished firm of John Forbes and Company. Josiah Blakeley of New Haven joined him later, after a six-year residence in Cuba. Joseph E. Sheffield of Southport, who had founded the Sheffield Scientific School at Yale, became a leading Mobile cotton merchant. Moses Austin left Durham for Philadelphia, failed to find his horn of plenty there, and went on to Virginia in search of a site for lead mining and smelting. Unsuccessful there, he changed his address in 1798 to Missouri, where he established the town of Potosi, set up a furnace and mill for making sheet lead, built a sawmill, a flour mill, and a store, helped to organize a bank, and having reached his limit, journeyed to Texas, where his son Stephen became a founding father of the Lone Star State.

Gospel ministers and missionaries abetted the cause of emigration more assiduously than they abetted the cause of maintaining a stable home front. With them, moving on was a good excuse for spreading the gospel. Apostle Hooker had set the example that they would never dismiss. "To Christianize the heathen in North America and to support and promote Christian knowledge in the new settlements of the United States" was the platform of the new missionary society that the Congregational Churches organized in 1798. Indians were not the only infidels on their list for conversion; they had in mind fully as much the callous dissidents who were the first to move into a new country.

The Connecticut *Evangelical Magazine* became the voice of the society, and it was so outspoken that the missionary movement was soon duplicated by other churches throughout New England. Missionaries went forth to carry the gospel to Ohio, Mississippi, Missouri, and, as settlers later moved into Iowa, Illinois, Washington, and Oregon, the Bible bearers were close behind them. Frequently they led the stampede into new lands, with a substantial segment of their congregations as company. Before a Yale graduate, the Reverend Asa Turner, set out for Iowa, he made an urgent plea that groups of families should accompany home missionaries to assist in "fixing the character of towns . . . spreading the moral power of New England, and effectually aiding to save the West."

These carriers of the Word were no physical weaklings. To hold their own they had to be jacks-of-all-trades, as handy at raising a barn as phrasing a proper prayer, quick with a gun, steady on horse-back. Representing the Connecticut Missionary Society, Thomas Robbins reached "Poland, Trumbull County, alias New Connecti-cut" on November 24, 1803, after a lonesome three-months' jour-ney of over eight hundred miles. His diary jottings, made as he went from settlement to settlement as an itinerant pastor, were only a faint indication of the demands placed upon him: "Preached all day; the meeting was serious and solemn; one per-son fell. . . . Rode with a company to Morgan, sixteen miles, without a house; snow and mud very deep. . . . A great fall of snow; it is now more than two feet deep on the level . . . very cold. . . . Worked with some of the people building a large bridge. . . . Preached all day; a good number of people; some pretty violently exercised. . . . Worked considerably, helping the people to clear a piece of ground for public uses. . . . Assisted in writing a notification of the incorporation of trustees for a college. . . . Rode to Vienna; attended the raising of a house, the first frame erected in the town. . . . Preached in the forenoon; after-noon Mr. Smith, a Baptist minister, preached, after which he bap-tized three persons in the river; A.M. I baptized a child . . . Can-field. Serious people here apprehensive of inroads by Methodists. . . . Conversed and disputed with the Methodist preacher; fear he is a dangerous character. . . . Rode through the woods to Cleveland. . . . The people rather loose in principles and conduct. . . . The most of them have not heard a sermon or a prayer in eighteen months. . . . Married a couple of persons. . . . Held meeting in an open new house; some of the people quite disorderly. . . . Wrote records for the church here. . . . Worked a little helping to raise a log house. . . . Rode to Hartford; twelve fam-ilies have lately moved into this town from Hartford, Conn. . . . Had conversation with a stupid, cross infidel; preached to a good number of people. Reproved some for trading on the Sabbath. . . . Worked some with the people on the road. . . . Met in a barn with very convenient accommodations. . . . About half the people came in just as I finished the sermon; I sat a few minutes, prayed and preached again. . . . Assisted in towing into the river a vessel of twenty tons' burthen. . . . Rode to Warren. . . . Some people here who have lately arrived from Connecticut feel pretty gloomy. Assisted in raising a heavy and valuable frame for a mill. . . . Assisted in laying a plan for a bridge. . . . Visited sick. . . . Rode to Somers. . . . Wolves something troublesome. . . . Preached and administered the sacrament; being disappointed of wine, made a composition of brandy, vinegar, water and brown sugar, which answered well." Robbins returned to his "dear native state" broken in health at the end of one year.

What had been so idealistically lauded as "the spirit of traffic and emigration" was not often so ordained to compassion and self-denial as the efforts of missionary Robbins. Escapists might set forth with high ideals and become diverted en route. The most incorrigible of all the Connecticut wanderers was John Ledyard. At the age of twenty-one he went to Dartmouth, class of 1776, in the prayerful hope of getting the classical education people told him he would need to serve as a missionary to the Indians. His father had been a sea captain out of Groton, and John inherited the paternal mobility. He lasted just one term at Hanover. Endurance of hunger, exhausting marches, and the hostilities of man came easy to him, but the confinement and discipline of academic Dartmouth he could not endure.

Secretly he constructed a fifty-foot canoe and, without a shilling in his pocket, made his getaway down the Connecticut to Hartford and New London. There he shipped as a sailor to the Mediterranean, starting the weirdest odyssey in which any Connecticut globe-trotter ever participated. He accompanied Captain James Cook on his third and fatal voyage around the world. In the Vancouver region he did enough exploring to see the unprecedented possibilities of fur trade in the far Northwest, and all but succeeded in interesting Philadelphia merchants in a great industrial venture there. His plans for a foot expedition across the continent from Washington to Virginia were foiled, so he substituted a walking trip across Siberia.

Then, as an agent of the Association for Promoting the Discovery of Interior Parts of Africa, "mad, romantic, dreamy Ledyard" explored the sources of the Niger, took a caravan trip from Cairo into the interior of Egypt, and won the acclaim of his British sponsors. Among his friends he numbered kings, ambassadors, Thomas Jefferson, and John Paul Jones. And he accumulated almost as many enemies. Empress Catherine of Russia assured him that "if he was found again in the Russian dominions, he would be hanged."

In general, however, he managed to establish easy rapport with feminine acquaintances. "Women in all countries are civil and obliging, tender and humane," he acknowledged. "With man it has been otherwise. In wandering over the barren plains of inhospitable Denmark, through honest Sweden and frozen Lapland, rude and churlish Finland, unprincipled Russia, and the wide-spread regions of the wandering Tartar, if hungry, dry, cold, wet, or sick, the women have ever been friendly to me."

Ledyard was the recognized Marco Polo of his day, yet all the thousands of miles he traveled were on the meager generosity of friends he made on the road. "I am accustomed to hardships," he summarized. "I have known both hunger and nakedness to the utmost extremity of human suffering; I have known what it is to have food given to me as charity to a madman; and I have, at times, been obliged to shelter myself under the miseries of that character to avoid heavier calamity. My distresses have been greater than I have ever owned, or ever will own, to any man. Such evils are terrible to bear, but they never yet had power to deter me from my purpose." He died in Egypt, possibly from a stroke brought on by "vexation occasioned by repeated delays in the departure of the caravan" that was to take him far into unknown Africa. Anything was within his Yankee endurance except remaining in one place.

Years later the far Northwest that visionary Ledyard wanted to open up was pioneered by other New Englanders, with the support of the "Washington Band," a group of Yale missionaries intent on leavening trade with Christian principle. Meanwhile, Connecticut was helping to push the West farther west. Whole regions in Indiana and Illinois were referred to as "New England" counties, and the ideas and ideals of men from towns like Fairfield, Lebanon, Hartford, Colchester, Wethersfield, and Windham had been transplanted there. The Collins brothers of Litchfield settled Collinsville, Illinois, and with traditional Yankee dexterity established a distillery alongside their union meetinghouse; they operated a sawmill, a cooper shop, a smithy, a wagon shop, a carpenter shop; had warehouses in both Collinsville and St. Louis; and the meetinghouse doubled as a public school during the week. By 1838 restless citizens of Norwich, Stamford, and New Milford were joining the throng moving to Michigan and Wisconsin through the Erie Canal and the Great Lakes; and a decade later came the Gold Rush and the peddler's rush from Connecticut to California—by ship from Mystic around the Horn, by the Santa Fé trail, by the Salt Lake and the old Oregon trails.

"Even our steady-going young men of Connecticut abandoned for the time their wooden nutmegs to sit at the feet of golden eloquence," a raconteur of the "California Ho!" era recalled. On the *Henry Lee* a delegation of distinguished Hartford youth, organized as "the Hartford Union Mining and Trading Company" set out, with an enormous cargo of mining implements, "merchandise on consignment from stoneware to garden seed, together with boots, shoes and clothing," enough provisions to last for two years, and enough tradesmen and wares to serve a complement twenty times the size of the company. "Divided into companies of three or four, they hopefully started out, many to encounter sickness, and find early graves; others to pluckily delve for a time and finally to join the ever increasing number of returning wanderers, some to settle down and call it 'home.'"

It was the coming of big industry to Connecticut that finally halted the two centuries of exodus. The discovery was made that there was more room for economic expansion in the state than fathers and grandfathers had dreamed of. The disease of wanderlust found a remedy in the lure of attractive mill-town wages and big-city business. At last the wandering Yankee tribes were ready to settle down and stay put. They had established little Connecticuts from coast to coast. At the hundredth anniversary of the founding of Western Reserve in 1896, Connecticut received its due tribute in the recognition that "there are townships on this Western Reserve which are more thoroughly New England in character and spirit than most of the towns of the New England of today. Cut off, as they were, from the metropolitan life that has been gradually moulding and changing the spirit of New England, they preserved here in the wilderness the characteristics of New England as it was when they left it at the beginning of the century. . . . The pioneers were a people who had been trained in the principles and practices of civil order, and those were transplanted to their new homes. They planted the institutions and opinions of old Connecticut in their new wilderness homes. . . . These pioneers knew well that the three great forces which constitute the strength and glory of a free government are the family, the school and the church. These three they planted here, and they nourished and cherished them with an energy and devotion scarcely equaled in any other quarter of the world."

What was true of Cleveland in 1896 later became more true of many a village in the Midwest, New York, or upper New England. These progeny are more Yankee than Connecticut. Vermont is credited with retaining more of the character of the nation established in 1789 than any of the original thirteen states or the other thirty-four that followed, but Vermont got its start as New Connecticut. The legacy is far reaching; it is found across the land, in remote islands and unexpected places. Even in Dutch Guiana there are New England houses with incongruous brick chimneys, green-painted shutters, cupolas, fanlights, and wooden pilasters, built by Yankee traders; and the Paramaribo town hall is constructed of brick shipped down in the 1700's by Captain Joshua Green of Glastonbury. Connecticut families once occupied those colonial houses.

The escapists completed their cycle. The course was reversed. From New York, from the four corners of the country, escapists from other confinements are flocking back to rescue the villages deserted a century or two ago by migratory great-grandparents. They want to restore some of the lost symbols, emulate the sturdy Yankee character, keep alive the tradition of enterprise and resourcefulness, revive some of the old-fashioned ideas of independence, democracy, or piety—and in time, perhaps, reassert the spirit of traffic and emigration.

QUOTATION

SOURCES

QUOTATION SOURCES

YANKEE OF THE YANKEES

P. ix—Mark Twain's Yankee: Twain, Mark, *A Connecticut Yankee in King Arthur's Court* (Harper 1917) pp. 14, 15. P. x—Bernard's observations: Bernard, John, *Retrospections of America* (Harper 1887) p. 37. P. x—Haliburton's observation: Haliburton, Thomas C., *Clockmaker* (London 1840), p. 57. Pp. x-xi—Ohio boatmen: "Great Western March," *Harpers*, June 1884, p. 125. P. xi—California Yankees: Froude, J. A., *Oceana* (1887), p. 316. P. xi—Yankeefied Japan: *Oxford Dictionary* (Yankee). P. xi—Mongolian Yankee notions: Keenan, George, "Ride Through the Trans-Baikal," *Century*, May 1889, p. 82.

1

FOREFATHERS

P. 3—"Jankins": Of course, there are other etymological explanations of the derivation of "Yankee," but *The Oxford Dictionary* notes that this is perhaps the most widely accepted. P. 4—Hooker's sermon: Archibald, W. S., *Thomas Hooker,** p. 7. P. 7—Griswold: Barber, J. W., *Connecticut Historical Collections* (1836), p. 331. P. 9—Litchfield wolf: Barber, *op. cit.*, p. 482. Pp. 9-10—Putnam's wolf: *ibid.*, pp. 439-40. P. 10—Hartford blackbird tax: *ibid.*, p. 47. P. 11—Pigeons: Goodrich, S. G., *Recollections of a Lifetime* (1857), I, 101. Pp. 11-12—Bethany bear: Barber, *op. cit.*, pp. 187, 188. P. 12—Price of Norwalk real estate: *ibid.*, p. 389. P. 12—Milford real estate: *ibid.*, p. 229. P. 12—Norwich real estate: *ibid.*, p. 290. P. 14—Idyl: *Connecticut: A Guide to its Roads, Lore, and People* (Houghton Mifflin 1938), p. 453. P. 15—Fitch's intercession: Barber, *op. cit.*, p. 337. P. 15—Buckley on Indian lands: *ibid.*, p. 304. P. 17—Enfield Shakers: Pease, J. C. and Niles, J. M., *Gazetteer of the States of Rhode Island and Connecticut* (1819), p. 69. P. 17—Christ-ians: Barber, *op. cit.*, p. 425. P. 17—Sarah Bishop: *ibid.*, p. 401. P. 18—Hannah Herman: *ibid.*, p. 409. P. 18—New Haven witches: *ibid.*, p. 208. P. 18—Moses Parker: *ibid.*, p. 56. P. 19—

**Titles followed by asterisks are pamphlets published by Yale University Press in commemoration of the Connecticut Tercentenary of 1935. Publication rights are now held by the Connecticut State Library, Hartford, Connecticut.*

Done's execution: *ibid.*, p. 58. P. 19—Goodman Love: *ibid.*, p. 163. P. 19—William Beadle: *ibid.*, pp. 118-19. P. 20—Cancer Quack: "On a Patient Killed by a Cancer Quack," *ibid.*, p. 268. P. 20— "Hideous wilderness": *ibid.*, p. 31.

2

LAWGIVERS

Pp. 22-23—Beecher on parson politicians: Beecher, Charles (editor), *Autobiography, Correspondence, etc. of Lyman Beecher, D.D.* (1864-'65), I, 259. P. 23—Ludlow's phraseology: *Fundamental Orders of Connecticut.** P. 23—Plantation Covenant: Hinman, R. R. (An Antiquarian), *The Blue Laws of New Haven Colony* (1840), p. 134. P. 24—Massachusetts laws on clothing: *ibid.*, p. 132. P. 24—Laws for holiness: *ibid.*, pp. 145-46. P. 24—Beer on Saturday: *ibid.*, p. 131. Pp. 24-25—Lord's Day: *ibid.*, p. 206. P. 25—Swearing: *ibid.*, pp. 206-07. Pp. 25-26—Barnum's yarn: Barnum, P. T., *Struggles and Triumphs* (Courier Edition, 1875), p. 53. P. 26—Wives and husbands: Hinman, *op. cit.*, p. 197. P. 27—Peters' complaint: Trumbull, J. H., *Blue Laws of Connecticut*, p. 33. Pp. 27-28—Peters' blue laws: *ibid.*, pp. 303, 307. P. 28—"Hard water": Clark, G. L. *History of Connecticut* (G. P. Putnam's Sons 1914), p. 95. P. 28—Trumbull on Peters: Trumbull, J. H., *op. cit.*, p. 31. P. 28—Critics' appraisal of Peters: *ibid.*, pp. 33, 34. Pp. 29-30—"Governor of River Connecticut": Clark, *op. cit.*, p. 14. P. 31—First example: *ibid.*, p. 62. P. 31 —Close identity of church and town: Lee, G. S., *About an Old New England Church*, p. 11. P. 32—"Uncommon grace and favor": Barber, *op. cit.*, p. 19. P. 32—Connecticut boundaries: Clark, *op. cit.*, p. 77. Pp. 33-34—Royal charter excerpts: *Charter of Connecticut,** pp. 15-21. Pp. 34-35—Adams' tavern: Clark, *op. cit.*, p. 58. P. 35—Complaint against lobbyists: Barber, *op. cit.*, p. 55. P. 38— Elbow room: Beecher, *op. cit.*, I, 395. P. 38—Ouster of ministers: *ibid.*, pp. 343, 344. P. 38—American constitution: Trumbull, J. H., *op. cit.*, p. vi.

3

PULPITEERS AND PROPHETS

P. 41—Proclamation of Independence: Todd, C. B., *In Olde Connecticut* (1906), p. 184. P. 41—Champion's prayer: Baldwin, A. M., *Clergy of Connecticut in Revolutionary Days,** p. 24. P. 43—Daggett's letter: *ibid.*, p. 7. Pp. 43-44—Johnson's letter: *ibid.*, p. 10. P. 44—Goodrich's advice: *ibid.*, p. 16. P. 45—Hop Meadow location: Simonds, W. E., "Canton," *Connecticut Quarterly*, 1:241. P. 48—"Jesticulous tone": Allen, N. H., "Old Time Music and Musicians," *ibid.*, p. 275. P. 48—Singing lecture: *ibid.*, p. 278. P. 48—

"If we once begin to sing": *ibid.*, p. 277. Pp. 48-49—Quavers: *ibid.*, p. 278. Pp. 49-50—Bill of rights: Munich, A. F., *Beginnings of Roman Catholicism in Connecticut,** p. 11. P. 50—Gay June: *ibid.*, p. 7. P. 50—Washington's reminder: *ibid.*, p. 8. P. 51—Fenwick retort: *ibid.*, p. 18.

4

HUSBANDMEN

Pp. 53-54—Neighbor Gay: Huntington, M. C., "Early Lebanon," *Connecticut Quarterly* 2:255. Pp. 55-56—Exodus: Pease and Niles, *op. cit.*, p. 11. Pp. 56-57—Father's plantings: Olson, A. L., *Agricultural Economy and the Population of Eighteenth Century Connecticut,** p. 28. P. 57—Whitefish: Barber, *op. cit.*, p. 533. P. 58—Scanty crops: Huntington, *op. cit.*, 2:252. P. 59—Shrinking cow's milk: Hyde, B. W., "Reminiscences of Bean Hill," *ibid.*, 3:303. P. 59—Weather predictions: Bates, A. C., "Connecticut Almanacs of Last Century," *ibid.*, 4:408-16. P. 60—Cider brandy: Pease and Niles, *op. cit.*, p. 9. P. 61—Gin: *ibid.*, pp. 13-15, 65-67. P. 62—Onions: *ibid.*, p. 89. P. 62—Advertisement for cornstalks: Barber, *op. cit.*, p. 179. P. 62—Oyster trade: *ibid.*, p. 158. P. 63—First tobacco law: McDonald, A. F., *History of Tobacco Production in Connecticut,** p. 3. P. 63—Amended tobacco legislation: Barber, *op. cit.*, pp. 17, 18.

5

MARINERS

P. 72—Horse jockeys: Todd, *op cit.*, p. 81. P. 73—Whaler supplies: *ibid.*, p. 86. P. 77—John North: Carrington, G. H., "In the Tunxis Valley," *Connecticut Quarterly*, 1:31. P. 77—Deacons' pilferage: *ibid.*, p. 30. P. 79—"God Almighty": Abbe, N. G., "Traffic on the Connecticut River," *ibid.*, 3:273. P. 81—"Bell of the Wreck": Sigourney, Mrs. L. H., *Western Home and Other Poems* (1854), p. 212.

6

HIGHWAY STRATEGISTS

Pp. 84-85—Surveyor's Report on Great Road: Wood, F. J., *Turnpikes of New England*, (Marshall Jones Co., Boston, 1919), p. 352. P. 86 —Hartford paradise: Brissot de Warville, J. P., *New Travels in the United States* (1792), p. 132. P. 86—Road to Rye: *ibid.*, pp. 138, 139. P. 87—Individualism: Mitchell, I. S., *Roads and Road Making in Connecticut,** pp. 31, 32. P. 89—Lebanon pariah: *ibid.*, p. 7.

P. 90—Freight movement: Wood, *op. cit.*, p. 26. P. 91—Caravan: Earle, A. M., *Stage Coach and Tavern Days* (Macmillan 1901), pp. 315-17. Pp. 91-92—Madame Knight: *Journals of Madam Knight* (1825), pp. 1-32. Pp. 92-93—Birket's travels: *Some Cursory Remarks Made by James Birket on His Voyage to North America 1750-1751*, pp. 33-39. P. 93—Hugh Finley: Mitchell, *op. cit.*, p. 25. P. 93—Rhode Island Lottery: *ibid.*, p. 26. P. 93—Traveler to Pomfret: *ibid.* P. 94—First post: Earle, *op. cit.*, p. 275. P. 94—Yale observer: *ibid.*, p. 276. P. 94—Sham bundles: *ibid.*, p. 277. P. 94—New York *Journal* quote: Wood, *op. cit.*, p. 27. P. 96—Yale's residence: *ibid.*, p. 350. P. 96—Woodstock and Thompson turnpike: *ibid.*, p. 380. Pp. 96-97—Straight turnpikes: *ibid.*, pp. 366, 370, 376-77. P. 98—Talcott Mountain Turnpike: *ibid.*, p. 345. P. 99—Robert Rankin: *ibid.*, p. 369. P. 99—Victory Tomlinson: *ibid.*, p. 366.

7

TINKERERS

P. 105—John Hay quote: *Letters of John Hay and Extracts from His Diary* (1908), I, 93. P. 107—Dr. Colton: Hartford *Courant*, December 10, 1844. P. 108—Horace Wells: Erving, H. W., *The Discoverer of Anaesthesia,** pp. 6, 7. P. 111—John Howe quote: Bishop, J. L., *History of American Manufacturers*, (Young 1861-1868), II, 563. P. 112—Eli Whitney quote: Roe, J. W., *Connecticut Inventors,** p. 21. P. 113—Simeon North quote: *Dictionary of American Biography* (Simeon North). P. 115—Buell's penalty: Barber, *op. cit.*, p. 531. P. 117—Whittling: Goodrich, *op. cit.*, I, 95.

8

PROSPECTORS

P. 120—"Silvar and coper": Carrington, G. H., "To the Hartlands," *Connecticut Quarterly*, 1:252. P. 121—Royalty: *ibid.*, p. 252. P. 121—Resolution: Clark, *op. cit.*, p. 439. P. 122—Washington's letter: Fitzpatrick, J. C. (Ed.), *Writings of George Washington*, IV, 155. P. 123—Baxter's self-label: *ibid.*, p. 164. P. 124—Legislative insults: *ibid.*, p. 167. P. 125—Prisoners' meal: *ibid.*, p. 171. P. 125—Convicts' health: Carrington, *op. cit.*, p. 254. P. 125—Prison description: Todd, *op. cit.*, pp. 169, 172-73. P. 125—Anburey's observations: Anburey, Thomas, *Travels Through the Interior Parts of America* (1789), II, 302-03. P. 126—"Curse, swear and fight": Clark, *op. cit.*, p. 441. P. 126—Apology: Carrington, *op. cit.*, p. 252. P. 126—Mill for rolling balls: Clark, *op. cit.*, p. 191. P. 127—Expropriation: Pynchon, W. H. C., "Iron Making in Connecticut," *Connecticut Quarterly*, 5:277. P. 127—Forbes' Description: Smith,

C. P., *The Housatonic*, (Rinehart and Co. 1946) p. 257. P. 127—
Allen's charge: *ibid.*, p. 260. P. 131—38,000 tons: Bartlett, E. S.,
"Salisbury," *Connecticut Quarterly*, 4:370. Pp. 131-32—Woodbury's
minerals: Todd, *op. cit.*, p. 198. P. 134—Durham coal bed: *ibid.*,
p. 201.

9

TRADERS

P. 139—Emma Hart's poem: *Antiquarian*, November 1951, p. 24.
P. 140—Shining coffee pots: Wright, Richardson, *Grandfather Was
Queer* (J. B. Lippincott Co. 1939), p. 28. Pp. 140-41—Subaltern's
complaint: Barber, *op. cit.*, p. 512. P. 141—Lyme tea party: *ibid.*,
p. 334. P. 142—Dwight's observations: Dwight, Timothy, *Travels
Through New England and New York* (1821-22), II, 53-55. P. 143
—Bernard on peddlers: Bernard, *op. cit.*, p. 42. P. 144—Divinely
ordained Negro: Weld, R. F., *Slavery in Connecticut,** p. 1. P. 145
—Slaves for sale: Barber, *op. cit.*, p. 179. P. 145—British Secretary
of State on slavery: Weld, *op. cit.*, p. 12. P. 145—Aversion to
traders: *ibid.*, p. 19. P. 146—Terry as peddler: Hoops, P. R., *Early
Clock Making in Connecticut,** p. 12. P. 148—"He wer hatched":
Wright, *op. cit.*, p. 30. P. 150—Yankee House of Commons: Cross,
Wilbur, *A Connecticut Yankee* (Yale University Press 1943), p. 36.

10

PEDAGOGUES

P. 153—Occum's preaching: Barber, *op. cit.*, pp. 339-40. P. 153—
Dartmouth: *ibid.*, p. 544. P. 154—Chateaubriand: Loomis, I. F.,
"Bacon Academy," *Connecticut Quarterly*, 2:121. P. 155—Kirk-
land's bequest: Trowbridge, J. P., "Life of a Connecticut Educator in
Civilizing the Indians," *Connecticut Magazine*, 12:244. P. 156—
Obookiah's inscription: Barber, *op. cit.*, p. 467. P. 157—Beecher's
aversion: Beecher, H. W., *Star Papers* (1855), pp. 189-93. Pp. 157-
158—Sturtevant's affection: Leete, W. W., "Away from the Railroad
in Connecticut," *Connecticut Magazine*, 5:359. P. 158—Barbarism:
Clark, *op. cit.*, p. 208. P. 158—Norwich indicted: *ibid.*, p. 222.
P. 159—Sewing circle: Bartlett, E. S., "Bits from Grandmother's
Diary," *Connecticut Quarterly*, 1:270. P. 160—Franklin Village:
Barber, *op. cit.*, p. 306. P. 160—Nott's Counsel: Backus, J. W.,
"A Ministry of a Hundred Years Ago," *Connecticut Quarterly*, 3:278.
Pp. 160-161—Mrs. Nott's school: *ibid.*, 3:279. P. 161—Noah Web-
ster: Clark, *op. cit.*, p. 221. P. 162—Bacon's bequest: Loomis, *op.
cit.*, 2:124. P. 163—Sigourney poem: *Connecticut Quarterly*, 2:121.
P. 164—Daggett's defense: Barber, *op. cit.*, p. 154. P. 165—Clap's
comment: *ibid.*, p. 165.

11

ARTISTS

P. 167—Yankee Doodle origin: *Connecticut Quarterly*, 2:284. P. 169—Endless excuses: Clark, *op. cit.*, p. 528. P. 170—Billings' fugue: *ibid.*, p. 529. P. 170—Parlor music: *ibid.*, p. 532. P. 171— Mozart of America: Allen, H. H., "Old Time Music and Musicians," *Connecticut Quarterly*, 3:288. Pp. 171-72—Complaint to Kentucky: Johnson, F. H., *Music Vale Seminary*,* p. 13. P. 173—Eliot's complaint: Allen, *op. cit.*, 3:71. P. 174—School for Morality: Barber, *op. cit.*, p. 56. Pp. 174-75—Appraisal of Hodgkinson: Bernard, *op. cit.*, p. 257. P. 175—Dunlap: Dunlap, William, *History of American Theatre* (1833), pp. 268, 295. P. 175—Long respite: Allen, *op. cit.*, 3:73. P. 175—Outcry: *ibid.*, 3:75. P. 176—Tarkington's comment: *National Cyclopoedia of American Biography* (Gillette). Pp. 178-79—Trumbull's modesty: Dexter, F. B. (editor), *Extracts from the Itineraries and Other Miscellanies of Ezra Stiles* (Yale 1916), IV, 578. P. 179—Dwight's tribute: *Greenfield Village*, Part VI, "The Vision" (1794), p. 182. P. 180—Waldo: Clark, *op. cit.*, p. 516. Pp. 181-82—Lack of genius: Morse, J. M., *Rise of Liberalism in Connecticut 1828-50*,* p. 37. P. 183—Recent Connecticut writers: Williams, S. T., *Literature of Connecticut*,* p. 21.

12

CONSERVATORS

P. 186—1635 hurricane: Morton, Nathaniel, *New Englands Memoriall* (1669), pp. 94-95. Pp. 189-90—Salisbury's barren land: Barber, *op. cit.*, pp. 486-87. P. 190—Wethersfield burnings: *ibid.*, p. 121. P. 190—Tasteless wilderness: *ibid.*, p. 31. Pp. 191-92—Eliot's instruction: Eliot, Jared, *Essays Upon Field Husbandry in New England* (1760—Columbia University Press reprint), pp. 29, 35-38. P. 192—Berkshire Plan: Morse, *op. cit.*, p. 8. P. 193—1880 farming: *ibid.*, p. 6. Pp. 193-94—Handbook: Gold, T. S., *Handbook of Connecticut Agriculture*, pp. 7, 8, 18, 62, 63. Pp. 194-95—Gold's challenge: Gold, T. S., "Notes on Forestry in Connecticut," *Connecticut Quarterly*, 4:373-75. P. 196—City lungs: Banks, J. W., "The Parks of Bridgeport," *ibid.*, 3:373. P. 197—Timber in state forests: State Park and Forest Commission, *Guide to Connecticut State Parks and Forests*, p. 8.

13

MERRYMAKERS

P. 200—Julia Cowles: *Diaries of Julia Cowles* (Yale 1931), p. 36. Pp. 200-01—Love-making scandal: Earle, *op. cit.*, p. 216. P. 201— Guernsey on dancing: *Discourse on the Evils of the Dance* (1850, pamphlet), pp. 3-12. P. 201—Lascivious dancing: Magriel, Paul, *Chronicles of the American Dance* (Holt 1948), p. v. P. 201—New London dance: Caulkins, F. M., *History of Norwich, Connecticut*, p. 332. P. 202—School of good manners: Fowler, W. C., *History of Durham, Connecticut*, p. 169. P. 202—Nomadic dance schools: Caulkins, *op. cit.*, p. 541. P. 203—Lyman on dancing: Lyman, William, *Modern Refinement of the Art of Dancing* (1800, pamphlet) pp. 4-19. P. 203—Dwight's catalogue: Dwight, *op. cit.*, IV, 354. P. 204—Hartford Theatre rules: Garvie, B. S., "Hartford's Early Theatres" (Ms., Connecticut State Library), p. 2. P. 204—Petition for entertainment: Morse, *op. cit.*, p. 28. P. 206—Dockstader: Rice, E. L., *Monarchs of Minstrelsy* (Kenny Publishing Co., N. Y., 1911), p. 340. P. 207—Tavern animals: Earle, *op. cit.*, p. 196. P. 207— Animal inspiration: Morse, *op. cit.*, p. 27. P. 208—Joice Heth: *Dictionary of American Biography* (P. T. Barnum). P. 208—Barnum's first bill: Garvie, B. S., "Early Circus Days in Hartford" (Ms., Connecticut State Library), p. 7. P. 209—Danbury circus: Bailey, J. M., *Life in Danbury* (Shephard and Gill, Boston, 1873), pp. 61-63. P. 211—"Fill Carter": Osborn, Mrs. P. E. (Aunt Derby), *Danbury Fair* (1894), p. 8. P. 211—Danbury Fair constitution: "Great Danbury Fair," *Connecticut Circle*, June 1946, pp. 44-46. P. 212—Survival: *ibid.* Pp. 212-13—Coasting at New Canaan: *Landmarks of New Canaan* (New Canaan Historical Society 1951), pp. 401-02. P. 213—Barrel-burning accident: Barber, *op. cit.*, p. 300. P. 214— Skimmington verse: Mead, D. M., *History of Greenwich*, pp. 204-05. P. 214—Fusillades: Bacon, E. M., *Connecticut River and the Valley of the Connecticut* (G. P. Putnam's Sons 1907), pp. 334, 335. P. 215—Wheel club: Hartford Wheel Club Constitution (Connecticut State Library).

14

BIG OPERATORS

Pp. 216-17—Connecticut in Washington: Countryman, W. A., "Connecticut's Position in the Manufacturing World," *Connecticut Magazine*, 7:323. P. 217—Monopoly machine: Clark, *op. cit.*, p. 366. P. 218—Mansfield silk: Barber, *op. cit.*, pp. 552-53. P. 218—Hitchcock chairs: Moore, M. R., *Hitchcock Chairs*,* p. 2. P. 218—Hitchcock revival: Catalogue Weston, Vermont, Country Store (1956), p. 39. Pp. 219, 220—Collins axes: Simonds *op. cit.*, *Connecticut Quarterly*,

1:247; Thayer, A. L., "The Axe and How it is Made," *ibid.*, 2:142. P. 221—Heaven-sent symbol: "The Railroad Enterprise, Its Progress, Management and Utility," *New Englander*, 35:344. P. 222—Railroad appurtenances: *ibid.*, pp. 3, 10, 11. P. 225—Waterbury Brass Company: Lathrop, W. G., *Development of the Brass Industry in Connecticut,** p. 21. P. 226—Imitator: Day, Clive, *Rise of Manufacturing in Connecticut 1820-1850,** p. 20. P. 226—Pomfret factory: *ibid.*, p. 9. P. 227—1819 oysters: Pease and Niles, *op. cit.*, p. 100. P. 227—Stratford oysters: Barroll, H. H., "Connecticut's Huge Industry under the Sea," *Connecticut Magazine*, 7:252-53. Pp. 228-29 —Terry's New York trip: Welch, A. A., *History of Insurance in Connecticut,** pp. 6, 7. P. 229—Jewell's address: *ibid.*, p. 10. Pp. 229-30—Locks in Paris: Daniel, E. G., "Connecticut at the Paris Exposition," *Connecticut Magazine*, 6:436.

15

OUTLANDERS

P. 232—WPA study: Koenig, S., *Immigrant Settlements in Connecticut* (Connecticut State Department of Education), p. 10. P. 232 —Yankeeism: Pratt, Magee, "Berlin: A Sketch," *Connecticut Magazine*, 6:170. P. 234—Connecticut law on slaves: Norton, F. C., "Negro Slavery in Connecticut," *ibid.*, 5:321. P. 234—Perkins' slaves: Caulkins, *op. cit.*, p. 328. Pp. 234-35—Negro churchgoers, recruits, and revelers: Norton, *op. cit.*, pp. 322-24. P. 235—Abby Kelley: Weld, R. F., *Slavery in Connecticut,** p. 24. P. 236—Canterbury resolution: Norton, *op. cit.*, p. 327. P. 236—Thomas Tisdall: Pease and Niles, *op. cit.*, pp. 54-55. Pp. 237-38—Lord's Bridge: Caulkins, *op. cit.*, p. 445. Pp. 238-39—Bavarian conversation: Boerstler, C., "Autobiography of a Bavarian Immigrant," *Connecticut Magazine*, 12:402-03. P. 240—New Haven Sabbath: Bernard, *op. cit.*, pp. 333, 334. Pp. 241-42—Stamford directory: *Stamford Advocate*, Tercentenary Edition, 1941, p. 14. P. 242—Taft quote: Koenig, *op. cit.*, p. 28.

16

HOSTS

P. 246—Adams on tavern keepers: Earle, *op. cit.*, p. 69. P. 247— Tea party: Bartlett, *op. cit.*, 1:267. P. 248—Babe's beverage: Earle, *op. cit.*, p. 125. P. 248—Ordination ball: *op. cit.*, p. 82. Pp. 248-249—Ridgefield Tavern: Goodrich, *op. cit.*, I, 20. P. 249—Uses of tavern: Earle, *op. cit.*, p. 199. P. 249—Balloons: *ibid.*, p. 196. P. 250—Grudge: Fowler, *op. cit.*, p. 170. P. 250—Training Day: Goodrich, *op. cit.*, I, 87. P. 250—Madame Knight: *Journals*, p. 39. Pp. 251-52—Nervous pastor story: Goodrich, *op. cit.*, I, 184, 185. P. 252 —Sinda's account: Larned, E. D., *History of Windham*, II, 592. P.

252—Stiles' letter: *ibid*, p. 562. P. 253—Anburey's account: Anburey, *op. cit.*, pp. 131, 132. P. 253—Poem on frog battle: Barber, *op. cit.*, p. 448. P. 253—Larned's account: Larned, *op. cit.*, I, 562. P. 253—Deduction: *ibid.*, p. 563. P. 254—Goodrich on whittling: Goodrich, *op. cit.*, I, 93-95. P. 254—Larceny at Vaille's: Barber, *op. cit.*, p. 459. P. 255—Murder at Horsford's: Simonds, *op. cit.*, I, 245. P. 255—Hourly: *Connectictut Quarterly*, 3:442. P. 256— Shore bungalow: Reckard, G. A., "Ella Wilcox and the Bungalow," *ibid.*, 1:220. P. 256—Mill Rock: Dickerman, J. H., "Hamden," *ibid.*, 4:389. P. 257—Stafford Springs: Barber, *op. cit.*, p. 556. Pp. 257-58—Pomfret: Porter, J. A., "Picturesque Pomfret," *Connecticut Quarterly*, 2:3-24. Pp. 258-59—Talcott Tower: Wadsworth, S. C., "Towers of Talcott Mountain," *ibid.*, 1:186-87. P. 260—Darien celebration: *Town of Darien*, p. 3.

17

ESCAPISTS

Pp. 261-62—Goodrich's recollections: Goodrich, *op. cit.*, II, 79, 80. P. 263—"What remaynes": Morrow, R. L., *Connecticut Influences on Western Massachusetts and Vermont*,* p. 2. P. 264—Vermont Declaration of Independence: Slade, William, *Vermont State Papers*, pp. 69-70. P. 265—Suffield complaint: Boyd, J. P., *Susquehanna Company: Connecticut's Experiment in Expansion*,* p. 6. P. 265 —Purpose of Company: *ibid.*, p. 8. P. 266—Adams on Dyer: *Dictionary of American Biography* (Dyer). P. 267—Deane's vision: Boyd, *op. cit.*, p. 2. P. 267—Lyman's travels: Pease and Niles, *op. cit.*, p. 88. P. 268—Obstacles: *ibid.*, pp. 11, 12. P. 269—Route West: Rosenberry, L. K. M., *Migrations from Connecticut Prior to 1800*,* p. 27. P. 269—Greatest land purchase: Pease and Niles, *op. cit.*, p. 88. P. 270—White's biographer: *ibid.*, p. 275. P. 270— Dwight on western New York: Dwight, *op. cit.*, III, 529-30. P. 271 —1200 sleighs: Earle, *op. cit.*, p. 234. Pp. 272-73—Knight's letter: Larned, E. D., "Notes on an Ohio Pioneer, 1788-89," *Connecticut Quarterly*, 2:244, 245. Pp. 273-74—Granger's reports: Granger, J. N., "Connecticut and Virginia a Century Ago," *ibid.*, 3:100-05. P. 275—Missionary Society platform: Rosenberry, L. K. M., *Migrations from Connecticut After 1800*,* pp. 16, 17. P. 275—Turner's plea: *ibid.*, p. 18. Pp. 276-77—Robbins' diary: Larned, E. D., "New Connecticut or Western Reserve," *Connecticut Quarterly*, 3:88-95. P. 277—"Mad, romantic, dreamy Ledyard": *Dictionary of American Biography* (Ledyard). P. 277—Empress Catherine's threat: Pease and Niles, *op. cit.*, p. 156. Pp. 277-78—Ledyard's women: Barber, *op. cit.*, pp. 327-28. P. 278—Ledyard's summary: Pease and Niles, *op. cit.*, p. 157. Pp. 278-79—Gold rush: Hamilton, F. L., "Henry Lee Argonauts of 1849," *Connecticut Quarterly*, 1:229-30. P. 279— Tribute: Larned, *op. cit.*, 3:99.

INDEX

INDEX

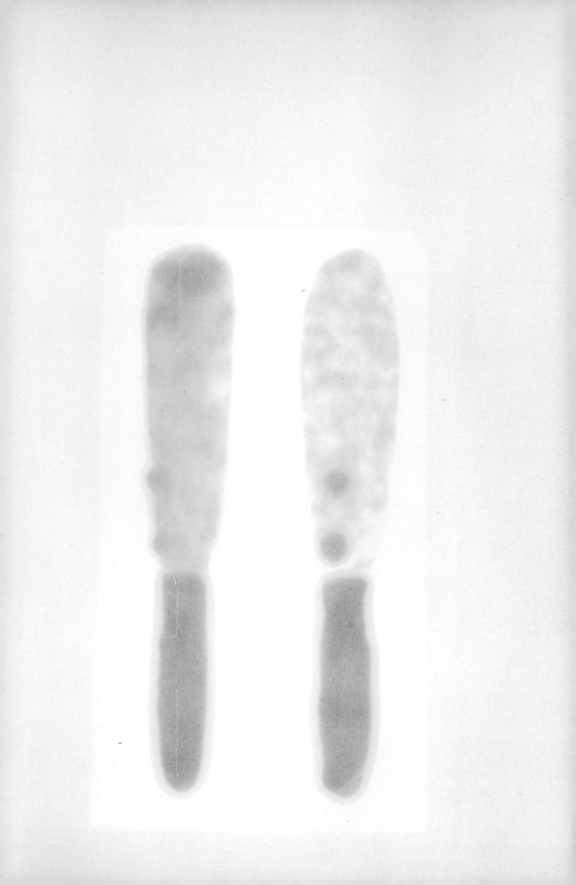

DATE DUE	

← Pocket Inside